# The Sciences Po Series in International Relations and Political Economy

Series Managing Editor

Miriam Perier
CERI-Sciences Po
Paris, France

Series Editor

Alain Dieckhoff
CNRS/CERI-Sciences Po
Paris, France

GW00645457

**Aim of the series**
The Science Po Series in International Relations and Political Economy consists of works emanating from the foremost French researchers from Sciences Po, Paris. Sciences Po was founded in 1872 and is today one of the most prestigious universities for teaching and research in social sciences in France, recognized worldwide. This series focuses on the transformations of the international arena, in a world where the state, though its sovereignty is questioned, reinvents itself. The series explores the effects on international relations and the world economy of regionalization, globalization, and transnational flows at large. This evolution in world affairs sustains a variety of networks from the ideological to the criminal or terrorist. Besides the geopolitical transformations of the globalized planet, the new political economy of the world has a decided impact on its destiny as well, and this series hopes to uncover what that is.

More information about this series at
http://www.springer.com/series/14411

Philippe Bonditti • Didier Bigo • Frédéric Gros
Editors

# Foucault and the Modern International

## Silences and Legacies for the Study of World Politics

*Editors*
Philippe Bonditti
European School of Political & Social
Sciences (ESPOL)
Université Catholique de Lille
Lille Cedex, France

Didier Bigo
CERI
Sciences Po Paris
Paris, France

Frédéric Gros
CEVIPOF
Sciences Po Paris
Paris, France

The Sciences Po Series in International Relations and Political Economy
ISBN 978-1-349-95098-0 (hardcover)     ISBN 978-1-137-56158-9   (eBook)
ISBN 978-1-349-95837-5 (softcover)
DOI 10.1057/978-1-137-56153-4

Library of Congress Control Number: 2016955950

Printed on acid-free paper

This Palgrave Macmillan imprint is published by Springer Nature
The registered company is Nature America Inc.
The registered company address is: 1 New York Plaza, New York, NY 10004, U.S.A.

# ACKNOWLEDGMENTS

Because this volume is the product of a collective work, I would like to thank all those who have devoted time and energy in this project.

The first that have to be thanked are my students at the *Instituto de Relações Internacionais* at PUC-Rio (IRI/PUC-Rio) in Rio de Janeiro (Brazil). I keep strong memories of our passionate discussions about Foucault during which the conference project took shape the first time.

I want to thank the members of the *Association pour le Centre Michel Foucault* (Paris)[1] who supported this project intellectually and financially. In particular, I want to warmly thank Philippe Artières, Research Director at the French CNRS and President of the *Association pour le Centre Michel Foucault* for more than 20 years until December 2013. There is little doubt that without his immense support neither the Conference organized in Paris,[2] from which this volume partly comes out, nor this volume would have come to material life.

At the Centre for International Studies (CERI-Sciences Po, Paris), I want to thank those who believed in this project and made it possible by hosting and partly funding the Paris conference and, later, by accepting

---

[1] The *Association pour le Centre Michel Foucault* is a nonprofit organization. Since its creation in 1988, its members have worked continuously at building the archive of the work of Michel Foucault. It is through their work that most of Foucault's immense work has been made available for French and non-French readership.

[2] *Biopolitics, Governmentality, (security) Dispositif. Concepts for the study of the International?* conference organized by Philippe Bonditti, Didier Bigo and Frédéric Gros, CERI-Sciences Po, Paris, January 14th and 15th, 2014.

the present volume in the *International Relations and Political Economy Series* at Palgrave Macmillan.

The *Centre d'études sur les conflits* (Paris) and its members must be thanked for having provided financial support for both the organization of the 2014 conference and the translation of some of the contributions to this volume. The support of the *Centre d'études sur les conflits* takes place within a broader line of intellectual and scholarly engagement that contributed since the early 1990s to the development and diffusion, in France and beyond, of a critical, reflexive and empirically grounded line of analysis of the International, especially through its quarterly Journal *Cultures & Conflits.*

At the European School of Politics and Social Sciences of the Catholic University in Lille, I would like to thank my colleagues for their encouragements, as well as all those who made possible the financial support these two institutions have provided to this project.

My gratitude also goes to all the contributors to this volume who I want to thank for their extreme patience that was only equaled by their constant support all along the fabric of this volume. Along with the contributors, I also would like to thank Gregory Elliot and Andrew Brown who translated some of the contributions in this volume.

Finally, a warm and special thank is due to Miriam Perier who, as the *International Relations and Political Economy Series* Managing Editor at CERI-Sciences Po, did more than just her job, especially when the time came to choose an appropriate title for this volume, and to find the most appropriate formulations when either Foucault or some of us in this volume were simply untranslatable.

Philippe Bonditti

# CONTENTS

# About the Editors and Contributors

## Editors

**Didier Bigo** is MCU Research Professor at Sciences-Po, France and a Professor of International Relations at Kings College London, UK. He is also the Editor-in-Chief of the French quarterly journal *Cultures & Conflits*, and the founding co-editor, with R. B. J. Walker, of the journal *International Political Sociology*. His research interests include security and liberty, biometrics identifiers and databases, antiterrorist policies in Europe after 9/11, the merging of internal security and external security, migrants and refugees in Europe, critical security studies, and international political sociology.

**Philippe Bonditti** holds a Doctorate in Political Science from Sciences Po Paris (2008) and is currently an Assistant Professor at the European School of Political and Social Science (ESPOL, UC Lille). Previously an assistant professor at the Institute of International Relations of PUC-Rio, Brazil (2010–2013), and a postdoctoral fellow at the Watson Institute, Brown University, USA (2008–2010), his research interests include, contemporary discourses on violence, war and security, the transformations of the modern state and the art of government, (critical) IR theory, (critical) security studies, contemporary French philosophy, and political theory.

**Frédéric Gros** is a Professor of Philosophy at Sciences Po Paris and a former student of the Ecole Normale Supérieure in the rue d'Ulm, Paris. His research focuses on contemporary French philosophy (especially the thought of Michel Foucault whose writings and courses at the College de

France he edited—*Subjectivity and Truth, The Hermeneutics of the subject, The Government of the self and others, The Courage of Truth,* etc); the foundations of the right to punish; issues of war and security; the ethics of political subject (particularly through the problem of obedience/disobedience).

## CONTRIBUTORS

**Jean-François Bayart** is a specialist of historical and comparative political sociology. A professor at the Graduate Institute (Geneva), he holds the Yves Oltramare chair (Religion and Politics in the Contemporary World). Bayart is also a director of the Comparative African studies chair at University Mohamed VI Polytechnique (Rabat), president of Fasopo (Fonds d'analyse des sociétés politiques) and of Reasopo (Réseau européen d'analyse des sociétés politiques), and associate fellow at CERI-Sciences Po (Paris).

**Mitchell Dean** is Professor of Public Governance at the Copenhagen Business School. He has held Chairs of Sociology at the University of Newcastle and Macquarie University, where he also was a Dean of Society, Culture, Media and Philosophy. He has published several books, including *The Constitution of Poverty: Towards a Genealogy of Liberal Governance* (Routledge, 1991), *Governing Australia* (edited with Barry Hindess, Cambridge University Press, 1998), *Governmentality: Power and Rule in Modern Society* (Sage, 1999/2010), *Critical and Effective Histories: Foucault's Methods and Historical Sociology* (Routledge, 1994), *The Signature of Power* (Sage, 2013) and *State Phobia and Civil Society: The Political Legacy of Michel Foucault* (with Kaspar Villadsen, Stanford University Press, 2016). His work is at the nexus between political and historical sociology and political theory and philosophy.

**Michael Dillon** is an Emeritus Professor of Politics in the Department of Politics, Philosophy and Religion at the University of Lancaster, UK. His last two books were *Deconstructing International Politics* (Routledge, 2012); and, *Biopolitics of Security: A Political Analytic of Finitude* (Routledge, 2015). His new book project is provisionally entitled *Political Spirituality and the Courage of Truth*. Michael Dillon is a co-editor of a new book series with Bloomsbury entitled *Political Theologies* and co-editor of *The Journal of Cultural Research* (Taylor and Francis).

**Stuart Elden** is a Professor of Political Theory and Geography at University of Warwick and Monash Warwick professor at Monash University. He is the author of seven books including *The Birth of Territory* (University of Chicago Press, 2013), *Foucault's Last Decade* (Polity, 2016) and *Foucault: The Birth of Power* (2017). He has been involved in editing several collections of Henri Lefebvre's writings, and has edited or co-edited books on Kant, Foucault, and Sloterdijk. He is now working on a project on territory in Shakespeare's plays, and the question of terrain. He runs a blog at www.progressivegeographies.com

**Paulo Esteves** is Director of the Instituto de Relações Internacionais (IRI) at PUC-Rio, holds a PhD (2003) in Political Science from IUPERJ. He has edited several books (in Portuguese) among which *International Institutions: Security, Trade, and Integration* (2004) and *International Relations: Theoretical and Meta-Theoretical debates* (2010, PUC-Minas). He is the author of *The Convergence Between Humanitarian Aid and International Security* (Del Rey/FUNAG, 2010). He is also a founding partner and director (2005–2009) of the Brazilian International Relations Association and active member of the IPS section of the International Studies Association. His current research focuses on the convergence among the fields of International Security, humanitarianism and development, and the participation of emerging and peripheral countries in the new architecture of international security.

**Marta Fernández** holds a PhD in International Relations at IRI/PUC-Rio (2011) with a scholarship from CAPES at the St. Andrews University, Scotland, (2010). Professor Fernandez' main areas of interest include International Relations Theory (especially: post-colonialism), Africa (mainly: Somalia), International Security (mainly: peace operations).

**Béatrice Hibou** holds a PhD in Political Economy from the Ecole des Hautes Etudes en Sciences Sociales (EHESS, 1995). She was member of the editorial boards of *Politique africaine* (1998–2001) and *Critique internationale* (1998–2003). She directs the "Africas" (Les Afriques) book series published by Karthala, Paris. She is a co-founder and vice president of Fasopo (Fonds d'analyse des sociétés politiques) since 2003. She is also in charge of the research group on historical sociology of economics at CERI. Her comparative research in political economy focuses, from a Weberian perspective, on the political significance of economic reform, based on cases from sub-Saharan Africa, the Maghreb and Europe. Her recent publications include *The Bureaucratization of the World in the Neoliberal Era* (Palgrave Macmillan, 2015).

**Armand Mattelart** is an Emeritus Professor of Information and Communication Sciences at the University of Paris VIII. From 1962 to 1973, he was a Professor of Sociology of Population and Communication at the Catholic University of Chile, Santiago, and United Nations expert in social development. During the Popular Unity period (1970–73), he worked with the Government of President Allende until the 1973 military coup, when he was expelled from Chile. His research interests include communication theory and history, media studies, and international communication. He has authored and co-authored numerous books, translated into many languages, including, *The Invention of Communication* (1996), *The Information Society: An Introduction* (2003), with Michèle Mattelart, *Rethinking Media Theory: Signposts and New Directions* (1992) and *The Carnival of Images: Brazilian Television Fiction* (1990), *Theories of Communication: A Short Introduction* (1998). His most recent book in English is *The Globalization of Surveillance. The origin of the securitarian Order* (2010) and, in French, *Le Profilage des populations* (2014), with André Vitalis.

**Laurence McFalls** is a Professor of Political Science at the Université de Montréal, where he directs the Canadian Centre for German and European Studies as well as the International Research Training Group "Diversity." Together with Mariella Pandolfi, he founded the Groupe de recherche sur les interventions militaires et humanitaires (GRIMH). His recent research and publications address Max Weber's epistemology and sociology of domination, Michel Foucault's political thought, the new forms of therapeutic domination that have merged under neoliberalism and humanitarian intervention, memory politics of East Germany, and post-unification German political culture.

**Nicholas Onuf** is a Professor *emeritus*, Florida International University, Miami, and an associate professor at the Institute of International Relations, Pontifica Universidade Católica do Rio de Janeiro. His latest book, *Making Sense, Making Worlds: Constructivism in Social Theory and International Relations (2013)* was published in conjunction with the republication of *World of Our Making: Rules and Rule in Social Theory and International Relations* (1989).

**Luca Paltrinieri** received his PhD in Philosophy from the Ecole Normale Supérieure de Lyon, France, and the University of Pisa, Italy. He is assistant professor in Political Philosophy at the University of Rennes 1 and program director at the Collège International de Philosophie. His research focuses on history of demographic knowledge, neoliberalism and political philosophy of the firm. He published *L'expérience du concept. Michel Foucault entre épistémologie et histoire* (Publications de la Sorbonne, 2012) and he co-edited with Christian Laval and Ferhat Taylan, *Marx & Foucault. Lectures, usages, confrontations* (La Découverte, 2015).

**Mariella Pandolfi** is a Professor of Anthropology at the Université de Montréal. She is a co-director of GRIMH (military and humanitarian research group). Her research interests include contemporary theories in anthropology, medical anthropology, body politics, violence and social passions, humanitarian and military intervention in post conflict and post-communist Balkans. She co-edited with Didier Fassin, *Contemporary States of Emergency. The Politics of Military and Humanitarian Interventions* (Zone Books, 2010).

**Michael J. Shapiro** is a Professor of Political Science at the University of Hawai'i at Manoa. His most recent book, *War Crimes, Atrocity and Justice* (Polity, 2015) is the 2015 recipient of the David Easton Award, given by the Foundations of Political Theory section of the American Political Science Association ("for a book that broadens the horizons of contemporary political science by engaging issues of philosophical significance in political life"). In press with Polity is his next book, *Politics and Time: Documenting the Event.*

**Ferhat Taylan** is a program director at the Collège International de Philosophie, France, and a post-doctoral researcher, University of Liège, Belgium. Taylan's research focuses on relationships between environmental and governmental knowledges, especially in France during the eighteenth and nineteenth centuries. He is the co-author, with Christian Laval and Luca Paltrinieri, of *Foucault & Marx. Lectures, usages, confrontations* (La Découverte, 2015).

**R.B.J. Walker** is Professor of Political Science at the University of Victoria in Canada and Professor of International Relations at PUC-Rio de Janeiro in Brasil. His most recent book is *Out of Line: Essays on the politics of boundaries and the limits of modern politics* (London and New York: Routledge 2016). He is the long-term editor of the journal

*Alternatives: Global, Local, Political* and the founding co-editor, with Didier Bigo, of the ISA journal *IPS: International Political Sociology*.

**William Walters** is a Professor of Political Sociology in the Departments of Political Science and Sociology & Anthropology at Carleton University, Ottawa. He has published widely in such areas as migration and citizenship studies, security and borders, and Foucault studies. His most recent book is *Governmentality: Critical Encounters* (Routledge 2012). He co-edits the book series *Mobility & Politics* (Palgrave Macmillan). His current research interests are secrecy, publicity, mobility and infrastructure. He is working on a new book provisionally titled *The Production of Secrecy*.

# CHAPTER 1

# Introduction: The International as an Object for Thought

*Philippe Bonditti*

This is not a book on Foucault, nor is it a book on "international relations." This edited volume is both more and less ambitious. It is less ambitious in the sense that it aims neither to advance an exegesis of Foucault's immense work nor to offer a systematic and empirically grounded analysis of "international relations" as the latter seem to be reconfiguring in our deeply and rapidly transforming world. It is more ambitious in that it tries to make a wide variety of Foucaults live and to build on all these possible Foucaults to suggest other ways of engaging with "international relations" and the implicit conception of the "international" that enabled the constitution of "International Relations" as a field of study (hereafter referred to as IR[1]) which somehow has gradually monopolized knowledge about deeply social and political phenomena that develop beyond the spatially situated sites of materialization of power. In other words, this volume is all about pluralization: pluralizing Foucault, rather than confining his multiple-thought (*pensée multiple*) to the arbitrary unity of a book *on* Foucault,[2] and pluralizing knowledge about the International—rather than *re*producing the kind of knowledge developed within IR.

P. Bonditti (✉)
ESPOL, Catholic University of Lille, Lille, France
e-mail: philippe.bonditti@gmail.com

1

© The Author(s) 2017
P. Bonditti et al. (eds.), *Foucault and the Modern International*,
The Sciences Po Series in International Relations and Political
Economy, DOI 10.1057/978-1-137-56153-4_1

In this spirit, for example, my own Foucault in this volume shares very little with the Foucaults of Nicholas Onuf, Frédéric Gros, Béatrice Hibou or Michael Dillon; and none of these Foucaults have anything to do with the neoliberal Foucault some have been striving to configure in order to make *The Birth of Biopolitics*[3] the textbook of neoliberalism, and the author of *The Archaeology of Knowledge*[4] its finest theoretician. Similarly, it is unlikely that the reader will identify an overarching conception of the "International" among the contributors to this volume. Didier Bigo, Mitchell Dean, Armand Mattelart or Rob Walker hardly share the same conception of it, although the four of them—indeed all contributors in this volume—oppose the unreflective character of both IR and the social practices of those who claim to work and act *internationally*.

It is therefore both the challenge and, I want to believe, the merit of this book to account for the multiple ways in which Foucault's concepts and methods have been and might be (re-)appropriated and (re-)deployed to address the difficult problems identified with the International, while simultaneously working against all forms of dogmatic appropriations of the work of Michel Foucault. This is also a challenge, a merit and a difficulty that confronts me in writing this introduction to a highly diverse array of contributions. I will thus limit myself to brief discussions of the genesis of the book, the problems it seeks to engage and how the present contributions offer to engage and (re)configure these problems.

## GENESIS AND CONSTRUCTION OF THE BOOK

The present volume is partly the product of a conference organized in January 2014 on the theme: *Biopolitics, Governmentality, (security) Dispositifs: Concepts for the Study of the International*[5] Originally, this conference was aimed at bringing together two groups of scholars in particular: on the one hand, people like Onuf, Dillon, Shapiro, Jabri and Walker who, starting in the mid-1980s and often drawing on Foucault's work, had developed a devastating critique of IR, and, on the other, a group of (younger) scholars—Paltrinieri, Taylan, Sibertin-Blanc, Sauvêtre—more particularly involved within the French academic field, all (trained as) philosophers, recognized specialists of the work of Michel Foucault. Despite their shared interest in Foucault's work, these two groups tended to work in "mutual isolation."[6]

Many reasons explain this mutual isolation. The working language, on which I shall not comment further here, is certainly one of them. The fact, also, that IR never became institutionalized in France as it did in the

Anglo-American world, where it had gained relative and yet sufficiently strong autonomy *within* the discipline of political science for some IR scholars to speak about IR as a proper *academic discipline*. Nothing comparable having occurred in France, the critique of IR did not receive the same attention and could therefore not have the same impact in the broader space of knowledge (*l'espace des savoirs*) despite the work of Didier Bigo, Jean-François Bayart and a few others around them. Finally, the *disciplinary organization* of knowledge, and the complex mechanisms by which knowledge became both specialized and compartmentalized, certainly also explain that these scholars have been kept distant from each other for so long: the study of IR being institutionally kept *under* political science, despite many initiatives to exceed it, while Foucault was kept under philosophy, despite his own intense resistance to this categorization. The ambition of the Paris conference was to initiate the dismantling of these disciplinary walls, and to work toward the emergence of a *critical and reflexive knowledge that would constitute the International as an object for thought*. The present volume extends this initial effort.

Yet, for this purpose, it was not enough to bring together the "Critical IR scholars" and those known as the foucauldians in France and in the field of Contemporary French Philosophy. To avoid the risk that discussions would eventually reproduce the division between the "practitioners of Foucault" and the exegetes of his work, they needed to melt into a wider group of scholars who would bring about their own uses of Foucault in their respective fields of study: Mitchell Dean, Jean-François Bayart, Fabienne Brion, Mariella Pandolfi, Béarice Hibou and Marc Abélès at the conference, later joined in this volume by William Walters, Laurence Mcfalls, Armand Mattelart and Stuart Elden who were brought into the project to pluralize not only the figure of Foucault but also the disciplines within which they had contributed to spread Foucault's concepts and methods.

## FOUCAULT: THE EXPLOSIVES EXPERT

In this process, both the conference and the present volume *strategically* built on one figure of Foucault in particular: the "subversive Foucault," that is, the Foucault who through his intellectual practice and his approach to knowledge, language and power, the modern subject, history and modernity obstinately refused all disciplinary affiliations. More than any other intellectual of his time, this Foucault in particular signaled—as much as he was himself a product of—the limits reached by the modern episteme and its empirico-transcendental doublet.

In many different ways, this volume seeks to extend the effort of this particular Foucault who presented himself as an explosives expert (*artificier*)—not without giving a glimpse of his own ambiguous relationship to politics and political praxis,

> I'm an explosives expert (*artificier*). I make things that can be used, when it comes down to it, for sieges, wars, destruction. I'm not in favor of destruction, but I'm in favor of being able to push through (*passer*); to move forward (*avancer*); to bring walls down. An explosives expert is first of all a geologist. He looks at layers of terrain, folds, fault lines. What sort of ground will be easy to dig into? What sort may prove hard? He observes how fortresses have been built. He identifies the features of the relief that could be used for concealment or launching attacks. Having done that, he goes on to the experimental, trial-and-error stage. He carries out reconnaissance, he posts sentries, he orders reports. Then he works out his tactic. Sapping? A siege? Explosives, or direct assault? The method, in the end, is nothing other than this strategy.[7]

It is no surprise therefore that Foucault's concepts of biopower, biopolitics and governmentality, as well as concepts that he invested with new meanings, like discourse, statement (*énoncé*), archive, discipline, *dispositif* and problematization, together with his methods of historical inquiry, have been put into practice by so many scholars and intellectuals throughout the world and the academic disciplines. It is no surprise either that Foucault has become one of the most quoted intellectuals, including in domains of knowledge in which he proved to have no particular interest.

## The International as an Object for Thought

Yet Foucault's fabricated posture as a "subversive intellectual," at least ontologically and epistemologically, does not in itself explain the multiple convergences on and appropriations of his name, his concepts and his methods. Perhaps, and this would be my view, the "enthusiasm" for the work of Foucault, as much as the skepticism which it encounters, stems from the ways in which Foucault interrogated and problematized modernity and what he called the "threshold of modernity,"

> I am not of those watchmen who always claim to be the first to have seen the sun rise. I am interested in understanding the threshold of modernity one can spot somewhere from the XVII[th] to the XIX[th] century. From this

threshold the European discourse has developed gigantic universalizing powers. Today, in its fundamental notions and its basic rules, it may be carrying any kind of truth, should this truth be turned against Europe, against the West. Basically, I have only one object of historical study, the threshold of modernity. Who are we, we who speak this language inasmuch it has powers that are imposed on ourselves in our society, and on other societies? What is this language that can be turned against us, that we can turn against ourselves? What is this formidable bolting transition to the universality of Western discourse? That's my historical problem. [8]

For Foucault, to take modernity as a historical problem first implied not (only) looking at modernity as a mere "historical period" and the very concept of modernity as simply a category of historical periodization.[9] Certainly, Foucault did come with his own mode of periodization, yet by backing it onto his concept of *episteme* he suggests that *temporal limits* or, better, limits *in* time, cannot be apprehended independently from the limits in and of knowledge.

In this perspective, perhaps "modernity" can be approached as a radically contingent set of arrangements and combinations which, under the impetus of the scientific and spiritual revolutions of the sixteenth and seventeenth centuries[10] (even possibly until the early twentieth century and the work of Poincaré and Einstein) eventually settled as a complex system of limits that has demarcated the secular from the religious, the scientific from the spiritual, culture from nature.[11] It is within this particular system of limits that the production of knowledge and truths (about Man, nature, the world, etc.) on the one hand, and political practices on the other were made possible, and thus for Man—that elusive figure—to appropriate and configure its immediate environment.

It is still under this historically situated and contingent system of limits, for which everything seems to indicate its radical mutation, that intellectuals and scholars wishing to overcome the disciplinary organization of knowledge are still struggling when trying to make sense of contemporary mutations of social and political life. In this regard, discussions about our possible entry into a new era (be it called postmodern,[12] liquid,[13] the anthropocene[14] or the "Earth System Regime (*régime du système terre*),"[15] "post-Westphalian," "global," the "world," "neoliberal," "biopolitical" or whatever) in which time and space, the human and the non-human, the living and the non-living, human beings and Earth collide at the same time as "geographical borders" are said to collapse, are all expressions of the intense work of abstraction and reconceptualization aiming at making sense of what modernity as a system of limits enabled and that now seem to surpass it.

In this picture, here drawing more specifically on Walker's work,[16] maybe the International can be understood as the specific regime of *spatio-temporal* limits deeply and firmly rooted in a geometrical and telluric model inherited from the seventeenth and eighteenth centuries, and within which *political life* has come to settle. Although it has become deeply unsatisfactory, especially regarding the particular way it has organized our practical engagement with and in the "world," the fact remains that as a regime of spatio-temporal limits embodied in the modern system of fixed borders, fixed territories and fixed individual (citizenship) and collective (national) identities, the International seems to have developed as a *solution* for human communities to cohabit on the planet—sometimes pacifically, sometimes not and always giving rise to relations of domination and exploitation. In this perspective, Walker might suggest, it seems especially difficult, perhaps impossible for those who want to make the *world*, the *planet* or the *earth* the new site(s) of/for politics (*after* the modern territorial state and the modern international), or bring the world into the *realm of politics*.

Whatever the *concept* of the International might refer to, it seems urgent to re-appropriate it, to interrogate and problematize it, in order to (possibly) re-orient and reconfigure the practices that have constituted the "international" as an abstract space distinct from the national space and supposedly governed by its own rules of functioning. For the most challenging phenomena of our contemporary era seem to establish transversally to the division between the "national" and the "international" (transnational violence, environmental degradations, economic financialization, etc.), they demand a better diagnostic, which itself calls for more than just *re*producing the International. Foucault's concepts and methods might possibly help in this task even though Foucault himself never *directly* engaged with the International.

## Foucault, the International and IR: Aborted Encounter

The International does not indeed present itself as a domain of special interest for Foucault, nor is the name "Foucault" *primarily* associated with the field of study known as "International Relations." Yet, as some in this volume remind us, Foucault clearly came close to "international relations" as an object of knowledge, and to IR as a field of study, especially in his lectures on March 22 and 29, 1978 at the Collège de France in which he encounters some of the most central concepts of IR: "the balance of power" and the "society of states."

> The idea that between themselves states form something like a society in the European space, the idea that states are like individuals who must have certain relations between them that the law must fix and codify, gave rise at this time to the development of what has been called the law of nations (*droit des gens*), the *jus gentium*, which becomes one of the fundamental points, one of the particularly intense focal points of the activity of juridical thought, since it involves defining juridical relations between these new individuals, the states of Europe, coexisting in a new space, or society of nations [...][17]

Here, two things are worth mentioning. First, at no moment in these lectures did Foucault seize upon the concept of the International, of which he has a rather normative use. Second, at no moment in these lectures did Foucault make reference to IR. It seems quite improbable that Foucault had never heard about it. By the time he gave these lectures, indeed, IR was clearly well established in the academic field, and even counted two French intellectuals—Raymond Aron and Pierre Hassner—among its canonical authors. Why did Foucault remain so silent about IR, despite having encountered its grammar and concepts in his own efforts to bring to light and analyze the governmental rationality that was emerging from the sixteenth century?

Even though he was clearly laying the foundations of an archaeological study of IR knowledge, especially when he described the transition from the right of the sovereign to a "physics of States" and evoked the encounter of politics and political science with the problem of thermodynamics (the problem of force),[18] Foucault abruptly interrupted his analysis.

> Obviously there is a problem here that I leave completely in abeyance and merely point out to you. You can see that this development that takes place entirely on the basis of a historical reality and identifiable historical processes—the discovery of America, the constitution of colonial empires, the disappearance of the Empire, and the withdrawal, the erosion of the universal functions of the Church—in short, all these phenomena, which are what they are and which have their own necessity and intelligibility, lead to the appearance in political thought of the fundamental category of force. All these phenomena lead to a mutation that means that for the first time we are faced with political thought that aspires to be, at the same time, a strategy and a dynamics of forces. Now you are well aware that at the same time,

and by completely different processes, the sciences of nature, and physics in particular, will also encounter this notion of force. So the dynamics of politics and the dynamics of physics are more or less contemporaneous. And we should see how all of this is connected through Leibniz [...][19]

Blaming Foucault for not having conducted either an archaeological study of IR or the genealogy of the whole range of practices (from war to diplomacy) that have constituted the International as an abstract space distinct from the national would make little sense. Interrogating this non-encounter or, rather this aborted encounter to try to understand what it teaches us of Foucault's intellectual and political trajectory, of its conceptual options and creations seems potentially more fruitful. This is another objective of this volume: wondering not merely how Foucault's concepts and methods might help us when interrogating the International but also what Foucault's silence about the latter tells us about him and his work.

## THE FIELD OF IR AND FOUCAULT

Although Foucault remained silent about IR, IR has not ignored the philosopher-historian, his methods and concepts. It is not my intention here to recall the multiple ways in which Foucault has been appropriated in this field. Others have done that already,[20] and some in this volume will do that again better than I would do it myself. Rather, I want to briefly recall the somehow initial subversive function Foucault's work inspired in the field of IR.

Indeed, as already suggested in the beginning of this introduction, Foucault is, in the Anglo-American world, one of those—with Derrida, Baudrillard, Virilio and more recently Bourdieu and Latour—whose work helped shape a somehow radical critique of IR. Starting at the end of the 1970s, some within IR found in *The Order of Things* and the *Archaeology of Knowledge*—that is, in the least positivist Foucault—as well as in his conceptualization of power as relational and productive, the arguments for a critique of the onto-epistemological options that had underpinned the different theorizations of "international relations." Now associated with the names of Shapiro, Ashley, Onuf, Dillon, Campbell, Connolly, Jabri, Walker and Der Derian among others, this critique worked within and called for a pluralist ontology, insisting on multiplicity instead of unity, difference instead of identity, heterogeneity instead of homogeneity. From an epistemological point of view, the archaeo-genealogical mood that was progressively being articulated in IR enabled various interrogations of the universalistic assumptions of epistemic realism that had, that far, come to dominate the field of IR.[21] Hence, it became possible to shed light upon the historical practices as well as the conceptual and discursive operations that have enabled the concepts of state, sovereignty,[22] diplomacy,[23] foreign policy[24] or security[25] to work unreflectively within IR.

The foucauldian line of this critique helped to raise questions about how "international relations" had been constituted as an object of knowledge, along with IR as a specific field of study within an academic discipline, even though its archaeological study remains an incomplete project. Overall, this critique helped establish the historically contingent character of the discipline itself, highlighting especially how the theories developed within IR were more an expression of a particular and historically situated spatial and political imaginary than of the explanations of world politics they purported to be.

By then, the works of Michel Foucault were performing a heterotopical and virtually emancipative function for critique, though they served more as a resource for a *political* critique than to mobilize any sustained archaeological study of IR. The political critique nevertheless contributed to open spaces in which many others, coming from various disciplines and fields of research, have developed other ways of using Foucault in order to renew the study of "international politics." From the 1990s on, and even more since the 2000s, uses of Foucault for the study of the "international relations" and "international phenomena" have shifted and pluralized. In order to study a world often taken to be "neoliberal," "biopolitical" or "global," it is no longer Foucault the epistemologist or Foucault the archaeologist of "discursive monuments" who is called in, but Foucault of the rationality of government, governmentality and the "dispositifs of security." The toolmaker philosopher who had wished to be used as a toolbox seems to have been heard, although not necessarily fully understood—especially when some *unreflectively* appropriate the concept of "governmentality" to simply transpose it and apply it to the "international" still perceived as something above and/or broader than the local sites of materialization of power.

With this multiplication and diversification of the uses of Foucault's concepts, a more critical reading of his work also came to emerge. Indeed, since the 2000s, Foucault is no longer just a resource for the critique but also an object of critique. Following Gayatri Spivak and others, some reproached him for having limited his analyses of power to the "western sphere." Others have come to regret not finding in his analysis the tools that may help understanding the increasing "virtualization" of the contemporary forms of violence or globalization.[26] These critiques draw our attention to the (urgent) need to reassess Foucault's thought, not so much, however, in the form of the exegetic commentary that would establish (again) the conditions of possibility of its emergence and uncover a thought that would have been kept secret to us, and even possibly to itself, but by trying to "update" that thought, its concepts and method(s) based on the multiple uses that have been made of them.

## LEVELS OF READING

With these multiple objectives in mind, the contributions to this volume work in three directions that suggest three levels of reading which I now would like to briefly expose, rather than presenting the formal structure of the book. A first possible line of reading explores the ways in which Foucault's methods of historical inquiry might help in the study of contemporary social and political phenomena or problems identified with the International. For example, what does an archaeological study of terrorism, the global or the *milieu* tell us about "transnational violence," "globalization" or the "environmental issue"?

Second, through various themes and concepts such as "modernity," "sovereignty," "liberalism," "human capital," "biopolitics" and "globalization," another possible line of reading suggests consideration more specifically of the contributions, and potential limits of foucauldian approach(es) for the problematization and understanding of the modern International. The question here is: what is the impact of foucauldian approaches on how so-called the international phenomena have been isolated, identified and eventually construed as objects of knowledge?

Third, the contributions to this volume offer to revisit Foucault's thought and to put it to the test of the multiple ways in which it has been appropriated since the 1980s in IR and beyond. A slightly different question underpins this third possible line of reading: how can Foucault's concepts be reconfigured, his lines of inquiry re-oriented and his theoretical practices specified once they have proved to be unfruitful in our own investigations of a given phenomenon?

With these three possible levels of reading, this volume not only suggests other "types of knowledge," modes of inquiries and practices of theorization for the study of the International taken as a problem for thought but it also seeks to interrogate four of the most taken for granted features of our contemporary world: "international" (Part III), "(neo) liberal" (Part IV), "biopolitical" (Part V) and "global" (Part VI), with the hope of refining our capacity to diagnose our challenging times.

## NOTES

1. Interestingly enough, this field of study called itself with the name of what it constituted as its object of study. It is an established habit in this field to differentiate both by capitalizing (IR) the name of the field of study.
2. Michel Foucault, *The Order of Discourse*, in Michael Shapiro (ed.), *Language and Politics* (New York: New York University Press, 1984), pp. 108–138.
3. Michel Foucault, *The Birth of Biopolitics. Lectures at the Collège de France 1978–1979*, transl. Graham Burtchell (New York: Palgrave Macmillan, 2008).
4. Michel Foucault, *The Archaeology of Knowledge & The Discourse on Language*, transl. Alan M. Sheridan Smith (New York: Pantheon Books, 1972).
5. *Biopolitics, Governmentality, (security) Dispositif. Concepts for the study of the International?* conference organized by Philippe Bonditti, Didier Bigo and Frédéric Gros, CERI-Sciences Po, Paris, January 14 and 15, 2014. Program available online: https://manyfoucaults.wordpress.com/2013/10/05/foucault-and-the-international/
6. It is not my intention here to suggest that each of these two groups constituted homogenous groups; indeed, quite the contrary, as I hope the present volume will show.
7. Michel Foucault, "Entretien avec Roger-Pol Droit [1975]," *Le Point*, n°1659, July 1, 2004: 84. My translation. The ambiguity lies in the twofold conception of politics that silently underpins this statement: politics as struggles, as confrontation of forces on the one hand, as the continuous attempt to "push things through" which reminds, if not approximates the "laissez-faire laissez-passer" on the other.
8. Foucault, "Entretien avec Roger-Pol Droit [1975]:" 91–92. My translation.
9. Peter Osborne, "Modernity is a Qualitative, not a Chronological Concept," *New Left Review*, 1/192, March–April 1992: 65–84; Mitchell, T., "The Stage of Modernity," in *Questions of Modernity* (Minneapolis: University of Minnesota Press, 2000), pp. 1–34; Stuart Hall, David Held, Don Hubert, Kenneth Thompson (eds.), *Modernity: An Introduction to Modern Societies* (Oxford: Open University, 1996).
10. Alexandre Koyré, *From the Closed world to the Infinite Universe* (Baltimore: John Hopkins University Press, 1957).

11. Philippe Descola, *Beyond Nature and Culture*, transl. Janet Lloyd (Chicago: The University of Chicago Press, 2013).

12. David Harvey, *The Condition of Postmodernity: An Enquiry into the Origins of Cultural Change*, (New York: Wiley-Blackwell, 1991).

13. Zygmundt Bauman, *Liquid Times* (Cambridge: Polity Press, 2007).

14. Bruno Latour, *The Anthropocene and the Destruction of the Image of the Globe*, Gifford Lectures; University of Edinburgh, February 25th, 2013, published in French under the title: "L'anthropocène et la destruction de l'image du monde," in Emilie Hache (ed.), *De l'Univers clos au monde infini* (Paris: Editions Dehors, 2014), pp. 29–56.

15. Déborah Danowski, Eduardo Viveiros de Castro, *L'arrêt du monde*, in Hache (ed.), *De l'Univers clos au monde infini*, pp. 221–339.

16. R.B.J. Walker, *After the Globe, Before the World* (New York: Routledge, 2009).

17. Michel Foucault, *Security, Territory, Population, Lectures at the Collège de France 1977–78*, transl. Graham Bruchell (New York: Palgrave Macmillan, 2008), p. 390.

18. Foucault, *Security, Territory, Population*, p. 382.

19. Foucault, *Security, Territory, Population*, pp. 382–383.

20. Nicholas J. Kiersey, Doug Stokes, Jason R. Weidner, "Introduction," in *Foucault and International Relations. New Critical Engagements* (Oxon, UK and New York, USA: Routledge, 2011), pp. xiii–xxi.

21. See especially: James Der Derian, Michael Shapiro, *International/Intertextual Relations. Postmodern Readings of World Politics* (New York: Lexington Books, 1989); Richard Ashley, R.B.J. Walker, "Speaking the Language of Exile: Dissident Thought in International Studies," *International Studies Quarterly* 34(3): 259–268.

22. Jens Bartelson, *A Genealogy of Sovereignty* (Cambridge: Cambridge University Press, 1995); R.B.J. Walker, *Inside/Outside. International Relations as Political Theory* (Cambridge: Cambridge University Press, 1993).

23. James Der Derian, *On Diplomacy. A Genealogy of Western Estrangement* (Oxford: Basil Blackwell, 1987).

24. David Campbell, *Writing Security. United States Foreign Policy and the Politics of Identity* (Minneapolis: University of Minnesota Press, 1998).

25. Michael Dillon, *Politics of Security. Towards a Political Philosophy of Continental Thought* (London/New York: Routledge, 1996); Ronnie Lipschutz, *On Security* (New York: Columbia University Press, 1996).

26. James Der Derian, "Critical Encounters in IR," *International Social Science Journal*, 59(191), 2008: 69–73.

# PART I

# De-disciplining Knowledge About the International

# CHAPTER 2

# The Figure of Foucault and the Field of International Relations

*Nicholas Onuf*

Michel Foucault only rarely wrote about specific people and their ideas. He wrote instead about relations among "institutions, economic and social processes, behavioural patterns, systems of norms, techniques, types of classification, modes of characterization," and the conditions that make a "system of relations" even possible.[1] When he did concern himself with individual thinkers, Ian Hacking tells us that he was inclined to call them figures: for example, the figure of David Hume.[2] Of course, he was deeply interested in the texts to which Hume put his name but only as the tips of discursive icebergs in that turbulent sea called the conditions of possibility.

In this essay, I write about an especially elusive figure whom we call Foucault. We might even say that every field of study in the social sciences has its own Foucault—a figure construed to serve the needs of scholars

I am grateful to Philippe Bonditti for teaching me more about Foucault, not to mention the subtleties of the French language, than I could otherwise have hoped to learn.

N. Onuf (✉)
Florida International University, Miami, FL, USA
e-mail: onufn@fiu.edu

© The Author(s) 2017
P. Bonditti et al. (eds.), *Foucault and the Modern International*,
The Sciences Po Series in International Relations and Political
Economy, DOI 10.1057/978-1-137-56153-4_2

in that field. My field of study is International Relations (hereafter IR). Yet few scholars in IR will recognize the figure of Foucault that I put forward here, for I have configured him—I should say: *re*configured *it*—to suit myself.

Before I address those needs, I should point out that IR has a substantial and ever-growing interest in Foucault as a textual phenomenon—the textual Foucault. Foucault's indifference to the field, or indeed to provincialized scholarship, deters no one. By necessity, the field's many Foucaults are the product of selective textual appropriation. Yet they seem to converge in significant respects. This convergent figure might be thought of as the normalized Foucault for the field as a whole. I also expect that every field in which Foucault is read has its own normalized Foucault. The actually existing Foucault would surely have appreciated the irony as well as the inevitability of this development.

In different fields, writers divide up the foucauldian oeuvre at different points, and sometimes at more than one point. Transcending fields and their specific needs is the textual Foucault mapped onto a stylized life story in several chapters. It looks something like this:

- Chapter 1, the young, brash Foucault, focused on discourse and method
- Chapter 2, the maturing Foucault, turning his attention to power and resistance
- Chapter 3, Foucault in his prime, reflecting on normality
- Chapter 4, an older Foucault, dispensing wisdom on diverse matters
- Chapter 5, Foucault in his last years, preoccupied with pleasure.

I am not competent to discuss, much less substantiate, the normalization of Foucault within any other field than my own. In the remainder of this chapter, I limit myself to two tasks. The first is to sketch the figure of Foucault as normalized in IR. The second is to sketch a figure that illuminates what interests me.

I take international relations, as IR's presumptive subject, to be a pastiche of "institutions, economic and social processes, behavioural patterns, systems of norms, techniques, types of classification, modes of characterization."[3] My concern is the place of this system in the larger, ever transforming "system of relations" that I and many other scholars call the modern world. This too was an enduring concern of the figure whom I call Foucault. For centuries, the former system has framed the latter. The textual Foucault's evident disinterest in IR is no obstacle to using foucauldian texts to explore the relations of systems of relations. It does mean that I will have to supply some of the necessary framing materials myself.

## IR AS A FIELD OF STUDY

To call IR a field of study is to imply that it is not a discipline. In the USA, IR is a field of study in the discipline of political science. Few IR scholars in the USA have the slightest interest in the figure of Foucault. This subject is left to the political theorists, who are themselves a disciplinary outlier. In the rest of the world, IR scholars invoke Foucault's name with palpable reverence and sing out his signature concepts (Genealogy! Power! Discipline! Governmentality!) with monotonous regularity.

One might wonder then why so many advocates of IR as a discipline invoke Foucault's name. Have they constructed a figure of Foucault that belongs to them, and them alone, in aid of validating the claim that IR is a discipline in its own right? Their indifference to Foucault's normalization in other fields of study suggests as much. I forego a literature review to assess the question. Instead, I proceed directly to my impressionistic sketch of the figure of Foucault as normalized in IR.

My sketch picks up the life story attributed to the figure of Foucault. It takes the chapters in this story and links them to developments in IR during the 1980s. At that time, leading scholars in IR were political realists who thought that social science could, and should, conform to the scientific method. They saw the relations of nation-states as dominated by rationally motivated violence. Progressive liberals had always contended that rational people could, and should, find alternatives to violence, most obviously by developing institutions addressing the sources of insecurity. Such liberals found their standing in the field to have all but disappeared by the 1980s. Because the field emerged as such in the USA after World War II, there had never developed a Marxist or critical contingent of scholars. Anyone so disposed went into some other field of study.

In the late 1970s and early 1980s, scholars in US universities in such disciplines as philosophy and literature "discovered" Continental social thought. Some few IR scholars, styling themselves dissidents, belatedly took notice. In the first instance, they did so to challenge hegemonic political realism, not as the study of organized violence on a large scale but as a would-be science.[4] Obviously, this meant attacking the assumption that people, including state leaders and scientists, are autonomous and rational beings. And mounting the attack meant drawing on a wide and diverse range of critical, post-Marxist European scholarship.

In this context, Foucault was just one of the many figures whose texts were invoked for the purposes of argument and authority. Foucault's arresting claims about the invention and possible end of "man" in *The Order of Things* gave many of the dissidents a splendid weapon with which to strike at rationality, slash political realism and salute the advent of the post-modern age. Once dissidents deemed the crusade against realism a success, talk of the end of man faded to an occasional rhetorical flourish.

The dissidents had also followed the so-called "linguistic turn." This was another, if indirect, way to strike at the rationality assumption, which is expressed in the view that the only function of language is to represent states of affairs. Once we concede that language has other functions, we readily come to see that language use substantially constitutes social reality. In this context, some scholars flirted with deconstruction. Others turned to *The Archaeology of Knowledge* and its careful exposition of methods by which to study discourse.[5]

This, I believe, is the link between Foucault as a young, brash figure, and IR as a field. It is a link, however, that says less about the figure than it does about the field. The young, brash Foucault used many texts to locate discontinuities in discourse and thus in social life. Most IR scholars who invoke the figure of Foucault study specific texts to interrogate discursive practices that seem to be locked in place. I suspect that they do so because their normalized figure of the maturing Foucault has taught them to think small about power. To the extent that discursive continuities imply that small displays of power have big effects, they think they can talk about IR.

On the evidence, however, they find very little to talk about. IR scholars have been obsessed with power from the field's beginning. When they try to fit Foucault's conception of "productive power" with their own, they mistakenly think that Foucault identified two kinds of power, one familar and the other Foucault was first to name. A much cited essay is illustrative: "productive power concerns the boundaries of all social identity, and the capacity and inclination for action for the socially advantaged and disadvantaged alike, as well as the myriad social subjects that are not constituted in binary hierarchical relationships."[6] As Foucault so memorably said, "power produces; it produces reality; it produces domains of objects and rituals of truth." This is *not* a distinctive kind of power, one opposed to power that "excludes," "represses," "conceals."[7] Power *always* produces reality and repression—these are different descriptions of the same effect; power *also* always produces resistance to its effects.

If some IR scholars genuflect to the figure of the maturing Foucault as a power theorist, many more simply wallow in what Foucault's texts have to say about governmentality and then worry how this concept applies to the globalized conditions of the last quarter century. While Foucault's lectures at the Collège de France in 1978 are much concerned with governmentality and his lectures in 1979 with neoliberalism, the textual Foucault offers no unified, integrated treatment of these two concerns.[8] This has not prevented scores of scholars from writing as if it were so. Jan Selby has argued that "scaling up" Foucault's conception of governmentality to suit global conditions has the effect of supporting "what are in essence reworked and reworded liberal accounts of international politics."[9] If this is the case, then it can hardly have been what most foucauldian scholars hoped to achieve (see Bigo and Walters in this volume). As I will explain presently, Foucault (and, of course, I mean Foucault as I have configured him) deserves a good deal of the blame for the confusion.

IR scholars have had little to say about the figure of Foucault in his last years.[10] This neglect should be no surprise, both because of the obsession with governmentality reinforced by the recent publication of lectures Foucault delivered in the late 1970s and because the concerns animating the second and third volumes of *The History of Sexuality* and other late materials direct attention to the self as subject and the relation between aesthetics and ethics—topics claimed by other disciplines.

So how then does the normalized figure of Foucault map onto the story that IR scholars tell about themselves?

- Chapter 1, one of many weapons in the struggle against realism, rational agency and science
- Chapter 2, an invitation to study discourse
- Chapter 3, a reminder that there is more to power than blunt force
- Chapter 4, a clumsy way to talk about globalization in the last quarter century
- Chapter 5, some murmurs of regret that the figure of Foucault was so wrapped up in the subject of (him)self in his last years that he never got around to talking about imperialism and colonialism.

## Foucault Reconfigured

Let me now present Foucault as I have reconfigured him to suit my scholarly concerns. Conversely, I present myself as reconfigured by the textual Foucault. My first exposure to the textual Foucault was in 1981 when I read *The Order of Things* and saw the modern world in a new light. I did not see any immediate relevance to my narrow field of study. After reading *The Archaeology of Knowledge*, I saw little advantage in studying discourse as Foucault recommended. Reading more and more Foucault, I was never quite sure about the methodological difference between foucauldian archaeology and genealogy. That most scholars speak of genealogy with no further ado may suggest that, in their opinion (however little considered), Foucault was no longer interested in large questions and great discontinuities, preferring instead to focus on local expressions of power and resistance. This seems right. Yet it is not so clear that this shift in his concerns required a shift in his method of inquiry.

I am convinced that the terms *archaeology* and *genealogy* are different metaphors for the same general method, which finds past and present in a stable relation. As a metaphor, archaeology suggests that whatever we excavate will be fragmentary—shards that resist assembly into recognizable objects. Foucault also talked about "genealogical fragments" that we "dig out of the sand."[11] The method is the same, the frame is fixed, the objects of inquiry are fragmentary. Yet there would seem to be a substantive discontinuity in Foucault's thought. The fragments to be excavated were fragments even before they were buried. However paradoxically, it is modernity's great discontinuities, and thus the piecing together of whole epochs, that secure the relation between method and substance.

### *Discontinuities*

"In any given culture at any given moment," Foucault wrote in *The Order of Things*, "there is always only one *episteme* that defines the conditions of possibility of all knowledge, whether expressed in a theory or silently invested in a practice."[12] An episteme is a set of rules telling people in that culture (I would say society) how to gain knowledge about their world and put that knowledge to use. By the same token, an episteme is a set of constraints on what people can possibly know. Must we take Foucault's epistemes as he found them? I think not. The first two he evoked brilliantly. The third is, in my view, misrepresented. A fourth he failed to identify at all.

Foucault has framed the Renaissance episteme as a world of "things visible and invisible," among which its inhabitants routinely made associations.[13] Knowledge is the methodical accumulation of similarities. Metaphor, analogy and repetition make the dissemination of knowledge no less methodical. Only in this epistemic space of inexhaustible resemblances was it possible for Renaissance humanists to situate themselves in relation to the ancients, find an alternative to cyclical or apocalyptic interpretations of the past and undermine the temporal unity and moral authority of medieval universalism.[14]

Resemblance was, however, not only a way for Renaissance minds to turn their experience of the world into knowledge about the world. Adjacency plays its part; things "come sufficiently close to one another to be in juxtaposition." Yet we should not think of adjacency as a geometric relation. Things are adjacent when "their edges touch, their fringes intermingle, the extremity of the one also denotes the beginning of the other."[15] Even less does it imply that cause is an abstract relation between things. Instead adjacency links proximity and familarity, valorizes what is convenient and customary in everyday life, smooths out the discontinuities that odd resemblances might suggest and produces local knowledge.

On Foucault's account, the classical episteme no longer limits thinking to similarities. Differences come to the fore because each thing has a nature uniquely its own. Yet things do not differ in every ascertainable property, and they can be sorted by the kinds of properties they have in common with some other things. Moreover, the relations among things can also be sorted by what they have in common, the ways in which they are identical. Even the relation between properties and relations has fixed properties. What we can know depends on how we represent the relation of things in relation. *The Archaeology of Knowledge* uses the term *representation* in a spare and not very helpful way: representations are "signifying elements referring to contents."[16] Throughout *The Order of Things*, the text associates representation and order.

Order lends itself to formal expression, most obviously as geometry. For the classical mind, nature has an order that we cannot appreciate directly but nevertheless can make sense of by ordering things and their relations. Yet classical order is neither order for its own sake nor order for practical purposes. It is an attempt to explain how the world works in the most general terms, on the assumption that the great classical thinkers of antiquity had the same ambition.

Foucault's understanding of the modern episteme is harder to convey. "History displaces order as the fundamental mode of being of empiricities." History is not simply "a compilation of factual successions or sequences"; it "*gives place* to analogical organic structures, just as Order opened the way to *successive* identities and differences." In the classical episteme, identities and differences succeeded each other as spatially imagined wholes. The modern episteme took analogy out of the Renaissance world of appearances and deployed it in time. By invoking development, evolution and dialectical reasoning, modern thinkers could bring together "totalities of elements without the slightest visible identity."[17]

The "empiricities" of history are the objects and events to which modern sciences applies its analytic procedures—an "analytic of finitude"[18] (see Dillon in this volume). Positivist methodology starts by isolating these things and measuring their properties. Only then can observers make causal inferences about the relations of things. Reduction displaces representation in the methodical pursuit of knowledge. When things are related with enough complexity to resist analysis, we often call these complex things organisms or, more abstractly, systems, to which we impute structure and make inferences about their functions. Modern physics and biology exemplify the possible trajectories of modern science.

The modern episteme developed a discontinuity, first manifest in the theory of evolution and on full display by 1900. Yet Foucault seems never to have acknowledged it. Many other scholars have paid it a great deal of attention as the modernist movement in arts and letters. I believe Foucault's resistance on this point stems from his close attention to the preoccupation with organisms and their functioning in the early nineteenth century. Foucault may not have seen a discontinuity develop later in the century because of its functional orientation. Or he may have read subsequent modernist functionalism, with its emphasis on adaptive differentiation, back into earlier investigations of organisms and the totality of their functional relations.

In any event, modernism issued science a methodological mandate: get below the surface of things, and not, as modern science demands, below some thing to the things beneath. Thus motivated, modernists instituted a new set of sciences: political science, sociology, psychology and anthropology. Insofar as modernist thought and the social sciences reaffirm "human finitude" and thus "the strange figure of knowledge called man," they remain, for Foucault, within the confines of the modern episteme. Thus, the imminent "disappearance of man" would mark the appearance of an entirely new post-modern episteme, and not merely a post-modernist moment.

For each episteme, there is a before and after, a pair of discontinuities, none of them easily identified. Foucault found these discontinuities in different "domains" of knowledge. Domain (*domaine*) is a conveniently loose metaphor, which we find Foucault having deployed in many contexts. Domains of knowledge are "discursive formations" or "unities"—Foucault used both formulations repeatedly. Treating such unities methodically, "what we discover is neither a configuration, nor a form, but a group of *rules* that are immanent in a practice."[19]

Do domains of knowledge, each defined by its own ensemble of rules, have common features when considered together? Foucault inveighed against "totalitarian periodization."[20] Yet discontinuities within discursive formations must have common features—a "totality" of cross-domain continuities—if they are to constitute an epistemic rupture. Foucault contradicted himself on this issue.[21] I suspect he was unsure as to whether some ensemble of rules unified the rules constituting each episteme and then at some point these meta-rules changed, or each ensemble of domain rules more or less paralleled the others in reaching a breaking point and losing their coherence. Here's how Foucault finessed the issue in *The Archaeology of Knowledge*:

> The idea of a single break suddenly, at a given moment, dividing all discursive formations, interrupting them in a single moment and reconstituting them in accordance with the same rules—such an idea cannot be sustained. The contemporaneity of several transformations does not mean their exact chronological coincidence: each transformation may have its own particular index of temporal "viscosity".[22]

### Domains

*The Order of Things* puts forward three discursive formations that Foucault took to have been "constituted in similar ways" in the seventeenth century.[23] These he called Natural History, General Grammar and the Analysis of Wealth, respectively oriented to speaking (*parler*), classifying (*classer*) and exchanging (*échanger*).[24] With the advent of the modern age, around 1800, these discursive formations became "what are for us the 'quasi-transcendentals' of Life, Labour, and Language."[25]

They are duly sedimented into "human sciences" of biology, political economy and philology. Representation gave way to the analysis of positivities, and the human sciences turned into positivities themselves.

When Foucault described the domains of Life, Labor and Language as "quasi-transcendentals," he created the impression that these three domains were not just obvious choices but the only choices. He never clarified what properties would elevate some domains over others in epistemic significance. Nor did he preclude the possibility of "other archaeologies." Indeed, he offered three possibilities: "the archaeological description of 'sexuality,'" an analysis of painting and an analysis of "political knowledge."[26]

The first of these possibilities Foucault would later begin as a multivolume project on the history of sexuality but not finish. The brief introductory volume proposes a return to archaeology in all but name: "In order to situate the investigations that will follow, let me put forward some general propositions concerning the objective, the method, the domain to be covered, and the periodizations that one can accept in a provisory way."[27] We find Foucault mentioning the classical age several times.[28] At no point in setting up this ambitious project did he suggest that sexual practices constitute a quasi-transcendental domain.

The second possibility would be to "reconstitute the latent discourse of the painter." Thus "one can try to recapture the murmur of his intentions, which are not transcribed into words, but into lines, surfaces, and colours; one can try to uncover the implicit philosophy that is supposed to form his view of the world."[29] Foucault's brilliant discussion of Diego Velásquez's *Las Meninas* to begin *The Order of Things* and a contemporaneous discussion of René Magritte's *Ceci n'est pas une pipe* pursue this possibility. The analysis of a single painting may tell us a great deal about one or another episteme but less when digging through an epistemic rupture, and much less when embarking on a full-scale archaeological expedition.

The third possibility calls for some comment. One might think that Foucault's genealogical forays into politics and power are so fragmentary as to defeat an archaeological assessment. The recent publication of Foucault's lecture series at the Collège de France for 1978 gives a rather different impression. Analysis of the pastorate takes four lectures, one lecture attends to the transition from the pastorate to the apparatus of the state, and then four lectures examine reason of state, reason taken to mean a rational attitude toward the condition of rule. As for the transition, Foucault reverted to an archaeological mode of expression:

An entirely finalist world, an anthropocentric world, a world of prodigies, marvels, and signs, and finally a world of analogies and ciphers, constitute the manifest form of God's pastoral government of the world. This is what disappeared. When? Precisely between 1580 and 1650, at the same time as the foundation of the classical *episteme*.[30]

The 1979 lectures resume the discussion of politics. Despite their title—*The Birth of Biopolitics*—they say remarkably little about the advent of modern age and its positivities, including the state, its population and government as apparatus of rule over enumerated people. Foucault explained why in the first lecture: "only when we know what this governmental regime called liberalism was, will we be able to grasp what biopolitics is"; reason of state gave way to liberalism as "economic truth."[31] Liberalism and its permutations dominate the eleven subsequent lectures (see Gros, and Pandolfi and Macfalls in this volume). That liberalism only slowly prevailed in the West over the course of two centuries and in the process gradually changed in character, not least in its relation to capital, militates against any sense of rupture in the conditions of rule. We are left instead with a genealogy of continuities in political economy and an unstated assumption that modern liberalism is a quasi-transcendental condition.

Defining politics in terms of power, which leaves its traces in every epoch and domain, yields a genealogy of fragments—a poor substitute for an archaeology of political knowledge. Defining politics by reference to law does more than help. It saves the day. Had Foucault made law the fourth domain when he worked out the plan for *The Order of Things*, he would have made place for political knowledge that is repeatedly transformed over the centuries but never diminished in importance.

Foucault's discussion of the pastorate amply confirms the fully transcendental position and unifying force of law in an otherwise fragmented Medieval world. While his treatment of the Renaissance as a "finalist world" minimizes the epistemic consequences of Humanist scholars' confrontation with Scholastic lawyers, it does comport with my own sense that Renaissance Europe remained a traditional society in its conditions of rule. The rupture following the Renaissance thrust law into the discursive foreground. Throughout the classical age, the law of nature and of nations linked philosophy and science as a quasi-transcendental frame for practical political knowledge. That frame transformed when writers abandoned natural law in favor of a fully secular law befitting the age of "man." Yet law maintained its quasi-transcendental position in theory and practice.

It did so chiefly by legitimating states as territorial monopolies of rule and the society of states as a mighty frame for the modern world. And it did so under the cover of a discourse of rights and the rule of law that had already come to the fore during the rupture of the classical episteme. Had Foucault come to appreciate modern, positive law as an infinitely extendable and adaptable set of rules constituting an apparatus of rule in diverse settings—some liberal, some not—he would have had no need to adopt that "ugly word 'governmentality.'"[32] Instead, he might have seen that modern rationalism and then modernist professionalization along functional lines gave the domain of law the very features that he found so difficult to articulate in the 1978 lectures on governmentality.

We might ask why Foucault never recognized law as a domain on a par with life, language and labor. He is well known for his interest in what people take to be normal and therefore abnormal. One might think that the domain of law extends to the normal and abnormal in social relations. Yet he saw law and norm at odds. Thus he held that the "development of bio-power" a consequence of "the growing importance assumed by the action of the norm, at the expense of the juridical system of the law."[33] Behind this point of view is an exceedingly narrow conception of law as an instrument of social control.

A defining feature of law is its normativity (and any social mechanism, no matter how informal, that relies on normativity for its causal efficacy falls within the domain of law). Normativity refers to all those social relations about which it is appropriate (in the English language) to use the modal auxiliaries "can," "may," "should" and "must." The use of these auxiliaries or their semantic equivalents results in some degree of obligation, or prescriptive force, whether accepted or resisted. On etymological grounds alone, normativity and normality are obviously related. How they are related would also seem to be obvious: what everyone does ends up being what everyone should do in the end.

Foucault's conception of norm reflects a background in the history and philosophy of science. Such a conception is so limited as to exclude obligation, law and perhaps even ethics as conventionally understood. When Foucault wrote about rules, they are crystalizations of routine practices lacking any discernible normative force. In my opinion, his treatment of normality is his greatest contribution to social theory. Conversely, his indifference to normativity was his greatest failing as a social theorist and the chief reason why he failed to recognize law as the fourth domain.

I have suggested that the domain of law helped to frame political knowledge. That frame survived a series of ruptures and periodically recast the limits of knowledge about power and politics, rules and rule. Over several centuries, the domain of law has contributed at least as much to the constitution of Western modernity as have the domains of life, language and labor. What Foucault described as neoliberal governmentality and I would describe as the effects of modern rationalization and modernist professionalization grants the domain of law even greater importance. Arguably, it now threatens to swamp the other three domains.

## CONCLUSION

Let me summarize. I reconfigured Foucault so as to have him complete the majestic plan of *The Order of Things* and then to modify it as he proceeds through the chapters of his life and sees what he did not adequately take into account. *This* Foucault, young and brash indeed, worked out a systematic conception of Western modernity from its beginnings and never abandoned it. His late remarks on pastoral power would place it in the Medieval age that gave way to the Renaissance. Long before, he had located the sovereign power of the crown in the Renaissance without having said so explicitly. His treatment of the classical age has sovereign power rationalized as the legal regime of the sovereign state. The advent of the modern age at the end of the eighteenth century marks "the birth of biopolitics" in company with positivist science. Disciplinary power finds a place in what I have called the modern*ist* age. In the domain of law, it adds functional differentiation and an implicit evolutionary logic to modern processes of positivist reduction and rationalization.

Thirty years after Foucault's death, whatever seems to be happening now in the domain of law and what it says about late or post-modernity do not make the Foucault whom we think we know—the normalized Foucault—the most insightful or prescient of observers. If I were to bring my reconfigured Foucault into the present (figuratively, of course) and he were to consider the convergence I just alluded to, he might conclude that epistemic discontinuities do not mean that old ways of thinking disappear. Instead, they pile up as the modern world sags under many burdens. Moreover, he might see that the domain of law and its highly disciplined technologists threaten to swamp the other three domains—all of them.

Perhaps not. Foucault as I have configured him put the modern world aside in his last years and went back to antiquity. There, in an epistemic context not ours but not entirely unfamiliar either, he hoped to find a subject, a self, so constituted as to care for itself in a way that is impervious to the convergence of modern and modernist conditions. The texts he consulted link the care of one's self to pleasure, thus leading from an "ethics of control" to an "ethics of pleasure."[34]

"A break with the traditional ethics of self-mastery?" A young Foucault might have said yes to his own question: There had been a break, a discontinunity, a rupture in the ethics of antiquity. Yet this is *not* what happened. "Clearly not, but rather a shift, a change of orientation, a difference in emphasis."[35] This abrupt sequence of incomplete sentences manages to convey a contemplative tone, a rueful awareness. The ethics of self-mastery has never gone away. Texts from that age linking self-control to good conduct, and good conduct to the common good, still resonate.

The Foucault that I have reconfigured to suit myself would have soon moved from self-constitution to its paradoxical double, that is, to self-control. To have done this would have brought his attention back to resistance and thus to normativity. In due course, he would have embraced what we now call virtue ethics and a republican conception of the domain of law. Such a turn is, I believe, the only possible antidote to late modern excesses and the impending collapse of the liberal world.

Of course, I have projected myself into this figuration of Foucault. I have no doubt that any number of foucauldians, armed with texts that I have never so much as laid eyes on, will dismiss it out of hand. I have reservations myself, spurred by Foucault's attachment to Nietzsche as a figure whose ethical claims would seem to have little or no relation to the virtue ethics descending from Greco-Roman antiquity. Yet it is Foucault's conception of limits and their transgression that gives me greater pause.

> And yet, toward what is transgression unleashed in its movement of pure violence, if not that which imprisons it, toward the limit and those elements it contains? What bears the brunt of its aggression and to what void does it owe the unrestrained fullness of its being, if not that which it crosses in its violent act and which, as its destiny, it crosses out in the line it effaces?[36]

Foucault wrote these words in 1963, only two years after he published *Folie et déraison*. I hear in them two contradictory impulses: one is the glorification of "pure violence" and the other is the absence of an agent. Transgression is "obstinate"; "aggression" is a property of transgression and not the act of a trangressor. Together these impulses deny the possibility of self-control, not to mention responsibility, the social function of limits, the domain of law and the point of resistance.

Taken together, these impulses define madness for many purposes. Indeed, they grant madness "a primitive purity."[37] Is this Foucault coming to grips with the possibility of his own madness? Or Foucault assuaging the pain that abnormality so often inflicts? Or a high-style fanboy's taste for such cartoonish figures as Sade and Artaud? Or, as Hacking has suggested, a "romantic fantasy"?[38]

We will never know. It seems likely that the man whom we call Foucault never knew himself (the double entendre is deliberate). Insofar as that man believed in the purity of madness and acted out his transgressive impulses, it would discredit both the normalized Foucault and the reconfigured Foucault that I have invoked in these pages. I prefer to think that he lived most of his life by an implicit code of self-control. How else to account for the sheer size and many layers of the foucauldian archive?

It seems fitting to end this essay with Foucault's definition of an archive:

> The archive is first the law of what can be said, the system that governs the appearance of statements (énoncés) as unique events. But the archive is also that which determines that all these things said do not accumulate endlessly in an amorphous mass, nor are they inscribed in an unbroken linearity [une linéarité sans rupture], nor do they disappear at the mercy of chance external accidents; but they are grouped together in distinct figures [figures distinctes], composed together in accordance with multiple relations, maintained or blurred in accordance with specific regularities; that which determines that they do not withdraw at the same pace in time, but shine, as it were, like stars, some that seem close to us shining brightly from afar off, while others that are in fact close to us are already growing pale.[39]

Madness resides in the domain of what cannot be said. Nothing that Foucault said accumulates endlessly and amorphously. All that he did say can be grouped together in distinct figures, of which he is indeed one. For so many of us, in so many fields, this figure shines more brightly the farther we are from its biographical singularities.

## NOTES

1. Michel Foucault, *The Archaeology of Knowledge*, transl. A.M. Sheridan Smith (New York: Pantheon, 1972), pp. 45.
2. Ian Hacking, *Historical Ontology* (Cambridge, MA: Harvard University Press, 2002), p. 90. Hacking was probably referring to this passage: "Et c'est lui qui a rendu possibles ces individualités que nous appelons Hobbes, ou Berkeley, ou Hume, ou Condillac." "Individualities" is too awkward

for English use; "individuals," which we find in the English translation, misses Foucault's obvious attempt to depersonalize individual thinkers, while Hacking's "figure" nicely captures it. Michel Foucault, *Les mots et les choses: Une archéologie des sciences humaines* (Éditions Gallimard, 1966), p. 77; *The Order of Things: An Archaeology of the Human Sciences*, transl. A.M. Sheridan Smith (New York: Pantheon Books, 1971), p. 70.

3. Michel Foucault, *The Archaeology of Knowledge*, p. 45.
4. See James Der Derian; "Critical encounters in international relations"; *International Social Science Journal*, 59(191) (2009): 69–73.
5. James Der Derian and Michael J. Shapiro, eds., *International/Intertextual Relations: Postmodern Readings of World Politics* (Lexington: Lexington Books, 1989).
6. Michael Barnett and Raymond Duvall, "Power in International Politics," *International Organization*, 59(1) (2005): 57.
7. Michel Foucault, *Discipline and Punish: The Birth of the Prison*, transl. Alan Sheridan (New York: Vintage Books, 1979), p. 194; scare marks in text.
8. Michel Foucault, *Security, Territory, Population: Lectures at the Collège de France, 1977–1978*, transl. Graham Burchill (Basingstoke: Palgrave Macmillan, 2007); Michel Foucault, *The Birth of Biopolitics: Lectures at the Collège de France, 1978–1979*, transl. Graham Burchill (Basingstoke: Palgrave Macmillan, 2008).
9. Jan Selby, "Engaging Foucault: Discourse, Liberal Governance and the Limits of Foucauldian IR," *International Relations*, 27(3) (2007): 334.
10. Brent J. Steele, *Defacing Power: The Aesthetics of Insecurity in Global Politics* (Ann Arbor: University of Michigan Press, 2012), is a conspicuous exception.
11. Michel Foucault, *Society Must Be Defended: Lectures at the Collège de France, 1975-1976*, transl. David Macey (New York: Picador, 2003), p. 11.
12. Foucault, *The Order of Things*, p. 183.
13. Ibid., p. 19.
14. Constantin Fasolt, *The Limits of History* (Chicago: University of Chicago Press, 2004), pp. 16–39.
15. Foucault, *The Order of Things*, p. 20.
16. Foucault, *The Archaeology of Knowledge*, p. 49.
17. Ibid., pp. 237, 288.
18. Ibid., pp. 340–7.
19. Foucault, *The Archaeology of Knowledge*, p. 46.
20. Ibid., p. 148.
21. Gary Gutting, *Michel Foucault's Archaeology of Scientific Reason* (Cambridge: Cambridge University Press, 1989), pp. 178–9.
22. Foucault, *The Archaeology of Knowledge*, p. 175.
23. Ibid.

24. Foucault, *The Order of Things*, ch. 3–5.
25. Ibid., p. 272.
26. Foucault, *The Archaeology of Knowledge*, pp. 192, 193.
27. Michel Foucault, *The History of Sexuality, Volume I: An Introduction*, transl. Robert Hurley (New York: Pantheon, 1978), p. 80.
28. See especially ibid., p. 143 on its rupture and the emergence of "modern man."
29. Foucault, *The Archaeology of Knowledge*, p. 193.
30. Foucault, *Security, Territory, Population*, lecture nine, p. 237.
31. Foucault, *The Birth of Biopolitics*, lecture one, p. 22.
32. Foucault, *Security, Territory, Population*, lecture five, p. 115.
33. Foucault, *The History of Sexuality*, p. 144. See Ben Golder and Peter Fitzpatrick, *Foucault's Law* (Abingdon: Routledge, 2009), pp. 34–9, for discussion.
34. Michel Foucault, *Care of the Self, Volume 3 of the History of Sexuality*, transl. Robert Hurley (New York: Pantheon, 1986), pp. 65, 67.
35. Foucault, *Care of the Self*, p. 67.
36. Michel Foucault, "A Preface to Transgression," in *Language, Counter-Memory, Practice: Selected Essays and Interviews* (Ithaca: Cornell University Press, 1977), pp. 34–5.
37. Michel Foucault, "Preface to the 1961 edition," *History of Madness*, transl. Jonathan Murphy and Jean Khalfa (Abingdon: Routledge, 2006), xxxiii.
38. Ian Hacking, "Foreword," in Foucault, *History of Madness*, p. xi.
39. Foucault, *The Archaeology of Knowledge*, p. 129; *L'archéologie du savoir*, p. 170.

# CHAPTER 3

# Michel Foucault and International Relations: Cannibal Relations

*Didier Bigo*

## INTRODUCTION: CANNIBAL RELATIONS

Political science has framed the issue of how people are governed and how they govern themselves by differentiating power *within* the state and power *between* states, thereby separating government studies and the study of international relations (hereafter called IR).[1] The distinction between an *inside* and an *outside* of the state has organized both sub-disciplines as Siamese twins who would hate each other while endlessly await for surgery.[2] This has become so "natural" for us—as scholars—that we seem to be forgetting this initial split despite its immense consequences for the study of dynamics of power and politics, and their inscription in space.

Michel Foucault, on the contrary, never considered this split as being relevant. For him, the French political science "discipline" was just something of a follow-up and an extension of a science of government in the service of the "state" and the "raison d'Etat," not a consistent domain of knowledge (*savoir*) to study politics. He never seemed to be interested in

D. Bigo (✉)
Sciences Po, Paris, France

Kings College London, London, UK
e-mail: didier.bigo.conflits@gmail.com

© The Author(s) 2017
P. Bonditti et al. (eds.), *Foucault and the Modern International*,
The Sciences Po Series in International Relations and Political
Economy, DOI 10.1057/978-1-137-56153-4_3

33

discussing with IR scholars and was not sure IR could be organized as a specific field of study that would grasp a form of knowledge of its own.

At the College de France, because a large group of students coming from political studies started populating the amphitheater during the mid-seventies, he felt obliged to explain that his disdain and indifference toward the discipline of political science and its rhetoric was the best way he had found to work seriously on the topic of territory, population and security, ignoring their assumptions from the beginning. Engaging a dialogue would have been hopeless indeed. He was, however, absolutely fascinated by the object of political science as a science of government and decided to conduct his own enquiry with other methods: genealogical ones. On several occasions, Foucault also insisted on the necessity to approach and study politics as a (series of) practice(s). "War is too important to be left to military studies, the same is true for politics, avoid political 'science' but engage with their topics, with their texts, not with their commentators; engage also with politics as practice and in practice, engage with their effects instead of resorting to abstract generalization, in search of an essence of politics." It was the same for IR. To those who criticized him—as some post-colonial scholars did (see Esteves & Fernández in this volume)—for not engaging with the international, Foucault had the very same answer: "You misrecognize what IR is because you always look for comparative politics and other states behavior. This is not what I am doing. But, think how analyzing death penalty, or studying prisons is a way to deal with the issue of the international—even if one does not admit it—by what it revealed about governing in different places."[3]

Later on (in 1982), he would insist on the "historical circumstances"[4] of his lectures in the seventies and their implicit international politics. As Alessandro Fontana and Mauro Bertani signaled in their presentation of his 1977 lectures (*Society must be defended*), it is necessary to read these lectures while having in mind Foucault's permanent back and forth between, on the one hand his activity of writing, and on the other the international conflicts of his time (in Vietnam, in Palestine, in Chile, in Northern Ireland) as well as the post-1968 social and political struggles in France. It was not necessary to give further details or examples. The audience understood immediately the implicit international references, which permeated the tone of Foucault's lectures, and also explained much of the metaphors he used. As surprising as it may be for some, I will contend that Michel Foucault has been a "politist" and an "internationalist," but of a different kind.

Therefore, as I will explain in a first part, despite the reciprocal indifference between Foucault and the political scientists of his time, his lectures have left profound traces in IR until today. The importance of Foucault for IR and his legacy for today exist, despite this initial non-encounter, and even hostility, whose conditions of possibility have to be examined.

Although Foucault avoided direct contact with political scientists in France, he nonetheless encountered some geographers while focusing on some of the key texts and concepts they were referring to and on which political science, IR and geography had based their assumptions about, and conceptions of space, war, power, subjectivation and freedom.

In a second part, I will return to the discussion about war and develop on why the conception of war Foucault proposed can be a way to escape today's extremely controversial, and somehow loosely framed debates on war, terrorism and radicalization. It is also during these formative years (1974–1978) that Foucault partly changed his earlier agenda, initially formulated in terms of an archaeology of knowledge (centered on concepts and discourses)[5], to engage more directly and more systematically with issues of politics, sovereignty, discipline and power. In their "Situation du cours," Fontana and Bertani[6] explain Foucault's intellectual trajectory as being in harmony with his practical engagements, and the implicit references to a political context that everyone understood at that time, but vanished in time and translations since then. For them, this partly explains why, unimpressed by the arguments developed in IR about a balance of power between states, Foucault coined terminologies and intellectual tools such as biopolitics, dispositif, governmentality, diagram of power, that so many scholars now use.

Hence, by proposing different "thinking tools," his work de facto *cannibalized* political science and IR by "devouring" their topics, by questioning differently sovereignty, territory, population, as well as criticizing the focus on state power, so often reduced to an essence and conceived as a unified and homogenous "actor." Foucault challenged and reformulated the dominant narratives without even discussing their (implicit) "theories," nor using their examples, but by simply showing how to think differently about power, subjectivation, at whatever scale could be imagined: from the self to the chains of interdependences that establish molecular relations in "moles" of molecules (to use Deleuze's terminology).

The newly institutionalized French political science—which inherited its schemes of analysis from US political science, while also having to cope with the powerful group of French law professors—did not survive the confrontation at a distance. Many French students of the late seventies left political sciences to choose history or sociology. But, more than 30 years later, a new generation of IR scholars (often of different countries), has reconnected Foucault with their discipline, welcoming his legacy of thought. Nevertheless, in return, Foucault's achievements in terms of thinking differently about how people are governed and govern themselves was made possible via multiple translations—linguistically as well as trans-disciplinary, that is from French to other languages as much as in terms of fields of knowledge (*savoir*): political theory, history, sociology, geography, cultural and gender studies... So, by an apparent paradox, after his death, a doppelganger of Foucault appeared in US political science. This other Foucault was a liberal thinker, apologetic toward Ronald Reagan and Margaret Thatcher and, more recently, even configured as a justification for counter-terrorism policies involving surveillance and predictive actions based on algorithms. This de-contextualization dismembered the coherence of his own body of work—even though that kind of re-appropriation might have satisfied Foucault himself who considered that creativity with his thinking tools was by far more important than transforming his ideas into doctrinal statements.

Therefore, as I shall suggest in conclusion, some of the terminologies Foucault developed have been in turn cannibalized by what gradually became known as a "foucauldian field of study," to be re-incorporated into academic disciplines that had hold him in contempt 30 years earlier, by their inner critics in quite surprising ways, especially around security. Are we therefore in a "cannibal democracy" of mutual eating and devouring?[7] Is Oswald de Andrade's "anthropophagist manifesto" (a narrative created for Brazil's modernity), the best metaphor to illustrate what happened between Foucault and the French IR inherited from US political science? What kind of "mulato" is French IR today? Has the mutual swallowing and absorbing of what is useful in a culture or a domain/form of knowledge eventually worked? I propose to proceed to Foucault's "death relevailles"[8] urging scholars daring to mitigate the philosopher and historian he was, to do so with a sociology and an anthropology of practices to perpetuate his fight to understand politics in the world against the renewed different disciplinary dogmas that claim to hold the appropriate knowledge of the way living beings are/ shall be governed and govern themselves.

## INTERNATIONAL RELATIONS AND POLITICAL SCIENCE IN FRANCE: WHY FOUCAULT NEVER MET DUVERGER

A post-war discipline, IR has been nurtured by schemes inherited from US political sciences in the fifties and sixties, and especially by security and strategic studies. Rational Choice Theory, understanding of the state as a unified actor represented by a government and acting on a specific "international" scene, ideas of a national interest made congruent with security understood as "*national* security," have led to a series of assumptions—especially regarding population and people, territory and borders, war and security—and a strong common sense equivalent to a doxa. IR scholars have effectively come to share such doxa despite their different structural or normative positioning regarding: first the stability of the system, second the specificities of the norms that would govern the international life of states, and third the future of international relations as either an exclusive domain of state actors or ineluctably pushed toward the blending of state and transnational actors in a global(ized) and supposedly borderless world.

In France, this construction of the discipline of IR as a realm apart from political theory and sociology, built on the idea of a two-faced Janus state organizing the internal and the external differently, developed as a wall built inside the Law faculties and with the support of the "école libre des sciences politiques," against the contamination of ideas introduced by the post-structuralist movement of the late sixties agitating humanities and social sciences. They were convinced their "fortress" was impregnable and that the new political elites they were training would not know what was going on a couple of blocks away.

Those who believed so were wrong. Political science was to be challenged because of its own situation in France and to fragment, pushing many students to change discipline or to quit university. Indeed, both the state and the status of IR and political science in France in the mid-seventies was still very fragile and very dependent on the US model. If the idea of moral and political sciences had existed since the 1880s within the "école libre des sciences politiques" as a science of, and for (entering) the state, the status of a specific field of knowledge called political science was still very much discussed a century later. Political science was still considered an appendix of the Law faculties and the *Treaty of political science* was mainly organized by constitutional lawyers, and edited by Georges Burdeau, himself a lawyer.

It is in this context that Maurice Duverger and Marcel Merle's initiative to create a "discipline" as such—with its own "Agrégation,"[9] different from public law, and based on a referential mainly coming from the US—was central. The duumvirate of government and IR studies represented by Maurice Duverger and Marcel Merle gradually gained autonomy to eventually become institutionalized: French "political science" as a proper discipline was born, with an orthodoxy even more stringent than in the USA, and so profoundly different from sociology, philosophy and French literature. The post-1968 cultural bubbling of ideas that had agitated sociology and philosophy was severely disavowed in most of the courses. In those years, students attracted by politics were at a lost: the discipline of political science was not really the place to discuss politics, quite the contrary. It created dissatisfaction and search for alternatives. These were just nearby, at the College de France where students from Sorbonne or the "Institut d'études politiques," including a few political scientists of the new generation, migrated and formed long queues to learn how to think differently.[10]

This is how Foucault saw his course more populated than ever and welcomed the "defectors" with a surprised smile when they evoked what they were being taught within the political science departments around. They became a diaspora having much in common with their new home, and almost banned or deprived of their professional citizenship of political scientist when they were quoting Foucault. Yet, the "contamination" had begun,[11] and the words of Foucault were to infiltrate the heart of the dogma of "political science" and IR, devouring the old conceptions of territory and space, security and sovereignty, population and people and proposing alternative frames of understanding.

It is certainly difficult to realize what political science and security were in France in the mid-seventies. Even those who lived this period are now uneasy to explain how they have been entrapped into a series of beliefs and assumptions, now regarded as caricatures. While an aggiornamento was asked to the communists who had believed in Staline and Thorez, a similar work of "remembrance" has not yet reached the discipline of political science despite some troubled moments in the 1990s.[12] Important and lively debates on foreign affairs and on the creation of moral statements for the cold state monsters certainly did exist around Pierre Hassner and Stanley Hoffmann, but the epistemological discussions in the IR theories' courses of the 1980s concerning the modalities of veridiction were, and are still extremely poor. Some pre-reflexive positivist statements that no social scientist of the late 1960s would dare to say continue to be presented as "evidence" in some courses of IR, even today.

Looking back at the mid-seventies courses and manuals first shows that IR was in fact more a history of foreign affairs, and/or what lawyers called "general culture," a sort of gloss allowing to speak beyond the technicalities of a specialty. Security studies were part of strategic and military studies, which were themselves part of International Relations, especially the branch of it in which the horizon of death carried by the Mutually Assured Destruction (MAD) doctrine of the time was considered to be more important than the horizon of equality, justice, welfare and development. In a context of competing ideologies setting up "blocks," the key discussions on security were limited to the political implications of the existence of nuclear power, and of the emergence of a perpetual situation of crisis Aron had coined as "impossible peace, improbable war."[13] For the newly born French political science and its IR specialty, the ambition was to become another *scientific* discipline by looking at what had been done in the USA and reproduce it.

At that time, security was a clear and uncontested concept for political science and IR. It was understood as the result of an accumulation of power, with a material conception of the latter so it could be conceived as something that could be possessed and to which means and goals could be attached. These goals were clear, at least for politicians and their top strategists and military advisors. Most, if not all, top political scientists at the time acted as strategists and experts, simultaneously working at defining "national security" and promoting their own academic discipline in which handbooks analyzing the arms race were the most popular readings. In this context, political science was presented as a useful discipline for political scientist to join the military-diplomatic apparatus, and for the latter to equip itself with scientific tools that would help calculating and determining the best positioning for the country national interests.

Assumptions regarding security as a *need* that would exist naturally for all humans, tightly connected to the protection a state would give to its population, were unchallenged. Security was about survival, about war, and not the endgame of multiple games of probabilities and risk. The fact that within sociology or law departments, security may mean *social* security and refer to the protection of individuals against accidents at work, or against unemployment by legal regimes of administrative norms, was just incomprehensible.

When some in the eighties started to challenge these beliefs, they did so through an IR inner critique, trying to expand security studies to other domains of social life, rather than by deconstructing these.[14] The paradox is that they have been called "critical security studies" (hereafter CSS) even though, ignoring how security was conceived outside IR, they eventually perpetuated a conception of security tightly connected to the notion of survival in which security remained a form of protection against the violence of others. Such a conception also kept relying on well-established distinctions (inside/outside, military/police organizations, enemies/adversaries) that Foucault had already discussed at length in his lectures. By the time, these lectures had not yet been translated and would only arrive in the English language "market" by the late eighties to become popular by the beginning of the 2000s only.

## Doing International Studies Differently: Foucault on War, Space, Territory, Population and Governmentality

My intention is neither to discuss the full context of Foucault's series of lectures in the 1970s, nor develop in details about each of these lectures. Others have done this very well: Mauro Bertani, François Ewald, Alessandro Fontana, Frédéric Gros and Michel Sennelart especially. I would like however to very briefly link these lectures with the topics that traditional IR scholars considered as their domain of expertise, and that Foucault questioned so differently. I will evoke two topics only. The first is the discussion about war, with Foucault's reading of Hobbes and his strong critique of the neo-Hobbesian school of thought characterized by its attitude toward deterrence. On several occasions, Foucault insisted on his view of war as colonization and production of a historical narrative. The second topic relates to the patient deconstruction of the dogma of states' attributes: territory, population, security, which begins as early as 1974 and will continue at least until 1979. It may not be a theory of power as IR scholars fancy it, but it offers a clear alternative to understand the "voluntary servitude," that shall not be reduced to a will to serve, but rather implies to understand how freedom, resistance and power are articulated into a micro-physics, and not through big structures and huge institutions.

As Bertani and Fontana emphasized: "Foucault's interest in power stems from the vigilance, attention and interest with which he followed what Nietzsche called 'die grosse Politik': the rise of fascisms around the world, the civil wars, the establishment of military dictatorships, the oppressive geopolitical aims of the great powers (and especially of the United States in Vietnam)."[15] They also insisted on how deeply Foucault's interest in power was rooted in his political practice that allowed him to ground his analyses on concrete situations such as the material living conditions of the prisoners for example. With the historical context in mind, made of wars, social struggles and rebellions, Fontana and Bertani interpret the *Society Must Be Defended* lectures series as "the point of articulation of the political problem of power and the historical question of race."[16]

On several occasions Foucault spoke of his determination to understand this polymorphic violence that runs through society, and what Bertani and Fontana remind the English speaking readership of, is Foucault's strategy not to explicitly refer to a country or a given situation, rather proposing tools to understand power practices in various contexts. In this regard, and contrary to what some post-colonial critique of Foucault suggested,[17] Bertani and Fontana insist on Foucault's high interest for dissent and post-colonial struggles. They evoke the book and movie *Moi, Pierre Rivière* and the testimony of Daniel Defert:

> As Daniel Defert reminds us in his 'Chronology,' Foucault was reading Trotsky, Guevara, Luxemburg, and Clausewitz in 1967 and 1968. He was also reading the writings of the Black Panthers at that time, and he remarks in a letter 'they are developing a strategic analysis that has emancipated itself from Marxist theory.' In a letter written in December 1972, he says that he wants to analyze power relations by looking at 'the most disparaged of all wars: neither Hobbes, nor Clausewitz, nor the class struggle: civil war.' And in another letter, written in August 1974, he writes: 'My marginals are incredibly familiar and repetitive. I feel like looking at something else: political economy, strategy, politics.[18]

Foucault will therefore invest time trying to understand the closest colonial situations; Northern Ireland especially to see how these dimensions explain the long occupation of Ireland by the English, and also detainment conditions for political prisoners.

As I mentioned earlier, even if Michel Foucault never engaged with the orthodox discipline of political science, he nonetheless engaged with the journal of geopolitics *Herodote* and Yves Lacoste. The journal was heterodox at that time, contending functionalism and systemism, IR dominant approaches and conflict studies (Marcel Merle). It also opened its columns to post-colonial battles, analyzing Cyprus, Chile, anticolonial struggles. Like Michel Foucault, Yves Lacoste questioned the practices of making war in relation to territory and population, refusing to forget war-making, and to transform governments into "protectors" ensuring security to the population. The discussion was intense but never concretized into an alliance of knowledge (*alliance des savoirs*).[19] Nevertheless, when Foucault's ideas were translated into English, the geographers inspired by *Herodote* abroad were the first to listen to what he had to say about war and also territory:[20] territory has no certainty and is not an organizing principle for control and order. It is the contingent result of struggles of power and knowledge. States fighting for territories to expand their power and security derive from a vitalist approach common to many expressions of racism. The criticism of orthodox political science could not be more damageable.

As often with Foucault, his analytics of war, power, space and territory began with some bold statements he presented as questions that occur as soon as someone takes on an "empirical mood." What are the relations between practices of war, space and territory? What are the effects of these wars on populations? Is it possible to think about them "strategically?" Do we necessarily have to begin with Hobbes? In a soft tone, he explained that Hobbes did not offer a description of wars and civil wars; rather he wanted to set up the spatial and temporal frame of understanding justifying a "sub-lunar" sovereignty for the state. Hobbes tried to find "the formulation of general principles of public law." "So, the art of government was caught between an excessively large, abstract, and rigid framework of sovereignty on the one hand, and, on the other, a model of the family that was too narrow, weak, and insubstantial."[21]

In this vision, war is the "horizon" of a struggle of every man against every man, not an effective practice. This is the vision Clausewitz developed after the Napoleonic wars, pushing the idea even further, with the possible escalation to total war if politics did not limit the game by imposing strategic goals. This is also the logic at work in Aron's narrative with the introduction of deterrence as a war against the will of the adversary; a will that can be destroyed without fighting *effectively* if capacities of retaliation exist, and there remains no doubt about the determination to use them. This elaborated story, however, does not analyze the exercise of power. Should it do so, war would then be about invasion, occupation and the colonization of a people by another.

This certainly explains why Foucault's discussion on Boulainvilliers is so interesting. Through him it is possible to do the analytics of competing narratives that insist on the existence of either one or two peoples, and to see how colonization and occupation are justified and organized as forms of historical knowledge.[22] In the *Society Must Be Defended* lectures series, this is obviously not without reminding of the USA in Vietnam, Israel in

Palestine, and the Northern Ireland case, but Foucault's thinking tools are sharp enough so he does not need to make specific reference to any of these contexts.

The February 1976 lectures therefore deal centrally with the objects of International Relations: war and the exercise of power, as well as their regimes of justification. At no moment, however, does Foucault use the terminology of political science of security, be it to talk about security as survival or security as a balance of power (see also Esteves and Fernández in this volume). He seems to carefully avoid this terminology of security in which violence appears as a protection of the people by the state. His critique of the nineteenth century interpretation of the Hobbesian narrative, which allows to escape the practices of war-making and to develop a discourse of war "hanging over," reduced to a duel of will, to a virtualization, to aerial warfare with defoliant technologies. Here, Raymond Aron is one of the obvious ghost figures.

Yet, when Boulainvilliers writes about Gaul, Romans, Frankish and the Germanic invasion, the reader may have the war in Vietnam or the Israël/Palestine situation in mind; it is up to him. The same can be said for the absent term of security in a military understanding of survival. Using the terminology would be accepting a certain narrative from the discipline of political science and IR. The term security is not used to analyze war practices, it has to be either rejected or exclusively used in relation to the protection of workers, with guarantees and welfare.

This is what most "critical security studies" scholars never understood for they have been searching for the lectures explicitly mentioning "security," and not the ones in which Foucault was in fact (intentionally) avoiding the term though dealing with the practices of violence that CSS and IR actually name(d) "security." I shall return on this productive misunderstanding concerning security, and would now like to focus on the two later moves I mentioned earlier.

As Foucault explained in his lectures, if colonization reframed the history of people, then processes of marginalization and exclusion were certainly not delimited by territorial borders and war-making. They were transversal. Unsurprisingly, nationalism goes hand in hand with the production of "abnormals" inside the territory, be they monsters, onanists or incorrigibles. Therefore, the model or matrix of war may be the best way to analyze, not the international, but society itself, reversing Clausewitz's approach on politics and war. Foucault therefore dared to question the relation between contention, war and state-making by analyzing how enmity is produced inside a society, and came back to the genealogy of biopower and state racism in its most extreme modalities (Nazism and fascism), however suggesting these were the exacerbation of a logic that all colonial countries had experimented. If politics is the continuation of colonial war by other means, then the rule of law and constitutional rules may be invested by this logic of enmity organized to target some insiders, who look like others. The war of occupation builds a political narrative of uniqueness justifying struggles and promoting a historical knowledge. This is how war and the international are not absent from Foucault's lectures. On the contrary, they are a red thread between the lectures, even when the "objects" look purely "national."

However, this can be clear only once it is assumed that doubts exist about the fact that a territory would be the result of a homogenizing function of the people inside, simultaneously working as a differentiating function that almost automatically produces outsiders, i.e. foreigners "belonging" to other states. Territory could certainly be multifunctional and, depending on the quality of the political institution of borders, delimit a sphere of control where bureaucracies could legitimately operate. But it could also be unfinished, spiked by holes, dependent on a milieu continually transforming, organized through multiple interventions on the freedom of movement, and thought of as millions of individuals not always recognizing themselves as "subjects."

By focusing on (the conduct of) conducts, Michel Foucault displaced once again the discussion from the means of power concentration (implicitly seen as a resource that can be hoard) to the conditions under which power circulates and flanks freedom in a way to act upon it. Mobility, circulation, associated with freedom of action and movement therefore become the *milieu* that sets up the conditions of possibility allowing for a series of interdependent relations to be encapsulated into a territory whose boundaries are acknowledged and lived as necessity (on the concept of *milieu*, see Taylan in this volume).

This movement of freedom (rather than a freedom of movement) organizes, at the "molecular" scale, a permanent and changing environment. The state, in this perspective, is the result of this organization of regularities. It becomes consistent as a "mole of molecules," and not because it would possess a quality or a will to power that would permit the concentration of the means of violence, and justify its use. In his book *Foucault* and the chapter "A New Cartographer" in particular, Gilles Deleuze insisted on this question of power that is not opposed to freedom but built on it, and that is never possessed and accumulated, but circulates, moves along the lines of resistance and their fluctuations, anticipating what Zygmunt Bauman would later call liquidity. More than Foucault himself, Deleuze considered that the state could not be an "actor" with territory, population, administration and government as its main attributes (see also Bayart in this volume). He accused political science of being reactionary and always on the side of order, through the creation of a puppet show, a shadow theater embodying the state, the people, the nation and assigning them their artificial life with the ideas of populations, administrations and governments.

For Foucault and Deleuze alike, it is necessary to understand the process at work, the doing, and not what has been done and constructed as done. What are the doings, the practices that organize a territory? How is a territory constructed through frontier segments joined together to close—at least in the imagination—a polygon geometrical figure, ideally a circle? What is the role of bordering and de-bordering in the process of constructing a territory? How can a territory be controlled via a map of strategically positioned checkpoints that cannot however be analyzed as a continuous wall or series of walls? How to cope with circulations? The space, the "milieu" organizes mobility and freedom by practically blocking the idea of territoriality as a body of a political organism called state and promoting the ideas of network and bifurcation. Yet, if a certain control of space is feasible, beyond coercion and violence, it is via the limits of freedom itself when applied in practice.

It is, I suggest, to avoid the term "necessity"—which he was objecting in his fight at a distance with Hobbes—that Foucault used the term security; a mistake, as we shall see, since this terminology of security was later interpreted as being related to the IR conception of security by some, as a justification of liberal economics by others. Central regarding the discussion on territory is that if political science scholars could ignore the questions raised by Foucault in the mid-seventies, these came back as a resurgence of the repressed by the end of bipolarity and in a context of growing claims about globalization and a world politics in the making. For an IR scholar, to be foucaldian became a way to understand his time, but that implied to accept that border, order and identity are myths to be deconstructed, and to seriously consider that power circulates, that freedom and power are not to be opposed, that states only exist as *loci*, as "moles" of molecular practices, as fields of actions, and not as the embodiments of political communities, whatever nationalist and liberal discourses might claim.

The idea that movement, mobility, interconnections and interdependences could render national territories inoperative as a set of practices of control despite the apparent beautiful homogeneity and complementary colors of the states on the maps of the geopoliticians, has introduced a series of doubts regarding the coherence of the assumptions of spatiality in political science, which have eroded the belief in a territorial state acting in his specific realm. It took time for the decay to generate its productive works and to have a rejuvenation of ideas regarding power and politics. This feeling was shared with French politists in charge of their new discipline. For them, the "essence" of the state and the "international" as a community of states was at stake, and it was dangerous. Many reactions aiming to re-affirm the canons of international relations were developed in different manuals and treaties of political science, in particular by the first generation of "agrégés" in France, rounding up the Sorbonne and Sciences-Po to stop the "noise" of these questions.

Nevertheless, in the immediate post cold-war period, discourses claiming that trans-national actors (multinational companies, NGOs, activist networks) were playing a role in trans-border activities, that states could be at risk with a dark side of globalization, that trans-governmental networks were a way to answer to the trans-nationalization of private actors, multiplied and came as a challenge for IR canons.

Beyond this however, the discussion raised the practical question of the trans-nationalization of all the so-called attributes of the state, therefore of its status. It implied a transformation of the political imagination organizing the discipline, including changing its name: world politics, international political economy and international political sociology. This new political imagination—maybe a slight transformation of an older episteme—was valorizing territory to such a level that geographers felt obliged to warn their IR colleagues of being prisoners of a "territorial trap" blocking their understanding of the world.[23] The set of geographical assumptions that have combined to obscure the historicity and mutability of political space and territory within international relations and comparative politics had to be deconstructed by raising the issue of borders, of the enclosures that form a territory and by questioning their governmentality.

## Using Foucault to Re-launch the Debate on Borders, Mobility and Freedom

William Walters, a contributor to this volume, was among the first to displace the questioning from territory to border and boundaries-making, and from the assumed naturality of the state to its modalities of governing borders. Building on Foucault's conception of power,[24] Walters proposed to use the notion of "diagram"—that Michel Foucault developed as a form of understanding of the possibilities that can emerge from different practices of governmentality that are never given and fixed in advance—also suggesting that Foucault may be useful to conceptualize the government of borders as "a way to think about governance not in institutional or structural terms, nor in ways limited to the image of the state, but in terms of concrete practices, schemes and spaces."[25] Here, what becomes central for the study of the movements of world population is not their entry/exit into/from territories controlled by states claiming sovereignty over these territories, but the kind of *regime of mobility* at stake, the forms of understanding of freedom and their limits as, for example, the study of the politics of visas suggests.[26]

As Foucault illustrated, modern liberal regimes do not govern through "security against threat," but through a regime of liberties, freedom and hence, circulation.[27] The art of government no longer consists in enforcing what is allowed and what is forbidden (power in societies of sovereignty), nor is it to mold bodies into workers, soldiers or reformed prisoners (power in disciplinary societies). It is to "produce" liberties and to encourage them to be "in motion," in order to cross borders, territories and many different forms of boundaries.[28] The "let it go" and "free pass" arguments of the liberal economical discourse are certainly not forms of anarchy. They work through a human capital and the apparent or imagined natural specificities of population characteristics, rendered visible through statistical tools, and separating the majority from the margins. Freedom produces its own limits and generates channels, roads and pathways into a milieu organized to condense flows around these pathways (see Paltrinieri and Mattelart in this volume).

## GOVERNANCE AND GOVERNMENTALITY, WELFARE, RISK AND (FLEXI)SECURITY

Rediscovering Foucault, a series of authors willing to discuss the practices of the European Union more specifically began to substitute "governance" by "governmentality." This triggered heavy criticism and ongoing controversy.[29] Ole Jacob Sending and Iver B. Neumann were among the most trenchant critics of the narrative of global governance and its subsequent multilevel EU governance, which began to prevail in some articles in which the name of Foucault and the term governmentality were quoted, but in which Foucault was used as equivalent to a traditional IR approach to power.[30] They detailed why the claim that the state had lost power to the benefit of non-state actors and that political authority was increasingly institutionalized in spheres not controlled by states was untenable. Along with others, they introduced the idea that the notion of governmentality is about the rationalities and processes that led to governance, and not an equivalent of a change from state power to multilateral governance.[31] Despite many warnings and critical approaches deconstructing the confusion about central Foucaldian terms, some scholars in the mid-2000s came to use the concepts of governmentality and conduct of conduct as if they were conveying the ideas of "being influent," of a "soft power" or, even more crudely, of "a way of lobbying in an open environment" as a member of the European Union (EU) Commission once claimed.[32]

Governmentality became a "talking point" for the EU Commission to describe "methods" to achieve governance, *de facto* referring to "policy tools" deployed in a neo-liberal framework of action. It was perceived as a capacity to "manage," as a "good multilevel-governance" more opened and more "productive" than the traditional intergovernmental sphere especially when it was claiming to "bring civil society" into the decision process. Along this debate, a portrait of a "managerial" Foucault emerged in support of a neo-institutionalist and pro-integrationist position against a state-power position in a very classic opposition reproducing both the traditional notion of transfer of power and the classic discourse on the teleology of the EU as an integration mode. Foucault's methodological struggles were ignored, and he was eventually enrolled for a "cause" he had clearly taken distance with.[33]

Fortunately, critics of this mid-2000 "Foucaultian turn" (as Foucaldian became foucaultian) in European studies, strongly claimed that Foucault's legacy was not, neither in his own work nor in the works that had popularized him in the English-speaking world,[34] to glorify neo-liberalism, but on the contrary a fierce and subtle critic of Thatcherism, Reaganomics and austere-Austrian policies (to come). The works of Nikolas Rose and Mitchell Dean were therefore mobilized by the critics to stop this diluting move that had configured governmentality as a mode of (democratic and good) governance—a rhetoric that a certain third way and post-Blairism continued to evoke by recovering their agenda with a Foucaldian superficial language.[35]

## Security, Biopolitics, Surveillance and Perfect Future: Dispositifs of Power and Resistance

The same mechanism of "regurgitation" of a Foucault—the Foucault as he had been reconfigured by the successive appropriations and translations of his works—, is at work with the issue of security. Apart from some brilliant exceptions,[36] a large number of IR scholars who had jumped on the post-2001 publications of Foucault's lectures at the Collège de France were quite surprised by his *Security, Territory, Population* lectures series. For they were prisoners of their own conception of security (as war, survival and state protection) on the one hand, of the discussion on the state of exception Giorgio Agamben had launched immediately after September 11 on the other hand, they hardly managed to make sense of Foucault's narrative on security. They could not realize that Foucault's conceptualization of security was radically different, in fact connected with the question of the emergence of responsibility and labor work struggles, and with the correlative emergence of new administrative laws accepting a responsibility without guilt of the state in terms of compensations. This was all what Foucault's seminar was about. By the time, François Ewald was preparing his Phd dissertation, and Robert Castel was publishing on the topic already.[37] What was gaining centrality in the study of security was in fact the emergence and transformation of economics in terms of risk, insurance, welfare. As I explained earlier, Foucault abandoned the idea of developing a triptych in which security would be added to sovereignty and discipline to avoid some sort of evolutionist, neo-weberian approach of different stages of power evolution marked by a combination of three ideal types.[38] Unhappy with these readings of his work, he reproached himself for his lack of clarity and shifted his attention to rationalities of government and the governmentality approach.

Paul Veyne—from whom he was very close—insisted at that time on the fact that the more Foucault tried to present the "novelty" of security in regard to discipline, the more he described a form of pastoral power practice. For Veyne, Foucault should rather look back at the Greeks and the Romans, before giving too much credit to seventeenth century liberal thought for having invented something new with a form of power acting upon freedom. Foucault first seemed to ignore these remarks, before changing his mind quite bluntly. He stopped working on security, and took the question of the conduct of conduct seriously to investigate again the government of the self out of an evolutionist canvas. This profound shift remained unnoticed to IR scholars who developed in the 2000s a new theorization of "critical" security that would connect the reading of risk and insurance with the rhetoric of incalculable risk the Bush administration developed at the same moment to justify a policy to "prevent" and anticipate terrorism (see Bonditti in this volume).

In these critical security works, terrorism and social security-welfare were creatively put under the label of security and very soon moved to risk "management" or "speculative" security. A crucial discussion about the state of exception, emergency, terror and prevention in times of anxiety or under a politics of insecurity and unease in the everyday life emerged and is still ongoing. In this debate however, quotations of Foucault serve more as invocations of the spirit of a dead grandfather than a proper analytics of the text—something Foucault himself might have been happy as I suggested in the introduction.

## Conclusion: For the Death Relevailles, a Warning and Some Questions

Nevertheless, for his "death relevailles," I may sound less enthusiastic than so many others, especially as I observe that the "creativity" with which Foucault's work and terminologies are appropriated is also masking the destruction of the notion of critique, in the name of a *necessity* to prevent and anticipate the future, as if this rationale was pre-empting hazard and was capable of anticipating forms of freedom. It is not necessary to invoke a plot against the critical views of Foucault, as sometimes it is also cultural misunderstandings, and the naïve belief that a foucauldian approach could be neutral in terms of value politics and used by right- as well as left-wing authors. But, here, I cannot escape the temptation to launch a warning against what I read as a profound depoliticization of Foucault, in particular when his name is used as a justification for reactionary politics with practices of exclusion, marginalization and the fabric of abnormals, that result from pre-emptive and speculative forms of security and surveillance.

Contemporary forms of (in)security that aimed at guaranteeing the highest possible security and freedom to the majority and to segregate it from an "abnormal" minority to be controlled and surveilled, have to be analyzed for what they are *diagrammatically*: logics of sacrifice, revenge and transversal struggles following a war matrix, and not for their apparent counter-terrorism program understood as a global security project with their pragmatic regime of justification evoking the taming of the future, the capacity to transform it into a perfect future through predictive policing techniques. This war matrix is now organized around *surveillance* as the optimum milieu for freedom.

Practices of surveillance for freedom and protection bear a long tradition related to colonialism, but it has been a more sub-terranean argument that may be called "differentialist freedom" (in contradistinction to "equalitarian freedom") in which the "laissez faire" of the market becomes the main practice of freedom, and where this freedom has to be "cherished" and monitored to make sure that its development does not create negative consequences in terms of freedom for criminals to act, or freedom of people to move across borders without authorization.

In his *Security, Territory, Population* lectures series Foucault deciphered this reasoning about freedom as it draws on the Austrian liberal approach inspired by Friedrich Hayek. He envisaged security as a different modality of power, distinct from sovereign and disciplinary encryptions. Central to understand Foucault's characterization of this approach of (hayekian) security as the limit of freedom in a specific area (milieu) is the way he approached the issue of limit. Indeed, he did not say a limitation of freedom opposing two different principles (freedom versus security) that have to be balanced from an arbitrary decision set up by a form of external (sovereign) power—be it the executive, the legislative or the judicial power. Foucault understood limit as a mathematical limit, in the sense of a point, a dot that is never fully achieved so that security reveals itself to be unachievable except under the benthamian dream of a utilitarian peaceful expression of all freedoms together.

This expression of security as the expandable conditions of possibility of freedom therefore opposes the traditional liberal understanding of security as exception and coercion limiting freedom by blocking its expansion. There is no balance here, only a subtle line where the last dot of a line connecting all the dots, changes function, and like in the famous Go game, transforms all the dots of freedom into a line of "freedom securitized," as a model of surveillance and organization of the trajectory of freedom. In this reasoning of a positive relation between freedom and surveillance, non-exclusive of the first one but used as a more general regime of justification, the justification of surveillance is therefore not only the answer to a potential aggression, to a threat, but the condition of possibility of "real" freedom in current open societies.

Inspired by Hayek, and now central in the argumentation of the defenders of the large scale "five eyes" surveillance system, this second line of thought needs to be further investigated collectively to develop a thorough critique of it as it may be the more successful and "doxic" one.[39] Contemporary practices of security cannot be analyzed in terms of disciplined bodies and forbidden movements only—as the "pessimist libertarian" stance in the surveillance literature argues for it remains stuck in the political imaginary of the Benthamian panoptic model. It should be analyzed in light of the diagrammatic and dispositif approach that Foucault came to articulate in the late 1970s to understand freedom in its "milieu."

What is happening is therefore more than just a misunderstanding. It is a proper re-appropriation of a work, which now appears to be at the heart of an IR "revival" expelling the specter of an IR mastered by US political science scholars becoming, as Ulrich Beck famously said in another context, the spoke-persons of a zombie institution, an institution that continues to believe that "she" is alive, but with a dead heart[40] and is finally replaced by a political sociology and a political theory in harmony with a post-1968 line of thought.

## NOTES

1. I would like to thank Miriam Perier for her editing of the initial version of this chapter.
2. R. B. J. Walker, *Inside/Outside: International Relations as Political Theory* (Cambridge [England]; New York: Cambridge University Press, 1993); Didier Bigo, "The Moebius Ribbon of Internal and External Security(ies)," in *Identities, Borders, Orders: Rethinking International Relations Theory*, edited by Mathias Albert, David Jacobson and Yosef Lapid, (Minneapolis London: University of Minnesota Press, 2001), pp. 91–116.
3. Conversation with a group of students after one of his lecture in 1977. See also Colin Gordon's discussions with Michel Foucault on death penalty and the left in: Colin Gordon, "Le possible: alors et maintenant. Comment penser avec et sans Foucault autour du droit pénal et du droit public," *Cultures & Conflits*, 94–95–96 (2014): 111–134.
4. Certainly a reference to Canguilhem's "historical circumstances:" Georges Canguilhem, "Qu'est-ce que la psychologie?," *Revue de Métaphysique et de Morale* (1) (1958): 12–25.
5. Luca Paltrinieri, *L'expérience du concept. Michel Foucault entre épistémologie et histoire* (Paris: Publication de la Sorbonne, 2012).
6. Alessandro Fontana and Mauro Bertani, "Situating the lectures," in Michel Foucault, *Society must be Defended* (New York: Picador, 2003), pp. 273–293.
7. Zita Nunes, *Cannibal Democracy* (Minneapolis, London: University of Minnesota Press, 2008).

8. In different parts of Central Africa, "relevaille of the dead" is the process by which a body is unburied after 40 years, put in a chair, observed and talked to by the grandchildren as a way of knowing the ancestor.

9. In France the "aggregation" is a civil service competitive examination for certain positions in the French education system.

10. In Paris, the College de France is located Rue des écoles, one block away from the Sorbonne.

11. Didier Bigo, "Gérer les transhumances," in Marie-Christine Granjon (ed.), *Penser avec Michel Foucault, Théorie critique et pratiques politiques* (Paris: Khartala et CERI, 2005), pp. 129–160.

12. Marie-Claude Smouts, ed., *The New International Relations. Theory and Practice* (London: Hurst Publishers, 2014 [1998]).

13. Raymond Aron, *Paix et Guerre entre les Nations* (Paris: Calman Levy, 1984 (1962).

14. Barry Buzan, *People, State and Fear. The National Security Problem in International Relations* (Brighton: Wheathsheaf Books Ltd, 1983).

15. Fontana and Bertani, "Situating the lectures," p. 285.

16. Fontana and Bertani, "Situating the lectures," p. 286.

17. See G. C. Spivak, and S. Harasym, *The Post-Colonial Critic: Interviews, Strategies, Dialogues* (Hove: Psychology Press, 1990). Spivak is often quoted for his critique of Foucault, but it should be reminded that her statement started by, "so clearly I will be doing some injustice to Foucault, but..." She felt uneasy when so many people had taken for granted that Foucault was not interested in colonial histories. She explained that she was not saying that, but indicating by this "silence" that Fontana and Bertani are suggesting here through the climate of the support or at least understanding to rebellion and the "reds" in academia during the mid-seventies where the "implicit" was considered a more subtle approach than Negri's.

18. Fontana and Bertani, "Situating the lectures," p. 282.

19. "Des questions de Michel Foucault à 'Hérodote'," *Hérodote*, 3 (July–Sept 1976): 9–10; reprinted in Michel Foucault, *Dits et écrits 1954–1988*, (Paris: Gallimard, Four Volumes, 1994, Vol. III), pp. 94–5. Translated into English in Jeremy W. Crampton, Stuart Elden. *Space, Knowledge and Power. Foucault and Geography* (Basinkstoke: Palgrave, 2007), pp. 19–25. In her introduction, Juliet Fall explains why French geographers did not follow when Foucault, after his interview, sent back his questions and was unsatisfied by their answers.

20. An obvious reference on territory who developed a powerful critique of Foucault on this issue is Stuart Elden, *The Birth of Territory* (Chicago: The University of Chicago Press, 2013).

21. Michel Foucault, *Security, Territory, Population. Lectures at the Collège de France 1977–1978*, transl. By Graham Burchell (Basingstoke: Palgrave MacMillan, 2007), p. 103.

22. Michel Foucault, *Society must be Defended. Lectures at the Collège de France 1975–1976*, transl. By David Macey (New York: Picador, 2003), p. 155–165.
23. John Agnew, J., "The Territorial Trap: The Geographical Assumptions of International Relations Theory," *Review of international political economy* 1 (1994): 53–80.
24. William Walters, "Border/control," *European Journal of Social Theory*, 9(2) (2006): 187–203.
25. Walters "Border/control," p. 145.
26. Didier Bigo and Elspeth Guild, "Schengen et la politique des visas," *Cultures & Conflits* 49 (2003): 5–21.
27. Didier Bigo, "Security: A Field Left Fallow," in M. Dillon and A. Neal (eds.), *Foucault on Politics, Security and War* (Basingstoke and New York: Palgrave Macmillan, 2011), p. 107.
28. Malcolm Anderson, Didier Bigo, and Eberhard Bort, "Frontiers, Identity and Security in Europe: An Agenda for Research," in Pratt M. and J. Brown (eds.), *Borderlands under Stress*, (La Haye: Kluwer Law International, 2000), pp. 251–274; Bigo, "Security: A Field Left Fallow."
29. Miguel De Larrinaga & Marc G. Doucet, *Security and Global Governmentality: Globalization, Governance and the State* (London: Routledge, 2010).
30. Ole Jacob Sending, Iver B. Neumann, "Governance to Governmentality: Analyzing NGOs, States, and Power," *International Studies Quarterly*, 50(3) (2006): 651–672.
31. See Chris Rumford, *The European Union: A Political Sociology* (Hoboken, NJ: John Wiley & Sons, 2008), or Thomas Lemke, "An Indigestible Meal? Foucault, Governmentality and State Theory," *Distinktion: Scandinavian Journal of Social Theory*, 8(2) (2007): 43–64.
32. "The Changing Landscape of European Liberty and Security" Concluding Conference, EU Framework Program 6, Brussels, 18 May 2009.
33. See his interviews in *Le Nouvel Observateur* journal. This was described by Michel Rocard, *Le Coeur À L'ouvrage* (Paris: Odile Jacob, 1987). See also Daniel Garcia, *Le Nouvel Observateur 50 Ans* (Paris: Les Arènes, 2014).
34. Nikolas Rose, O'Malley, P. and M. Valverde, "Governmentality," *Annual Review of Law and Social Science*, 2 (2006): 83–104. See also Nikolas Rose, *Powers of Freedom: Reframing Political Thought* (Cambridge University Press, 1999) or Peter Miller and Nikolas Rose, "Political Thought and the Limits of Orthodoxy: A Response to Curtis," *British Journal of Sociology* 46(4) (1995): 590–597.
35. Ian Loader and N. Walker, "Policing as a public good: Reconstituting the connections between policing and the state," *Theoretical Criminology* 5(1) (2001): 9–35; see also Petersen, A., "Risk, governance and the new public health," in Petersen A. and R. Bunton (eds.), *Foucault, Health and Medicine*, (London: Routledge, 1997), pp. 189–206; John Ploger, "Public

participation and the art of governance," *Environment and Planning B*, 28(2) (2001): 219–242.

36. See especially Vivienne Jabri's work and her concept of War Matrix: Vivienne Jabri, "War, Security and the Liberal State," *Security Dialogue* 37 (1) (2006): 47–64.

37. Castel synthesized his late 1970s/early 1980s works in: Robert Castel, "From Dangerousness to Risk," in Burchell G., C. Gordon, and P. Miller (eds). *The Foucault Effect: Studies in Governmentality* (Chicago: The University of Chicago Press; 1991); pp. 281–298.

38. Didier Bigo "Security: A Field Left Fallow."

39. Zygmunt Baumann, David Lyon, *Liquid Surveillance: A Conversation* (Cambridge and Malden: Polity, 2013); Zygmunt Bauman et al. "After Snowden: Rethinking the Impact of Surveillance," *International Political Sociology* 8(2)(2014): 121–144.

40. Ulrich Beck, *Risk Society: Towards a new Modernity* (London: Sage,1997 [1986]).

# CHAPTER 4

# The Microphysics of Power Redux

*William Walters*

## PROLOGUE: THE JAWS OF MIGRATION

We could speak of jaws of migration control in a metaphorical way. In 2014 alone more than 3000 migrants drowned while attempting to cross the Mediterranean:[1] the reference to jaws would signify that for many migrants the borderzones that connect and separate the zones of prosperity and poverty that we have come to designate, however unsatisfactorily, as global north and global south, have today become places of unspeakable cruelty and death. But we could also be very literal about the jaw.[2] Most scholars of migration would puzzle at the claim that the regulation of the migration of people bore any connection to the jaw. Likewise more than a few scholars of international relations would frown at the suggestion that there is anything faintly mandibular about the making and the policing of borders. But there is.

> [T]he mandibular angle technique is a safe technique. The risks deriving from its correct application are small and the margin for error sufficiently wide as to make the risks of incorrect application similarly small.[3]

W. Walters (✉)
Carleton University, Ottawa, ON, Canada
e-mail: william.walters@carleton.ca

© The Author(s) 2017                                                    57
P. Bonditti et al. (eds.), *Foucault and the Modern International*,
The Sciences Po Series in International Relations and Political
Economy, DOI 10.1057/978-1-137-56153-4_4

So wrote the Independent Advisory Panel on Non-Compliance Management (IAPNCM), the expert committee of doctors, prison experts and magistrates recently convened by the UK Home Office to look into the management of "non-compliant" people undergoing deportation. While concerns about the abuse suffered by deportees during "removal" from the UK had circulated for some time,[4] matters were brought to a head by a fatal incident involving a man being expelled from the UK to Angola. In 2010, Jimmy Mubenga died while being restrained by three Detainee Custody Officers (or "escorts," to use the rather benign term of deportation experts) on a British Airways plane waiting to depart Heathrow airport. The escorts were employed by G4S, the multinational security company which then held the contract for policing removals in the UK. Among its findings a Coroner's report lamented the culture of "pervasive racism" among the escorts, a system of performance points which appeared to penalize escorts for failed deportations, and the inadequate "scenario-specific" training given to escorts for managing recalcitrant deportees in the cramped space of an aeroplane journey.[5] So when the Independent Advisory Panel met, it was the need for a "bespoke approach to safe escorting" that it sought to address, a "restraints package" that "avoids force whenever possible" and "minimises harm and maximises safety."[6] By no means an easy circle to square.

The mandibular angle is not a method of control that just happens to produce pain in the course of restraining people. "Pain inducing techniques are not painful as a side-effect: they use pain in order to secure compliance." The Panel went on to note that exercising pain in this way did raise "clear ethical issues." Yet, this exercise could be justified if it was the "safest and most appropriate way of dealing with an incident, or of gaining control of a violent subject;" it was reasonable if it was less risky than other means of de-escalating the situation. Typically it might be used when the subject was resisting being placed on or removed from an aircraft, operating as "the least risky way of releasing a detainee's grip on a person or on a railing or similar object."[7] Used according to proper guidelines as to the occasion and the duration ("five seconds") pain-inducing techniques could be rationalized as "reducing the risk of injury to detainees and to staff."[8]

The mandibular angle technique appears in the report as part of a whole package of "core techniques" which the Panel was recommending for the management of deportees. In the report the body is broken down into an ensemble of head, limbs, torso, digits, wrists etc, each of which offers potential pressure points for the calculated application of particular holds, twists and flexes. These moves appear in the report framed as a "risk assessment matrix"[9] wherein the experts review each one in terms of the likelihood it might result in incidents of "airway, breathing and circulation," "fracture or dislocation," "soft tissue injury" and other complications. The mandibular angle came out as "low," "nil" and "low" respectively, though it was noted that if "misapplied, a minor risk of causing cardiac complications due to compression of carotid sinus" was a possibility.[10]

While such a reference to risk places this calibration of "control and restraint" squarely within very contemporary rationalities of governance, I think it is also possible and useful to place this expert discourse about power and the body of the deported within a somewhat different lineage, that of political anatomy. It was Michel Foucault who brought this term into contemporary use by borrowing and adapting it from the economist and physician Sir William Petty. To speak of political anatomy as Foucault repurposes it is not to commit the anthropomorphic error of treating the state as a unified body. Instead, "[o]ne would be concerned with the 'body politic,' as a set of material elements and techniques that serve as weapons, relays, communication routes and supports for the power and knowledge relations that invest human bodies and subjugate them by turning them into objects of knowledge."[11]

Foucault proceeds to explain that the project of a political anatomy would emphasize that the human body does not exist in a purely external relationship to the political field. Nor is the body to be regarded as a kind of ever present biological substrate, a foundation for human subjects who engage in politics, alongside countless other activities. Rather, "the body is... directly involved in the political field; power relations have an immediate hold upon it; they invest it, mark it, train it, torture it, force it to carry out tasks, to perform ceremonies, to emit signs."[12]

If Petty made his mark on political anatomy by mapping Ireland for the purpose of its colonization under Cromwell it is instead the migrant body that is being mapped here. One could open up new aspects of deportation by examining it from the angle of political anatomy. While political science might approach deportation as a state policy—asking perhaps what social and institutional factors explain the effectiveness of different national programs—a political anatomy would examine the heterogeneous powers involved in deportation on a more molecular scale, revealing that a whole set of mechanisms is at play at the level of the body of the deportee, its relationship with the bodies and actions of the escorts and other authorities, and within specific milieux such as the detention center, the airport and the aircraft. These mechanisms are typically overlooked by political science and international relations (IR), but they merit our attention: without a means to control the deportee in transit, the entire project of deporting people would lose much of its efficacy and viability.

The political anatomy I have in mind would no doubt show that it is not just migrants who cross borders but these many little practices of control: they too are mobile. For the kinds of pacification and neutralization techniques examined by the Panel are often invented in one setting or country and then migrate across a national and transnational web of expertise that connects prisons, remand schools and migration control facilities, despite the fact of their different populations, functions and jurisdictions.[13] It would also show how each little practice has its own complicated history—how, for instance, at some times and in some places immigration enforcement has used powerful drugs like Haldol and Stesolid to sedate deportees while in other jurisdictions this practice has been deemed illegal.[14] Or how the mandibular technique replaced the nose control technique since the latter was causing too many nosebleeds in young people.[15] This political anatomy would doubtless show that a variety of public as well as private actors are implicated in this ecology of control. So, when the Panel wanted to test the effectiveness and safety of different methods it was to the Virgin Atlantic airline simulator training environment at Gatwick airport that their field trip took them.[16] Finally, one would also need to examine the relationship between political anatomy and political economy. As the Panel noted with an air of satisfaction, the majority of deportations do not require the use of force.[17] The majority are "voluntary" in the very minimal sense that their targets leave without being physically and bodily removed. The schemes of "assisted voluntary return" managed by agencies like the International Organization for Migration represent an important factor in such voluntary departures. These offer cash incentives and bureaucratic assistance with the migrant's relocation. Here the deportee is located within a matrix of economic interest rather than pain and restraint. That said, the boundary between the political economy of voluntary return and the political anatomy of enforced removal is distinctly blurry. This is not least because of the nature of the choice on offer: voluntary return is "offered as a less painful alternative to continued destitution followed by (inevitable) compulsory return."[18]

As is well known, Foucault raises the theme of a political anatomy—or as he sometimes puts it, anatamo-politics—in the context of the rethinking of power which he advances in *Discipline and Punish*. It is in this work that he gives the theme of a "microphysics of power" its fullest and most systematic expression. However, with the phenomenal growth of interest in themes of governmentality and biopolitics (the latter a notion he first introduced as the counterpart to anatamo-politics), the theme of the microphysics of power has somewhat receded from view—both in Foucault studies and commentaries, and in the considerably wider domain of post-foucauldian political sociology. It seems that studies of governmentality "are everywhere the most living part of [Foucault's] *oeuvre*."[19]

In the extensive literature that has developed connecting themes of bio-power and governmentality to world politics one can discern at least two broad branches. One is exemplified by works like Hardt and Negri's *Empire* which draw Foucault into the orbit of grand theory.[20] Here, the detailed analysis of the micro-powers is even less prominent than in Foucault's reflections on governmentality. In a second branch, the microphysics of exercising rule over great distances and territories is placed front and center—a move nicely illustrated by Andrew Barry's masterful account of the art of empire in terms of the development of electrical standards and the challenge of engineering transoceanic telegraph cable.[21] The development of the study of political anatomy might be situated in this second branch.

This chapter can be read as something of a thought experiment. I argue for revisiting the microphysics of power and demonstrate this can be useful for the analysis of particular issues and contexts within global politics.[22] In particular, and as intimated in this opening discussion which situates medical and police know-how about the jaw within the power/knowledge of state enforced migration, I am interested in what microphysics brings to our understanding of the kinds of power that circulate in the domain of deportation. Following a brief contextualization of Foucault's thinking on microphysics, I make two arguments about the value of microphysics redux. First, a concern with microphysics can serve as a counter-weight to the tendency in many studies of governmentality to focus on indirect forms of power while downplaying or overlooking the presence of relations of force, violence and struggle.[23] In particular, this move can foreground the materiality and place of everyday violence in the fabrication of global order. Second, I argue that a microphysics of power can help to give a focus on the body a more prominent place in scholarship on international relations and security studies. Throughout the chapter, I use examples drawn from the study of deportation and migration control to illustrate my claims. My call is not for a general re-adoption of the microphysics but rather sensitivity for contexts where it does provide effective and appropriate tools. Forced deportations are one such context. In my conclusion I call for disentangling the microphysics of power from the specific locations and regimes in which Foucault developed it. I argue that microphysics is not a synonym for disciplinary power. If anything the powers that invest deportation are suggestive of a *microphysics of police*.

## FROM MICROPHYSICS TO GOVERNMENTALITY... AND BACK?

If the thematic of the microphysics of power has fallen out of favor within foucauldian-inspired research, this is probably due to a perception that it was superseded with Foucault's turn toward governmentality. That is certainly one conclusion we might draw from Bröckling, Krasmann and Lemke's important attempt to situate both microphysics and governmentality in the overall trajectory of Foucault's political thought. "Foucault's interest in studying government signals a far-reaching correction and refinement of his analysis of power."[24] At one level it corrected for the impression that his analytical focus on the individual body and its imbrication in mechanisms of discipline allowed insufficient room to consider "more comprehensive processes of subjectification."[25] Gordon notes that Foucault seems to have found fault afterwards with the rhetorical style in *Discipline and Punish*, which may have given the impression of a power that possessed "an almost absolute capability to tame and subject individuals."[26] With this shift to governmentality, Foucault would open space to rethink power in terms of the interface between the government of the self and the government of others. Alive to the multiple and always historically formed ways in which individuals have conducted themselves, and how these diverse practices of the self might connect up with, support, but also conflict with attempts to govern collectivities, governmentality would allow for a multi-faceted appreciation for the complexities of subjectivity in relation to political power, an appreciation that was largely undeveloped in the microphysics.[27]

The move to governmentality appears to have operated as a corrective and clarification on a second level as well. Foucault had developed microphysics in part as a challenge to what he saw as the state-centrism of modern political analysis, as well as its juridico-legal understanding of power as repressive and negative. Yet, this microphysics, developed as it was in the context of studies of specific institutional locales like the prison and the asylum, exposed Foucault to a second charge. Formulated in its most sympathetic form, this was that Foucault's thought offered some very precise tools for the study of power and domination on the scale of bodies, places and organizations. Yet, it furnished little that might assist scholars and practitioners concerned with the so-called bigger structures of state and international order. True, Foucault did call for an "ascending analysis"[28] that worked its way from the "infinitesimal mechanisms" of power to the more general. But in books like *Discipline and Punish* his readership could find insufficient concepts and guidelines that might assist in conducting such an ascent. While he offered a wealth of tools to analyze the subtle movements, mechanisms and reversals, it seemed the toolkit was wanting when it came to the question of how the micro-practices were aggregated into projects of power and domination on the scale of states and other "big" formations.

Here it seems Foucault's lectures on governmentality provided at least a partial response to such criticisms.[29] Framed as a series of investigations into the history of the art of government, the lectures revealed that far from ducking the question of the state, Foucault offered a nuanced if fragmentary account of its birth and transformation as an effect of practices. This was not state theory in the sense practiced by his Marxist critics since it refused to seek or utilize any essential properties or tendencies in explaining the state.[30] Indeed, what made this "genealogy of the modern state"[31] so novel was precisely its aspiration to think the history of political power without resort to any universals whatsoever.[32] (For the methodological implication of this approach, see Shapiro in this volume).

No doubt the double correction which Bröckling et al. highlight helps to explain the largely positive reception that governmentality has enjoyed in studies of world politics in the past 15 years or so. By bringing a distinctive approach to questions of practice, subjectivity, materiality and historicism, and by opening a thought space between and across the restricted materialism of realism and the thin discursivity of liberal constructivism, governmentality studies has resonated with many theoretical and political concerns animating IR scholarship today (see Onuf in this volume). For example, its attention to the nexus of governance and self-governance, or a politics of control and a politics of freedom, has proved valuable for theorizing those particular styles of rule associated with neoliberalism. Why, then, should we give more attention to the microphysics of power? Is it not redundant, surpassed by these theoretical advances?

## FORCES AND STRUGGLES

From the outset, and following Sennelart,[33] I want to stress that it is not a matter of choosing between *either* a microphysics of power, *or* governmentality. At the very least this stark binary can be rejected for the fact that microphysics and governmentality are not self-contained and opposed theories of powers. On the contrary, they have many points of contact and complimentarity. For example, consider the remarks Foucault offers part way through his lectures on *The Birth of Biopolitics* when explaining his new found interest in governmentality. "[T]he analysis of micro-powers, or of procedures of governmentality, is not confined by definition to a precise domain determined by a sector of the scale, but should be considered simply as a point of view, a method of decipherment which may be valid for a whole scale, whatever its size."[34] Note that here Foucault uses the terms "micro-powers" and governmentality interchangeably, and suggests that these points of view are equally valid for examining "the conduct of mad people, patients, delinquents, and children" as they are for "phenomena of a completely different scale, such as economic policy."[35]

As I see it the debate about microphysics and governmentality is better understood as a tactical matter. Governmentality and microphysics embody different and distinctive idioms for talking about power. Both are capable of attending to the little details, the molecularities, the subtle shifts in ways of caring, punishing, administrating and so on. It is just that the former frames these zones in terms of conducts of conduct, of relations of persuasion and co-option. The latter brings to the fore the aspect of force relations, and the hypothesis that, inverting Clausewitz, politics can sometimes be read as the continuation of war by other means. Under what political or intellectual circumstances might the latter emphasis, the idiom of the microphysics of power, be more useful or even timely?

For all its accomplishments, the spread of governmentality studies as a perspective on world politics has come at a certain cost. The necessary emphasis which these studies have placed on indirect governance, or governance through the self-governing capacities of subjects, has somewhat occluded the many ways in which illiberal powers persist or re-emerge.[36] While the exclusionary and violent underside of neoliberalism is often rightly noted in Foucault studies, insufficient attention is still paid to all the contexts and mechanisms in which people are subjected not to subtle or indirect forms of control but rather violent measures such as hunting, herding, branding and isolation. All those situations where authority does not seek to harness agency but constrain, confine, repel and shut out have not been sufficiently regarded as situations calling for their own dedicated modes of understanding. As Merlingen has put it in specific reference to the use of governmentality in international studies, "it seems odd that many governmentality writings pay little attention to the dark side of modern life. Their welcome programme to go beyond a conception of power as merely repressive and to bring out its productivity tends to result in somewhat sanitised accounts of governance in which elements of domination, exploitation and violence (figuratively and literal) become largely invisible."[37]

However, in calling for foucauldian scholarship to pay greater attention to relations of violence and force it is not my intention to suggest a dichotomy: force on one side, consent on the other. Instead, the great value of the microphysics of power as a theme is that it calls attention to the ways in which modern rule involves the imbrication of force and consent. The governance of contemporary deportation illustrates precisely this point. In the UK case, it transpires that most removals take place without the accompaniment of security personnel, and in only perhaps one in ten cases is physical restraint exercised upon the deportee.[38] Should we conclude that deportation is a largely consensual practice, that physical violence is exercised by the state and its delegates only in a minority of cases? Surely not. It would be more accurate to observe that the exercise of force casts a long shadow: directly operative in a minority of cases it is still present everywhere else, insinuating itself into the behavior of the subject. All those deportees who decide to go quietly, under their own steam as it were: is their decision not made in full knowledge of the powers that can be mobilized otherwise? Force and consent exist not as diametrically opposed states of affairs but as flip sides of the same coin.

The tendency in foucauldian scholarship to downplay relations of force and violence has been offset by certain counter-tendencies. Despite their differences of emphasis and concern, what the growing interest in themes of biopolitics and sovereign power,[39] necropolitics,[40] illiberal liberalism,[41] power as war/struggle,[42] or the politics and techniques of securitization[43] all share is the insistence that relations of rule cannot be reduced to the games of indirect governance. So if the revival of microphysics which I am urging here signals a renewed interest in themes of force, domination, violence and a power that operates at the level of bodies and at the threshold of life and death, it would do so not alone but in ways that resonate with these ongoing lines of research.

And yet I want to insist that a microphysics brings something distinctive and important to this wider concern with illiberalism within liberal societies. It is not just the foregrounding of relations of force, but also the attention to detail. It is the *micro* as much as the *physics*. The microphysics enjoins us to take seriously the most seemingly marginal and insignificant things, the capillaries of power, because often they reveal much about the governance of the world. It's a matter of resolution: a micro-*scopic* view of power. The little things matter: the five seconds that are specified as the maximum time that the mandibular angle technique is to be applied; the guidelines that recommend that if a deportee is to be manacled, such restraints should be hidden from the view of other passengers by a blanket.[44] The devil really is in the details. These little things matter not because they offer the factual truth about what happens when people are deported. Indeed, recent reports suggest that despite official recommendations regarding the need to improve conditions surrounding deportation flights, various guidelines are frequently being flouted.[45] These details matter instead because they give a sense of the texture of power, including its knowledges and technical norms that political analysis misses if it confines itself to the more general level of policy or logics of government.

One example of why a concern with detail matters will have to suffice here. Consider the testimony given by a managing director of G4S's Care and Justice Services division to a UK House of Commons hearing on restraint in deportation. The managing director distinguished between the transport of prisoners and deportees. Prisoners are typically moved in "cellular vehicles" and the use of handcuffs is routine. By contrast, handcuffs and dedicated cellular vehicles are not routine in the movement of deportees "[s]o there are some quite distinct differences in terms of what staff have to do."[46] The value of a microphysics of power in this instance is that it would caution against any generalization about the logics of migration control becoming subsumed within rationalities of criminalization. While there can be no doubting that there exist all sorts of ways in which the fields of crime and migration have been brought much closer together, in the case of UK deportations it seems significant that in very real and material ways the state seeks to maintain a distinction between deportee and criminal. So there is a political desire to see deportees leave the territory wherever possible like regular travelers rather than convicts. Whether this is a matter of legitimizing deportation, economizing on its cost, or related to other factors is a question further research might pursue.

A focus on the microphysics is important not just out of a concern to render a more textured and nuanced account of the exercise of authority and violence. Were it to confine itself to the details of devices, restraints, and holds mobilized around the deportee —as I have to this point—it would offer a very gloomy, monotonous and fatalist view of the world. The microphysics is equally valid and equally relevant for the purposes of understanding power relations and struggles in a fuller, multi-dimensional sense. Indeed, were it not the case that many deportees resist their deportation through a whole range of actions, which extend from public campaigns for residence and refuge to the most visceral struggles with escorts and security personnel in detention settings, airports and planes, then the whole political anatomy of deportation would be unnecessary.[47] What the microphysics promises, particularly through its attention to little details, is an appreciation for the dynamism and relationality of power. Seen on the scale of the microphysics, the conduct of deportation is anything but static. It is because every practice has its points of reversibility, and every technique its lines of contestation, that the state must remain inventive and experimental in its approach to the forcible movement of people—just as migrants and their allies will be inventive and creative in the ways they seek to obstruct and evade powers of deportation. [48]

## BODIES

The second reason why a renewed dialogue with the microphysics of power would be valuable has to do with the precise locus and object around which Foucault first developed the concept. I speak, of course, of the body. It should be clarified at this point that, at least in Foucault's thought, there is no intrinsic or necessary relationship between microphysics as an orientation for research and bodies. If, as Foucault suggests, something like economic policy is also a viable focus for a perspective of microphysics, then clearly this perspective is not confined to a focus on bodies as the contact point of the capillaries of power.

That being said, there is a strong case for reviving this connection between microphysics and modes of analysis which foreground a politics of the body. For a concern with bodies and embodiments is marginal both in governmentality-oriented political studies as it is in the wider field of IR. Recent research highlights the fact that questions of embodiment and corporeality are rather neglected in much political science. They are particularly muted in international relations and security studies. For Lauren Wilcox, this is paradoxical to say the least. "Bodies have long been outside the frame of International Relations (IR)—unrecognizable even as the modes of violence that use, target, and construct bodies in complex ways have proliferated."[49] Drawing attention to such issues as drone warfare, suicide bombers, biometric identification, and the revelation of torture as a mode of power within the US-led war on terror, Wilcox notes that the body could not seem more central—whether as a stake in debates about collateral damage, a weapon in its own right, an object to be inscribed, read and identified, or a capacity for pain that is to be utilized. Yet, whereas feminist theory has long seen gendered and race-d bodies as a principal concern and a problem for de-naturalizing, the political sciences have tended to regard bodies as inert, merely organic, as brute facts. Bodies, as such, have little place in IR; what matters instead are the interests and motivations of agents.[50]

A renewed engagement with the theme of a microphysics of power could certainly help to bring questions of corporeality more fully into security studies and IR. That said, let us note at this point that the microphysics, at least as Foucault set it out in *Discipline and Punish*, is alone not adequate to the task. It offers nothing like a general framework under which to carry out such work. That is hardly surprising. If it is a question of bringing the sensing, feeling body into IR then scholars would do better to follow the lead of key studies in affect theory, and work on the sociology of emotions, and technologies of perception. If it's the question of how actors comport themselves, how they reveal and conceal, then surely it is to the traditions of phenomenology and performance that we might turn.[51] If the question is the cultural or scientific practices by which the bodies of the dead, the maimed or the missing become resurrected as political issues and controversies then we should look to studies of modes of forensic truth-telling[52] or sociologies of haunting.[53] The list could go on. In short, the question of the body is not singular and does not lend itself to a general theory. Instead, one is confronted with an extremely heterogeneous domain for which, fortunately, there already exist rich traditions of social and philosophical thought as well as methods.

Nevertheless, there would seem to be a whole dimension of contemporary regimes of power for which the microphysics of power *would* appear to be well suited; a set of issues for which the microphysics does provide an appropriate set of tools. Let us return to the whole domain of migration, security and borders. Political science tends to treat migration control as a matter of states, economies, ideologies, public opinions, bureaucracies and officials, networks, demographics and other powerful forces. But what is quite remarkable is that in many ways migration control today involves some very particular instruments and finely-detailed actions which achieve their impact by configuring a "machine-readable body"[54] (see Bonditti in this volume). States have long used papers, files and photographs in an attempt to determine identities and regulate movements inside as well as across their borders. There is however something profoundly corporeal about the policing of borders and boundaries that makes control today qualitatively different.

Dijstelbloem and Meijer[55] use the term "migration technology" to draw attention to the various ways in which "technological borders" are emerging in Europe and elsewhere. What they emphasize is not so much the role of old military technologies of helicopter, fast boat or even satellite to enhance the visibility of borders and territories but a new technology. What distinguishes this new migration technology of X-rays, DNA tests, retinal scans, bone scans and gait identifications is the way these practices interface with population in all its corporeality. "Control of citizens, travellers, migrants, and illegal aliens is coming closer to their bodies."[56] Migration technology swarms around us all, but it targets the most vulnerable—the stateless, the undocumented, the criminalized—with a particular intensity.

This chapter began with a deportation practice that operates through a political map of the living body, cross-referencing its most vulnerable pressure points with considerations of risk and legitimacy. We noted how the jaw becomes, in the hands (quite literally) of the escort, a site where state power really makes its presence felt. But the jaw is just one of a great constellation of points at which migration control plays itself out around the body. A more expansive political anatomy would register how blood, saliva, iris and hair now become identification papers, how age and thus one's status as a minor becomes a matter of bone scans, how fingerprints cross borders faster than any human, and how the most vital and elementary facts of breathing or the possession of a beating heart are turned by detection technologies into a trace, a sign, a catch (see Bonditti and Mattelart in this volume).

A revived political anatomy could certainly make a contribution by tracing the lines that connect the power of states and other organizations to bodies, lines of connection and force organized by knowledges and machines. And one should not overlook how these vital connections are in turn mediated, how they shape the mediascapes of migration. Yet, this anatamo-politics is not confined to the analysis of the attempts to sort, settle, speed, shepherd and suppress population movements. Our understanding of subversion, resistance and contestation in the domain of borders and migration will also be advanced the more that we acknowledge the various ways an anatamo-politics is also practiced by migrant subjects. If migration is a social struggle, it proceeds not just or even primarily as a confrontation between social forces or raw humans. Things happen at a very molecular level, the moving composition of a thousand little acts and capacities by which the mobile body is forged, and forges itself as a site of insistent presence[57] and of resistance. Whether it is the training a body requires if its bearer is to travel across mountains, the pain you must silently endure to remain undetected in a hidden compartment in a truck when crossing a border,[58] the pills you take to suppress bowel movements when traveling covertly by sea,[59] or the skills required to fix an old jalopy—[60] through these very different experiences, it is quite evident that there is a microphysics of border subversion just as there is a microphysics of migration control, and that they exist in a state of mutual provocation. In sum, migration studies offers one of many sites where a revived focus on microphysics would undoubtedly advance understanding of international processes. And if whole governments and even regimes are sometimes brought down by the gradual or sudden outflows of people that these micro-practices enable, then clearly the little things matter. They change the world.

## CONCLUSION

This chapter has argued for a renewed focus on the project of a microphysics of power and suggested such a move might enrich understanding of key issues in world politics. Throughout I used examples drawn from the field of migration and borders research. My interest in this microphysics is not to cast it as an alternative to what is today the more common extension of Foucault, namely in terms of governmentality. Rather, it is to suggest that microphysics can serve as a provocation and a correction to certain problematic tendencies in governmentality studies. Not the least of these is the neglect of dynamics of struggle and the marginalization of relations of force.

One last point is in order. We should not overlook the fact that Foucault's thinking about microphysics was conducted in a specific historical and thematic context. It came amidst his interest in the phenomenon of disciplinary power, a constellation he traced out across institutional sites of school, hospital, prison and so on. As such, his main emphasis was on the micro-practices by which persons were drilled, trained, segmented and recombined so as to become productive individuals and collective energies.

In highlighting deportation and other forms of migration control I have not, for the most part, been engaging with disciplinary power. Microphysics and discipline are sometimes conflated. This is mistaken, just as it is mistaken to think that neoliberal economic policy cannot be thought from the perspective of a microphysics. The analytical distinction between microphysics and particular logics of power is necessary. If I were to characterize the wider pattern at stake in the preceding discussion, it would be a microphysics of police. These little techniques are not for the most part motivated to train, domesticate or enhance the productive capacities of the migrant bodies that are their target. Instead, they aim mostly to pacify, neutralize, order, contain and remove. The idea of a microphysics of police has yet to be properly formulated as a research agenda.[61] I hope this chapter offers sufficient grounds to suggest this would be a worthwhile undertaking.

## NOTES

1. *The New York Times*, "Migrant Deaths in the Mediterranean," January 5, 2015.
2. I juxtapose the literal and the metaphorical here for convenience. But see Onuf who reminds us that "so-called literal concepts are generalized, conventionalized and naturalized metaphors." Concepts are, in other words, "metaphors that are no longer fresh." Nicholas Onuf, "Polemics: Fitting Metaphors—The Case of the EU," *Perspectives: Review of International Affairs* 18(1) (2010): 65.
3. IAPNCM (Independent Advisory Panel on Non-Compliance Management), *Report of the Independent Board on Non-Compliance Management*, 2014: 40.
4. For example, Birnberg, Peirce and Partners, "Outsourcing Abuse: The Use and Misuse of State-Sanctioned Force During Detention and Removal of Asylum Seekers" (London: Medical Justice and the National Coalition of Anti-Deportation Campaigns, 2008); Liz Fekete "Accelerated Removals: The Human Cost of EU Deportation Policies," *Race & Class* 52, no.4 (2011): 89–97.
5. Karen Monaghan, *Inquest into the Death of Jimmy Kelenda Mubenga. Report by the Assistant Deputy Coroner, Karon Monaghan, QC, Under the Coroner's Rules 1984, Rule 43* (2013). Available at http://inquest.org.uk/pdf/narratives/Mubenga_R43_Final_copy.pdf.
6. IABNCM, *Report of the Independent Board...*, p. 3.
7. Ibid, p. 33.
8. Ibid, p. 34.
9. Ibid, p. 31.
10. Ibid, p. 39.
11. Michel Foucault, *Discipline and Punish: The Birth of the Prison* (London: Allen Lane, 1977), p. 28.
12. Ibid, p. 25.
13. For example, note how the Independent Panel took an interest in the Canadian approach to deporting people which "places greater emphasis on the use of mechanical restraints than do the Prison Service's Control and Restraint techniques." These "mechanics" include zip-lock style flexible wrist restraints, rigid handcuffs and a waist restraint belt. IABNCM, *Report of the Independent Board*. p.11. Canada is, apparently, typical of other jurisdictions.

14. *Washington Post*, "Some Detainees are Drugged for Deportation," May 14, 2008. Available at http://www.washingtonpost.com/wp-srv/nation/specials/immigration/cwc_d4p1.html (verified on October 8th, 2015); Radio Sweden, "Deportees given Illegal Forced Injections," October 24, 2014 http://sverigesradio.se/sida/artikel.aspx?programid=2054&artikel=6000012 (verified on October 8th, 2015).
15. Inquest into the Death of Jimmy Kelenda Mubenga. Monaghan, *Inquest into the Death of Jimmy Kelenda Mubenga. Report by the Assistant Deputy Coroner, Karon Monaghan, QC, Under the Coroner's Rules 1984, Rule 43* (2013), p. 21n.
16. IABNCM, *Report of the Independent Board...*, pp. 24, 51.
17. Ibid., pp. 5–6.
18. Frances Webber, "How Voluntary are Voluntary Returns?" *Race & Class* 52(4) (2011): 103.
19. Jacques Donzelot, "Michel Foucault and Liberal Intelligence," *Economy and Society* 37(1) (2008): 116. John Allen has argued that Foucault's work on disciplinary power is significant for its detailed accounting of the spatial and temporal practices that mediate the exercise of power. By contrast, in Foucault's work on governmentality, "we have scant detail of the spatial assemblages involved in the management of dispersed populations." John Allen, *Lost Geographies of Power* (Oxford: Blackwell, 2003), p. 82.
20. Michael Hardt and Antonio Negri, *Empire* (Cambridge: Harvard University Press, 2001).
21. Andrew Barry, "Lines of Communication and Spaces of Rule." In *Foucault and Political Reason: Liberalism, Neo-Liberalism and Rationalities of Government*, edited by Andrew Barry, Thomas Osborne and Nikolas Rose (Chicago: University of Chicago Press, 1996), pp. 123–142.
22. What is global politics? No doubt for many scholars it refers to a politics of the now, a politics of "our" time, a politics defined by multiple relationships to the risky, speedy and interconnected time-space of the planet. When he writes about the tricky work of assemblage that is necessary to make effective any claims about the macro, Bruno Latour suggests an altogether more modest and empirical understanding of "global" which I prefer. "Macro no longer describes a *wider* or a *larger* site in which the micro would be embedded like some Russian Matryoshka doll, but another equally local, equally micro place, which is *connected* to many others through some medium transporting specific types of traces. No place can be said to be bigger than any other place, but some can be said to benefit from far safer connections with many more places than others." See Bruno Latour, *Reassembling the Social: An Introduction to Actor-Network-Theory* (Oxford: Oxford University Press, 2005), p. 176. For an extensive discussion on the "global," see Mattelart in this volume.
23. For example, see Allen and Goddard who argue that post-foucauldian governmentality has effected a certain "domestication" of Foucault by

foregrounding themes of governing at the expense of a concern with struggle. Ansgar Allen and Roy Goddard, "The Domestication of Foucault: Government, Critique, and War," *History of the Human Sciences*, 27 (5) (2014): 26–53.

24. Ulrich Bröckling, Susanne Krasmann and Thomas Lemke "From Foucault's Lectures at the College de France to Studies of Governmentality: An Introduction," in *Governmentality: Current Issues and Future Challenges*, ed. Ulrich Bröckling, Susanne Krasmann and Thomas Lemke (New York: Routledge, 2011), p. 1.

25. Ibid.

26. Colin Gordon "Governmental Rationality: An Introduction," in *The Foucault Effect: Studies in Governmentality* edited by Graham Burchell, Colin Gordon and Peter Miller (Chicago: University of Chicago Press, 1991), p. 5.

27. In Foucault's work we can distill at least three different emphases which he gives to the term governmentality—a point I have argued elsewhere (Walters, *Governmentality: Critical Encounters*, Abingdon: Routledge, 2012). First, and in its broadest sense, governmentality functions as a way to study power at the level of its rationalities, reflections and technologies and from the angle of "actions upon other actions," "conduct of conducts" and a "management of possibilities." (Foucault, "The Subject and Power" in *Michel Foucault: Power*, edited by James Faubion (New York: The New Press, 2000), p. 341). Second, Foucault often uses governmentality in a way that associates it with the project of writing the "genealogy of the modern state and its different apparatuses" (Foucault, *Security, Territory, Population*, Basingstoke: Palgrave Macmillan, 2007, p. 354). While he acknowledges that governmentality analysis can be undertaken on any scale, it is the question of governing on the scale of "the management of the whole social body" (Foucault, *The Birth of Biopolitics*, Basingstoke: Palgrave Macmillan, 2008, p.186), that is, governing within the framework of the state, that largely interests him in the lecture series of 1977–1978 and 1978–1979. Third, there are places in those lecture series where Foucault seems to define governmentality as being very close to one particular art of government, namely liberalism. This is especially evident in the lecture of February 1, 1978 where, famously, he speaks of a specific and complex power that has "population as its target" and "political economy as its major form of knowledge" (*Security, Territory, Population*, p.108). It should be noted that the point that power can be rethought in terms of the interface between the government of the self and the government of others can be worked in different ways through each of these three readings of governmentality. In this chapter when I speak of governmentality it is largely in the first sense, that is, as the conduct of conduct. For a more extensive discussion about governmentality, see especially Bigo, Gros and Bayart in this volume.

28. Michel Foucault, "Two Lectures," in *Power/Knowledge: Selected Interviews and Other Writings, 1972–1977, by Michel Foucault* edited by Colin Gordon (New York: Pantheon, 1980), p. 99.
29. Foucault, *Security, Territory, Population*, 2007; *The Birth of Biopolitics*, 2008.
30. Gordon, "Governmental Rationality: An Introduction," p. 4.
31. Michel Foucault, *Security, Territory, Population*, p. 354.
32. Paul Veyne, *Foucault, his Thought, his Character* (Cambridge: Polity, 2010).
33. Michel Senellart, "Course context." In Foucault. *The Birth of Biopolitics,* pp. 327–330.
34. Foucault, *The Birth of Biopolitics*, p. 186.
35. Ibid.
36. Sven Opitz "Government Unlimited: The Security Dispositif of Illiberal Governmentality," In *Governmentality: Current Issues and Future Challenges* edited by Ulrich Bröckling, Suzanne Krasmann and Thomas Lemke, pp. 93–114 (New York: Routledge, 2011); Mitchell Dean, "Powers of life and death beyond governmentality," *Cultural Values* 6(1) (2002): 117–136; Judith Butler, *Precarious Life: The Powers of Mourning and Violence* (London: Verso, 2004).
37. Michael Merlingen, "Foucault and World Politics: Promises and Challenges of Extending Governmentality Theory to the European and Beyond," *Millennium* 35 (December 2006): 191.
38. House of Commons, *Rules Governing Enforced Removals from the UK. 18th Report of Session 2010–12* (London: The Stationery Office, 2011): p. 4.
39. Dean, "Powers of life and death beyond governmentality."
40. Achille Mbembe, "Necropolitics," *Public Culture* 15(1) (2003): 11–40.
41. Barry Hindess, "The Liberal Government of Unfreedom," *Alternatives* 26 (2001): 93–111.
42. Allen Ansgar and Roy Goddard, "The Domestication of Foucault: Government, Critique, War," *History of the Human Sciences* 27(5) (2014): 26–53.
43. Didier Bigo and Anastassia Tsoukala, *Terror, Insecurity and Liberty: Illiberal Practices of Liberal Regimes after 9/11* (London: Routledge, 2008).
44. ECPTIDTP, *13th General Report of the CPT's Activities* (Strasbourg: Secretariat of the CPT, 2003), §36).
45. *The Guardian*, "Deportees Treated as Commodities by Security Staff, Says Prison Inspector," June 02, 2014.
46. House of Commons, *Rules Governing Enforced Removals*, p. Ev3.
47. Helen Hintjens, Richa Kumar and Ahmed Pouri., "Pro-Asylum Advocacy in the EU: Challenging the State of Exception," in *Transnational Migration and Human Security* edited by Truong Thanh-Dam and Des Gasper (Berlin: Springer-Verlag, 2011), pp. 209–223.

48. Take the example of seatbelts. Planes cannot take off if passengers do not wear them. Acting out of concern and protest, the refusal by some passengers to observe this little disciplinary practice of air travel has sometimes proved sufficient to halt certain deportations by air. See Sydney Morning Herald, "Qantas Bans Student Who Stood Up for What She Believed In," March 7, 2015. http://www.smh.com.au/national/qantas-bans-student-who-stood-up-for-what-she-believed-in-20150306-13xosl.html (verified on October 8th, 2015). One reason states are looking to special charter flights as a way to deport migrants, rather than placing them on regular commercial flights, is to insulate deportation practice from the gaze and possible intervention of fellow passengers. I discuss charter flights at length in Walters, "The Flight of the Deported: Aircraft, Deportation, and Politics," *Geopolitics* 21(2) (2016): 435–458.

49. Lauren Wilcox, *Bodies of Violence: Theorizing Embodied Subjects in International Relations* (Oxford: Oxford University Press, 2015), p. 1.

50. Wilcox, *Bodies of Violence*, p. 2.

51. Diana Coole, "Experiencing Discourse: Corporeal Communicators and the Embodiment of Power," *British Journal of Politics and International Relations* 9(3) (2006): 413–433.

52. Thomas Keenan, "Getting the Dead to Tell Me What Happened: Justice, Prosopopoeia, and Forensic Afterlives," in *Forensis: The Architecture of Public Truth.*, edited by Forensic Architecture (Oberhausen: Sternberg Press, 2014), pp. 35–55.

53. Avery Gordon, *Ghostly Matters: Haunting and the Sociological Imagination* (Minneapolis: University of Minnesota Press, 1997).

54. Irma van der Ploeg, *The Machine-Readable Body* (Maastricht: Shaker, 2006).

55. Huub Dijstelbloem and Albert Meijer, *Migration and the New Technological Borders of Europe*, (Houndmills: Palgrave Macmillan, 2011).

56. Ibid, p. 7.

57. Martina Tazzioli, *Spaces of Governmentality: Autonomous Migration and the Arab Uprisings* (London: Rowman & Littlefield International, 2014).

58. Noelle Brigden and Cetta Mainwaring, "Matroyshka Journeys: Im/mobility during Migration," *Geopolitics* 21(2): 407–434.

59. Ruben Andersson, "Hunter and Prey: Patrolling Clandestine Migration in the Euro-African Borderlands," *Anthropological Quarterly* 87(1) (2014): 119–149.

60. John Steinbeck, *The Grapes of Wrath* (New York: Penguin, 2002 [1939]), pp. 118–122.

61. But see Seantel Anaïs' genealogy of non-lethal force which could certainly be read as a contribution to the study of the microphysics of police. *Disarming Intervention: A Critical History of Non-Lethality* (Vancouver: University of British Colombia Press, 2015).

# PART II

# Between Philosophy and Method

# CHAPTER 5

# Political Spirituality: Parrhesia, Truth and Factical Finitude

*Michael Dillon*

## FACTICAL FINITUDE

Given the amount of effort, inspired by the work of Michel Foucault, that I have devoted to interrogating how and why it is that modern politics is essentially a politics of security, it was a relief to concentrate upon those lectures in which Foucault's work interrogates what he calls the politics of truth. The relief lies in how Foucault's analytic of the politics of truth, of the courage of truth (*parrhesia*), and of political spirituality in particular, begins to disclose an entirely different way of posing the questions that modern politics addresses to modern times and modern subjects. It is a project that holds out the prospect of loosening the ties that bind us individually and collectively as subjects of modern rules of truth and truths of rule dominated by security politics, its lethal dangers and the constant global surveillance to which it necessarily subjects us.

---

The objective of truth telling is therefore less the city's salvation than the individual's ethos (Michael Foucault, *The Courage of Truth, The Government of Self and Others II, Lectures at the College de France 1983–1984*, ed. Frederic Gros and Arnold I. Davidson (London: Palgrave Macmillan, 2011), p. 65.

M. Dillon (✉)
University of Lancaster, Lancaster, UK
e-mail: m.dillon@lancaster.ac.uk

© The Author(s) 2017
P. Bonditti et al. (eds.), *Foucault and the Modern International,*
The Sciences Po Series in International Relations and Political
Economy, DOI 10.1057/978-1-137-56153-4_5

I detect a quite different project of thinking politically emerging in these later lectures of Foucault concerning *The Courage of Truth*, *The Hermeneutics of the Subject*, *Wrong-Doing Truth-Telling*, *The Government of Self and Others*, and *On the Government of the Living*.[1] It is a project of thought that critically engages the veridico-political matrix of modern politics as a theatrical political economy in which rules of truth and truths of rule are intimately connected. It requires a dramatic sensibility as much as it does an epistemic and veridical political awareness. It is sutured through and through by an overriding sense that truth and rule, both and equally, must take place together, and that this taking place is, in its essence, performative.

The truth at issue is not, however, truth as such. It is not any form or expression of truth. It is alethurgical truth, a truth, among other things, in which governors and the governed, alike, tell the truth about themselves. Moreover, thinking with and beyond Foucault in a foucauldian way, the alethurgical truth at issue in modern times differs from that of the alethurgical truth of Classical and Christian times to whose exploration the later Foucault devoted himself. The reason is that different modes of truth telling take place in different temporal political economies. Moreover, the rules of truth and truths of rule that they tell, and how these are told, enact temporal political economies of truth which are distinguished as much by their regimes of representation and figuration as they are by their rituals, liturgies and doctrines. Alethurgy was temporally posed on the one hand in terms of the temporal political economy of Greek cosmology and on the other in terms of the temporal political economy of Christian soteriology. Not so with the alethurgical truth of modern times. Modern alethurgical truth is posed—and problematized—in terms of the temporal political economy of modern factical finitude. Finite things exist *sub specie aeternitatis* for Christianity, for example, whereas factically finite things exist *ad infinitum* for the modern. (Not all of those who live in modern times are, of course, moderns or modernizers, just as not all those that lived in Christendom were Christians.)

Modern alethurgical truth therefore continues to display the same occulting character—the same excessive and ultimately even opaque character—as does that of Greek and Christian alethurgy. But it does so for very different reasons. The excess of truth over appearance that continues to characterize modern alethurgy is not, for example, a function of cosmological mystery or Christian divinity. It is a matter of how the rules of truth and truths of rule of modern factical finitude are comprised of an infinity of finite rules of truth and truths of rule. The excess lies in the relation between the finite and the infinite not the mortal and the divine. The infinite is very much not the eternal. The eternal holds out a promise of redemption. The infinite holds out no such promise. *Sub specie aeternitatis*, the mortal is distinguished from the divine by an eschatological break that nonetheless serves to reconnect the two. Religious eschatology separates this world from the next and promises a return from the one to the other. Life everlasting is on offer. Amid the infinity of finite things, however, factical finitude immanentizes the eschaton. There is no division of worlds. There is one world. It is comprised of an infinity of finite things that continuously come and go. This world is also sewn and sown together eschatologically, but differently. The eschatological break, here, lies within, and persists between, the death of the old and the birth of the new. There is no such thing as life everlasting. For all its promises, everlasting life is not on offer factically. Renewal, however, is. It comes in an infinity of finite forms, one of which is currently called resilience governmentally, but it is necessarily also as violent as it is infinite. The infinite is then more a positivistic device that allows the finite to be mapped, quantified and brought to presence in its very measurable specificity. Modern veridico-political government thus takes place as an exercise in the infinite government of finite things. The shift is fundamental.

My title grandly gestures toward what this new thought must think. In this short chapter I can, however, do little more than point down the track of upon which it has to proceed. The task is ultimately that of thinking about the courage of truth and political spirituality in the modern age. Since Foucault doubts whether or not there can be political spirituality and the courage of truth under modern conditions of truth and rule, the thinking here has to be conditional.

It must first proceed by asking IF there is such a thing as *parrhēsia* under the terms and conditions of modern rules of truth and truths of rule, what conditions of possibility and what conditions of operability would these modern rules of truth and truths of rule set for the exercise of *parrhēsia*? Since *parrhēsia* is traditionally connected both to truth and rule, since it was in fact linked to the alethurgical account of truth just as it was to the tyrannical as well as democratic practice of rule, and since the expression of alethurgical truth to which it was allied was that of an alethurgical truth access to which required forms of spiritual training, we have also to ask, secondly, in what ways would modern truths of rule and rules of truth condition the very possibility of political spirituality as well today?

How also would it condition their very taking place? Such alethurgical truth is avowedly also a performative truth that seeks manifestation, finite modes of appearance in which alethurgy is given voice, aspect and face. We have then to ask, thirdly, what figurative regimes characterize the theatrical political economy of truth and rule that obtains under modern conditions? And, how might this theatrical political economy together with its regimes of figuration, imaging and gesture (decorum) impinge upon the possibility and operation of the courage of truth and of political spirituality? For, manifestly, alethurgy finds its expression in appearance—finite spatio-temporal manifestations of truth—its taking place is thus, essentially, figurative. Before we address any of these questions, however, we have therefore to attempt some summary of Foucault's exploration of these two critical terms—*parrhēsia* and political spirituality. Since Foucault devoted years and several lecture courses to pursuing these reflections this summary is bound to be inadequate. Again it can only gesture toward what must be done in a more sustained interpretative exegesis.

## POLITICAL SPIRITUALITY AND *PARRHĒSIA*

"It is the parrhesiastic standpoint, which tries precisely, stubbornly, and always starting over again, to bring the question of truth back to the question of its political conditions and the ethical differentiation which gives access to it... This is the parrhesiastic discourse...it is the discourse of the irreducibility of truth, power and ethos, and at the same time the discourse of their necessary relationship, of the impossibility of thinking truth (aletheia), power (politeia), and ethos, without their essential, fundamental relationship to each other."[2]

From Kant and Hegel, through to Heidegger and Derrida, the term spirit has a central as well as disputed history in modern European thought. Similarly, it has a long and bloody history in the record of modern European politics. In neither instance could Foucault have been unaware of this history. Indeed he was not, and by the late 1970s he was in any event already deeply committed, also, to exploring the Christian as well as the Classical tradition in which spirituality, together with many other related themes, comprised the semantic field of formation of alethurgical truth. Foucault clearly knew that spirit, spirituality and political spirituality, in particular, were therefore terms with a contemporary as well as a Classical and a Christian heritage, and that they would inevitably attract criticism. Thus, having first floated the idea of political spirituality in particular, in an article published by *Le Nouvel Observateur* on 6 November 1978 concerning the Iranian insurrection, he observed that political spirituality is a, "possibility that we have forgotten since the Renaissance and the great crisis of Christianity." Speculating that something like political spirituality was on display in the Iranian insurrection, he concluded, "I can already hear the French laughing, but I know that they are wrong."[3]

Foucault's interest in alethurgical truth and political spirituality was no turn to religious mysticism. Spirituality, in Foucault, is not to be conflated with religiosity. It arises in relation to practices that a subject undergoes in order to gain access to alethurgical truth. Most especially it arises when, not being preformed to receive access to the truth, a subject must train itself in those practices which will allow it to attain some measure of the truth: "The truth is not given to the subject by a simple act of knowledge (*connaissance*) which would be founded and justified simply by the fact that he is the subject and because he possesses this or that structure of subjectivity," records Foucault in *The Hermeneutics of the Subject*. Practices of spirituality postulate "that for the subject to have right of access to the truth he must be changed, transformed, shifted and become, to some extent and up to a certain point other than himself."[4] And so: "Spirituality postulates that the subject as such does not have right of access to the truth and is not capable of having access to the truth. It postulates that the truth is not given to the subject by a simple act of knowledge (*connaissance*), which would be founded and justified simply by the fact that he is the subject and because he possesses this or that structure of subjectivity. It postulates that for the subject to have right of access to the truth he must be changed....The truth is only given to the subject at a price that brings the subject's being into play. For, as he is, the subject is not capable of truth."[5]

Foucault thus defines spirituality in contradistinction to modern *connaissance* in as pithy an observation as any that he made. It is one that also raises a profound question mark over the possibility of *parrhēsia* in modern times as well: "If we define spirituality as being the form of practices which postulate that, such as he is, the subject is not capable of the truth, but that, such as it is, the truth can transfigure and save the subject, then we can say that the modern age of relations between the subject and truth begins when it is postulated that, such as he is, the subject is capable of truth, but that, such as it is, the truth cannot save the subject."[6] Modern knowing thus presupposes the accessibility of truth to a subject pre-engineered for it, pursuing it very largely through positivistic practices while immersed in a regime of knowing reliant upon the self-certainty and transactional doubting of the Cartesian subject, the very limits of whose postulated epistemic certainty Kant nonetheless disclosed as lying foundationally within the structure of the *cogito* itself.

In short, and to emphasize three definitive features of Foucault's analytic of spirituality in general and of political spirituality in particular: First, the opacity of alethurgical truth, perhaps it is better to say its excess of truth over its finite appearance, is the prevailing condition of possibility for an account of spirituality as the practices by means of which the subject becomes the subject of alethurgical truth. Second, the excess of alethurgical truth over its appearance is compounded by the structures of the subject of alethurgical truth itself. Such a subject does not come into the possession of alethurgical truth by a simple act of knowing of which it is, *a priori*, capable in itself. Third, spirituality is not to be conflated with a religious experience. Spirituality concerns the practices that a subject must pursue in order to make it more receptive and capable of evolving itself, as a subject of truth, in relation to alethurgical truth, a truth that will never be transparent to it because there is always an excess of alethurgical truth over its finite appearance. Above all, the truth here concerns the ethos of the subject. The courage of truth even more so. Political spirituality refers to the practices, experience and occasions on which truth is spoken back to power in a discourse that, recalling the ineliminable link between truth, power and the subject, challenges the *doxa* or prevailing orthodoxies currently governing their triangulation.

It is here that the question of political spirituality is linked with that of *parrhēsia*, the courage of truth. Thus, Foucault emphasizes that the courage of truth is not a matter of epistemic technique. Neither is it a question simply of learning or responding to mentoring. He says very precisely that the courage of truth is ultimately a matter of timing. I would add, given my earlier reference also to the temporal enframing of modalities of truth, that it is timing which gives specific figuration to finite manifestations of the veridical landscape of alethurgy's field of formation and application. Foucault observes also that this matter of timing is especially related to how "a crisis of political institutions" arises as a "possible site for *parrhēsia*." That this moment shifts the subject's attention from the life of institutions—where rules of truth and truths of rule are installed and a *mentalité du gouvernment* associated with them cultivated—directly back to the ways in which one lives one's self (*hontina tropon teze*). Thus, the courage of truth appears to occur at, and in, a certain moment. It finds its expression in the freedom to say no to rules of truth and truths of rule. This is a dangerous veridical game for both parties—governed and governors alike, since governors are also "subjects of truth"—because it involves a potentially lethal challenge to the rules of truth and truths of rule that each tell about themselves. In challenging the veridical contract through which they are engaged, it challenges their very sense of self as both rulers and ruled. However, just as truth telling—prophetic, technical and otherwise—might take place in a single historical moment, its telling resist ascription to that single moment. To acknowledge this fact is not to deny that truth telling is historical and evental. It is to recognize the philosophical, scientific and political complexity of time, of historicality, and of the moment.

However, generically suspicious it may, therefore, be of truth and rule, this politicizing parrhesiastic refusal of rules of truth and truths of rule is no principled anarchy. It is as idiomatic as rules of truth and truths of rule themselves. It refuses this or that rule of truth, this or that truth of rule. It is a refusal of certain specific truths and certain specific truth tellers, of certain specific historically operating governmental systems of rule or rulers. If truth and rule are thus both historic and idiomatic, the moment when truth strikes, and an allied political spirituality arises, characterize the response to a current *doxa* of rules of truth and truth of rule. *Parrhēsia* therefore finds its idiomatic and historical mode of expression in the process of it being contoured by, and forcefully contesting, prevailing rules of truth and truth of rule. It, too, has to find its voice, face and aspect. Such truth telling is as potential lethal to the *tyrannos*, *politikos* or democratic assembly to which it is addressed as it is to the parrhesiast who engages in it. *Parrhēsia* poses a lethal threat to both sides of the veridical equation.

Recall, in conclusion, then, the defining features of spirituality and of how these are related to *parrhesia* as the set of practices that cultivate and test the subject's capacity for truth telling, especially in relation to politics, government and rule. If modern knowing is therefore a modern *dispositif*, alethurgical truth is a scandal to it. The scandal of this truth lies in the *factum brutum* that alethurgy is never transparent and is not a function or expression of the operation of the structure of the modern's account of the willing, reasoning subject and of the subject–object distinction governing modern accounts of rules of truth and truths of rule.

## The Ethos of the Subject of Truth

Modern politics of security are of course a certain politics of truth, a certain problematization of rules of truth and truths of rule that arise when finitude itself is problematized and positivised *ad infinitum* rather than *sub specie aeternitatis.* Here, rules of truth become an infinity of finite rules of truth. Correlatively, such rules of truth become an infinity of finite truths of rule. The rule of truth becomes the infinite excess of truth over its finite manifestation, while the truth of rule becomes the infinite government of finite things.[7] In that respect, the truth of modern rules of truth and truths of rule display the qualities of alethurgical truth at issue among the Classical as well as Christian accounts of truth telling: "a drama of multiple truths, of abundant truths, of truths in excess."[8] The drama is, however, one in which the subject has become a very particular kind of subject, and a very specific point of application, for the rules of truth and truths of rule of modern security politics. Here, also, the modern security state becomes a *Katechon* whose very foundational task is to hold back the end of which it is, nonetheless, integrally comprised as the very factically finite entity that it is. And that is why modern security politics are by definition both indefinite and comprehensively intrusive. If the subject of modern truth and rule is to escape its entrapment by the rules of truth and truths of rule of its prevailing security politics, if its ethos is to escape that of the animal depicted in Kafka's story of "The Burrow,"[9] the very ethos imparted by its rules of truth and truths of rule has to be re-thought. That means re-thinking the rules of truth and truths of rule of which it is a subject. This can only be done if its current constitution—its conditions of operability as well as possibility—are re-framed. Such a projects is precisely one that Foucault's lectures initiate.

## Alethurgy

The truth of *parrhēsia,* and of its allied spirituality, does not therefore concern any form of truth much less truth as such. It is the operation of alethurgy that is at issue. But if truth has a history then so also, however, does alethurgical truth. That of the Greeks was enframed cosmologically. That of the Christians was enframed soteriologically. The alethurgical truth of the moderns is neither Greek nor Christian. And it is not the neo-metaphysical truth of the disclosure or sending of Being either (Heidegger).

The alethurgical truth of the moderns is framed by a different temporal political economy or problematization of truth and rule. It is that which is introduced by the modern preoccupation with the positivity of factical finitude, rather than the salvational finitude of Christianity or, indeed, the cosmological finitude posited by the Greeks. Albeit that in each instance one of the single most important points of application for both truth and rule has been the constitution of the subject of truth and rule, as the character of alethurgical truth changed in response to the temporal political economy of factical finitude in which it is posited by moderns, so also did the constitution of the modern subject of truth change in its relation to truth. If neither truth, rule nor the subject is a historical constant, its triangulation is equally subject to historical transformation and change. Similarly, if such factically finite rules of truth and truths of rule find their alethurgical manifestation in modern times they must do so through the figurative regimes by which modern times gain their very expression. Foucault's project, if it were to be pursued, would therefore not only have to concern itself with the triangulation of truth, subjectivity and power to which Foucault calls our attention, it would also have to locate that triangulation in the figurative drama within which its taking place takes place. In short, since, as Foucault teaches in these lectures, alethurgy must have its manifestation, then modern regimes of figuration associated with its performative enactment must enter the analytic somehow as well. *Parrhēsia* and political spirituality arise, therefore, not simply as responses to alethurgical truth that dangerously recall the intimate triangulation of truth, subjectivity and power. They simultaneously also draw attention to the representational and figurative regimes without which neither truth or rule can gain purchase on the subject and thereby lend face, voice and aspect to it as the modern factically finite subject of both truth and rule.

That we are ruled does not therefore mean that we are ruled in the same ways historically. That we are subjects of truth does not mean that we are subjects of the same orders of truth. That we are subjects of both truth and rule does not mean that we are subjects of the same unchanging historical orders of truth and rule, or indeed the same subjects. Finally, since truth and rule must find their expression, then regimes of representation and figuration are not incidental to and neither can they simply be diversions from or mere ornament to the taking place of rules of truth and truths of rule. This ensemble is a complex drama, one that demands performative wit as much as analytical expertise. The changing fields of formation comprising modern regimes of representation and figuration, their genealogies together with the operation of their principles of formation, from geometry to the algorithm, for example, and from single point perspective to digitalization, are part of the challenge as well (see Bonditti and Elden in this volume).

All this is manifestly the case, also, with rules of truth and truths of rule that claim universality over us. Consider only the degree to which the Catholic Counter-Reformation expressed itself through the Baroque as much as it did the doctrinal teachings of the Council of Trent or the Papal Offices introduced to regulate hagiography, miracles, sainthood, liturgy and worship. For they, too, are not only comprised of rules of truth and truths of rule—every rule of truth expressing itself also in terms of the injunction to rule and be ruled according to the truth. They manifestly change in the very process of their operationalization. Both truth and the subject of truth, governed through and by the truth, as well of course as the power relations obtaining within the veridico-political matrix of rules of truth and truths of rule, are historical. Consequently, as the quotation from Foucault's lectures on *The Courage of Truth* so epigrammatically put the point: the objective of parrhesiastic truth telling and the practices of political spirituality—IF such things exist in the modern age—would therefore be less that "of the city's salvation," with which modern government appears to be so foundationally preoccupied in modern political theory and practice, than with "the individual's ethos."[10]

Foucault took many years and many lecture courses to pursue the question of the intimate correlation, in their very in-eliminable heterogeneity of truth (*aletheia*), politics (*politeia*) and the subject (*ethos*). Heterogeneity matters here. It does not simply mean plurality. It means that these three things while ineliminably related are nonetheless also ineradicably different. There is truth. There is power. There is singularity. They cannot be reduced to each other. Neither can they be reduced to some common denominator introducing a background unity to their plurality. They are not simply plural, they are heterogeneous. It is vitally important to note, also, that their compatibility is, therefore, by no means automatic and cannot be assumed. Foucault's reflections are located at the center of this complex problematization of subject, truth and rule, just as it is of the equally complex intersection of knowledge, time and the moment.

If there is an excess of truth over its manifestation, so also is there an excess of power over its appearance and an excess of singularity over its subjectivation. At the same time, however, rules of truth always inspire truths of rule just as truths of rule invoke rules of truth. Each finds their point of application in processes of subjectivation that nonetheless also figuratively locate their subjects in a performative enactment of both truth and rule. Always operating together, truth, rule and the subject continuously correspond and correlate with one another. In many respects, this is what Foucault means by the politics of truth. Truth always already in veridical correspondence with rule (power) finds its expression through processes of subjectivation. All I would add is that, since rules of truth and truths of rule must find their expression, then figuration in the widest sense of the term is simultaneously at issue also. Such processes of subjectivation are therefore as much figurative as they may be rational. Their very rationalism itself comprises a figurative regime.

The triangulation of truth, subject and the power relations of which they are also comprised necessarily, then, includes the staging and the setting as well as the soul: "We are dealing with a pure, fascinating manifestation whose principal intention is not so much to demonstrate or prove something, or to refute something false, but simply to show, to disclose the truth."[11] If truth must find its manifestation as Foucault claims in the lectures, *On the Government of the Living* in particular, that it must and does, modern rules of truth and truths of rule find their expression in the special effects of modern spectacle as much as they do in the disciplinary and other processes of self-subjectivation. Here, from a foucauldian perspective, and despite some of Foucault's exaggerated dismissals of spectacle as well as of sovereignty, truth must show itself. Its sociality is as much a society of the spectacle as it is of disciplinary or other relations of power. But it is a function less of ideological deception than it is of the imperatives of veridiction, and of the veridico-political necessity of having both truth and rule appear, become, or be made, manifest as an operating force in and throughout our lives.

Schmitt's miracle of decision, to take one dominant modern trope of truth and rule, may therefore be re-cast less as an un-conditioned event than the outcome of carefully contrived and staged special (veridico-political) effects, the growth of whose sanction and regulation had as much to do with the institution and elaboration of papal as it did of statal power and governance. Just as the example is never fully exemplary, so also the exception is never wholly exceptional. These days it has in fact become almost entirely a matter of governmental routine. No miracles to determine, no hagiography to compile, no miracles and hagiography to translate into doctrine, ritual and liturgy, then no Pope, no Church and no Ecumene of Belief (religious or national). No contest, either between

Concilliarists and Papal Imperialists, for example, together with the impact that this had on the development of modern democratic representation and constitutional theory in Europe and North America.[12]

It is remarkable how long Schmittean scholarship has been allowed to get away with talking about the miracle of decision without asking about the changing history of the miracle, and of how much the regulation of the miraculous, of miracle workers and their hagiographical record contributed to the development of modern as well as medieval (papal) governance. No modern State either, then, without the regulation of the event in the form of the miracle of decision and the compiling of political, national and martial liturgies and hagiographies as well. Once we take Foucault's injunction to recognize the ways in which truth—alethurgical truth—seeks manifestation, it is a short step to reinvigorating the analysis of spectacle and the reintegration of the theatrical political economy of rules of truth and truths of rule into a powerful analytic of modern politics of truth. As Hobbes, for one modern, noted from the outset of modern rules of truth and truths of rule, the triangulation of truth, rule and subjectivation is inescapably a theatrical political economy of truth and rule. The modern continues to transact relations between mystery and manifestation. In doing so it remains a drama. The question remains what kind of drama: Tragedy, *Trauerspiel*, or Farce? There are, of course, other candidates.

## PROSOPOPOEIA: FIGURING TRUTH AND RULE

Truth has to be made manifest. It requires personification, of sorts. It is precisely the absence of a truth that must be brought to presence that necessitates the use of figurative language. In rendering finite the infinity of finite things, factical finitude must also figure the infinite itself. Thus, the necessity for figuration is itself absolute.[13] Alethurgic truth has therefore to be given its figure, its voice and its face. Hobbes, again, knew this, and knew how critical it was to the personating characteristic of power relations in modern times. Hobbes also knew that the Greeks called this rendering, *prosopopoeia*, although he also refers to it, recalling the frontispiece to his great book *Leviathan*, as the masque of power. No mere inert mask, therefore, but a mask play in which something of the truth that is disclosed by masquing is simultaneously also held in reserve. Let "mask" then stand for the figurations without which alethurgical truth, without figure, face or voice—without aspect—would simply not become manifest. The figure of *prosopopoeia* is indeed metaphorical insofar as it involves a transfer of properties from one entity to another, but resemblance is not the principle that authorizes such transfers. What is instituted through *prosopopoeia* resembles nothing, nothing other than itself.[14] There is, then, an additional feature of alethurgical truth telling to add to that of its multiplicity and its dramatic taking place. For all that it takes place, and for all that access to alethurgical truth may also be gained via strenuous training, alethurgical truth is also characterized by an excess of truth over its appearance. The alethurgic drama is, then, that of the masque. Like all drama, it is characterized by a continuous figurative transactions between mystery and manifestation. The mask is the *sur-face*—the more than one face, aspect or voice—upon which rules of truth and truth of rules are projected and find their manifestation. As any actor or director would tell you, acting with a mask, acting out a masque, is an uncanny thing.[15]

This point emerges early in Foucault's *On the Government of the Living* lectures. There he rehearses a story about the Roman Emperor Septimus Severus who was reputed to have had a large ceremonial hall on whose ceiling was painted the stars precisely as they would have appeared on the date of his birth, thus providing an astral record of his fate. There was, however, a small element missing. It was the astral recording of the Emperor's "sky of death." This was recorded instead in one of the emperor's private rooms. Foucault works this story into an account of this other aspect of alethurgy.

Alethurgical truth telling is not a matter of finally making its truth transparent to the initiate who has undergone the spiritual training necessary to gain access to it, even at the price of their exposure, in the parrhesiastic expression of it, to death. Alethurgical truth is excessive. In its excess over appearance lies something of the mystery, obscurity and perhaps even final opacity of alethurgical truth. Access comes to its initiate at a price. But it does not seem as if, the price paid, unreserved access is fully and totally secured. It does not seem to be that kind of truth. Training for it does not seem to be that kind of training. Alethurgical truth clearly keeps something in reserve (shades of both Heraclitus and Heidegger here). There is, we might say, always an excess of alethurgical truth over its manifestation. It is, therefore, not merely a question of alethurgical truth being made manifest: "Essentially it was a question of making truth itself appear against the background of the unknown."[16]

For that very reason alethurgical truth is not only historical, or indeed consequently also figurative and gestural, it effects a novel transaction, within its truth telling, between the manifestation and retention of the truth. If there is to be truth there has to be a finite manifestation of it. But such manifestation never exhausts what there is. Whatever happens to become manifest, finitely, is freighted with the possibility of the indefinite supplement of the infinite. The astonishing fecundity of modern facticity, not least in relation to modern cosmology, itself testifies to this. The very finite technological appearance to which it subjects the infinity within which, and with which, it works, continuously extends, it does not exhaust but constantly subverts, deconstructs, extends and transforms, the grounds and boundaries of its own technological knowing. Whatever you call this peculiar phenomenon, even modern scientific knowing does not escape it.

We might, therefore, go further. However ascetic it must be, a masque of both truth and power seems necessarily also to be in play via the very ascetic spiritual training that the initiate into alethurgical truth undergoes. However, much it may also be comprised of self-consciously contrived special effects, the drama of alethurgical truth telling is not merely contrivance. It is inescapably a contrivance. Figuration and gesture—changing modes of representation as such including also language, of course—are integral to its very veridical political economy. Alethurgical truth telling seems thus to be a theatrical political economy of truth and rule not because it seeks to simulate, dissimulate or mask its truth but as a consequence of the very character of the truth it is bound to tell, and of the subject of truth that tells it: "So I won't say simply that the exercise of power presupposes something like a useful and utilizable knowledge in those who [govern]. I shall say that the exercise of power is almost always accompanied by a manifestation of truth understood in this very broad sense... there is no exercise of power without something like an alethurgy."[17]

Call this "ritual of manifestation of the truth and of power," a transaction between mystery and manifestation if you will. Many will of course routinely recoil from such terms. But it is simply a fact. One for which the grounding of modern knowing in the infinity of finite things cannot account, but continuously discloses instead. Fearing that such a concession would re-admit a religiosity that it struggled to escape, modern knowing merely concedes more to the religious, a monopoly over this excess of truth over appearance, than the religious itself warrants.

The masque of alethurgical truth telling is consequently a showing that necessarily also withholds as it manifests its truth. It has something of the negative about it. In modern times this is less a function of mystification than the sheer excess of the infinity of finite rules of truth and truths of rule over their appearance. It is in the nature of alethurgical truth, therefore, to be characterized by this definitive duality. Can there really be a power, Foucault therefore provisionally concludes by asking, "that would do without the play of light and shadow, truth and error, true and false, hidden and manifest, visible and invisible? In other words can there be an exercise of power without a ring of truth. Without an alethurgical circle that turns around it and accompanies it?"[18] We could do worse than repeat what he had to say about the existence of a modern form of *parrhēsia*: "*parrhēsia*.... And what about the modern epoch you may ask? I don't really know. It would no doubt have to be analyzed."[19] The masque of modern rules of alethurgical truth and truths of rule? It would no doubt have to be analyzed.

## Conclusion

*Democracy is not the privileged site of parrhēsia, but the place in which parrhēsia is most difficult to practice.*[20]

I end by repeating the important caveat with which I began. There may be no such thing as a contemporary form of *parrhēsia* or a contemporary form of political spirituality. Foucault seemed deeply ambivalent on the matter.

Since *parrhēsia* is a mode of truth telling that arises in relation to the *polis* we would therefore have to say that modern *parrhēsia*, if there is such a thing, would be expected to arise in relation not to the rules of truth and truths of rule of the *polis* but in relation to those of the modern state. It could not arise in relation to the rules of truth and truths of rule of the modern state alone, however, since, Foucault long taught, modern power relations are plural and diverse, and their primary point of application is the modern subject. But, if they ever were, they are no longer simply a matter of the subject being regulated by a superior power. The modern subject attains its status as subject through the degree to which it regulates and disciplines itself. If there is such a thing, then modern *parrhēsia* would be expected to arise in relation to the political and governmental matrix of modern power relations *tout court*.

More than that, however, and again as Foucault teaches in these lectures, the trope of being tested is a classical one. So also, Foucault teaches, is the modern subject a subject of (self) testing. But differently. Let us say that as a subject the modern subject is a subject that continuously serves-out a probation. The object of that probation is to demonstrate that the modern subject is worthy of being a governable—ideally, a self-governable—subject. However, since the government of modern factical finitude is the infinite government of finite things, it is not possible for the modern subject to serve out the terms of its probation because the very terms of that probation are simultaneously not only infinite they are thereby indefinite. There is no end to them, but there is also no limit to their properties either. That being so, if there is such a thing as a modern form of *parrhēsia*, we would expect to look for it in a refusal of this very conditioning of the modern subject of truth and rule. It would be a refusal of the infinite and indefinite probationary conditioning that now defines the very being of modern subjectivation.

There is, one might also add, a further definitive feature of the indefinite probationary terms that the modern subject must serve-out, and to whose definitive rules of truth and truths of rule one might expect a modern form of *parrhēsia* to have the courage to refuse. Eschatologically fractured from beginning to end as a finite creature, the modern subject is a specific instance of the infinity of finite things existing in an imperious universe indifferent to its fate, and, like the modern state, equally also a subject of security. Theirs is an infinite and indefinite probationary existence defined in terms of securing a survival that is beyond their measure and their means. For that reason they simultaneously govern, and are themselves also governed, in terms of an infinity of finite rules of truth and truths of rule. Resisting the end of which they are nonetheless integrally comprised they submit to its endless rule seeking only to prove themselves governable in terms of it. The relation between the modern state and the modern subject is therefore not contractual at all. It is homologous. Each is a function of the factical finitude that construes them as katechontic, obsessed with securing a survival that is outwith their composition, their competence and their cognition except in the form of the endless rule that governs them.

I could go on. I should go on. But there is no space to carry on. Perhaps enough has been said already, however, to gesture toward the path down which this reflection will have to proceed. But there is a final note on which I would like to conclude. Foucault observes in these lectures, notably those of *The Courage of Truth*, that one of the legacies of the Classical account of *parrhēsia* is the observation that democracy, in particular, does not especially favor the practice of *parrhesia*. On the contrary, the conclusions of the classics was that democracy was one of the most difficult sites upon which *parrhesia* could be practiced. Since *parrhēsia* was always a matter of both politics and spirituality, the practice of political spirituality did not find a privileged site in democracy either. For these reasons, modern democracy would be the place to begin looking for a courage of truth and a political spirituality that it historically claims to possess, but in which it currently seems to be so deficient.

## NOTES

1. *The Courage of Truth, The Government of Self and Others II, Lectures at the Collège de France 1983–1984*, ed. F. Gros and A. I. Davidson, transl. G. Burchell (London: Palgrave Macmillan, 2010); *The Hermeneutics of the Subject. Lectures at the College de France, 1981–1982*, ed. by Frederic Gros and Arnold I. Davidson (London: Palgrave Macmillan, 2005); *Wrong-Doing Truth-Telling. The Function of Avowal in Justice*, ed. Fabienne Brion and Bernard E. Harcourt (Chicago: Chicago University Press, 2014); *The Government of Self and Others, Lectures at the College de France 1982–1983*, ed. Frederic Gros and Arnold I. Davidson (London: Palgrave Macmillan, 2010); *On The Government of the Living. Lectures at the College de France, 1979–1980*, ed. Frédéric Gros and Arnold I. Davidson (London: Palgrave Macmillan, 2014).
2. Foucault, *The Courage of Truth*, p. 68.
3. Michel Foucault, "What Are the Iranians Dreaming [Rêvent] About?" [1978], transl. Karen de Bruin, in Janet Afary and Kevin B. Anderson, *Foucault and the Iranian Revolution. Gender and Seductions of Islamism* (Chicago and London: The University of Chicago Press, 2005), p. 209.
4. Foucault, *The Government of Self and Others*, p. 15.
5. Foucault, *The Hermeneutics of the Subject*, p. 17.
6. Foucault, *The Hermeneutics of the Subject*, p. 19.
7. Michael Dillon, *Biopolitics of Security: A Political Analytic of Finitude* (London: Routledge, 2015).
8. Foucault, *On The Government of the Living*, p. 25.
9. Michael J. Shapiro, *Reading the Postmodern Polity* (Minneapolis: Minnesota University Press, 1991).
10. Foucault, *The Courage of Truth*, p. 65.
11. Foucault, *On The Government of the Living*, p. 5.
12. Stefan Kuttner, *History of Ideas and Doctrines of Canon Law in the Middle Ages* (Varium, 1980); Francis Oakely, *The Politics of Eternity: Studies in the*

*History of Medieval and Early Modern Thought* (Brill, 1999); Brian Tierney, *Foundations of the Conciliar Theory: The Contribution of The Medieval Canonists from Gratian to the Great Schism* (Cambridge, Cambridge University Press, 2010).

13. Adrian W. Moore, *The Infinite* (London: Routledge, 2001); Andrew D. Irvine (Ed.), *Philosophy of Mathematics* (Amsterdam: Elsevier, 2009); Brian Rotman, *Ad Infinitum* (Stanford: Stanford University Press, 1993); and *Mathematics as Sign* (Stanford: Stanford University Press, 2000).

14. Ian Balfour, *The Rhetoric of Romantic Prophecy* (Stanford: Stanford University Press, 2002), p. 64.

15. Michael Dillon, "Le masque et le courage de la vérité," Program note to *Un Ballo in Maschera* performed by The Royal Belgian Opera Company at De Munt/La Monnaie, Brussels, 2015; Peter Hall, *Exposed by the Mask* (London: Oberon Books, 2000); David Wiles, *Mask and Performance in Greek Tragedy* (Cambridge: Cambridge University Press, 2014).

16. Foucault, *On The Government of the Living*, p. 6.

17. Ibid, pp. 6–7.

18. Ibid, p. 17.

19. Foucault, *The Courage of Truth*, p. 29.

20. Ibid, p. 57.

CHAPTER 6

# Power as *Sumbolon*: Sovereignty, Governmentality and the International

## Mitchell Dean

Michel Foucault was concerned with power throughout his entire intellectual career. Yet it is in the 1970s that it received his most explicit treatment. As a way of summarizing his contribution, I offer a figure, the *sumbolon*, which operates according to "the rule of halves," through which we can understand his investigations on power.[1] I next use that figure to present an overview of the trajectory of his analysis of power and its principal concepts. I shall then suggest how international politics is approached in his investigations, and how we might think with but go beyond Foucault himself. I conclude by suggesting how we might remain loyally unfaithful to his approach to power more broadly.[2]

My general argument concerns the need to reconnect the many halves of Foucault's work to address international politics and government, including especially his approaches to sovereignty and the government of life (variously called "governmentality" and "biopolitics"). I further identify two relevant "dispositifs" in his work—one diplomatic-military and the other liberal-international—and suggest three ways of extending his contribution. The first is the extension of his characterization of the features of

M. Dean (✉)
Copenhagen Business School, Copenhagen, Denmark
e-mail: md.mpp@cbs.dk

© The Author(s) 2017
P. Bonditti et al. (eds.), *Foucault and the Modern International*,
The Sciences Po Series in International Relations and Political
Economy, DOI 10.1057/978-1-137-56153-4_6

a domestic liberal government to an analysis of current liberal-international politics and governance. The second is to challenge the idea that liberalism is a form of governmental reason that seeks to limit governing in the international domain. The third is a revaluation of the early modern invention of sovereignty as not only a "right of death," that wraps itself in glory, but also as a condition of a politics of life, a biopolitics.

## SUMBOLON

In the recently published lectures of 1980, *On the Government of the Living*, Foucault returns to the etymology of the symbol, the Greek *sumbolon*, a platter in which two halves have been broken.[3] The context is a discussion of the excessive manifestation of truth beyond the effective exercise of power (see Dillon in this volume). The same figure appears without name in a comparison of the structure of two plays in the 1983 lectures on *parrhesia* and forms of truth telling, and had been discussed at length on several previous occasions in his readings of Sophocles's *Oedipus Rex*.[4] The first, in a 1971 lecture in his initial series at the Collège de France, actually contains a table of the *sumbolon* in that drama reproduced from the notes of an auditor. It appears in the extended version of this lecture appended to the same lecture series, delivered in Buffalo and at Cornell in 1972. Then it appears again in the second of his 1973 Rio lectures.

In the earliest of these lectures, Foucault provides a counter reading of the play to that of Freud. By the Rio lecture, he notes that this is somewhat redundant given the intervening publication of *Anti-Oedipus* by Deleuze and Guattari.[5] However, what is striking for our concerns here is not that Foucault offered an explicit link between the *sumbolon* and power. Rather it is simply that at the beginning and at the end of his most intensive reflection on concepts and relations of power during the 1970s, he raises this figure of ancient Greek thought. And after a decade of deliberation on power, he continues to pose the question of the "non-economic" manifestation of truth.[6]

The *sumbolon* for Foucault is however closely related to sovereignty. It was Oedipus himself, he remarks in 1971.[7] The story of Oedipus, like so many others in Foucault, is one of the disempowerment of the sovereign. Yet the *sumbolon* is both a form of organization of the play and a mode of investigation. Each character in the play, whether god, seer, royalty, servant or shepherd, holds or presents only half a truth that requires complementing by another. Some of these halves break into further halves.

It is only by fitting all these pieces together that the truth emerges that challenges the sovereign's exercise of power by revealing his ignorance— of the identity of his real parents and of his murder of Laius. So the *sumbulon* is like a platter whose two halves are joined, or a mosaic in which all the tesserae are aligned, or a kaleidoscope in which all the pieces of glass are shifted into a particular form. It is a mechanism of truth that conforms to the "rule of halves."[8] As Foucault commented in 1973, "Power manifests itself, completes its cycle, maintains its unity by means of this little game of separate fragments of the same whole, a unique object whose overall configuration is the manifest form of power."[9] For the Greeks, it is a juridical, political and religious technique. In Sophocles, it marks a transition in regimes of veridiction from an oracular-prophetic one to a juridical-investigative one based on the evidence given by witnesses. Ten years later, this organization of the play is itself a mode of veridiction, a "dramatics of truth telling."[10]

My wager here is that if we want to understand Foucault's conception of power, we can regard each concept according to this rule of two halves and work out the overall configuration, the *sumbolon*, if you like, that results from an arrangement of all these pieces, all these tesserae. This applies not simply in an analytical and formal way, as if these pieces can be arranged in a system or a totality, but as a process of investigation that follows the trajectory of his thought. For while we think that we know the main terms of this thought in a vocabulary that includes discipline, sovereignty, biopolitics, governmentality and the pastorate, none of this makes sense except in relation to that which can be known only on the basis of the arc of an investigation. The truth effect of Foucault's investigations into power does not concern particular statements or concepts but an entire set of relations established by them. My second wager is that it is only by assembling these elements that we can begin to grasp the implications for what he would call the "great diplomatic-military apparatus [*dispositif*]"[11] or the current liberal-international dispositif.

## FOUCAULT'S TRAJECTORY ON POWER

It is not possible to identify the day that Foucault first spoke of power in a way that could be described as foucauldian, although it would perhaps be sometime after his inaugural lecture at the Collège de France in 1970. There, he announced his intention to conduct, as well as archaeological or "critical" studies, genealogical ones that would study positivities, the power to constitute objects about which one could make true or false propositions.[12] A kind of "rule" or "law of halves" is quickly found at work in these early elaborations and indications on power: of power and knowledge, of power and truth, of positive and productive power and power as repression, of power and the subject, of relations of power and rituals of truth, power and resistance, and so on. These pieces, tiles or halves are given their methodological enunciation as a microphysics of power and an analytics of power in his major books of the 1970s. Here the pieces come together as an analytical toolbox that allows a diagnostic of the present (see Bonditti in the volume). But Foucault would also seek to assemble the halves of this *sumbolon* both from a narrative about the past and an attempt to make intelligible the appearance of the new. Like the *sumbolon* in *Oedipus Rex*, the questions and answers of Foucault's approach to power have a precise temporality: they take a *diagnostic* form that gives us an ontology of the present, a *genealogical* form that distinguishes that present from the past and a *prospective* form that asks what the future can bring.

In terms of the relation to the past, Foucault is usually considered to be a thinker who wanted to introduce a fissure or a break in forms of power, and this is certainly true of the first part of his conceptual elaboration. He first sought to show that sovereignty and its spectacular and violent relation to the body had been displaced by the less visible, mute and petty dominations of disciplinary normalization.[13] He would soon after contrast a symbolics of blood and an analytics of sexuality, the right of death and the power of life, the deductive power of the sovereign with the productive powers of biopower and discipline.[14] But if both the "anatomo-politics" of the body and the biopolitics of the population are defined in contradistinction to sovereignty, they would be bound together as the functionally interrelated axes of biopower. The corporeal body of discipline would find a new half in a power aimed at the population, the species body.

In all this, Foucault would seek to think about power relations outside the vocabulary of juridical-political theory, with its concepts of sovereignty, legitimacy, representation and so on—thus introducing a new breakage. In concurrent lectures in 1976, he would test the historico-political discourse of the "race wars" as a potential model for rethinking power relations outside the proclaimed universalism of the state.[15] He would experiment with inverting Clausewitz, or at least returning to that which the latter inverted, so that politics became a continuation of war.[16] He would soon find that the law "operates more and more as a norm," and later as a "technology of government."[17] He would call for the decapitation of the king, at least in political thought and analysis.[18] He would provide narratives of the movement of power from its sovereign to its disciplinary and biopolitical forms. He would describe a microphysics of power rather than a theory of the state (see Walters in this volume). There is clearly a process of breaking, of splitting and of cutting, which is quite violent, in Foucault's search for a characteristic way to think about power.

Perhaps it is doubtful whether Foucault succeeded in putting this *sumbolon* back together. But he was aware of a problem this earlier strategy of breaking leads to. Having made a set of distinctions, he would then try to specify the relationships between the terms. Sometimes these relationships are overly functional and integrative, with diverse effects. In the last lecture in 1976, he would suggest that it is the combination of biopolitics and sovereignty that ensures that all modern states have the diabolical potential only manifest in the most pathological of them, such as the Nazi state.[19] But soon he finds that this does not seem to lead anywhere and could lend itself to a politics of denunciation practiced by militants and those advocating violent confrontation with the state in Germany and Italy at the time. His excavation of "state phobia" over the next couple of years seems to indicate a concern that his analytics of power could be tied to such a politics of denunciation.[20]

Thus beginning in 1979, we find Foucault insisting that his concern has been, and will be with "the government of men insofar as it appears in the exercise of political sovereignty", that is to say, his concern was *not* the displacement of sovereignty by something else.[21] The transformation of political sovereignty would now be accomplished not by the arc of a historical narrative but by a critical ethos invested in liberalism or, at least, in the liberal art of government. This art of government would promote new sites of veridiction, grounded in political economy, of the market and of civil society. Similarly, the analysis of the dispositifs would not dispense with sovereignty but turn it into one dispositif of law, among several, including discipline and security.[22] What would count now would be "the dominant characteristic" or "the system of correlations" within "complex edifices" made up of "juridico-legal mechanisms, disciplinary mechanisms and mechanisms of security."[23] Law would no longer be the expression of the sovereign will but a mechanism, a device or a technology of power, depriving the sovereign of its claim to transcendence and supremacy within a particular domain. Law and sovereignty would be one heterogeneous and contingent assemblage among many, no longer the expression of a centralized, uniform and supreme power within a domain. Foucault would reverse the critique of liberalism, traceable to German jurisprudence, as an ethical, economic and technical reduction of the political. Liberalism itself would be a critique always concerned with too much governing, which embodies new forms of truth and offers new rituals of veridiction, and makes possible and works through new forms of freedom. Liberalism promises an ethical, economic and technical opening up of the field of the political even as it closes human subjectivity within *homo œconomicus*.

This investigation into modern forms of power comes to a dramatic end, a *finis* rather than a *telos*, but perhaps both, with the lectures on neoliberalism, itself divided into two parts—German and American.[24] It is the most radical form of neoliberalism—of the Chicago School—that presages a new kind of regulation or power which, though not without dangers, seeks to modify variables in the environment, allows the maximum tolerance and the greatest degree of difference, and regulates without the creation of subjects, without "subjectification" (*assujettissement*).[25] This has given rise to some debate over Foucault and the course of French neoliberalism.[26] If there is a *telos* to this investigation, it is one in which power, now transmuted into governing, bases itself on the "rationality of the governed," as Foucault himself said or, as some of his followers put it, governs through freedom, through self-governing.[27] Some have claimed that it is American neoliberalism and the idea of human capital in which each individual is an entrepreneur of the self that forms a passage to Foucault's investigations into the care of the self in antiquity (see Gros and Paltrinieri in this volume).[28] Whether or not Foucault offered an "apology of" Gary Becker and his economic theories, as François Ewald has argued,[29] there is certain flattening out of power along a plane of immanence in these investigations of Foucault. The movement from the spectacular and symbolic elements of power, which was found not simply in historical reality but in literature and art, to a certain dull uniformity of the rationalities of government indicates a thesis of disenchantment reminiscent of Max Weber. Nonetheless, the halves proliferate: technologies of government and techniques of the self; relations of power and games of freedom. It is certainly noteworthy that the idea of power as "games of freedom" only appears *after* his study of liberalism and neoliberalism. But does this movement toward an immanent domain of governing, in which government will be limited by means of its own internal economy, only capture one half of that which Foucault had initially set himself to understand?

Here we can assemble an entire set of references that indicates that the other side of the *sumbolon* is still present even in those lectures where Foucault offers the most rationalized view of power. First, there is the eminence of theology and religious practice. Consider his long excursus in the lectures of 1978 on the passage of the pastorate in Judaeo-Christian civilization and his later insistence at Stanford on the defining relationship between its shepherd-flock game and the Greek-derived city-citizen game.[30] It is the pastorate that allows him to pose the problem of modern expertise, and the theme of government as the "conduct of conduct" is introduced in relationship to Gregory of Nazianus and the *oikonomia pyschōn*, the economy of souls.[31] Secondly, there is also the recurrent thematic of eschatology in his narrative of governmentality. The "government of men" emerges in between two eschatologies: one imagined as an actuality and the other as potential. There is a medieval eschatology that seeks the restoration of the Roman Empire as it awaits the coming of the Last Days. Then there are also the "counter-conducts" formed around an anti-governmental eschatology based on the notion of civil society in liberal government.[32] Thirdly, there is Foucault's analysis of the science of police and its concern in Mayerne and Hohenthal for the "splendor" of the state, encompassing the "visible beauty of the order and the brilliant radiating manifestation of a force."[33] Here we are reminded of the role of the spectacle and the symbolic in his earlier accounts of sovereignty and of the excessive manifestation of truth accompanying forms of power. Fourthly, there is Foucault's evident and manifold relation to the state of exception tradition. He analyzes the *coup d'État* in writers such as Naudé, Le Bret and Chemnitz as encompassing necessity, violence and theater, and as being continuous with raison d'État. Foucault calls the classical theater of Shakespeare, Corneille and Racine a theater of the *coup d'État*, and suggests that the *coup d'État* itself is a form of political theatricality that "brings this tragedy into play on the stage of reality itself."[34] Further, liberal reason itself is described as introducing an exception into the juridical order of sovereignty: the market as a "free space," or, more exactly, a "free port" (*franc port*) or what we would call a special economic zone.[35] Even in the most "economic" of his thought figures, that of the dispositif, he invokes the condition of "urgency" such as the mass vagabondage of the seventeenth century that shaped the dispositif of discipline, and the famines of the eighteenth century that were the condition of a new security dispositif.[36] Underlining his interest in the state of exception, Foucault cites Le Bret, for whom the exception creates a necessity, a force so great that like a "sovereign goddess, having nothing sacred in the world but the firmness of its irrevocable decrees, it ranks everything divine and human beneath its power."[37]

In these passages, Foucault connects the study of power and government with, respectively, an economic theology, a political eschatology, the question of splendor and glory, and the state of exception. In regard to the latter, Foucault joins with the state-of-exception tradition from Jean Bodin to Carl Schmitt. In all these respects, there is a possible communication with the most recent work of Giorgio Agamben beyond what many of Foucault's followers would allow.[38]

Now, we can ask a series of paired questions that illustrate the halves of his thought:

1. Does the arc of Foucault's investigation of power reveal a thesis of secularization, rationalization and disenchantment, a movement from a transcendent power around the sovereign, and behind him, God, to the immanent practices and rationalities of government? Or does Foucault already suggest a continuing economic theology eminent in our practices of governing today, particularly concerning the role of professionals and experts, inherited from the earliest pastors and Fathers of the Church?

2. Does Foucault's discussion of the state's splendor in the science of police and political theatricality in reason of state not indicate a continuing concern for practices of political glorification and acclamation, for the spectacle and symbolics of power, and for its ceremonial and ritual form? Or is his narrative one of the progressive and dialectical emergence, against various transcendent authorities (whether God, the King, the Father, the Expert, the State), of a form of power rationalized according to the rationality of the governed?

3. Are the politico-religious and excessively violent dimensions of power mostly aligned with the genealogically revealed past? Or is the potential for fanaticism and anti-state eschatology made possible by liberal notions of limited government acting through civil society?

4. Does Foucault reveal a concept of the political in his notion of governmentality that is disconnected from sovereignty and the state of exception? Or, is it only possible to think of innovations of governmentality and its characteristic dispositifs in relation to crisis, emergencies, events and decisions?

If, despite their apparent antinomical structure, we can answer *all* of these questions affirmatively, then we can see that a kind of rule of halves is at work here. Whatever findings Foucault reports at any one moment, his questions about power concern in part the theological and the secular, the glorious and the rationalized, the genealogical and the prospective, the economic-governmental and the juridical-decisionist.

## FOUCAULT AND INTERNATIONAL POLITICS

It is here that we can introduce Foucault's contributions on international politics. There is a three-part story of the government of the international contained in his lectures of 1978 and 1979. The first is that of the "theological-cosmological continuum" in which governing would be conducted in a medieval chain of being linking God, the king, the pastor and the family.[39] Foucault cites Aquinas's *De Regno*. Here earthly government would be conducted while awaiting the Second Coming and would be dedicated to the restoration of the Roman Empire. In this sense, the worldly government of *respublica Christiania* is always driven by an imperial ambition and the opening of a permanent eschatological bureau.

This "theological-cosmological" continuum is shattered by the emergence of raison d'État or reason of state that introduces "an open time and multiple spatiality."[40] This is the second part of the story. Reason of state imposes a limitation on the ambition of states and a disenchanted view of interest of state. Foucault speaks of reason of state as a "practico-reflexive prism" through which relations between states can be viewed and analyzed and by which strategies and tactics can be planned and devised.[41] The "rivalry of princes," with its concerns for the treasures and possessions of the sovereign, and his familial and dynastic alliances, is replaced by "competition between states," with its interests of state and their combination. It is linked to multiple technologies of governing including war (which is no longer under the sign of justice but of politics), a conscious, constant and permanent art of diplomacy, and standing armies and permanent military apparatus.[42] What is at stake is thought of in terms of force, the balance of forces and the balance of Europe.[43] There is no more waiting for the end of history. Politics and political conflicts, the need for alliance and the balancing of large and powerful states with combinations of smaller and less powerful ones, and for the prevention of war, will always be with us. At its best, "one of the most fundamental mutations in the form of both Western political life and Western history" promises an end to the idea of a just war and the organization of states according to the rule of a *jus gentium*, and thus resonates in many respects with Schmitt's account of the *jus publicum Europæum* characterized by the moral "bracketing" of war and the relation between equal sovereigns.[44]

Foucault proceeds in the following year (1979) to discuss the "international space of liberalism."[45] This is the third part of the story. Just as reason of state is a rationality that can be used to govern the international ordering or "police" of states and the relationship between them, so liberalism extends the internal benefits of the legitimate game of natural competition to the trade between countries and individual freedom leads to the mutual enrichment of all the states of Europe.[46] Liberalism is undoubtedly related to colonialism and the division between Europe and the rest of the world in which "the game is in Europe, but the stake is the world."[47] But liberalism does this through the globalization of the market and new forms of globality. Liberalism has an affinity with new forms of global "juridification" such as that of maritime law, the combatting of piracy and the space of the free sea. Projects of perpetual peace, such as those envisaged by Kant, base themselves on the natural propensities of human beings to exchange and to associate with one another in separate regions.[48] The "guarantee of perpetual peace is therefore actually commercial globalization [*planétarisation*]," remarked Foucault.[49] According to this logic, if you want an end to war, you must take liberalism and its game of economic competition instead.

Foucault was concerned to stress the (post-) theological dimension of both reason of state and liberalism, and hence of this movement from the Christian empire to the Europe of balance and then the Europe of progress. He notes that reason of state was denounced by Pope Pius V as "the devil's reason" (*ratio status* as *ratio diaboli*) and that, later, political economy was an "atheistic discipline with neither God, totality, nor the possibility of a sovereign point of view over the totality of the state he has to govern."[50] Foucault rejects the interpretation of Adam Smith's "invisible hand" that links it to providentialism such as found in Malebranche. Knowledge of economic totality is denied to participants in the market or any political agent.[51] Nevertheless, in relation to the international sphere, he indicates the potentiality for what he calls a "relative eschatology" in both reason of state and economic liberalism.[52] Reason of state offers a critique of the absolute eschatology of the waiting for the Kingdom of the Final Days. In doing so, it opens the possibility of a kind of "relative eschatology" of a perpetual peace that is "expected to come from a plurality without major unitary effects of domination."[53] The plurality of course is a world of very different but formally equal sovereign states. Kant's narrative of perpetual peace is a kind of liberal version of this relative eschatology: the human propensity to exchange leading to the civil law of the separate states; the separate states in turn to international law; and the movement of exchange across borders to cosmopolitan law.[54] Liberal economic government initiates, in other words, the possibility of a kind of commercial eschatology, a perpetual end of history in the ceaseless circulation of goods, money and services around the globe.

There are three features of Foucault's admittedly sketchy account of these international rationalities of government that provide us with analytical openings.

The first is that Foucault indicates a genealogical basis for the distinction between the domestic and the international. He locates a first international dispositif inherited from reason of state. The four characteristic elements of liberal government—the practice of economic veridiction, population management, law and respect for freedom and rights, and modern police forces—are joined with the "great diplomatic-military apparatus [*dispositif*] which has hardly been modified since the eighteenth century."[55] Thus, while liberal domestic government continues to be a site of innovation, international governing largely relies on these older technologies. The opening thus allows us, beyond Foucault, to investigate how liberal governing has reshaped the international along these four allegedly domestic dimensions. We can thus observe the development of international agencies that seek to regulate the economic governance of nations, the attempted management of populations across borders and in international spaces, the growth of international law and human rights principles, and the view of military intervention as form of international policing.[56] Moreover, just as liberal government seeks to limit itself domestically by invoking the historical-natural reality of civil society, so liberal internationalism closely aligns itself with what it calls "transnational" or "global civil society." As David Held observed some time ago, the contemporary liberal international regime brings about changes that "in many respects... represent the extension of the classical liberal concern to define the proper form, scope and limits of the state in the face of the processes, opportunities and flux of civil life."[57] By shifting Foucault's analysis of the art of domestic liberal government to the international domain, we can achieve a certain felicitous description of the kinds of rationalities and technologies operative within the current liberal-international dispositif. We might then distinguish two dispositifs of international politics: the diplomatic-military one that emerges with reason of state and the liberal-international dispositif that emerges in the twentieth century.

The second feature that provides an opening is Foucault's view of the fecundity of limitation. Reason of state confronts an external "principle of the state's self-limitation"—that of the existence of other states, some stronger and some weaker in effect, but equal in principle.[58] It is the plurality of states that also puts an end to the millennial dream of the restoration of Empire awaiting the Final Kingdom. International governing in this sense is a kind of external limitation of a police governmentality that domestically wants to proceed with no such limitation. Indeed, it is the competition between states that requires the intensive regulatory development of states and their populations in reason of state. While the internal regulation of the police state knows limits set by theology, natural law and imprescriptible natural rights, these are merely extrinsic to reason of state[59] (see Gros in this volume).

Liberalism, by contrast, faces a general, de facto, internal principle of limitation that determines the adequacy of government, rather than its legitimacy. This principle constitutes a rational division between the agenda and non-agenda of government, and between what is to be done and what is not to be done.[60] The principle of right that balanced reason of state internally is replaced by the "age of critical governmental reason."[61] But again, these observations allow a thought experiment beyond what Foucault had to say. What if we hypothesize that a liberal art of government knows no external limits in the international sphere and seeks to erase the specificity of states and their interests and imposes a regime that can facilitate and transform global capitalism? What if the general, rational, critical governmental reason that constitutes its own internal limits knows no limit in its desire to be spread externally? The domestic danger of reason of state, which was held in check only by right and juridical reason, was an overgoverning of populations within its territories, in part due to external concerns. In a kind of reverse symmetry, there is an international danger of liberalism that seeks to impose a global uniformity on all states in such a way as to warrant a detailed domestic police of individual and institutional conduct within them. In this sense, the liberal international imperative to reform conduct undermines its domestic limitation of sovereignty. This observation yields a critical insight: liberalism as an art of government that claims to be self-limiting within states warrants an international liberal governmentality that requires detailed forms of governing not only of states but of the forms of conduct within them.

Thirdly, Foucault's approach to the international shows in broad terms how rationalities of government traverse the boundary between national and international governing. They appear to put together the two halves.

Foucault in this respect challenges a conception of the international founded on a categorical distinction between inside and outside, between a Hobbesian state of nature and the space of civil or civilized society. But we should push this further than a concern with governmental rationalities such as reason of state and liberalism and seek to bring together the internal and external components of sovereignty.

If we do this, sovereignty itself is not simply a form of power grounded in the exercise of violence. Both Weber and Foucault share this insight: the former in his definition of the state as a claim to a monopoly of legitimate violence and the latter in his gloss on sovereign power as founded on "a right of death."[62] But the system of sovereignty can also be viewed as a form of power that would claim two life-affirming achievements: on the domestic front, to protect subjects from the violence that inheres within an unfettered (un)civil society and particularly its confessional fanaticisms, and internationally, to tame an external state of nature by means of the juridical recognition of formally equal sovereigns, the demoralization of war and the regulation of the conduct of bellicose parties. In both these senses, this system is a condition of biopolitics, a politics of life, as much as it is its other, a right of death.[63] The modern sovereignty of the territorial state could be viewed as a juridical-political improvisation that established the protection of corporeal integrity, the foundation of other rights and of security. In this sense, despite his excursus into what he calls "state-phobia," Foucault tends to see sovereignty in "thanatopolitical" terms, and as entering into "demonic" combinations with other powers, including pastoral power and biopower, which are inscribed in the workings of all modern states.[64] In this respect, his view of sovereignty is perhaps too close to the liberal critique of the state as his genealogy of forms of neoliberalism in fact shows. Just as we can explore the reverse symmetry of reason of state and liberalism, we can link more closely the internal and external dimensions of sovereignty and connect the idea of sovereignty to a positive conception of biopolitics.

Foucault allows us to distinguish between a diplomatic-military dispositif, invented in relation to reason of state, and a liberal-international dispositif. Moreover, his thought about the international opens up three ways (at least) of thinking about the liberal-international dispositif beyond what he himself did: the translation of liberalism from the domestic to the international domain; the reverse symmetry of the dangers of liberalism and reason of state; and the putting together of apparent opposites of internal and external aspects of sovereignty and of sovereignty and biopolitics.

Perhaps we can paraphrase Max Weber's definition of "politically oriented action" here and say that liberalism is not only an art of government that limits itself by its internal economy but also a form of action oriented to the appropriation of the powers of the state and international organizations in order to implement a detailed conduct of life.[65] In this respect, while the first aspect of liberalism distinguishes it from the police state, as Foucault shows, the latter is continuous with reason of state, including its relative eschatology.

## CONCLUSION

By focusing on the image on an omnipotent and omniscient sovereign power as a right of death, Foucault accedes too much to a liberal understanding of sovereignty, which mistakes its glorious and transcendent form for its operation as a set of practices and capacities. Foucault in this sense never puts together the immanent and transcendent parts of sovereignty, its "economic" dimension as a dispositif with its glorious one of radiant splendor. State sovereignty allows the constitution of domestic spaces of peace and order while claiming a transcendence within a territorial domain and, at the same time, makes possible the juridical and governmental regulation of the international including a detheologized conception of war. Transcendent within one domain, immanent to another, the territorial and sovereign state claims transcendence at home and exercises immanent capacities both at home and abroad. While Foucault shifted his study of power away from the rejection of the juridical-institutional conception of sovereignty toward its immanent operation as a dispositif, he has left it to others to reconnect these two halves. The best form of loyal infidelity to Foucault in the study of international affairs is to continue this assembly of the *sumbolon*, and reconnect a series of halves: the juridical and the economic, the internal and the external, sovereignty and biopolitics, liberalism and reason of state, the governmental and the glorious.

The great achievement of Foucault's journey into power relations was to produce analytically coherent concepts of government, governmentality, security and the dispositif. But he did this through a series of displacements of sovereignty, state and law. It is up to us to bring these halves back into alignment. Recently, I have suggested that the field of attraction and repulsion between the juridical-institutional pole of sovereignty and the economic-managerial pole of governmentality constitutes the contemporary form of the *signature* of power.[66]

## NOTES

1. I am grateful to Jeffrey Bussolini and Marius Gudmand-Høyer for their comments on an earlier draft of this piece. It was the former who drew my attention on Foucault's use of the term "*sumbolon.*"

2. I am thinking of Pasquale Pasquino's comment about Foucault that while "he affected each one of us deeply, he kept those closest from remaining faithful," in "The Political Theory of War and Peace," *Economy and Society* Vol. 22, No. 1 (1993): 84.

3. Michel Foucault, *On the Government of the Living. Lectures at the Collège de France, 1979–1980* (New York, Basingstoke: Palgrave Macmillan, 2014), pp. 32–33. Jeffrey Bussolini, "Governmentality, *Oikonomia*, Form of Life: Agamben and Foucault on Being and Acting," presented at the Government of Life workshop, Copenhagen, April 2013.

4. "Lecture of 17 March 1971" and "Oedipal Knowledge," in Michel Foucault, *Lectures on the Will to Know: Lectures at the Collège de France, 1970–1971*, transl. Graham Burchell (London: Palgrave Macmillian, 2013), pp. 183–201 and 229–57. "Truth and juridical forms," in Michel Foucault, *Power, The Essential Works*, Volume 3 (New York: The New Press, 2000), pp. 1–89.

5. Foucault, "Truth and juridical forms," pp. 16–17.

6. Foucault, *On the Government of the Living*, p. 5.

7. Foucault, "Lecture of 17 March 1971," p. 199.

8. Foucault, "Truth and juridical forms," p. 19.

9. Ibid., p. 22.

10. Michel Foucault, *The Government of Self and Others, Lectures at the Collège de France, 1982–1983*, transl. Graham Burchell (London: Palgrave Macmillan, 2010), p. 84.

11. Michel Foucault, *Security, Territory, Population. Lectures at the Collège de France 1977–1978*, transl. Graham Burchell (London: Palgrave Macmillan, 2007), p. 254.

12. Michel Foucault, "The order of discourse," in Robert Young ed. *Untying the Text: a Post-Structuralist Reader* (Boston, MA: Routledge and Kegan Paul, 1981), p. 73.

13. Michel Foucault, *Discipline and Punish: the Birth of the Prison*, transl. Alan Sheridan (London: Allen Lane, 1977).

14. Michel Foucault, *History of Sexuality, Volume 1: An Introduction*, transl. Robert Hurley (London: Allen Lane, 1979).

15. Michel Foucault, *Society Must Be Defended. Lectures at the Collège de France, 1975–1976*, transl. David Macey (New York, Picador, 2003).
16. Ibid., pp. 15–16, pp. 47–48.
17. Foucault, *History of Sexuality*, 144. Michel Foucault, *The Birth of Biopolitics, Lectures at the Collège de France, 1978–1979*, transl. Graham Burchell (London: Palgrave Macmillan, 2008), p. 321.
18. Foucault, *History of Sexuality*, pp. 88–89.
19. Foucault, *Society Must Be Defended*, 260: "Nazism alone took the play between the sovereign right to kill and the mechanisms of biopower to this paroxysmal point. But this play is in fact inscribed in the workings of all States."
20. See Mitchell Dean and Kaspar Villadsen, *State Phobia and Civil Society. The Political Legacy of Michel Foucault* (Stanford CA: Stanford University Press, 2016).
21. Foucault, *The Birth of Biopolitics*, p. 2.
22. M. Foucault, *Security, Territory, Population, Lectures at the Collège de France, 1977–1978*, transl. Graham Burchell (London: Palgrave Macmillan, 2007), pp. 1–86.
23. *Ibid.*, p. 8.
24. Foucault, *Birth of Biopolitics*. On the distinction between *finis* as the end of a process and *telos* as its definite goal, see Karl Löwith, *Meaning in History* (Chicago, IL: University of Chicago Press, 1949), p. 18.
25. Foucault, *Birth of Biopolitics*, pp. 259–260.
26. See the various contributions to Daniel Zamora and Michael Behrent eds. *Foucault and Neoliberalism* (Cambridge: Polity, 2016).
27. Foucault, *Birth of Biopolitics*, p. 312.
28. Andrew Dilts, "From 'Entrepreneur of the Self' to 'Care of the Self': Neoliberal Governmentality and Foucault's Ethics," *Foucault Studies* 12 (2011): 130–146.
29. See Ewald's evaluation of Foucault's "apology" in Gary S. Becker, François Ewald, and Bernard Harcourt, "Becker on Ewald on Foucault on Becker: American Neoliberalism and Michel Foucault's 1979 'Birth of Biopolitics' lectures," Coase-Sandor Institute for Law and Economics Working Paper No. 614 (Chicago, IL: University of Chicago Law School, 2012), pp. 5–6. On the debate on Foucault's supposed affinities with neo-liberalism, see Gros in this volume and Zamora and Behrent, *Foucault and Neoliberalism*; for a thorough analysis of "human capital" in Gary Becker's analysis, see Paltrinieri in this volume.
30. On the city-citizen and shepherd flock games, see Michel Foucault "*Omnes et singulatim*: towards a criticism of political reason", in *The Tanner Lectures on Human Values*, volume 2, edited by S. McMurrin (Salt Lake City, UT: University of Utah Press, 1981), pp. 223–254. There are four

and a half lectures on the pastorate in Foucault, *Security, Territory, Population*.

31. Foucault, *Security, Territory, Population*, pp. 150–151.
32. On the potential for eschatological counter-conducts based on the idea of civil society, see Foucault, *Security, Territory, Population*, pp. 355–357.
33. Ibid., p. 314.
34. Ibid., pp. 261–267, 266.
35. Foucault, *Birth of Biopolitics*, p. 297.
36. Michel Foucault, "The Confession of the Flesh" in C. Gordon ed. *Power/Knowledge: Selected Interviews and Other Writings 1972–1977* (Brighton: Harvester, 1980), p. 195; and Foucault, *Security, Territory, Population*, p. 30.
37. Ibid., p. 263.
38. For example, Giorgio Agamben, *The Kingdom and the Glory: For a Theological Genealogy of Economy and Government*, transl. L. Chiesa with M. Mandarini (Stanford, CA: Stanford University Press, 2011).
39. Foucault, *Security, Territory, Population*, p. 234.
40. Ibid., p. 290.
41. Ibid., p. 294.
42. Ibid., pp. 302–306.
43. Ibid., pp. 295–298.
44. Ibid., p. 294, pp. 299–304. Carl Schmitt, *The Nomos of the Earth in the International Law of Jus Publicum Europaeum*, transl. Gary L. Ulmen (New York: Telos Press, 2003), pp. 140–148. For a comparison of Foucault with Schmitt on these points, see Mitchell Dean, *Governmentality, Power and Rule in Modern Society* (London: Sage, 2010), pp. 239–240, and, more broadly, Mitchell Dean, *The Signature of Power: Sovereignty, Governmentality and Biopolitics* (London: Sage, 2013), Chapters 5 and 6.
45. Foucault, *Birth of Biopolitics*, p. 51.
46. Ibid., p. 52.
47. Ibid., p. 56.
48. Ibid., pp. 57–58.
49. Ibid., p. 58.
50. Foucault, *Security, Territory, Population*, p. 242. Foucault, *Birth of Biopolitics*, p. 282.
51. Ibid., p. 278.
52. Foucault, *Security, Territory, Population*, p. 300.
53. Ibid.
54. *Birth of Biopolitics*, pp. 57–58.
55. The original formulation is found at Michel Foucault, *Sécurité, territoire, population*, p. 362: "Pratique économique, gestion de la population, un droit public articulé sur le respect de la liberté et des libertés, une police à fonction

répressive…quarte éléments qui viennent s'ajouter au grand dispositif diplomatico-militaire qui, lui, n'a guère été modifié au XVIIIe siècle."

56. Dean, *Governmentality*, pp. 242–7 for elaboration.
57. David Held, *Global Convenant: the Social Democratic Alternative to the Washington Consensus* (Cambridge: Polity, 2004), p. 132.
58. Foucault, *Birth of Biopolitics*, p. 6.
59. Ibid., pp. 8–10.
60. Ibid., pp. 10–12.
61. Ibid., p. 12.
62. Max Weber, *Economy and Society: an Outline of Interpretative Sociology, volume 1*, edited by G. Roth and C. Wittich (Berkeley, CA: University of California Press), p. 54. Foucault, *History of Sexuality*, Part 5.
63. See Blandine Kriegel, *The State and the Rule of Law* (Princeton, NJ: Princeton University Press, 1996).
64. On "state-phobia", see Foucault, *Birth of Biopolitics*, pp. 75–79. On "demonic" combination of power games, see Foucault, *Omnes et singulatim*, p. 239. On its inscription within all modern states, see quote at note 19 above. On "thanatopolitics" as a counterpart of biopolitics, see Michel Foucault, *Technologies of the Self: A Seminar with Michel Foucault*, edited by L. H. Martin, H. Gutman and P. H. Hutton (London, Tavistock, 1988), p. 160.
65. Weber, *Economy and Society*, p. 55.
66. Dean, *Signature of Power*.

# CHAPTER 7

# Foucault and Method

## Michael J. Shapiro

### Introduction: "Tools"

My title is inspired by Fredric Jameson's *Brecht and Method*, where he suggests that rather than offering a doctrine, [Brecht's] "'proposals' and his lessons—the fables and proverbs he delighted in offering—were more on the order of a method than a collection of facts, thoughts, convictions, first principles and the like." He adds that for Brecht "science and knowledge are not grim and dreary duties but first and foremost sources of pleasure: even epistemological and theoretical dimensions of 'science' are to be thought in terms of *popular mechanics* and the manual amusement of combining ingredients and learning to use new and unusual tools."[1] Foucault also evokes the tool metaphor to articulate his work with method. Referring to his analysis of prisons and asylums, he writes, "I would like my books to be a kind of tool-box which others can dig in to find a tool with which they can make good use, in whatever manner they wish, in their own area."[2] Certainly, many have dug in effectively; there is no stronger testimony to Foucault's hopes for the value of his toolbox than the various essays in the edited volume, *The Foucault Effect*, where

M.J. Shapiro (✉)
University of Hawai'i, Manoa, HI, USA
e-mail: shapiro@hawaii.edu

© The Author(s) 2017
P. Bonditti et al. (eds.), *Foucault and the Modern International*,
The Sciences Po Series in International Relations and Political
Economy, DOI 10.1057/978-1-137-56153-4_7

diverse scholars make use of Foucault's concepts—"the rationality of government" ("governmentality"), "the microphysics of power," "risk," "insurance technology," and "genealogy," among others.[3]

Doubtless we can connect Brecht and Foucault on a number of conceptual dimensions, not the least of which are practices of space and strategies of distanciation. For example, inventing an innovative model of spatiality, Foucault placed critical value on what he called heterotopias, "sites that have a general relation of direct or inverted analogy with the real space of Society." Such sites function, among other things, he writes, "in relation to the space that remains," and one such function, which gestures toward the role of the theater (as Brecht understood it), is "to create a space of illusion that exposes every real space, all the sites inside of which human life is partitioned, as still more illusory."[4] Brecht's use of the theater echoes that sentiment and adds the dimension of distanciation. For him the theater, "as an institution microcosmic of society as a whole (…) offers an experimental space and collective laboratory" where "the classical questions and dilemmas of political philosophy can be 'estranged' and rethought."[5] Similarly, Foucault avowedly employed strategies for distancing oneself from familiar problems. For example, he noted that he would often attend to "the history of successive forms in order to show how peculiar the contemporary form is" and thereby "to stand detached from it, bracket its familiarity, in order to analyze the theoretical and practical context with which it has been associated."[6] And in his lectures on *Security, Territory, Population*, where he notes that his method has involved a "triple displacement," he speaks of the necessity of transferring to the "outside," by looking at institutions from a point "off-center," by employing an "external point of view in terms of strategies and tactics [instead of] the internal point of view of the function," and by "free[ing] relations of power from the institution, in order to analyze them from the point of view of technologies."[7] In the next section, I want to pursue these aspects of his method and treat the epistemological issues that he has always added to them.

## PARALLEL PRACTICES

As one of my citations suggests, an important part of Foucault's method is to provide a history of the present in a way that makes contemporary arrangements peculiar—for example, showing that modernity's will to truth with respect to sexuality (the demand that people give and account of who and what they are as sexual beings) constitutes a radical break with how sexuality had been problematized in early periods.[8] But perhaps his most accessible illustration is contained in his brief analysis of another historical episode of the will to truth, his gloss on the problem of the so-called dangerous individual in nineteenth-century legal psychiatry. There he refers to "the gradual emergence in the course of the nineteenth century of [an] additional character, the criminal." Whereas in previous centuries, there were merely crimes and penalties, the nineteenth century witnessed the emergence of a new subject, which, having become an object of knowledge, was to be professionally interrogated and asked to tell truths about itself. As a result, conversations about the criminal/subject began taking place between doctors and jurists. Psychiatry had entered the courtroom because it was part of a new medical *dispositif*, focused on "a sort of public hygiene" applied to a new target of governance, the social order.[9]

Foucault's account in his treatment of the "dangerous individual" points to a crucial aspect of his method. He incessantly surveyed complicit epistemological discourses, especially those of psychiatry and other "human sciences," that ran parallel to the manifestations of the will to truth in changing modes of governance. For example, in his lectures under the title, *Security, Territory, Population*, he refers not only to an emerging governmentality—connected to new techniques of power focused on managing the new collective object, the "population" (a collectivity subject to calculations)—but also to the role of the "human sciences." He shows that while governance had shifted from a focus on sovereign power to one of managing the social order, those "sciences" had become concerned with the population's individual subjects, whose living, working, and speaking had to be comprehended.[10]

Elsewhere, in a reflection on an issue that arose in Australia in the 1970s, I elaborated the implications for inquiry of Foucault's evocation of that new subject, "the population."[11] Concerned with a high rate of infant mortality among its Aboriginal "population," the Australian government commissioned a social science investigation to explain what they viewed as a statistical aberration. Employing a social psychological idiom, their investigators attributed the problem to the Aborigine's recalcitrance, their insistence on continuing to move about while their women were pregnant. As I pointed out, the presupposition of the investigation was assimilationist. Rather than recognizing Australia as a bicultural state and thereby taking on the responsibility to mobilize health care services—putting them in vehicles instead of having only the fixed spaces of the hospital—the investigators expected Aborigines to curtail their nomadic cultural practices (they referred to an Aboriginal "failure to assimilate to our norms").[12]

As I added, however, a foucauldian gloss on the issue gives it a deeper, more historically sensitive political resonance. Adopting his genealogical approach, in which he investigates changing problematizations rather than problems, I observed that Australia had become assimilated to the modern governmentality, so that the governmentalization of health issues was responsible for absorbing Aborigines into "the techniques of power" (which had emerged in the eighteenth century), turning what was a solution for them into a problem for white Australian governance. This passage from Foucault's initial investigation of the politics of sexuality remains both politically and methodologically perspicuous:

> One of the great innovations in the techniques of power in the eighteenth century was the emergence of "population" as an economic and political problem: population as wealth, population as labor capacity, population balanced between its own growth and the resources it commanded. Governments perceived that they were not merely dealing simply with subjects, or even with a "people," but with a "population."[13]

## PHILOSOPHY AND METHOD

At a general level, Foucault's method is owed to his persistent affinity with Kantian philosophy in which he breaks with representational thinking and seeks always to explore the conditions of possibility for that which emerges as an object of representation. Consistently, Foucault's affinity with Kant lends him his "primary but unstated aim [i.e.] to articulate the theoretical underpinnings of his own analysis," a philosophical-historical enterprise shaped by "an attitude of criticism" that is inspired by Kant's idea of critique as an attitude.[14] In contrast, to witness an instance of Foucault's *breaking* of a philosophical affinity and at the same time to observe how Foucault's philosophical perspective shapes his methods more concretely—for example, to appreciate Foucault's approach to such collective subjects as the "population"—we need to heed his philosophical turn away from phenomenology. That turn is a shift from ways of seeing (or the phenomenology of perception) to a focus on the "statement" (*énoncé*) or collection of statements (discourses). An emphasis on the "statement" (*énoncé*) pervades his earlier account of his method in which discourses instead of mentalities or modes of consciousness had become his units of analysis as well as the locus of his accounts of subjectivity.[15]

Yet even in the Foucault associated with a politics of discourse, where the statement is foregrounded, we can discern the later Foucault who mapped the various *dispositifs* involved in implementing forms of power. For example, within his earlier musings on method in *The Archaeology of Knowledge*, which concern themselves with what it is that gives a discourse its coherence—primarily the conditions of the emergence of its objects—he also concerns himself with "group of relations" which, "independently of all discourse or all objects of discourse, may be described between institutions, techniques, social forms, etc."—for example, the "relations [that] existed between the bourgeois family and the functioning of judicial authorities and categories in the nineteenth century."[16] They are the relations that Foucault has theorized to turn discourse from mere language into practices involving complex interrelationships among agencies and institutions.

Whereas Foucault was concerned primarily with "what remains silently anterior" to discursive formations,[17] eventually he became more interested in the material effects of discursive formations, as he shifted from "the gaze" (*The Birth of the Clinic: An Archaeology of the Medical Gaze*, 1963) and his focus on discourse (*Archaeology of Knowledge* and *The Order of Things*, 1969) to disciplinary practices (*Discipline and Punish*, 1975), and ultimately, as his lectures at the Collège de France progressed, to the *dispositifs* through which forms of power are implemented and modes of subjectivity are administered. That progression articulates with Foucault's stated aversion to universalist philosophical positions. The beginnings of that philosophically encouraged methodological migration are already evident in his investigation of the emergence of the "clinic." Although his approach to the displacement of family assistance and the individualized perception of the healer by the teaching hospital involves the interarticulation of discourse and perception, exemplified in his expression, "the loquacious gaze,"[18] much of his analysis also involves agencies of implementation and control. Thus, in his observations about a "medicine of epidemics," he points out that such a medicine "could exist only if supplemented by a police: to supervise the location of mines and cemeteries, to as many corpses as possible cremated...to supervise the running of abattoirs and dye works, and to prohibit unhealthy housing.[19]

By the time he is delivering his lectures entitled *The Birth of Biopolitics*, his remarks about his method foreground *dispositifs* of implementation rather than the discursive practices emphasized in *The Archaeology of Knowledge*. He had shifted his focus from emergence to consequence, a shift that provides the opening to his turn from a primary concern with the history of ideas to a concern with technologies of power and domination. Referring in the first lecture (January 10, 1979) to his "choice of method," which he summarizes as a "radical break with traditional analyses of political concepts," he remarks, "instead of deducing concrete phenomena from universals, or instead of starting with universals as an obligatory grid of intelligibility for certain concrete practices, I would like to start with the concrete practices and, as it were, pass these universals through the grid of these practices."[20]

Discussing the implementation of that method in an analysis of the functioning of governmentalities, Foucault refers to "the state" as "that which exists, but which does not yet exist enough," such that the practice involved in raison d'état "places itself between a state presented as a given and a state presented as having to be constructed and built."[21] Among other implications, Foucault's approach provides a very different understanding of what constitutes "the state"—and by extension of "international relations" that some in mainstream International Relations had come to reduce to merely "relations between states." The state does not preexist in a coherent way its implementing agencies, rather it becomes something "constructed and built" *through* various implementing practices. To illustrate that understanding of the process of construction and the questions it raises, Foucault pointed out that the appropriate question for situating the "new programming of liberal governmentality," involving "an internal reorganization," implies that one "does not ask the state what freedom it will leave to the economy," but should ask instead how that "freedom," as it is implemented by various agencies, can have a state-creating function and role, in the sense that "it will really make possible the foundation of the state's legitimacy."[22]

## DISPOSITIFS

What then is a *dispositif*? Before rehearsing a variety of definitions, Foucault's among others, I turn here to an example—a passage in a novel—that inaugurates my recent investigation of war crimes, atrocities, and justice.[23] In his novel *Zone*, Mathias Énard's protagonist, Francis Servain Mirković, a former Croatian militia fighter, witnesses his former commander Blaškić on trial for war crimes at The Hague and says,

> Blaškić is in his box at The Hague among the lawyers the interpreters the prosecutors the witnesses the journalists the onlookers the soldiers of the UNPROFOR who analyzed the maps for the judges commented on the possible provenance of bombs according to the size of the crater determined the range of the weaponry based on the caliber which gave rise to so many counter-arguments all of it translated into three languages recorded

automatically transcribed 4,000 kilometers away from the Vitez Hotel and from the Lasva with the blue tinted water, everything had to be explained from the beginning, historians testified to the past of Bosnia, Croatia, and Serbia since the Neolithic era by showing how Yugoslavia was formed, then geographers commented on demographic statistics, censuses, land surveys, political scientists explained the differential political forces present in the 1990's, it was magnificent, so much knowledge wisdom information at the service of justice, "international observers" took on full meaning then, they testified to the horrors of the slaughter with a real professionalism, the debates were courteous, for a time I would have volunteered as a witness....I thought about what I would have said if they questioned me, how I would have explained the inexplicable, probably I would have had to go back to the dawn of time, to the frightened prehistoric man painting in his cave to reassure himself, to Paris making off with Helen, to the death of Hector, the sack of Troy, to Aeneas reaching the sores of Latium, to the Romans carrying off the Sabine women, to the military situation of the Croats of central Bosnia in early 1993 to the weapons factory in Vitez, to the trial as Nuremberg and Tokyo that are the father and mother of the one in The Hague - Blaškić in his box is one single man and has to answer for all our crimes, according to the principle of individual criminal responsibility which links him to history, he's a body in a chair wearing a headset, he is on trial in place of all those who held a weapon...[24]

Clearly, Énard's account of the trial's context maps The Hague's justice *dispositif* in a way that conforms to Foucault's most elaborate rendering of the concept. For Foucault, a *dispositif* is "a thoroughly heterogeneous ensemble consisting of discourses, institutions, architectural forms, regulatory decisions, laws, administrative measures, scientific statements, philosophical, moral and philanthropic propositions (...) the said as much as the unsaid (...) the elements of the apparatus (*dispositif*)."[25] Gilles Deleuze's Foucault-influenced version of the concept adds a crucial nuance that lends the *dispositif* its historical dynamism. He refers to the mutations in the assemblages constituting a *dispositif*—for example, those historical events that have shifted the "lines of force" involved in structures of command (over others and/or over oneself).[26] And Giorgio Agamben's version of the *dispositif* provides a useful way of relating the concept to Foucault's later focus on the politicization of ontologies of life. After tracing the emergence of the concept from Foucault's Archaeological investigations through to his later works, Agamben states that the ontology-*dispositif* relationship can be summarized as, "anything that has in some way the capacity to capture, orient, determine, intercept, model, control, or secure the gestures, behaviors, opinions, or discourses of living beings."[27]

These two supplements to the concept help me to pick up on the discursive component of the justice *dispositif* mapped in Énard's description of Blaškić's trial. Evoking another foucauldian methodological gesture, I refer here to a specific mutation that created the conditions of possibility for war crimes trials, ranging from those at Nuremberg through the contemporary ones at The Hague. Since Nuremberg, crucial to the prosecution of war criminals has been the elaboration of a new collective subject, "humanity." The emergence of that subject resulted from a collaboration among states, international agencies, and juridical authorities, all concerned with producing a counter-anthropology to the Nazi death apparatuses, whose anthropological legitimations functioned as part of a necropolitical *dispositif*.

The most notorious atrocity-justifying anthropological contribution was Alfred Hoche's concept of "life unworthy of life."[28] The intent of the counter-anthropology was to create the equalizing collective identity of "humanity as a whole" in order to delegitimalize hierarchical versions of human worthiness and to provide the basis for prosecutions.[29] To put it in foucauldian terms, the mutation in juridical discourse (an alteration in the process of subjectivation) that stemmed from the official recognition of crimes against humanity created a legacy that was in evidence in the Blaškić trial observed by Mirković in Énard's novel. What Énard adds is an account of the rest of the juridical "circus"—the other components, discursive and non-discursive that constitute what I have called "the global justice *dispositif*," as it is disclosed in the fictional Mirković's long reflection.

## TRUTH WEAPONS, *PARRHESIA* AND CRITIQUE

To situate that *dispositif* more comprehensively within the ambit of Foucault's methodological contributions, we must heed another of Foucault's concepts, what he calls "regimes of veridiction." Developing that concept elaborately in his investigation of the history of punishment, Foucault refers to relationships between juridical and veridictional practices and suggests that what is to be understood is "how a certain practice of veridiction was formed and developed in... penal institutions."[30] Foucault also illustrated the concept of truth-as-veridictional practice in his treatment of medical discourse, noting for example, "what is currently politically important is to determine the regime of veridiction established at a given moment that is precisely the one on the basis of which (...) doctors said so many stupid things about sex. What is important is the regime of veridiction that enabled them to say and assert a number of things as truths."[31]

Crucially, in pointing to "regimes of veridiction," it is important to note that methodologically, Foucault is not offering explanations. As he has stated, his analyses do not "partake of (...) so-called explicative procedures to which are attributed causal value (...)."[32] Instead, he saw himself undertaking "the critique of knowledge," which "consists in determining under what conditions and with what effects a veridiction is exercised."[33] Without using the concept explicitly, Énard effectively describes, in a further observation, the regime of veridiction that determines what is sayable and by whom at Blaškić's war crimes trial. His protagonist, Mirković, says, "in the great trial organized by the international lawyers immersed in precedents and the jurisprudence of horror, charged with putting some order into the law of murder, with knowing at one instant a bullet in the head was a legitimate de jure and at what instant it constituted as grave breach of the law and customs of war."[34]

Thus, in contrast with Foucault's explicit narration of his method, Énard's analysis proceeds through juxtaposition, through what Walter Benjamin famously called "literary montage."[35] This passage, in which Mirković observes some of his fellow passengers on a train to Rome (where Mirković is headed with an archive of atrocities to sell to the Vatican), has a subtle connection with the long quotation about the trial, earlier in the novel; it implies a different mode of responsibility for the atrocities during the Balkans Wars, for it alerts the reader to the role of arms trading,

> Egyptian, Lebanese, and Saudi businessmen all educated in the best British and American prep schools, discretely elegant, far from the clichés of colorful, rowdy Levantines, they were neither fat nor dressed up as Bedouins, they spoke calmly of the security of their future investments, as they said, they spoke of our dealings, of the region they called "the area," the zone, and the word "oil"...some had sold weapons to Croats in Bosnia, others to Muslims.[36]

Given Mirković's prior observation about Blaškić, "one single man (...) has to answer for all our crimes, according to the principle of individual criminal responsibility which links him to history," the reader is in effect asked to reflect on the supply side of technologies of violence and thus to focus on weapon dealers who play a significant (albeit unacknowledged within the trial) role in creating the conditions of possibility for atrocities. The unindicted, commercially predatory entrepreneurs observed by Mirković operate in a world in which global capitalism is redrawing the map as it secures its various clienteles, profiting from global antagonisms, ethno-national among others. Novelist Michel Houellebecq (who like

Foucault is a "new cartographer")[37] describes that map: "(...) free-market economics redrew the geography of the world in terms of the expectations of the clientele, whether the later moved to indulge in tourism or to earn a living. The flat isometric surface of the map was substituted by an abnormal topography where Shannon was closer to Katowice than to Brussels, to Fuerteventura than to Madrid."[38]

The characters/entrepreneurs, whose activities create that map, are not governed by cultural or political allegiances (as Énard's passage implies). Nevertheless, their conduct is at least as connected to atrocities as are those who hold the weapons they sell. As Énard's Mirković puts it, "our businessmen from the Zone didn't see the threat behind the outstretched hand, the deadly games that would play out in the course of the years to come (...)."[39] Thus, although victims and perpetrators are arrayed throughout Énard's novel, he (like Foucault) eschews universals. He does not offer a definitive judgment about justice. Instead of becoming absorbed into a moralistic affirmation of legal justice, his writing opens the issue of justice as he maps the lines of force that make possible both atrocities and the apparatuses that emerge to confront them. In effect, Énard offers a critique that challenges the pursuit of truth that tribunals seek. In this sense, his writing affirms Foucault's critical method.

## THE METHOD OF CRITIQUE

As he undertook his various critiques of knowledge, Foucault increasingly observed the importance of critique in various non-academic media as well and designated some of the ripostes to oppressive aspects of governance as "fearless speech" or *parrhesia,* which he defined as "a kind of verbal activity where the speaker has a specific relation to truth through frankness, a certain relationship to his own life through danger, a certain type of relation to himself or other people through criticism...."[40] Ultimately, *parrhesia* was central to Foucault's methodological approach, especially as his later writing became more explicitly political. *His* fearless speech was increasingly deployed against what he referred to as the "truth weapons" of official discourse. Referring to such weapons in his essay on critique, he raised the question, "what is the principle that explains history [and right]?" and answered that it is to be found in "a series of brute facts" such as "physical strength, force, energy," in short in "a series of accidents, or at least contingencies."

However, as he goes on to note, governments dissimulate the events of global violence by interpolating the use of raw force into the implementations of rationality and right: "The rationality of calculations, strategies and ruses; the rationality of technical procedures that are used to perpetuate the victory, to silence (...) the war (...) [and he adds that] given that the relationship of dominance works to their advantage, it is certainly not in their [the government's] interest to call any of this into question."[41] Foucault's approach to calling it into question was to counter the truth weapon with "critique (...) the movement by which the subject gives himself the right to question truth on its effects of power and question power on its discourses of truth."[42]

Among the inspirations I have drawn from Foucault's *parrhesia* is an analysis I undertake of the issues involved in the narco trafficking taking place in the USA and Mexico border zones. Perhaps the best critical analyst of both the trafficking and the governmental policies under the rubric of "the war on drugs" is Charles Bowden, whose hybrid text, *Dreamland: The Way Out of Juarez* (containing critical commentary, ethnographic interviews and images), is an example of fearless speech.[43] Investigating the "war" ethnographically (with many face-to-face interviews) in such dangerous cities as Juarez (aka "murder city"), Bowden challenges official proclamations, pointing out that on the Mexican side of the war, "Presidents come and go and pretend to be in charge"[44] and that while both the USA and Mexico act as if they exercise effective sovereign power and that the war is either under control or being won, their "truth weapons" are missing the mark: "One nation is called the United States, the other Mexico. I find it harder and harder to use these names because they imply order and boundaries, and both are breaking down," so much so that Bowden says he has to "try not to say the names," even as they continuously appear "right there on the maps and road signs."[45] In effect, to oppose the official truth weapons, Bowden finds himself suggesting a different cartographic imaginary:

This is a new geography, one based less on names and places and lines and national boundaries and more on forces and appetites and torrents of people. Some places, parts of Europe, island states here and there, remain temporarily out of play in this new geography. But the Bermudas of the planet are toppling one by one. The waves wash up now into the most ancient squares by the most solemn cathedrals.[46]

## NEW CARTOGRAPHERS

The spatial imagery in Bowden's critique of the "war on drugs" has strong resonances with another aspect of Foucault's method, best captured in Gilles Deleuze's characterization of Foucault as a "new cartographer": "In brief, Foucault's functionalism throws up a new topology which no longer locates the origin of power in a privileged place, and can no longer accept a limited localization (this conception of social space...is as new as contemporary physics and mathematics)."[47]

The topography to which Deleuze is referring is based on Foucault's approach to exercises of power, which (quoting from Foucault's *History of sexuality*) "are not in a position of exteriority with respect to other kinds of relationships (...) [they] are not superstructural positions (...) they have a directly productive role, wherever they come into play."[48] In short, for Deleuze, Foucault's approach to power, like his approach to discourse, stresses non-representational immanence. In the case of discourse, what is stressed is not what statements are about but how they create their objects and the interrelationships among them. Just as Bowden's "new geography" stresses appetites and forces, Deleuze suggests that Foucault's new geography/cartography is best understood through the figure of the diagram, which is a map of forces, "a display of the relations between forces."[49] Thus, for Foucault, the history of geographic forms constitutes a series of events of power/knowledge. For example, as he noted in his conversation with geographers, their "metaphors" are best understood as strategic rather than descriptive,

> *Territory* is no doubt a geographical notion, but it's first of all a juridico-political one: the area controlled by a certain kind of power. *Field* is an economico-juridical notion. *Displacement*: what displaces itself is an army, a squadron, a population, *Domain* is a juridical-political notion, *Soil* is a historico-geographical notion. *Region* is a fiscal, administrative, military notion. *Horizon* is a pictorial, but also a strategic notion.[50]

## STRATEGIC GEOGRAPHY AND LITERARY SPACE

Here I want to return to Foucault's concept of the heterotopia and apply that geographic metaphor to a politics of literature. How do Foucault's methodological gestures apply to literary discourse? And what does that tell us about the geography of "world politics"? There have been a variety of answers, and one of the most explicit and effective applies Foucault's concept of surveillance to the nineteenth-century novel. In that application, D. A. Miller shows how in the Victorian novel the prevailing policing functions—surveillance, identity impositions, and controls of circulation—are reproduced, not only through what the novels describe but also through the ways in which their representational practices constitute the characters and their *milieux* (see Taylan in this volume).[51] Alternatively, if we heed Foucault's approach to discourse, literature's objects of reference (its mimetic aspects) become less significant than what is immanent—the rules and mechanisms by which texts make their objects and worlds. As Simon During puts it, Foucault "attempts to drag Western thought out of the logic of mimesis as far a possible (...) by presenting discourse and other domains of representations" are events [by] (...) "presenting discourse and other domains of representation as ordered by immanent rules."[52] For example, if we regard history as a literature, we find that contrary to the Weberian thesis that historians shape events on the basis of their subjective values, what constitutes the way of representing historical events at any historical moment are the rules by which the genre of writing history is shaped.[53]

However, rather than drawing on either of those models—a literature's reinforcements of modes of power or governance or a genealogy of its genre effects—I want to illustrate the ways in which the creation of novelistic space, especially in a novel that contests mainstream forms of national and international space, enacts a politically inflected critique, without explicit reference to Foucault on critique (as is the case with my approach to the novel, *Zone* treated above). For this purpose, my focus is on the counter-spatiality of Salman Rushdie's novel *Shalimar the Clown*, which effects a critique of the ethno-national violence involved in India and Pakistan's struggle over Kashmir.

Rushdie's *Shalimar the Clown* is very much a critique of the geopolitics of securitization. Historicizing the India-Pakistan conflict over Kashmir, the novel juxtaposes the former exuberant life of cultural sharing—*Kashmiriyat* (which had once obtained in Kashmir)—to the subsequent ontologies and apparatuses of a security oriented, fear-mongering that substitutes forms of coercion for Kashmir's formerly playful, theatrically oriented life world. Early in the novel, that former world is represented with a description of a festival commemorating a mythical story ("the day on which Ram marched against Ravan to rescue Sita"):

Today our Muslim village, in the service of our Hindu maharaja, will cook
and act in a Mughal—that is to say Muslim—garden (…) two plays are to be
performed (…)Who tonight are the Hindus? Who are the Muslims? Here in
Kashmir, our stories sit happily side-by-side on the same double bill, we eat
from the same dishes, we laugh at the same jokes.[54]

Crucial to the homology between Rushdie's valorization of festivals and
Foucault's politics of space, Kashmir's festivals take place in a garden, a
special space internal to Kashmir, "the great Mughal garden of Kashmir,
descending in verdant liquid terraces to a shining lake (…)The name
meant 'abode of joy.'"[55] As I noted above, Foucault has addressed himself
to this kind of space, referring to it as a heterotopia:

> There are also, probably in every culture, in every civilization, real places—
> places that do exist and that are formed in the very founding of society—
> which are something like counter-sites, a kind of effectively enacted utopia in
> which the real sites, all the other real sites that can be found within the cul-
> ture, are simultaneously represented, contested, and inverted (…) Because
> these places are absolutely different from all the sites that they reflect and
> speak about, I shall call them, by way of contrast to utopias, heterotopias.[56]

Strengthening the case for a homology between Foucault and Rushdie
on space, Foucault cites gardens among heterotopias: "perhaps the oldest
example of these heterotopias that take the form of contradictory sites is
the garden."[57] And Rushdie goes beyond the mere fact of the garden's
reprieve from the coercive management of identity spaces and lends it a
performativity. His Mughal garden is constituted as the space of performative exuberance, a space that preceded the encroachment of the violent
securitization wrought by the Indian army and other agencies involved in
constituting Kashmir as an object within a global security *dispositif*, which
drew Kashmir into the ethno-national map.

Moreover, as is the case in Foucault's analyses, Rushdie uses other spatial metaphors to achieve a distanciating effect from the dominant governmentality. Two of his main characters operate in heights, above the
geopolitical ground plan. Max Ophuls was a pilot in his better days (before
being corrupted by his vocation as an intelligence and security operative).
He avoided the ethno-national boundaries (which Rushdie abhors) by fly-
ing above them. And the eponymous Shalimar, in his better days (as a
performer before he turned murderer), also operated above the geopolitical, boundary-policed ground plan. As a tightrope walker, his exuberant

life-affirming vocation contrasted powerfully with the securitizing, life-narrowing practices of the occupying Indian army.

## Conclusion: Foucault and the Ethico-Politics of Aesthetics

The role of the intellectual is not to tell others what they must do. (Michel Foucault)[58]

Why do literary texts articulate a foucauldian methodological sensibility so well? The writer, Maurice Blanchot, whose work resonated with Foucault's (noted in their commentaries on each other),[59] sees literature as critically disruptive. Literature's "purpose—even its mission—'(...) a term Blanchot somewhat startling employs'—is to interrupt the purposeful steps we are always taking toward a deeper understanding and a surer grasp upon things."[60] Blanchot's sentiment about literature echoes Foucault's well known privileging of historical ruptures in discursive practices: "rupture is the name given to transformations that bear on the general rules of one or several discursive formations," which he focused on to make modernity a peculiar set of arrangements rather than a period witnessing a deeper human accord, stemming from a progressive more enlightened understanding of who we are.[61] At its critical best, fiction achieves the critical distance that Foucault's critical methods prescribe. As Gayatri Spivak puts it, "the protocols of fiction give us a practical simulacrum of the graver discontinuities inhabiting (and operating?) the ethico-epistemic and ethico-political (...) an experience of the discontinuities that remain in place in 'real life.'"[62]

Concerning the "ethico-" parts of the two hyphenated expressions: near the end of the novel, Rushdie's main protagonist Shalimar is on trial. However, although Shalimar will be sentenced, his lawyer points out that the legacy of violence that had descended on Kashmir might just as well be on trial. Thus, Rushdie's novel enacts ethico-aesthetic and ethico-political perspectives, as Shalimar's trial becomes counter juridical. Ultimately the novel juxtaposes literary justice to legal justice, a contrast for which Shoshana Felman has provided the relevant gloss. After posing the question, "What indeed is literary justice, as opposed to legal justice," she answers, "Literature is a dimension of concrete embodiment and a language of infinitude that in contrast with the language of the law, encapsulates not closure but precisely what in a given legal case refuses to be closed and cannot be closed. It is to this refusal of the trauma to be closed that literature does justice."[63] Methodologically, Foucault was also resistant to closure. In a subtle beginning to his treatise on the genealogical approach to history, he uses a conceptually pregnant term: "Genealogy is gray, meticulous, and patiently documentary."[64] When he refers to patience, he is hinting that rather than moralizing about a particular mode of conduct, we should situate it, asking not what our judgment is but rather what are/were its conditions of possibility, and what alternative ways of living are displaced by those conditions. As Rushdie's novel describes Kashmir before securitization had eclipsed its former life world, what was displaced was exuberance. Kashmir had been a place of culinary arts and a playful theatricality. That other kind of life world also lurks in Foucault's "gray, meticulous, and patient" historical accounts. He addresses that world in his later writings in which he valorizes expressive, unconstrained bodies involved in artistic self-fashioning.

Resistant to moral codes (which provides a lot of fodder for his critics), foucauldian ethics is focused on "the manner in which one ought to form oneself as an ethical subject acting in reference to the prescriptive elements that make up the code."[65] For Foucault, the aestheticization of ethics is not a recipe for "undisciplined sensuality": "*This* aesthetics—aesthetics as sensibility-formation—[is a] sensibility [that] establishes the range of possibility in perception, enactment, and responsiveness to others."[66] As is the case with Brecht, Foucault's ethico-political sensibility suggests that it is to be staged (although its theatricality—its focus on style—is to be part of a "balanced self," an "artistic arrangement of its parts").[67] Finally, we can observe that there is an intimate connection between Foucault's aestheticization of ethics and his politically perspicuous use of the concept of the *dispositif*. As Jane Bennett points out in her gloss on Foucault's aestheticization of ethics, "Insofar as 'art' is thought to call for a special mode of perception, that is an attention to things as sensuous *ensembles* (scenes, songs, stories, dances), an artistic representation of ethics may reveal with special force its structural or network character" (where a "network" stands in for the *dispositif*). To return to my first novelistic example, Mathias Énard's *Zone*: Doubtless Énard abjures war crimes, but his ethical "attitude" is articulated aesthetically, through his style (pen), through the way he maps the conditions of possibility for war crimes. Similarly, in Foucault's account of the Greco-Roman aestheticization of ethics, he saw the ethical as intrinsic to their style, in the practices of the self through which they observed "the necessity of respecting the law and the customs…[and] more important was the *attitude* [my emphasis] that caused one to respect them."[68]

# NOTES

1. Fredric Jameson, *Brecht and Method* (New York: Verso, 2011), p. 2.
2. Michel Foucault, *Dits et Ecrits Vol II*. (Paris: Gallimard, 1970–1975), 523 (my translation).
3. Graham Burchell, Colin Gordon, and Peter Miller (eds), *The Foucault Effect* (London: Harvester Wheatsheaf, 1991).
4. The quotations are from: Michel Foucault, "Of Other Spaces" on the web at http://foucault.info/documents/heterotopia/foucault.heterotopia.en.html (verified on October 5, 2015).
5. Jameson, *Brecht and Method*, p. 11.
6. Michel Foucault, *The Use of Pleasure* transl. Robert Hurley (New York: Pantheon, 1985), p. 3.
7. Michel Foucault, *Security, Territory, Population*, transl. Graham Burchell (New York: Palgrave Macmillan, 2007), pp. 116–118.
8. See Michel Foucault, *The History of Sexuality*, transl. Robert Hurley (New York: Vintage, 2012).
9. See Michel Foucault, "About the Concept of the 'Dangerous Individual' in 19th-Century Psychiatry," *International Journal of Law and Psychiatry*, 1(1) (1978) On the web at http://schwarzemilch.files.wordpress.com/2009/02/foucault_dangerous_individual.pdf (verified on October 5, 2015).
10. Foucault, *Security, Territory, Population*, p. 79.
11. Michael J. Shapiro, *Studies in Trans-Disciplinary Method: After the Aesthetic Turn* (New York: Routledge, 2012), pp. 20–21.
12. See Colin Tatz, "The Politics of Aboriginal Health," *Politics* (The Journal of the Australian Political Studies Association) 7(2) (November, 1972): 8.
13. Foucault, *The History of Sexuality*, p. 25.
14. The quotations are from Marc Djaballah's thorough analysis of the Kantian influence on Foucault: *Kant, Foucault, and Forms of Experience* (New York: Routledge, 2008), p. 163. For Foucault's elaboration of the critical attitude, see Michel Foucault, "What is Enlightenment," in Paul Rabinow ed. *The Foucault Reader* (New York: Pantheon, 1984), pp. 32–50.
15. Foucault's focus on the statement, a turn away from phenomenology, is emphasized in Deleuze's treatment of Foucault. See Gilles Deleuze, *Foucault* transl. Sean Hand (Minneapolis, MN: University of Minnesota Press, 1988), p. 49.
16. Michel Foucault, *The Archaeology of Knowledge*, transl. A. M. Sheridan Smith (New York: Pantheon, 1972), p. 45.
17. Ibid., p. 47.
18. Michel Foucault, *The Birth of the Clinic: An Archaeology of Medical Perception*, transl. A. M. Sheridan Smith (New York: Pantheon, 1973), p. xii.
19. Ibid., p. 25.

20. Michel Foucault, *The Birth of Biopolitics*, transl. G. Burchell (New York: Palgrave, 2008), p. 3.
21. Ibid., p. 4.
22. Ibid., pp. 94–95.
23. Michael J. Shapiro, *War Crimes: Atrocity, Justice and the Archives* (Cambridge, UK: Polity, 2014).
24. Mathias Énard, *Zone*, transl. Charlotte Mandell (Rochester, NY: Open Letter, 2010), pp. 72–73.
25. Michel Foucault, "The Confession of the Flesh," A conversation in Colin Gordon ed. *Power/Knowledge: Selected Interviews & Other Writings 1972–1977*, transl. Colin Gordon, Leo Marshall, John Mepham and Kate Soper (New York: Pantheon, 1977), p. 194.
26. Gilles Deleuze, "What is a *Dispositif*," in *Two Regimes of Madness*," transl. Ames Hodges and Mike Taormina (New York: Semiotext(e), 2006), p. 342.
27. Giorgio Agamben, *What is an Apparatus?* transl. David Kishik and Stefan Pedatella (Stanford, CA: Stanford University Press, 2009), p. 14.
28. See Alfred Hoche, *Arztliche Bemerkungen* in Karl Binding and Alfred Hoche, *De Freigabe der Vernichtung Lebensunwerten Lebens: Ihr Mass und ihre Form* (Leipzig, 1920), pp. 61–62.
29. The notion of crimes against humanity in fact pre-dated the pre-trial Nuremberg negotiations. It was evoked in 1906 by E. D. Morel, in reference to the atrocities in the "The Congo Free State." In his History of the Congo Reform Movement, he refers to King Leopold II of Belgium's conduct in the Congo as "a great crime against humanity." Quoted in William Roger Louis and Jean Stengers, eds. *E. D. Morel's History of The Congo Reform Movement* (Oxford, UK: The Clarendon Press, 1968), p. 167.
30. Michel Foucault, *Discipline and Punish: The Birth of the Prison*, transl. Alan Sheridan (New York: Pantheon, 1977), p. 34.
31. Foucault, *The Birth of Biopolitics*, p. 36.
32. Michel Foucault, "What is Critique," in *The Politics of Truth* transl. Lysa Hochroth & Catherine Porter (New York: Semiotext(e), 2007), p. 63.
33. Foucault, *The Birth of Biopolitics*, p. 36.
34. Énard, *Zone*, p. 75.
35. Walter Benjamin, *The Arcades Project*, transl. H. Eiland and K. McLaughlin (Cambridge, MA; Harvard University Press, 2002), p. 460.
36. Énard, *Zone*, pp. 21–22.
37. That characterization of Foucault belongs to Gilles Deleuze in his *Foucault*, pp. 23–44.
38. Michel Houllebecq, *The Map and the Territory*, transl. Gavin Bowd (London: William Heinemann, 2011), p. 98.
39. Énard, *Zone*, p. 23.
40. Michel Foucault, *Fearless Speech*, ed. Joseph Pearson (New York: Semiotext(e), 2001), p. 19.

41. Michel Foucault, *Society Must Be Defended*, transl. David Macey (New York: Picador, 2003), pp. 54–55.
42. Michel Foucault, "What is Critique?", p. 47.
43. Charles Bowden and Alice Leora Briggs, *Dreamland: The Way out of Juarez* (Austin: University of Texas Press, 2010).
44. Bowden and Briggs, *Dreamland*, p. 2.
45. Ibid., p. 6.
46. Ibid., pp. 138–139.
47. Deleuze, *Foucault*, p. 26.
48. Ibid., p. 27.
49. Ibid., p. 36.
50. Michel Foucault, "Questions on Geography," transl. Colin Gordon, Leo Marshall, John Mepham, and Kate Soper in Colin Gordon ed. *Power/Knowledge: Selected Interviews and Other Writings* (New York: Pantheon, 1980), p. 68.
51. D. A, Miller, *The Novel and the Police* (Berkeley CA: University of California Press, 1988).
52. Simon During, *Foucault and Literature: Towards a genealogy of writing* (New York: Routledge, 1992), p. 197.
53. This is the argument of Paul Veyne who has internalized Foucault's method for treating discourse and other genres of representation in his *Writing History: Essay on Epistemology*, transl. Mina Moore-Rinvolucri (Middletown, CT: Wesleyan University Press, 1984).
54. Salman Rushdie, *Shalimar the Clown* (New York: Random House, 2005), 71.
55. Ibid., p. 12.
56. Michel Foucault, "Of Other Spaces," at http://foucault.info/documents/heteroTopia/foucault.heteroTopia.en.html. (Retrieved September 9, 2012).
57. Ibid.
58. Michel Foucault, "The Concern for Truth," in *Foucault Live,* transl. John Johnston (New York: Semiotext(e), 1989), p. 305.
59. See Michel Foucault *and* Maurice Blanchot: *Michel Foucault: Maurice Blanchot: The Thought from Outside/Maurice Blanchot: Michel Foucault as I Imagine Him*, transl. Jeffrey Mehlman and Brain Massumi (New York: Zone Books, 1987).
60. The quotation is from Ann Smock's "Translator's Introduction," in Maurice Blanchot, *The Space of Literature* (Lincoln: University of Nebraska Press, 1982), p. 3.
61. The quotation is from Foucault, *The Archaeology of Knowledge*, p. 177.
62. Gayatri Spivak, *An Aesthetic Education in the Era of Globalization* (Cambridge, MA: Harvard University Press, 2012), p. 317.

63. Shoshana Felman, *The Juridical Unconscious: Trials and Traumas of the twentieth Century* (Cambridge, MA: Harvard University Press, 2002), p. 8.

64. Michel Foucault, "Nietzsche, Genealogy, History," in Donald F. Bouchard ed. *Language, Counter-Memory, Practice*, transl. Sherry Simons (Ithaca, NY: Cornell University Press, 1977), p. 139.

65. Foucault, *The Use of Pleasure*, p. 26. Here I am following the critical discussion of Foucault's aestheticization of ethics by Jane Bennett, "'How is it Then That We Still Remain Barbarians': Foucault, Schiller, and the Aestheticization of Ethics," *Political Theory* 24(4) (1996): 653–672.

66. The quotations are from Bennett, Ibid.: 654.

67. Ibid.: 663.

68. Foucault, *The Use of Pleasure*, p. 31.

# PART III

# International?

# CHAPTER 8

# Silencing Colonialism: Foucault and the International

*Marta Fernández and Paulo Esteves*

Postcolonial perspectives are indebted to Foucault's writings in many important ways. In fact, since the publication of Edward Said's major work *Orientalism*, postcolonial thinkers often invoke Foucault's notion of the power-knowledge nexus. Drawing on Foucault, they argue that the way we frame events necessarily involves relations of power that serve dominant interests.[1] Although Foucault wrote extensively about, and certainly contributed to refine our conceptions of power, he remained quite silent about the ways in which power operated in the colonial arena.[2] Our aim in this contribution is to further explore the political implications of such an omission for a critical understanding of how politics have come to develop under "modernity." Mainly, we argue that the intervention of the colonial in the genealogical exploration of the European modern[3] complicates Foucault's account of the emergence of a "European international society." In this purpose, the chapter is divided into three parts. In the first part, we suggest that when Foucault came to approach the issue of an "international society" in his work,[4] he overlooked the role played by the colonial world in its constitution. As we argue in the second section, it appears that Foucault also regarded Europe as a homogeneous

M. Fernández (✉) • P. Esteves
IRI, Pontifical Catholic University of Rio de Janeiro, Rio de Janeiro, Brazil
e-mail: martafygarcia@gmail.com; esteves.pauloluiz@gmail.com

© The Author(s) 2017
P. Bonditti et al. (eds.), *Foucault and the Modern International*,
The Sciences Po Series in International Relations and Political
Economy, DOI 10.1057/978-1-137-56153-4_8

space merely ordered by a unique temporality. In our concluding remarks, we suggest that while taking the European frontiers of international society for granted, Foucault had in fact ignored crucial bifurcations (a term we shall further explain below) that came to be constitutive of the world divided into a center—a system of sovereign states regulated by the balance of power—and a periphery—an unchecked group of belated societies articulated as a civilizational or developmental space.

## International Society and Its European Alterities: Silencing Colonialism

In his March 1978 lectures at the Collège de France, Foucault engaged with a language very familiar to students and scholars of International Relations. In particular, there lie some striking similarities between these lectures on *Security, Territory, Population* and the central "English School" textbook, Hedley Bull's *Anarchical Society*,[5] which was published one year prior, only.[6] In his lecture given on March 8, 1978, Foucault refers to the disappearance of some sort of a great spiritual and temporal pastorate: the two great poles of historical-religious sovereignty—the Empire and the Church—that had dominated the West for so long, promising salvation, unity and the fulfillment of time. This disappearance leads to a new reality that Foucault extensively discusses in his March 22 lecture. It is striking in our view how much this "new reality" has in common with Bull's anarchical society. Indeed, not only Foucault argues that states, from Westphalia onward, came to form something like an international society in the European space, but he also stresses that this society is sustained by five key institutions: diplomacy, international law, the great powers, war and the balance of power,[7] the exact same five institutions Bull had identified in his account of an international society. Like Bull, Foucault also assigns a privileged role to the balance of power in this "society of states" and regards the treaty of Westphalia as the "first complete, conscious, explicit expression of the politics of a European balance."[8] For both authors, the balance of power emerged in the post-Westphalian context as an institution that, in Bull's view, reflects the existence of a collective commitment to the survival of that society.[9] Bull acknowledges that for the balance of power to operate as an institution, there has to be a self-conscious recognition of how power is distributed among all of the great powers.[10] According to Bull, stability requires an accurate perception of power; therefore, any considerable mismatch between the objective and the subjective balance of power could lead to a fragile balance.[11] In a similar vein, Foucault argues that the effective preservation of a European equilibrium requires that each state is in a position to assess its own forces as well as those of others, thus permitting a comparison that makes it possible to uphold the equilibrium.[12] Foucault goes one step beyond Bull by arguing that states, in this context, measure their own forces as well as those of the other states through a new science, namely statistics, by means of which each state produces a knowledge about its own capacities as much as about other states' capacities.

In this picture, Foucault understands colonization as contemporaneous with the emerging European regime of power-knowledge for it provides extra resources to European states which also needed to be measured to better assess their impact upon the dynamic of forces within the European space itself. Thus, Adam Watson noted,[13] European colonial possessions were taken into consideration in the very calculation of the European balance of power.

Despite some similarities between Bull's and Foucault's ideas of an international society, as Chamon reminds us,[14] it is crucial not to lose sight of the fact that Bull takes the state—from which the international society emerges—for granted, and does actually affirm the possibility for such an international society to exist, while Foucault conceives the society of nations as a specific problematization that emerged as an effect of a specific art of governing as much as of something that came to be named "international politics." As such, Foucault suggests, this problematization can and should be traced.[15]

While tracing the emergence of the idea of an international society however, Foucault does it in ways that overlook the role played by the colonial world in its constitution. The colonial world is seen here as merely a *space* of conquest or plunder for European powers.[16] With and against Foucault, one could raise the foucauldian objection that the analysis of power should take into account that "relations of power are not in a position of exteriority with respect to other types of relationships (economic processes, knowledge relationships, sexual relations), but are immanent in the latter."[17] This rule of immanence assumes that the economic relationship between a given metropolis and its colony has been made possible by strategies of power and techniques of knowledge that have objectified the colonized, the colony and even the colonizer.

It is not our priority herein to interrogate *why* Foucault and so many international theorists and historians have disregarded colonial relations of power as relevant to neither the emergence of the modern international nor the constitution of the modern subject. What we do know, though, is that "silence and secrecy are a shelter for power."[18] Therefore, it is not a matter of interrogating why colonial relations of power were forgotten while narrating "how the force relationships which for a long time had found expression in war, in every form of warfare, gradually became invested in the order of political power."[19] Instead, one should proceed in the following manner: first, problematize the "tactical efficacy" of this silence; second, interrogate the specificity of colonial relations of power vis-à-vis the metropolitan ones; finally, interrogate the silence's multiple effects upon the ways that we conceive and narrate the emergence of the modern international, the sovereign state and the autonomous subject.

For Foucault and many International Relations analysts, the ideas of Europe and of a modern international system, which emerged during the seventeenth century as an object of thought, were constructed exclusively against European references.[20] According to Foucault, Europe was constructed, first, against the universal vocation of the Empire and the Church and, second, against the German Empire.[21] Thus, the only alterities Foucault regarded as crucial for the construction of the European self were internal to Europe or, more precisely, to an outdated Europe. From Westphalia onwards, Europe was defined against any form of international hierarchy. According to Foucault, Europe is fundamentally plural because each sovereign is emperor within his own domain.[22]

According to the principle of raison d'état, the state is organized only in reference to itself and therefore seeks its own good, having no external purpose.[23] (See especially Gros in this volume.) It must lead to nothing but itself, that is, neither to any individual sovereign nor to man's salvation. Hence, raison d'état imagines a world characterized by a plurality of states "that have their own law and end in themselves."[24] The European space is defined as a multiple territoriality entailing a homogeneous temporality, which was no longer oriented toward a final unity or Empire. Raison d'état exists within a world of indefinite history without any form of fulfillment or eschatology.[25] Instead of a sort of absolute eschatology that posits an empire as a *telos*, we have, according to Foucault,[26] what could be called a "relative eschatology," precarious and fragile: peace[27]; it is a peace no longer guaranteed by an unchallenged supremacy like that of the Empire or the Church, but by the states themselves through the balance of power. Therefore, one can infer that raison d'état and the European equilibrium function within a single European space that is temporally coeval but excludes the Empire as part of its horizon.[28] It is the emptied conception of time that allows Foucault to speak about the *dispositif* of the balance of Europe and about Europe itself as quite interchangeable. The meaning of the past, where a specific eschatology prevailed, is constructed in terms of modern time's differentiating function because the present is judged in terms of the past from the space of Europe.

Surprisingly, Foucault overlooks the main manifestation of Empire that remains on course and very much alive during that period in the colonial world. By neglecting this important (colonial) dimension of global politics, Foucault regards Empire as an anachronism, as a form of political organization left behind by the European history.

## THE HOMOGENEOUS TIME OF THE INTERNATIONAL SOCIETY

As noted by Timothy Mitchell,[29] the narrative of history in Foucault is the story of Europe: homogeneous in terms of time and space, without any interruptions from the non-West. Through this narrative, Foucault disavows the "time-lag" of Empire as a signal of cultural difference and overlooks the temporal disjunctions the colonial empire introduced into the discourse of raison d'état.

Homi Bhabha introduces the notion of "time-lag" to account for the temporal disjunctions in modern global politics. Such disjunctions are evidenced, for instance, by the fact that the colonial powers were, in the nineteenth century, establishing the foundations for democracy and citizenship in Europe while also engaging in economic exploitation, authoritarianism and abuse of human rights in the colonies.[30] Bhabha[31] draws attention to the fact that the advent of Western modernity during the eighteenth and nineteenth centuries coincides with another history, namely, the history of the West as a colonial power. Bhabha sheds light on this last repressed history to reveal the contradictions of Western modernity that spread itself through the colonial world as a despotic power at the very moment of the birth of democracy and citizenship at home.[32] The point Bhabha makes is in fact not just that the history of colonialism is the silenced history of the West, but also that this history is "a *counter-history* to the normative, traditional history of the West."[33] The inconsistencies between these two histories of power relations—one told in terms of progress and *civitas*, the other experienced in terms of repression and despair, undermine the very ontology of the white world with its assumptions of rationality and universality.

In this sense, European powers did not extend their supposedly enlightening claims of universal rights and freedom to the colonial world. During the eighteenth century, discipline in Europe became a general formula of domination different from slavery for it was not grounded on a relationship of appropriation of bodies[34] in contradistinction to the practices colonial powers resorted to in their colonies in the nineteenth century, such as forced labor; practices that were to impact violently upon the bodies of the colonized. This contradiction shows that to deal with its "Others," European colonial powers were resorting to outdated ways of punishment, that is, to practices that had been made unacceptable in the European modern context.

In *Discipline and Punish*, Foucault actually describes in detail how, by the end of the eighteenth century, the punishment mechanics of body torture inherited from medieval times were gradually replaced, by more subtle punitive practices whose "functional ambition" was to create docility, and to extract utility from body strength, through disciplinary power. Thus, torture and torment increasingly became hidden from the public view and replaced by new and more efficient organizations with the power to punish. This is how, in modern Europe, Foucault observed, the abominable spectacle of body torture acquired a negative connotation, equating and even surpassing crime in terms of savagery. Hence, the replacement of the old executioner by an entire army of technicians: guards, chaplains, psychiatrists and educators, who were to guarantee to the Court that body and pain were no longer the final object of punitive action. During the Enlightenment, physical suffering and body pain were replaced by penalties that translated into an economy of suspended rights aimed at correcting and reeducating the (emerging figure of the) criminal—rather than punishing a human being. In this new economy of punishment, the body was no longer something to be branded and even possibly destroyed but, instead, arrested and isolated, for it was carrying a soul that could be disciplined. A new legislation defined the power of punishment as a general function of society that was to be exerted in the same way upon all members of the society, now understood as equals before the law. Thus, in a society in which everyone is provided with freedom, prison—understood as a temporary privation of the rights to individual freedom—came to be conceived of a "civilized" and equalitarian punishment. As Akerstrom Andersen pointed,[35] Foucault's *Discipline and Punish* is not a book only about prisons but also about a particular means of normalization: discipline, with vigilance molded along with the growth of prison. This is how, for Foucault: "The judges of normality are present everywhere."[36]

These new polished means of punishment, so deeply anchored in modernity, were not, we want to argue, employed by metropolitan states in their colonies where they kept resorting to non-modern punitive practices. Frantz Fanon describes this *bifurcated nature*[37] of the world in the following way:

> The colonized world is a world divided in two. The dividing line, the border, is represented by the barracks and the police stations. In the colonies, the official, legitimate agent, the spokesperson for the colonizer and the regime of oppression, is the police officer or the soldier. In capitalist societies, education, whether secular or religious, the teaching of moral reflexes handed down from father to son, the exemplary integrity of workers decorated after fifty years of loyal and faithful service, the fostering of love for harmony and wisdom, those aesthetic forms of respect for the status quo, instill in the exploited a mood of submission and inhibition which considerably eases the task of the agents of law and order. In capitalist countries a multitude of sermonizers, counselors, and "confusion-mongers" intervene between the exploited and the authorities. In colonial regions, however, the proximity and frequent, direct intervention by the police and the military ensure the colonized are kept under close scrutiny, and contained by rifle butts and napalm. We have seen how the government's agent uses a language of pure violence. The agent does not alleviate oppression or mask domination. He displays and demonstrates them with the clear conscience of the law enforcer, and brings violence into the homes and minds of the colonized subject.[38]

Here, Fanon clearly demonstrates the ambiguous behavior of colonial powers. On the one hand, consistent with Foucault's notion of disciplinary power, the colonial powers relaxed oppression at home, hiding domination from the European eyes with the help of several institutions. On the other hand, the metropolitan powers, despite their physical distance from the colonial world, exerted direct and non-mediated violence upon the bodies of colonial subjects, violence akin to the medieval punitive practices abolished in Europe during that same time.

Unable to resolve the aforementioned contradiction, the history of the West as a despotic colonial power "has not been adequately written side by side with its claims to democracy and solidarity."[39] Colonial powers tried to resolve, at least to mask this contradiction through the dehumanization of the native, regarding him as an absolute "Other." This is the vision Fanon denounced when saying that the colonizer paints the native as "a sort of quintessence of evil."[40] According to him,

The "native" is declared impervious to ethics, representing not only the absence of values but also the negation of values. He is, dare we say it, the enemy of values. In other words, absolute evil. A corrosive element, destroying everything within his reach, a corrupting element, distorting everything which involves aesthetics or morals, an agent of malevolent powers, an unconscious and incurable instrument of blind forces.[41]

One example of this process of dehumanization and of conceiving a radical "Other" can be found in the Haitian case.[42] Conceived by colonial discourse as not properly human, Haitians were seen as not ready to understand, or even to mimic, the "true" (French) revolution. The embedded racism of this colonial discourse made it impossible for Europeans to conceive of the *subhuman* slaves of the Caribbean as being prepared to have the inalienable rights, which, according to French Revolution ideals, all *human* beings should enjoy. In this sense, Haiti exposed the limits of the French Revolution, the ideals of which were not considered to be applicable to the colonial world that the colonial discourse enabled as a space where violent practices over the black slave bodies of Haitians were possible. The 1791 Haitian Revolution thus exposed the limits and ambiguities of French universalism—that Aimé Césaire called the "false universalism" of the French Revolution.[43] The Haitian Revolution was dissonant with the "regime of veridiction"[44] of the time, which (re)produced the imagined superiority of the colonizer vis-à-vis the colonized and made it unthinkable for the colonized to occupy the same discursive space as the colonizer. To the extent that Haitian revolutionaries defied the Western imaginary, they were silenced in and by European narratives.[45]

This strategy was informed by the medieval idea of what Arthur Lavejoi has called *The Great Chain of Being*,[46] according to which every form of existence has its place in an orderly cosmos. God was at the top of the hierarchy, followed by the angels, people on other planets, human beings, animals and inanimate objects. Each being is subordinate to that which comes after it.[47] In the European context of the eighteenth and nineteenth centuries, biological racial theories were introduced in this *Chain*, hierarchizing *Homo sapiens* and locating black colonial beings at the lowest rank of that identity.[48] The *Great Chain of Being* was understood as eternal and immutable, as a perfect and complete divine creation.[49] As such, the *Chain* was time(less) in that it did not imply any notion of progressive or evolutionary temporality. Referring to the rigidity of the *Chain*, Lavejoi noted the following:

[I]nconsistent with any belief in progress, or, indeed, in any sort of significant change in the universe as a whole. The chain of being, in so far as its continuity and completeness were affirmed on the customary grounds, was a perfect example of an absolutely rigid and static scheme of things.[50]

This "location of race" in an allegedly natural and unchangeable order given by God authorized, during colonization, several inhumane and despotic practices over black colonial bodies inconceivable in the European space during the eighteenth and nineteenth centuries. In this sense, the colonized was constructed as a population of degenerated types on the basis of its origins to justify European conquest.[51]

The colonial stereotypes are inconsistent and ambivalent, however. In this sense, the black body is seen not only as an intractable "Other" but also as an innocent child who can become mature under (and only under) the guide of its European parents.[52] While the latter suggests a teleology, according to which the native can be modernized under certain conditions of colonial domination, the first idea, anchored in a biological racist science, denied the colonized the capacities of self-government and Western modes of civility.[53] Accordingly, the modernizing, progressive, teleological narrative coexisted, in colonial discourses, with biological racist narratives that suggested the immutability of the "native."

Thus, side by side with the colonial discourse that represents the colonial subject as an irreparable "Other," there is another discourse that temporalizes difference, regarding the colonial "Other" as a backward version of the European Self.[54] In this sense, the colonial discourse articulates a discontinuous temporal gap between the white world of the colonizer and the black world of the colonized.[55] In Fabian's terms, they are not coeval, which means either that these worlds are not contemporaneous or that they do not exist in the same timeframe.[56] This gap, according to Brett Nicholls, reveals that "the black world arrives too late, it is always one step behind in the myth of progression that sustains the white sense of superiority."[57] If the colonized arrives too late in the modern world, then it is said that the colonized speaks from Europe's past or from the "time-lag" of cultural difference.[58]

Edward Keene[59] helps us to identify the disjunctures of the so-called Wesphalian system. While within Europe the leading purpose of international order was to promote peaceful coexistence in a multicultural world through the *toleration* of other political systems, cultures and ways of life beyond Europe, international order was dedicated to a different purpose:

the promotion of *civilization* and white racial supremacy.[60] Hence, in the colonial world, Europeans believed that they knew how other governments should be organized, and they actively worked to restructure societies that they regarded as uncivilized to encourage economic progress and stamp out barbarism and corruption that they believed to be characteristic of most indigenous regimes. In contrast to the Westphalian system, Europeans were "quite prepared to entertain the possibility of violent actions and other interventions might have to be made in order to civilize savage peoples, or to prevent them from retarding the civilization of the wilderness that they insisted on treating as their homelands."[61]

Nevertheless, this bifurcation did not lead to two separate and disconnected worlds, but to a unique and single world full of ambiguities and contradictions, in which the colonial world was to develop as an entity fully constitutive of the West. This leaves no other possibility for a genealogy of the European modern but to include the colonial world in which, during the very emergence of the "Westphalian system," a "great spiritual and temporal pastorate" was operating through the agency of the European colonial powers even though it was disappearing in Europe. This explains why Europe simply *cannot* be defined exclusively against an old version of itself (the Empire and the Church), and must also be defined against its colonial "Others."

Postcolonial thinkers, such as Fanon and Aimé Césaire, help us to understand these extra-European origins of modernity. For both authors, Europe is dependent. Anticipating Fanon's famous proposition that "Europe is literally the creation of the Third World."[62] Césaire argues that colonizers' sense of superiority and their sense of mission as the world civilizers depended on turning the "Other" into a barbarian.[63] Fanon calls attention to the binary structure of power and authority that produces the black man as the opposite side of the white man. By rejecting the "belatedness" of the black man, by refusing to locate him in the past of which the white man is the future, Fanon destroys the two time-schemes from which the historicity of the modern human is conceived.[64]

Postcolonial agency emerges, precisely, in terms of disrupting time by destabilizing the gap between these two supposedly insulated histories (the history of progress and modernization of the colonizer and the history of belatedness and tradition of the colonized). Thus, agency emerges in an enunciative space that contradicts the metaphysical idea of progress so that "Western modernity does not pose as *History*."[65]

Pondering on the role of the "Other" in the production of the European self, several authors emphasize the dual behavior of the colonial powers. Mitchell, for instance, argues that "to govern new forms of disorder, colonial discourse bec[a]me preoccupied with establishing distinctions of race, sexuality, culture and class."[66] These issues became available to be transferred back to the metropolis where, in the later nineteenth century, they helped create the racial, cultural, class and sexual identities that defined the modern bourgeois self. Césaire also emphasizes this "boomerang effect" by showing how Fascism should be read as colonial totalitarianism brought to Europe.[67] Far from civilizing Africans, colonialism "uncivilized" the civilized.[68] Concerning Nazism, for example, he says: "What he [the European or white man] cannot forgive Hitler for is not the crime in itself, the crime against man (...) it is the crime against the white man (...) the fact that he applied to Europe colonialist procedures which until then had been reserved exclusively for the Arabs (...) the 'niggers.'"[69] In a similar vein, Edward Keene[70] argues that it was in the context of World War II and for the first time that Europeans experimented the uncomfortable feeling of being themselves the target of racial discrimination on behalf of Germany. In this new context, it would be strange, he argues, to affirm the supremacy of the white race over the African or Asian races while simultaneously denying the validity of Nazi efforts in demonstrating Aryan supremacy. By projecting civilization against Nazism, its defenders were inevitably questioning the old assumptions about the racial frontiers of the civilized world. Hence, both authors blur the clear demarcation between Europe and the colonized world, or between European progress and colonial backwardness, by calling attention to the presence of the colonized and of backwardness in the European self.

## CONCLUSION

European-centered dualism has characterized the modern state system since Grotius's conception of an outer circle that embraced all humanity and an inner circle bound by the law of Christ.[71] Scholars of the English School tradition such as Hedley Bull presuppose the occurrence of historical progression from one set to the next that result from normative changes in international society according to the criteria for statehood and sovereign recognition.[72] Accordingly, as stated by Siba Grovogui,[73] "the end of European empires through decolonization completed the transformation of the international system into one of fully autonomous states, dependent upon a Western-based political ethos which is encoded albeit imperfectly into a singular regime of sovereignty." The conclusion is that European conquest and colonization facilitated the convergence in international morality that laid the groundwork for the international society.[74]

Diverging from Bull, Roxanne Doty[75] understands the above dualisms as structures of exclusion consisting of a privileged inner core and inferior peripheries. Drawing on Foucault, Doty[76] suggests that one structure of exclusion creates the niches for others; just as, for Foucault, the poor vagabond, the criminal and the deranged person took up the niche previously occupied by the leper, the members of each of these circles were characterized alternatively through time.

In this same way, a new dyad has emerged from the end of World War II onwards, replacing the old one that had distinguished the "civilized" sovereign states from their uncivilized dependences. The "core and periphery" new dyad underpinned the practices that supplemented the Cold War dynamic by establishing another axis of political action between North and South. The construction of peripheral states was dedicated to those communities whose evolution led to the acknowledgement of their own national identity and, therefore, made them independent of the metropolitan rule. Joining international society implied that nations should forge themselves as sovereign states by following the techniques of sovereignty, which are: (i) to recognize its rights and duties as a sovereign state; (ii) to differentiate itself from the other states by expressing an essential, singular and irreducible identity; (iii) to recognize the rights and duties of the great powers; (iv) to share a diplomatic vocabulary that was already disseminated among the members of the society; (v) to sustain the already established balance of power and (vi) to support the use of force in order to guarantee peace. To be a national sovereign state meant to become a subject of international society. Former colonies that once stood on the borders of the colonial powers were attracted to the center of the society of sovereign nation-states in order to share and adhere to their allegedly common interests and values.

However, the colonizing machinery and its techniques had as their objects not only space—the imperial space in this case—but also time. In fact, as a modern artifact, the colonizing machinery incorporated time and history into a new relationship in which time produced change; time meant evolution. The colonizing machinery had created cleavage within international society: on one side, there were the states which had long been sovereign—the founding fathers of international society—and on the other, the colonized states whose history and culture had to be translated into international society's vocabulary.

From an evolutionist perspective, colonized states were condemned to experience a time-lag due to their problematic and always belated inscription in the symbolic order of international society. In fact, to the states that had just joined international society, the effects of the time-lag appeared, historically, under a variety of labels: lateness, dependence, underdevelopment, transition, developing. Those labels are historically constructed stereotypes used as a tactic to produce subjects—in this case, states that were *becoming* sovereign but that were not sovereign *just yet.*

*Center* and *periphery* were distinct discursive instances that were articulated by a rhetorical authority that made being the condition of existence that may be found in the very idea of international society—and in the international regime of power which articulates it. The cleavage between "center and periphery" is an instrument-effect in which the international colonizes time, creating a synchronic and homogeneous presence of international society's subjects inside its own order. As Bhabha perceives it, there was an economy of affects between colonizers and the colonized that encompassed their identities in a process of productive ambivalence.[77] The colonizing machinery's transcendental mode of operation and its techniques created a "time-lag" and, therefore, *center* and *periphery* as discursive instances.

Since the end of the Cold War, critical scholars have exhibited a growing interest in the concept of "failed states" and have debated how these new discursive instances are taking up the niche previously occupied by the uncivilized and the periphery during the Cold War. In the failed state discussion, a number of categories and metaphors are used to represent difference as backwardness, creating a temporal distance between Europeans and non-Europeans that reproduces a pattern of the first encounters between Europeans and non-Europeans. Taking into account this temporalization of difference, the discourse on "failed states" produces the temporal identity of the so-called successful states. Thus, "successful states" are able not only to guarantee security through the monopoly of the legitimate use of force, to respect democratic principles and to ensure the efficient functioning of their administrative machine but also to construct themselves as temporally advanced in relation to their "failed" and "backward" counterparts.

As demonstrated herein, the main limitations of Foucault's approach reside in the fact that he did not devote enough attention to the process by which the colonial "Other," or the colonial alterity, centrally participated (and participates) in the production of the European self. As observed by the postcolonial thinker Achille Mbembe, "It's as if the colonial event belonged to another age and another place, and as if it had absolutely nothing to teach us about how to understand our own modernity, about citizenship, about democracy, even about the development of our humanities."[78] Thus, the uncivilized, the periphery, the failed states and, more recently, the fragile states, create, over time, modern European subjectivities.

## NOTES

1. Robert J. C Young, "Foucault on race and colonialism," *New Formations* 25 (Summer 1995): 57–65.
2. Ibid.
3. Timothee Mitchell, "The Stage of Modernity", in *Questions of Modernity* (Minneapolis: University of Minnesota Press, 2000).
4. Especially in Michel Foucault, *Security, Territory, Population, Lectures at the Collège de France 1977–1978*, (New York: Palgrave MacMillan, 2008).
5. Hedley Bull, *The Anarchical Society: A Study of Order in World Politics* (New York: Columbia University Press, 1977).
6. See especially Paulo Chamon, "Foucault crosses the English Channel: Interpreting the 'international politics' in *The Anarchical Society* and *Security Territory Population*," Paper presented at the Doctoral Workshop *Foucault and International Politics*, IRI/PUC-Rio, September 25–27, 2013.
7. Foucault, *Security, Territory, Population*, pp. 398–407.
8. Ibid., p. 407.
9. Richard Little, "Hedley Bull's The Anarchical Society," in *Balance of Power in International Relations: Metaphors, Myths and Models* (Cambridge: Cambridge University Press, 2009).
10. Ibid.
11. Ibid.
12. Foucault, *Security, Territory, Population*, p. 424.
13. Adam Watson, *A Evolução da Sociedade Internacional: Uma Análise Histórica Comparativa* (Brasília, Editora Universidade de Brasília, 2004).
14. Chamon, "Foucault crosses the English Channel".
15. Ibid.
16. Foucault, *Security, Territory, Population*, pp. 391–400.

17. Michel Foucault, *The History of Sexuality. Volume 1: An introduction* (New York, Pantheon Book, 1978), p. 94.
18. Ibid., p. 101.
19. Ibid., p. 104.
20. On The archeology of International Society, International system and International community metaphors, see Nicholas Onuf, "Escavando a 'comunidade internacional': por uma arqueologia do conhecimento metafórico," *Contexto Internacional* 32, no. 2, 2010: 253–296.
21. Foucault, *Security, Territory, Population*, p. 408.
22. Ibid., p. 399.
23. Ibid., p. 389.
24. Ibid., p. 389.
25. Ibid., p. 398.
26. Ibid., p. 402.
27. Ibid., p. 402.
28. R.B.J. Walker, "Lines of Insecurity. International, Imperial, Exceptional", *Security Dialogue*, 37(1), 2006: 65–82.
29. Mitchell, "The Stage of Modernity."
30. Ilan Kapoor, "Acting in a tight spot: Homi Bhabha's postcolonial politics," *New Political Science* 25, no 4, 2003: 561–577.
31. Bhabha, Homi. "The Third Space: Interview with Homi Bhabha," in *Identity, Community, Culture, Difference*, ed. J. Rutherford (London, Lawrence & Wishart, 1990), p. 218.
32. Ibid.
33. Ibid, p. 218.
34. Michel Foucault, *Discipline and Punish. The Birth of the Prison*, transl. Alan Sheridan (New York, Vintage Books, 1977).
35. Akerstrom Andersen, *Discursive analytical strategies. Understanding Foucault, Koselleck, Laclau, Luhmann* (Chicago: University of Chicago Press, 2003).
36. Foucault, *Discipline and Punish*, p. 304.
37. The expression is from Edward Keene, *Beyond the Anarchical Society: Grotius, Colonialism and Order in World Politics* (Cambridge University Press, 2002).
38. Frantz Fanon, *The Wretched of the Earth*, transl. by Richard Philcox (New York, Grove Press, 2004 [1963]), pp. 3–4.
39. Bhabha, *The Third Space*, p. 218.
40. Fanon, *The Wretched of the Earth*, p. 6.
41. Ibid., p. 6.
42. Marta F. Moreno, Carlos C. Braga, Maíra S. Gomes, "Trapped Between Many Worlds: A Post-colonial Perspective on the UN Mission in Haiti (MINUSTAH)," *International Peacekeeping* 19, no. 3 (2012): 377–392.

43. Martin Munro, Robbie Shilliam, "Alternative Sources of Cosmopolitanism: Nationalism, Universalism and Creolité in Francophone Caribbean Thought," in *International Relations and Non-Western Thought: Imperialism, Colonialism and Investigations of Global Modernity*, ed. Robbie Shilliam (London: Routledge, 2011), pp. 159–77.
44. Michel Foucault, 'Poder e Saber, 1977', in Michel Foucault, *Estratégia, Poder-Saber*, (Coleção Ditos Escritos IV), Rio de Janeiro: Forense Universitária, 2006.
45. Susan Buck-Morss, "Hegel and Haiti," *Critical Inquiry* 26, no 4 (2000); Marta F Moreno, Carlos C. Braga and Maíra S. Gomes, "Trapped Between Many Worlds…"
46. Arthur Lavejoi, *The Great Chain of Being: A Study of the History of an Idea* (Cambridge: Harvard University Press, 1936).
47. David Boucher, *Political Theories of International Relations. From Thucydides to the Present* (Oxford: Oxford University Press, 1998).
48. Ali A., Mazrui, "From Social Darwinism to Current Theories of Modernization. A Tradition of Analysis," *World Politics*, 21(1), 1968: 69–83.
49. James Ferguson, *Global Shadows. Africa in the Neoliberal World Order* (Durham and London: Duke University Press, 2006).
50. Ibid., p. 181.
51. Homi Bhabha, "A questão do 'Outro': diferença, discriminação e o discurso do colonialismo," in *Pós-Modernismo e Política* ed. Heloisa Buarque de Hollanda (Rio de Janeiro: Editora Rocco, 1991).
52. Ashis Nandy, *The Intimate Enemy. Loss and Recovery of the Self under Colonialism* (Delhi, Bombay Calcutta, Madras, Oxford University Press, 1983).
53. Bhabha, "A questao do Outro."
54. Naeem Inayatullah and D. L Blaney, *International Relations and the Problem of Difference* (New York, Routledge, 2004).
55. Brett Nicholls, "Disrupting time: Post-colonial politics in Homi Bhabha's The Location of Culture," *Southern Review* 30, no 1, 1997: 4–25.
56. Fabian Johanes, *The Time and the Other: how anthropology makes its objet* (New York: Columbia University Press, 2002).
57. Nicholls, "Disrupting Time," p. 9.
58. Ibid.
59. Keene, *Beyond the Anarchical Society*.
60. Ibid.
61. Ibid., p. 99.
62. Aimé Césaire, *Discourse on Colonialism*, transl. by Joan Pinkham (New York, Monthly Review Press, 2000), p. 58.
63. Robin D.G Kelley, "Introduction. A Poetics of Anticolonialism," in *Discourse on Colonialism*, Aimé Césaire (New York University, 2000), p. 9.

64. Homi Bhabha, *The Location of Culture*, (London: Routledge, 1994), pp. 237–8.
65. Ilan Kapoor, "Acting in a tight spot: Homi Bhabha's postcolonial politics," *New Political Science* 25, no 4 (2003): 574.
66. Mitchell, "The Stage of Modernity": 5–6.
67. Aimé Césaire, *Discourse on Colonialism*.
68. Ibid.
69. Ibid., p. 36.
70. Keene, *Beyond the Anarchical Society*.
71. Roxanne Lynn Doty, *Imperial Encounters* (Minneapolis, University of Minnesota Press, 1996); Bull, *The Anarchical Society*.
72. Doty, *Imperial Encounters*.
73. Siba N. Grovogui, "Regimes of Sovereignty: International Morality and the African Condition," *European Journal of International Relations* 8, no 3 (2002): 15–38.
74. Ibid.
75. Doty, *Imperial Encounters*.
76. Ibid., p. 155.
77. Homi Bhabha, *The Location of Culture* (London: Routledge, 1994).
78. Achille Mbembe, "What is Postcolonial Thinking: An Interview with Achille Mbembe", *Esprit*, 2008. Available online at http://www.eurozine.com/articles/2008-01-09-mbembe-en.html (site verified on October 27, 2015).

# CHAPTER 9

# Violence and the Modern International: An Archaeology of Terrorism

## Philippe Bonditti

"I start with a problem as it is currently posed and try to construct its genealogy. Genealogy means I conduct the analysis starting out from a contemporary issue."[1] This sentence from Michel Foucault is doubly informative about the aim of the philosopher-historian's work. On the one hand, it involved treating a *problem*—in fact, as we shall see, particular *historical forms of problematization* of a phenomenon. On the other hand, the history of those problematizations was intended to inform the present in action; this is the role of diagnosis of the present.

The list of "problems" tackled by Michel Foucault is impressive: madness—in fact, its equation with illness and incorporation into the general domain of medicine with the development of psychiatric knowledge (*savoir*); the criminalization of certain kinds of behavior, with the prison-form as the solution; sexual practices installed by the "dispositif of sexuality" as the fulcrum for a whole set of strategies of power. There is also the problem of government, which, strangely enough, Foucault ignored in that 1984 interview, when he pulled his extraordinarily varied research enterprises together under the concept of "history of problematizations."

P. Bonditti (✉)
ESPOL, Catholic University of Lille, Lille, France
e-mail: philippe.bonditti@gmail.com

© The Author(s) 2017                                                    155
P. Bonditti et al. (eds.), *Foucault and the Modern International*,
The Sciences Po Series in International Relations and Political
Economy, DOI 10.1057/978-1-137-56153-4_9

Having gradually made an appearance in his massive oeuvre from the mid-1970s, the problem of government acquired genuine centrality in the 1978 course, which did not actually start with a question about government, but what Foucault at the time called the "security society." We now know that these analyses of security did not issue in a satisfactory conclusion,[2] and Foucault fairly rapidly abandoned the theme in favor first of Christian pastoral power and then liberalism and neo-liberalism (see Bigo, Pandolfi and McFalls, and Gros in this volume). The question of government was the most irksome impasse in which Foucault found himself; he was unable to escape it.

The silent hypothesis behind these pages is that this impasse in fact stems from a double over-determination of Foucault's historical inquiries by his own hypothesis of bio-power, formulated from 1974. On the one hand, this hypothesis led him to associate the general problem of security too closely with that of illness and health. On the other hand, in his historical research it seems to have led him to single out elements that could confirm the hypothesis of life as a new target of technologies of power. Hence, the continuity in Foucault's analyses in these years: security—illness—population—human capital—Gary Becker—neo-liberalism (see especially Paltrinieri in this volume).

In what follows, I propose to reengage with the problem of government by reappropriating Foucault's investigation of security, but examining it from the more particular standpoint of its relationship to the general problem of violence. I shall show that contemporary changes in security, conceived from the standpoint of the radical heterogeneity of its constitutive practices, are closely connected with, and even *made possible* by, a new problematization of violence since the 1950s. This is attributable to discourses on "terrorism" rather, to the "terrorism-discourse"—which is in fact a discourse on and about *violence*—that, with this concept of "terrorism" (I shall suggest), has segmented violence in a new way: no longer in accordance with the spatial division between the internal and the external—with crime and police on one side and war and the military on the other—but in line with a temporal division between the effectivity of violence and the possibility of its irruption. I shall then show how this new problematization of violence is accompanied by a profound transformation in the art of governing with the advent of *traceability as a technology of government*, betraying the emergence of "societies of traceability."

## PROBLEM(S), PROBLEMATIZATION, ARCHAEOLOGY

Before coming to the heart of my argument, I need to spell out my research method in order to indicate what an approach—that might be called foucauldian in its method and concepts—can tell us about contemporary societies.

### Problem (s), Problematization and Theoretical Practice

When, from 1980 onwards, Foucault returned to his work to pull it together under the concept of "history of problematizations," a number of slippages occurred in his discourse. In fact, Foucault continually oscillated between the history of "problems" and the history of "problematizations." These slippages raise a number of legitimate questions, first about what Foucault calls "problematization," and then about the status and place of a problem in a history of (forms of) problematizations.

### From Problem to Problematization

It will be remembered that in his reflections on problematization Foucault seeks to distance his work from a history of solutions and, even more, from a search for alternative solutions. Neither search for solutions nor history of solutions, the history of forms of problematization is much more focused on *problems*, without being reducible to the history of a problem. Instead, the history of problematizations consists in showing how a problem—which will be called *specific* here—expresses a particular form of problematization of a *more general* problem.

That is what Foucault is referring to in the quotation with which I began, when he says that he wanted to "start with a problem and construct its genealogy." Faced with a general problem (illness, punishment, security, violence, etc.), his stance is not moral, but *analytical.* Furthermore, the analyst is not faced with a problem that arises in its specificity and whose history he or she proposes to construct, so as to show how it was constituted as such. There are domains of practices bound up with very general problems and, on the basis of the *established forms of knowledge* (*savoir*) *at the time*, they seize on a *specific problem* encountered by the deployment of *savoir faire* in practice.

Starting with a very general problem (illness, punishment, sex, security and, in our case, violence), and the questions that are attached to it, the history of problematizations will therefore consist in showing how, *when dealing with a specific practical problem*, these practices give rise to a redistribution of the *constitutive elements* of a more general problem—that is, to a new form of problematization. We can also infer from this that a problematization is the outcome, not the starting point, of analytical-interpretative work; the interpretative dimension of the analysis enabling the possibility to bring out the urgency associated with a new form of problematization.

*Problem, Concept and Theoretical Practice*
Thus construed as a history of the ways in which the constitutive elements of a general problem come to be redistributed in a particular period, the history of (forms of) problematization(s) should, from a methodological viewpoint, first result in the identification of the *specific problem* encountered by a domain of practices in this period: an encounter that will possibly give rise to the formation of one or more new concepts and, where necessary, lead to the formation of a new type of knowledge (*savoir*). This is what is at stake in a concept-centered method of historical inquiry. We must therefore introduce the importance of concepts in a history of (forms of) problematization, in particular clarifying their relationship to "problem" and practice.

I shall not seek to demonstrate here the close link between knowledge and concepts, but simply accept with Kant that all knowledge requires a concept, and with Gaston Bachelard that concepts are the "centres around which knowledge of reality is concentrated,"[3] on the premise that concepts are a matter of knowledge. A concept emerges of *necessity* in a field of knowledge and practice faced with *a practical problem*. Here we touch on a crucial characteristic of the concept identified early on by Jean Cavaillès, for whom "the invention of concepts is a requirement on the part of problems."[4] In fact, a concept always emerges in connection with a problem—that is, as suggested by the etymology of the word, in connection with an *obstacle* to knowledge (*connaissance et savoirs*), and hence to the deployment of the forms of *savoir faire* invested by them in practice. Faced with a problem encountered by practices, which existing concepts in their constituted form are unable to solve, the emergence of a new concept is how the *movement* of knowledge (and, therefore, *practices*) can be restored—and this through the new segmentation of realities operated by the network of concepts as recomposed in response to the emergence of a new concept.

As the fruit of the specific practice of abstraction—more specifically, of "conceptualization," as opposed to abstraction through language and its *words*—a concept is in fact the vehicle through which the thinking/acting subject appropriates the world. This is why Althusser could claim that we continuously live *in* and *under abstraction*,[5] and also why, for my part, I maintain that *abstraction is our practical relationship to the world* (on abstraction see also Hibou in this volume). Faced with a specific practical problem encountered by a sphere of practices in a given period, the specific practice of abstraction intensifies, possibly inducing the emergence of a new concept which a definitional work will make it possible to specify and to situate in the conceptual matrix within which it emerges. This is the work peculiar to the *theoretical practice*, which the archaeological method makes it possible to view close up, capturing the emergence of a new concept and describing the process of knowledge (*procès de connaissance*) of which this new concept becomes the object with, where necessary, the formation of a new knowledge (*savoir*).

This domain of radically heterogeneous practices (practice of abstraction, theoretical practice, discursive and nondiscursive practices, etc.) is fixed on by the analyst, who describes them in the *historical* complexity of their respective, mutual implications and thus accounts for their *problematization*. At the heart, then, of the history of (forms of) problematizations are a general problem, a specific problem—to be isolated in the particular way it is bound up with the general problem—and a domain of radically heterogeneous practices, with their *savoir faire* and the technico-practical knowledge to be found in them. Such are the factors that intellectuals must fix on in their self-appointed task of establishing the history of problematizations, which is also a way for them to problematize their present.

### The Role of the Intellectual and the Archaeological

#### Problematizing a Domain of Practice

We know that from the second half of the 1970s, Foucault made problematization the rationale for the *critical* and *political* activity of the intellectual. If not at the time, today at any rate, an emphasis on problems—as opposed to solutions—makes it possible to distinguish between the work of intellectuals and that of experts, whose major failing is their inability to pose a problem. Obsessed by solutions, unembarrassed by questions, experts do not know how to construct a problem or make a *diagnosis*—the twofold ambition of a history of problematizations. Although Foucault's 1978 course on security was not placed squarely under the sign of problematization, Michel Senellart is right to say that what was at stake for Foucault was historical and political in as much as it concerned a diagnosis of the present.[6] In Foucault's intellectual and political trajectory, the connection between problematization and diagnosis is an extension of his analyses of Kant's text "Was ist Aufklärung?" and of the role philosophy allocated to itself thereafter: pronouncing not on the eternal verities but on the nature of the present—an ontology of ourselves.

For intellectuals the point is not to arrive at a diagnosis authorizing them to state that a problematization is good or bad, desirable or undesirable, but to successfully *spot the danger* contained in the particular configuration of knowledge(s) (*savoirs*) and practices created in and by a new problematization: "My point is not that everything is bad, but that everything is dangerous, which is not exactly the same as bad. If everything is dangerous, then we always have something to do. So my position leads not to apathy but to a hyper- and pessimistic activism."[7]

Such is the intellectual's positive, strategic intervention in the process of problematization: an intervention that will twist this process by turning into a problem what had come to be historically constructed as a solution—making a problem of psychiatric practice, of prison, of the dispositif of sexuality and so forth. Intellectuals do not occupy some over-arching position with respect to problematization. Always already situated *in* problematization, they work within it and, through their own (theoretical) practice, turn it against itself, conducting a critique of practice by practice, an immanent critique whose strategic objective is to counter the movement of problematization by making a problem of solutions that claim to be "self-evident."

*Archaeology as Method*

For these purposes, the intellectual will deploy an *archaeological* method of historical inquiry, whose *concrete method* we shall not describe here, opting instead to say something about the "domain of empiricity" peculiar to an archaeology of the present. More specifically, this involves identifying the immediate object of the method, its subject matter (*matériau*) and the way that archival work (in the historians' sense of the word) organizes access to the archive in Foucault's sense—that is, to a system of rules authorizing the emergence of one statement (*énoncé*) rather than another in a given period.

Construed as a form of discourse analysis centered on concepts,[8] archaeology "finds the point of balance of its analysis in *savoir*."[9] In 1976,

Foucault presented it as "the method specific to the analysis of local discursivities,"[10] in the service of genealogy understood as a tactic for the dis-subjection of local knowledges. Let us recall here that discourse is to be understood in contradistinction to language, and *savoir* in contradistinction to *connaissance* (particularly scientific). By contrast with the latter, a subject/agent is never the "bearer" of *savoir* in Foucault's work, any more than discourse refers to a speaking subject. *Savoir* cannot be said to be "true or false, exact or inexact, approximate or definite, contradictory or consistent."[11] There is nothing subjective about discourse(s) and *savoir(s)*. On the contrary, they are what installs the subject in a kind of subjectivity peculiar to the occasion of the process of *appropriation* of *savoir* (*savoir* being *appropriable*), which is also the process of knowledge whose object is the concepts around which this *savoir* is articulated. For Foucault, concepts, *savoir* and discourse are inseparable.

The concepts I attended to in my own research are not scientific or philosophical, but those that might be called "general." In a given domain of practices (here security in relation to violence), they organize an era's *technical savoir* on which the *technico-practical knowledge* is built and then deployed in all the different types of security *savoir faire* (especially the police, military and intelligence *savoir faire*. We shall find these concepts in what is sometimes called "grey literature," mainly *written* output composed of institutional reports, guidelines or "guides to best practices," doctrine documents, armed forces field manuals, administrative glossaries and other dictionaries, where this knowledge (*savoir*) is recorded. This material must be systematically collected so as to reconstruct the fullest possible series for each type of document, and thereby identify chronological continuities that will facilitate the study of concepts and their variations over time. This method, a serial one, should make it possible to reconstruct the textual network that forms the *base of the archive peculiar to a domain of practices*, which a specifically archaeological inquiry will then fix on to identify the forms of rationality that organize and govern ways of doing and acting.

In this chapter, an attempt will therefore be made to locate and describe the emergence of new concepts and the mutation of the conceptual network it potentially prompts, and then to see if and how these new concepts are bound up with the formation of a new *savoir* and, where necessary, describe the way that the latter is connected with established *savoirs*. This is what I have been endeavoring to do since undertaking an archaeology of the *savoirs* of security and the concept of terrorism.

## THE EMERGENCE OF TERRORISM
## AND THE PROBLEMATIZATION OF VIOLENCE

### *The Counter-Insurgency Matrix of Terrorism*

The concept of "terrorism" is not immediately found in the settled form it takes today, in the vicinity of the concepts of *enemy*, *threat* and *network* with which it articulates the grand narrative of "terrorist networks as political and strategic enemies of states." Terrorism—initially as plain *word* and then as *concept and category* (see below)—did not spring up out of nothing in the 1950s. It emerged in the context of doctrinal reflection on what at the time were called "irregular" wars, referring to armed confrontations in which US military forces were thwarted by guerrilla movements (said to be) characterized by extreme mobility, reticular forms of organization and a capacity for surprise. Irregular warfare confronted the military with a very concrete practical problem—*asymmetry* in combat. This consists in an *imbalance* between the means—powerful—and structure—rigid—of conventional forces, on the one hand, and the unconventional methods of irregular warfare used by guerrilla movements, on the other. Here we have the *specific problem* on the basis of which the more general problem of violence was going to be problematized anew.

In the US Army's Field Manuals of the 1950s and 1960s, the *word* terrorism refers to a guerrilla "weapon" (the use of fear to secure the support of local populations) or combat tactic in an account whose general formulation (*énoncé*) William Colby—successively head of the Central Intelligence Agency's (CIA) Far Eastern Division (1962–68), deputy to the commander of CORDS (Civil Operations and Rural Development Support) in Vietnam, and Director of the CIA (1973–76)—rendered perfectly some years later:

> There is another level of security at which this new kind of war must be fought. In Vietnam, there is a secret Communist network within the society which tries to impose its authority on the people through terrorism and threat. This network, or as it is called in Vietnam, the VC infrastructure, provides the political direction and control of the enemy's war within the villages and hamlets.[12]

The word terrorism, whose reference is restricted to fear here, thus emerges in a lexical field also containing the concepts of security, network, threat and enemy, which would gradually find their point of equilibrium in that of "terrorism." And the latter would break the mold not only of the conceptual matrix which Clausewitz's theorization of war had made the first principle of military *savoir faire* but also of the very structure of *savoirs* of security as a whole.

## Terrorism as an Object of Knowledge

The mutation in the *savoirs* of security accelerated at the start of the 1970s—in particular, following revelations of the abuses committed by US Special Forces in Vietnam, which led to abandonment of the terminology of counter-insurgency and the emergence of that of terrorism. The latter was based on a series of "research programs" whose *immediate object* was acts of violence hitherto associated with guerrilla activities: sabotage, political assassination, hostage taking, bomb attacks, soon joined by the hijacking of aircraft and then all *non-state* acts of violence directed against the rulers of states. Among these programs, those conducted within the Rand Corporation and the CIA from 1968 and 1972 would have a significant impact. The databases of "international terrorism" they constructed, and the numerous publications they generated, represented a significant resource readily accessible to governmental agencies, academics and experts specializing in the issue of terrorism.

In the same period, in fact, a field of expertise on terrorism and political violence started to develop, composed of self-proclaimed "experts on terrorism."[13] Hailing from, or close to, intelligence circles in some cases and military circles in others, they were all widely consulted by US congressional committees, collaborated in the same think tanks, and published prolifically on the themes of terrorism, (political) violence and conflicts—in particular, in the journals *Studies in Conflict and Terrorism* and *Terrorism and Political Violence*, which they founded in 1977 and 1989, and that significantly contributed to the consolidation and diffusion of the particular *savoir* on terrorism forged since then, as well as to the development of what some years later became "Terrorism Studies" (a subject in which a student can now receive an education leading to a degree).

Statistical tools are essential in this firming up of terrorism as an *object of knowledge*. They are the means whereby the experts translate the positivities of the violence they study into figures, graphs and maps, and eventually establish these positivities of violence as a sui generis reality different from other forms of violence. Statistical knowledge enables them to establish typologies of terrorism (domestic, international, extreme left/right, pro-independence, separatist, religious, etc.), to identify "terrorgenic" zones (Latin America, Europe, the Middle East) and, above all, to isolate and establish criteria (fear, type and number of victims, the cost of the destruction, modalities of action, forms of organization, etc.), presented as *absolutely distinctive about*, and *characteristic of* "terrorist" violence. Terrorism as a singular form of violence was born and, with it, a new problematization of violence and a profound transformation in practices of security could commence.

### Security in the Modern Problematization of Violence

Hitherto, in effect, security was understood differently depending on whether the concept referred to law enforcement and punishment of crime on the one hand, and the protection of the national territory and national interests against potential aggression by other states on the other hand. Work in historical sociology has made it possible to clarify the constitution of these two domains of security, showing how the nascent sixteenth- and seventeenth-century state had to assert its physical power on two fronts at once: faced with other developing states, in and through war for land, with the creation of powerful armies for inter-state competition, and faced with local resistance, with the construction of police forces to maintain order and ensure tax collection. Thus, the formation of these two domains of security and, correlatively, of historically differentiated *functions*, *cultures* and *savoirs* of security (police, military and also intelligence) was intimately bound up with the socio-genesis of the modern territorial state—with which it is identified—and its *particular problematization of violence*.

The peculiarity of the *modern* problematization of violence consists not so much in the process of (de)legitimation of violence (which settled the problem of violence by turning violence against itself), as in the less studied process of *spatialization* whereby violence, grasped from the standpoint of its positivities, has been distributed *in* space by situating crime and police activity (rather) *inside* borders, and war and the military (rather) *outside* them. This helped to establish and reproduce the "modern spatiality" of the political so meticulously articulated around the spatial division between the inside and the outside,[14] which remains the first principle of all the features generally regarded as characteristic of political modernity: national/international, citizen/foreigner, home affairs/foreign policy, law enforcement/national defense and criminal/political enemy.

But this modern imperative of spatialization also *incorporates* a *temporal* dimension via the conception of a *spatialized time* inherited from the scientific revolutions of the sixteenth and seventeenth centuries. The upshot was a relationship to violence organized not only in space but also in time, with a whole set of mechanisms that made it possible to *restrict the legitimate use of violence in time* so as to wrest it from the domain of contingency and counter-pose it more firmly to the randomness of delegitimized violence. Thus, in a regime of the rule of law (not suspended by the declaration of a state of emergency), at any rate, the police can proceed to their investigative activity and possible use of violence only *after* the law has been broken. Military force was likewise progressively contained in a reactive role, being activated only in the case of an armed act of aggression (principle of legitimate defense), as a result of which, from a legal standpoint, war in the modern sense obtains only *after* a formal declaration of war, which is the condition of possibility of its closure in time.

The *modern* form of problematization of violence may therefore be understood as the procedure whereby violence and its apparatuses have been spatially and temporally configured, making possible a certain processing of violence and a relative "mastery" of it. It is precisely this spatio-temporal configuration, and its associated system of concepts, which is disappearing today *in and under the impact* of the emergence and consolidation of the *concept* of terrorism in the *savoir(s)-faire* of security.

## The Archaeology of Terrorism and the Genesis of "Traceability Societies"

We find this "spatio-temporal configuration" of violence in the conceptual matrix that guides, arranges (*dispose*) and organizes the security *savoirs* and *savoir faire* in the modern era, for example, in the division between the concepts of criminal—bound up with domestic criminal law and the focus of policing practices—and political enemy—bound up with the concept of the state and the target of military apparatuses and foreign intelligence agencies. It is also to be found in the distinction between aggression—actual perpetration of violence—and threat—potential violence—against which states mobilize different apparatuses: police and military forces in response to aggression, and intelligence agencies (police or military) which work in and on the peculiar domain of the threatening by collecting information as widely as possible and in the hope of anticipating violent acts.

I shall not attempt an exhaustive description of this conceptual matrix here, but instead attempt to show how the emergence of the *concept of terrorism* involved a series of conceptual shifts which, taken together, re-problematize violence and help reorientate the security *savoirs* and *savoir faire*. Such is the other possible history of terrorism: the history of the concept and its integration into a conceptual matrix by means of and during the intensive definitional work that fixed on the *word* terrorism in the late 1960s.

### The Emergence of the Concept of Terrorism and Associated Conceptual Variations

This definitional work was mainly done by experts on terrorism and then governmental security agencies. While it did not make it possible to fix the concept of terrorism in a single and definitive definition,[15] it afforded an opportunity for three series of key operations that *problematized* violence anew.

#### Terrorism as Political Violence

The first of these series made it possible to specify the relationship between terrorism and violence and the state, both conceptually and in terms of the positivities of the violence singled out by the concept of terrorism: kidnapping, hostage taking, aircraft hijacking, attacks and so on. Conceptually, terrorism was initially subsumed under the concept of violence: a crucial operation because it facilitated an understanding of terrorism as *violence* rather than, for example, as the combat *tactic* referred to by the *word* terrorism (cf. above). A second operation then made it possible to differentiate such "terrorist violence" from state violence: an extraordinary coup by the "discourse-expert" of the 1970s and 1980s whereby "terrorist violence" came to be understood exclusively as *violence by individuals*, while being fixed in a singular relationship to the state since it was presented as directed *against* it. Thus, "terrorist violence" was identified as and dubbed fundamentally *political* because, over and above its direct victims, it targets the "quintessential" institution of political modernity.

This specification of "terrorist violence" by the criterion of the political had two major consequences. The first was that it ruled out any possibility of subsuming the concept of terrorism under that of crime—and thus, in the case of the police, resorting to criminal law to fight terrorism. Hence, the recourse by governments to "regimes of exception," whose declaration stems not so much from the allegedly exceptional nature of the violence as the maladaptation of the law when faced with a violence that has gradually been exceptionalized, because it was extruded from the register of criminal violence—which is completely different. The second consequence of the specification of terrorist violence by the concept of "political" was to establish the figure of the "terrorist" in discourse alongside that of the criminal, with which it is not to be confused. Even so, this figure of the "terrorist" could not be rendered equivalent with the figure of the political enemy as it had hitherto functioned in the modern problematization of violence, precisely because a terrorist is not the agent of any state. Hence, the concept—as legally fluid as it is ideologically dangerous—of "unlawful combatant," developed by the neoconservatives in the Bush administration to permit the imprisonment on Guantanamo of individuals captured in the many theaters of the "Global War on Terror."

Neither criminal nor political enemy, since the mid-1980s and initial attempts to theorize an "enemy criminal law,"[16] the terrorist has been the figure on which local/national legal orders (criminal law) and the supranational legal order of international humanitarian law (laws of war) can converge. As for terrorism, it may be understood as the concept that, in and through the new segmentation of violence it has operated from the late 1960s in the modern problematization of violence, *has opened up* an area of indeterminacy of crime and war "between" individual violence and state violence where, consequently, the aforementioned *category* of terrorism could develop. An area of indeterminacy which is also a site of redifferentiation of legitimate violence, for the violence assigned to the category of terrorism will in return legitimate anti-terrorism as a *specific* domain of intervention by the coercive state apparatuses, with the constitution of a specific anti-terrorist apparatus gradually equipped with its own *savoir*. Neither precisely police nor specifically military, the latter draws on the *savoir* of intelligence as regards information collection—a *necessary* consequence of a new spatialization of violence.

*Terrorism as a Spatially Distributed Potentiality of Violence*
In an extension of the reference to fear (see above), the positivities of violence thus abstracted in and through the concept of terrorism are no longer defined solely by reference to the *actual* use of physical violence, but also by "the *threat* of use of violence." We find this reference to threat in most of the definitions of terrorism by US government security agencies. From the late 1970s onwards, it made possible a new segmentation of violence, placing not only the *violent act* (the physical violence *perpetrated* in breaking a law or armed aggression) at the center of an understanding of

terrorist violence, but also the *possibility* of its irruption, therewith freeing historically legitimized violence from the temporal limits to which the modern problematization of violence had confined it.

This assimilation of the concepts of terrorism and threat has had two major consequences. On the one hand, it has tilted the organized relationship to violence in time in the direction of its potentiality. As a result, the violent act is no longer understood as what opens up the possibility of the legitimate use of violence by the state, but as the *tipping point* from a *generalized state of threat* into a *state of emergency*. The former—the generalized state of threat—is the time prior to the irruption of violence when individuals are enjoined to subjectify themselves as "vulnerable subjects," while governments work to legitimate the means of anticipating such violence.[17] The state of emergency then becomes the time immediately following the irruption of violence, when the means of resilience, and for managing the consequences of a violent act are activated.[18]

The second consequence was the particular spatiality attributed to terrorist violence via the assimilation of the concepts of terrorism and network. We encounter the concept of network in various strata of discourse: in the 1950s and 1960s, when terrorism was associated with guerrilla activities in an account that described insurgents as "underground networks concealed among populations" (see above); in CIA reports, which from the 1970s evoked terrorism in terms of a *transnational* violence cutting across the structures of the modern international; in legal definitions of terrorism as well—in the USA, where it is defined as violence "transcending national boundaries," or in France where it is characterized as an "*association* of criminals *bound up in* a terrorist enterprise."[19] Since the mid-1990s, all the talk has been of "terrorist networks." The network is thus identified as the spatiality peculiar to "terrorist violence"—regarded, let us remember, more in its potentiality than its actuality. The *network form* (see Mattelart in this volume), in fact, imposed as the image of the special space of the threat. This is the meaning of warnings about "terrorism liable to strike anywhere at any time."

The divorce of the concept of terrorism from territory mirrors the growing proximity between the concepts of terrorism and network. In accounts of terrorism, territory is neither what terrorists build their authority and power on nor is it that which contains them or limits their reach. For clandestine organizations that derive their extreme mobility from their agents, territory is now merely an interchangeable base/support. Thus, the "global war on terrorism" has taken the form of a defense of "modern spatiality" and its inter-state system as the exclusive form of organization of human societies, in accordance with the watchword: "no future outside the state-form ... even when the state is called upon to radically transform itself in order to fight this new form of violence effectively."

The discursive operation whereby, from the mid-twentieth century onwards, the emergence of the concept of terrorism opened up a new problematization of violence is also that whereby the security architectures of modern states have themselves molted into a rhizomatic structure, which would enable them—or so the argument goes—to respond to the security imperatives of a world that is apprehended and represented less via the territorial model and its state-form than by means of a technical model and its network form. So it is no surprise if the computer science and information technology *savoir*—whose assignment of centrality to the concept of network is well known—connect up so compliantly with those of security and the emergent anti-terrorist *savoir*. It is not because their computational mode is "naturally" more apt to respond to an alleged new kind of threat. If the anti-terrorist *savoir* and that of information technology and computer science seem so disposed today to connect up, it is because they have come to share the concept of network around which the *savoirs* of security, hitherto so firmly attached to the tutelary figure of the state, have been reconfigured, along with the concrete practices of their agents—networked police, network-centric warfare, electronic intelligence—to the point of inducing a new technology of government wholly geared toward anticipation.

### The Networking of Security Structures and the Emergence of Traceability as a Technology for Governing "Traceability Societies"

The connecting up of the *savoir* of information technology and computer science with the emergent anti-terrorist *savoir*—to the extent that the first seems on the point of becoming *the savoir* of security—fits well with what Foucault called the process of governmentalization of the state, which has led to "the pre-eminence over all other types of power ... of the type of power that we can call 'government.'"[20] For the past half-century, I would like to suggest, another process has worked itself into this process of governmentalization of the state: computerization. "Governmentalization of the state" and now "computerization of government." The computerization of government[21] does not simply betoken what is sometimes referred to as "e-government" or "electronic administration." Government in

Foucault's sense is not what is commonly denoted by this term—in other words, the political administrative body in charge of conducting state affairs. As is often the case with Foucault, "government" is not a stable, precise concept that delimits a specific category of practices, but an elastic one that ends up referring to "a mode of action," a "way in which the conduct of individuals or groups might be directed... to structure the possible field of action of others."[22]

As mentioned in the introduction, Foucault began developing this notion of "government" in the mid-1970s, in the framework of a broader inquiry that led him to explore transformations in the art of governing. In this context, the idea of government came to function in a conceptual framework hinging on a few key notions: "governmentality"—denoting "the strategic field of power relations"[23] within which various "forms" of government (of souls, individuals, etc.) can be established; "bio-politics"—understood as the set of power procedures over the living who make up the category of "population." Government, governmentality, bio-politics, population—four concepts that mark Foucault's endeavor to fashion a conceptual apparatus with which to analyze historical changes in the exercise of power so as to identify what is replacing "disciplinary societies." By the late 1970s, the outlines of a "contemporary governmentality" had already been traced, structured around the sovereignty/discipline/governmental management triangle and, associated with each of these poles, a set of technologies of power which, as they deployed various techniques, instruments and types of knowledge (*savoir*), historically helped to forge their respective targets, their own specific political subject: *territory*, which the practices associated with state sovereignty try to capitalize on; *body-individual*, which disciplinary techniques train and educate; and *population*, which bio-political technologies seek to maintain in its multiple aspects. The articulation of this ensemble forms the contemporary art of governing: an art of governing on the verge of being totally reconfigured by the process of computerization mentioned above, which innervates the entire social body and participates in the restructuring of security apparatuses into a reticular architecture assembled by means of computerized database systems to meet the necessity to anticipate the irruption of violence.

This security architecture structured as a network should enable the information now collected *in relation to*, and *by means of*, everything that moves to be assembled and put into circulation. Virtually no circulation today takes place without the intervention or mediation of electronic and computer devices. Mobility generates multiple electronic traces and activates monitoring and surveillance mechanisms whose effectiveness is based on the most systematic data collection possible, as well as the storage and full *circulation* of this information among state apparatuses charged with the security of geographical territories and populations. Traceability, understood both as the nature of what is traceable and the technical ability of legitimate authorities to trace individuals, goods, capital and even digital data, is thus emerging as *the* main technology of government of the living and nonliving. In a world increasingly understood in terms of flux, this technology is to be construed as the capacity for marking flows at various points of passage—in other words, tagging them in order to retrace the trajectories of their constitutive units in time and space, and even possibly anticipate violence, as so many now seem so much willing to believe.

Unlike the techniques and judicial-legal knowledge of sovereignty, the main target of traceability is not territory. Nor does it target the body-individual—as in the cell techniques of disciplinary societies—or the population—unlike bio-political technologies—but everything that is set in motion, the human and the nonhuman, the living and the nonliving. In the new governmental configuration, the status and role of "geographical territory," the "body-individual" and "population" are displaced: no longer political subject or target of technologies of power, but instruments with which to tag, (geo)localize and track people, goods, capital and digital data. The emergence of traceability as a technology of government is not without its impact on the art of governing. It participates in the production of a new political subject: mobility and, more profoundly, movement. Therein lies the significance of the restructuring of state apparatuses: an operation of deterritorialization and reconfiguration that gradually gives rise to a rhizomatic architecture of information collection and circulation, and *traceability* as the technology of government of what Foucault had called "security societies." I suggest clarifying the latter with the concept of "societies of traceability," where the rationality of the government of human beings and things, as reconfigured in our age, draws not so much on the idea and organization of pastoral power, with its figure of the shepherd, as on the imaginary of the sailor and the metaphor of the pilot so tersely excluded by Foucault in his course on *Security, Territory, Population.*[24]

*Translated by Gregory Elliott*

NOTES

1. Michel Foucault, "Le souci de la vérité" (interview with François Ewald), *Magazine littéraire*, no. 207 (May 1984): 18–23; reprinted in Foucault, *Dits & Écrits* (Paris: Gallimard, 2001), pp. 1487–1507.
2. See Didier Bigo, "Security: A Field Left Fallow," in Michael Dillon and Andrew Neal (eds), *Foucault on Politics, Security and War* (Basingstoke and New York: Palgrave Macmillan 2011), pp. 93–114.
3. Gaston Bachelard, *Essai sur la connaissance approchée* (1927) (Paris: Vrin, 2000), p. 19.
4. Jean Cavaillès, *Philosophie mathématique* (Paris: Hermann, 1962), p. 29, quoted by Ferhat Taylan in *La Rationalité mésologique. Connaissance et gouvernement des milieux de vie (1750–1900)*, PhD thesis, Bordeaux University, 2014, p. 72.
5. Louis Althusser, *Initiation à la philosophie pour les non-philosophes* (Paris: PUF, 2014), pp. 123–160.
6. Michel Senellart, "Course Context," in Michel Foucault, *Security, Territory, Population: Lectures at the Collège de France 1977–78*, transl. Graham Burchell (Basingstoke and New York: Palgrave Macmillan 2009), p. 391.
7. Michel Foucault, "On the Genealogy of Ethics: An Overview of Work in Progress," in Hurbert Dreyfus and Paul Rabinow, *Michel Foucault: Beyond Structuralism and Hermeneutics*, 2nd edn, (Chicago: University of Chicago Press, 1983), pp. 231–2.
8. See Luca Paltrinieri, *L'expérience du concept. Michel Foucault entre épistémologie et histoire* (Paris: Publications de la Sorbonne, 2012), pp. 133–4.
9. Michel Foucault, *The Archaeology of Knowledge*, transl. A.M. Sheridan Smith (New York: Pantheon, 1972), p. 183.
10. Michel Foucault, *Society Must be Defended: Lectures at the Collège de France 1975–76*, transl. David Macey (New York: Picador, 2003), p. 10.
11. Michel Foucault, "Sur l'archéologie des sciences. Réponses au cercle d'épistémologie" (1968), *Dits & Écrits*, p. 751; Ian Hacking, "Michel Foucault's Immature Science" (1979), in *Historical Ontology* (Cambridge (Mass.) and London: Harvard University Press, 2002), p. 77.
12. William Colby, Hearings before the Committee on Foreign Relations, United States Senate, 91st Congress, Second Session on Civil Operations and Rural Development Support Program (CORDS), February 17–20 and 3,4, 17 & 19 March 1970, pp. 26–30.
13. See Edward S. Herman and Gerry O'Sullivan, *The "Terrorism Industry: The Experts and Institutions that Shape our View of Terror"* (New York: Pantheon Books, 1989); Philippe Bonditti, *Antiterrorism in the United States: A Foucauldian Analysis of the Transformation of the Practices of Sovereignty and of the Art of Government*, PhD Thesis, Sciences Po, Paris

2008; and Lisa Stampnitsky, *Disciplining Terror: How Experts Invented Terrorism* (Cambridge: Cambridge University Press, 2013).

14. See R.B.J. Walker, *Inside/Outside: International Relations as Political Theory* (Cambridge Cambridge University Press, 1993) and John G. Ruggie, "Territoriality and Beyond: Problematizing Modernity in International Relations," *International Organization*, 47 (1) (1993): 139–74.

15. See Philippe Bonditti, "Violence, 'Terrorism', Otherness: Reshaping Enmity in Times of Terror," in Roderick Campbell (ed.), *Violence and Civilization* (New York: New York University Press, 2013), pp. 192–214.

16. See Jakobs Gunthers, "On the Theory of Enemy Criminal Law," available at http://www.law-lib.utoronto.ca/bclc/crimweb/foundation/Jakobs%20current.pdf (accessed 6/12/2015).

17. Hence, the centrality now accorded to Intelligence in the struggle against terrorism, in an attempt to anticipate violence by massive, large-scale information collection and its automatic processing. This follows the old tendency to the autonomization and automation of intelligence agencies, through the formalization since the 1970s of intelligence communities (first of all in the USA and today in France) and increased use of the tools, techniques and *savoirs* of information technology.

18. This was the significance of Presidential directive PDD95 in the USA in 1995. It distinguished between "crisis management"—understood as the set of measures "to anticipate, present, and/or resolve a *threat* or *act* of terrorism"—and "consequence management," which refers to the measures implemented in response to a terrorist act. This is also the sense of proposals for the constitutionalization of the "state of emergency" by the French government in the wake of the violence of 13 November 2015.

19. "Association de malfaiteurs en lien avec une enterprise terroriste."

20. Michel Foucault, *Security, Territory, Population*, p. 144.

21. Armand Mattelart's work is invaluable to situate the computerization of government in relation to "the birth of communication": Armand Mattelart, *Mapping World Communication: War, Progress, Culture* (Minneapolis: University of Minnesota Press, 1994); *The Invention of Communication*, (Minneapolis: University of Minnesota Press, 1996) and *Networking the World 1794–2000* (Minneapolis: University of Minnesota Press, 2000). See also his contribution in this volume.

22. Michel Foucault, "The Subject and Power," in Dreyfus and Rabinow, *Michel Foucault*, p. 221.

23. Michel Foucault, *The Hermeneutics of the Subject: Lectures at the Collège de France 1981–82*, transl. Graham Burchell (Basingstoke and New York: Palgrave Macmillan, 2006), p. 252.

24. See Foucault, *Security, Territory, Population*, p. 168.

# CHAPTER 10

# Foucault and the Historical Sociology of Globalization

*Jean-François Bayart*

I will here limit myself, as an old user of Foucault's work, to just setting it within the context of the historical and comparative sociology of globalization, the main topic in the study of international relations—indeed, it has fed into a sub-discipline of the latter, namely global studies, which can be better understood if we examine it in this light.[1]

However circumscribed the viewpoint taken by the historical and comparative sociology of the political, it should not be neglected in any reconsideration of the thought of Foucault. After all, Foucault quite obviously never stops talking about this issue. In his personal dealings with history, to begin with. In his exchanges of ideas with historians who focused on the political, starting with Peter Brown and Paul Veyne—historians who saw the political as the "inventory of differences." In his constant concern to apprehend the historicity of the *episteme*, of subjection and the experiences of subjectivation. In his insistence on sticking to a study of practice. In his rejection of any essentialist and metaphysical definition of power. And in his reminders to us that power cannot just be reduced to the state and its structures.[2]

J.-F. Bayart (✉)
Graduate Institute Geneva, Geneva, Switzerland
e-mail: jeanf.leguilbayart@sciencespo.fr

© The Author(s) 2017
P. Bonditti et al. (eds.), *Foucault and the Modern International,*
The Sciences Po Series in International Relations and Political
Economy, DOI 10.1057/978-1-137-56153-4_10

We also need to take into account the formidable convergence between the thought of Michel Foucault and that of Max Weber (see Hibou in this volume), if we accept that the latter is the totem of the historical and comparative sociology of the political and is mainly concerned with the relationship between capitalism and universality, grasped through the prism of the West and its *Sonderentwicklung*. This is not, of course, the Weber of Talcott Parsons or Julien Freund, but the Weber we are now discovering thanks to his new translators into French, especially Jean-Paul Grossein. Although Foucault only rarely quotes or refers to Weber, hailing him as the sociologist of contingency but demurring from his alleged essentialism, the "elective affinities" between the two writers are clear.[3] The "causal multiplication"[4] of the one thinker echoes the untangling of "concrete genetic sets of relations" (or, in Kalberg's translation "tangible, causal connections"[5]) in the other. The ideal type needs to be understood as part of a process, not a typology.[6] Weber's "conduct of life" (*Lebensführung*) and "type of human being" (*Menschentum*) prefigure Foucault's "subjectivation"; the "becoming like every day" (*Veralltäglichung*) looks forward to Foucault's "dispositifs" or "apparatuses," and "domination" (*Herrschaft*) anticipates "governmentality."

My more learned colleagues may draw up fuller lists, but these different concepts are, so to speak, interchangeable. Anyone who doubts this need only read *The Protestant Ethic and the Spirit of Capitalism* and the texts related to it with a modicum of attention to realize that this is the case. Weber writes:

> We have intentionally decided here *not* to commence our discussion with a consideration of the objective social institutions of the old Protestant churches and their ethical influence. We have especially decided not to begin with a discussion of *church discipline*, even though it is very important. Instead, we will first examine the effects of *each believer's* organization of life that are possible when *individuals* convert to a religious devoutness anchored in asceticism. We will proceed in this manner for two reasons: this side of our theme has until now received far less attention, and the effect of church discipline cannot be viewed as always leading in the same direction. (...) In those regions where a Calvinist state church held sway, the authoritarian monitoring of the believer's life was practised to a degree that rivalled an inquisition. This supervision *could* work even *against* that emancipation of individual energies originating out of the believer's ascetic striving to methodically acquire a sense of certainty as belonging among the saved. (...) The church's regimentation of asceticism could have the same effect. Wherever the church developed too far in a harshly authoritarian direction, it coerced believers into adhering to specific forms of external behavior. In doing so, however, under certain circumstances the church then crippled the individual's motivation to organize life in a methodical manner.[7]

And Weber insists on "the great difference between the effects of the despotic-authoritarianism of the state *churches* and the effects of the despotism of *sects*. The latter rests upon voluntary subjection."[8] As we see, Weber is here prefiguring the definition of governmentality as Foucault had come to define it in the 1980s, that is, as a place where the techniques of domination exercised over others and the techniques of the self meet.[9] And he already sets within their historicity the "style of life" of ascetic Protestantism, that is, the Puritans' daily method of subjectivation, and the "individualism" involved (an expression which "encompasses the most heterogeneous phenomena to be imagined")[10].

In his turn, and in his own way, Foucault takes up the crucial question of obedience. This is a question which obsesses those authors whom the historical sociology of the political inevitably treats as reference points: Weber, of course, but also La Boétie and his "voluntary servitude," Marx and his concept of "appropriation," Gramsci and his "hegemony," and more contemporary scholars such as the "subalternists" who focus on Indian history, the historian Alf Lüdtke and the anthropologist Maurice Godelier. At present, it is doubtless Béatrice Hibou[11] who, in the field of the historical and comparative sociology of the political, most clearly illustrates the relative fungibility of such theoretical notions. Thus, in Foucault, political science is on familiar territory, and it is surprising that the members of the political science "establishment" have persisted for so long in viewing him with suspicion, even more than they do with Bourdieu, in whom several of them, recognize a kindred spirit (see Bigo in this volume).

In any case, as far as I am concerned, I found it quite natural to draw simultaneously on the concepts of Weber and Foucault to problematize contemporary globalization as a mode of governmentality, in the context of the historical and comparative sociology of the political, and especially of the state, thus going against most global studies which postulated a zero-sum game between the state and globalization.[12]

## CONVERGENCES

The convergence between the preoccupations of the historical and comparative sociology of the political and Foucault's investigations seems to me to rest especially upon six points. As a philosopher-historian of practices and of *raritas*, Foucault supports a conception of comparativism that is also found in Paul Veyne and Giovanni Levi, and that consists in sharing questions rather than answers or solutions (see Bonditti in this volume)—the polar opposite of the smooth, ahistorical comparativism that characterized the "developmentalist" trend of political science in its study of "cultural areas" in the 1960s. His relational definition of power as an action on actions is limpid and, until proved otherwise, irreplaceable. The concept of governmentality that he draws from it allows us to grasp the state in its own dynamic historicity, both in a given "cultural area" and on a global scale, while avoiding the dead end of culturalism.[13] The way he emphasizes the dispersal of power and the heterotopias constitutive of political community sheds light on the consubstantial incompletion of this same community. The—very Bergsonian—way in which he manipulates long periods of time (*durées*) casts doubt on the great established periodizations, such as Antiquity and the Christian Middle Ages, and combines lines of continuity and lines of discontinuity. Finally, his view that the Enlightenment represented an "emergence from minority" is the foundation stone of the historical and comparative sociology of the political insofar as it is a critical reflection on the political: such a move is made possible by the idea of writing as a "letting go" or "detachment" (*déprise*). This helps us, at last, to understand more fully the reticence of canonical political science, which is still so normative, edifying and prescriptive! A reading of "What is Enlightenment?" should indeed be made obligatory in all departments of political science in a sulphurous and salubrious counterpoint to the Gospel of Good Global Governance which they dispense.

The analysis of "cultural areas," one that is too marginal within the discipline to be altogether honest, decent company, has not, for its part, hesitated to resort to Foucault in a pragmatic way, using him as its "toolbox." In France, Foucault was initially of great help, in the early 1980s, when it came to envisaging the political "from below," and as a process of utterance (*un processus énonciatif*), in a scholarly movement that drew on the work of certain historians—Michel de Certeau, the trend represented by Italian *microstoria*, the British journal *Past and Present*—and concomitant with the research being carried out by others, in the context of German *Alltasgsgeschichte*, the subaltern studies of specialists in India, and medieval Japanese history.[14]

As a result, the reference to Foucault was very much in evidence in the new wave of thinking aimed at "deciphering" domination in non-Western cultures. Curiously, the influence of Foucault was not actually at its most productive in connection with colonization, that major episode in globalization, in spite (or because?) of the success of *Discipline and Punish*. This was not because the colonial period was something of a blind spot for Foucault, as Ann Stoler regretted (1995). Rather, the use that has been made of his writings, especially in the United States, in work on colonial situations, has been too unequivocal to be fully convincing. The notions of discipline and confinement have been highlighted to the detriment of the notions of subjectivation and governmentality. Thus, the practices of appropriation of the colonial state carried out by the colonized have been under-estimated. The result has been an interpretation very similar to the determinist interpretation found in postcolonial studies, which are decidedly far from foucauldian in their tropical Calvinism, which sees the effect of predestination as stemming from an ahistorical, undifferentiated essence of "coloniality"[15] (See Fernández and Esteves in this volume).

Much more interesting is the way Foucault has been called on in the study of contemporary forms of domination, in the context of globalization, for example, in China,[16] in Tunisia[17] and in Iran.[18] Yet using his themes relevantly has sometimes led to difficulties, and authors who have made the attempt have found themselves in tricky situations. Indeed, militant pieties will find little of benefit here. Woe betides anyone who talks of the active consent of the dominated to the scorned regimes of the Chinese Communist Party, the Tunisian dictatorship of Ben Ali or the Islamic Republic of Iran! Foucault was met with furious criticism when the revolution broke out in Iran in 1979—a taste of things to come, and still emblematic.[19] The critics who lambasted his views were mistaken in two regards: they were both anachronistic (the allegedly wrong-headed articles and interviews dated from autumn 1978, the revolutionary Terror from the beginning of 1979) and ethnocentric (why should anyone wax indignant at the term "political spirituality" as used of Shiite Islam, while in the same period admiring the Catholic faith of the workers of Solidarność?; on political spirituality, see Dillon in this volume). Not only that, they also revealed their failure to understand the concept of subjectivation, one that is after all crucial when trying to analyse domination from a new standpoint. It represents the real added value of Foucault vis-à-vis Weber, so long as we take the argument to its logical conclusion, as I shall be suggesting shortly. Indeed, this is the approach—as well as the very notion of "political spirituality"—which Ruth Marshall picks up and uses in her study of Pentecostalism in Nigeria, a global phenomenon from any point of view, thereby providing us with one of the most illuminating works on the relation between the religious sphere and contemporary state formation in sub-Saharan Africa.[20]

It has proved heuristically fruitful to use Foucault's work in the area of the historical and comparative sociology of the political in a situation of globalization because his work represents two major advances. First, in *The*

*Order of Things,* it breaks away from every form of historicism, while making a grasp of historicity its main focus. This explains why Dipesh Chakrabarty (2000), eager to "provincialize Europe," found a reading of Foucault so interesting. The latter's work, after all, helps us not just to "rescue history from the nation," as another proponent of subaltern studies, Prasenjit Duara (1995), desires us to do, but also to save it from revolution and the "transition" (to the market economy and democracy). The outrageously normative and teleological scholarly literature that seized on the "Arab Springs" in 2011 demonstrated that this theoretical argument was not always won, in spite of the disillusionment felt by the sycophantic devotees of the said "transitions" in the former Soviet sphere, in China and in Indochina.[21]

Secondly, Foucault dissuades us from arguing in terms of "origin," causality or intentionality. The very problematic of "state formation"—if we accept the distinction between the "formation" and the "construction" of the state as introduced by two historians of Kenya, Bruce Berman and John Lonsdale (1992) in a book that is much more foucauldian than you might expect, given the way these writers skirt Foucault's work[22]—depends on it. This problematic focuses on the "descent" (*Herkunft*) and "emergence" (*Entstehung*) of the state as it depends not just on public policies, but on the muddled actions of the whole set of social actors. This distinction chimes in with the approaches of "the political from below" and the "utterance of the political," and it has largely been accepted by the adepts of this trend; it has fostered the birth of a disparate and yet consistent body of work in the historical and comparative sociology of the political, with its epicentre in the CERI (Centre de recherches internationales) at Sciences Po in Paris from the 1980s onwards, and, more recently, the FASOPO (Fonds d'analyse des sociétés politiques) and its REASOPO (Réseau européen d'analyse des sociétés politiques—European Network for the study of political societies).[23] The focus here is less on political science in the strict meaning of the term and more on the social sciences of the political, which bring social science together with history, anthropology, political economy, sociology and various other disciplines. Students who wish to explore this path need to reread Foucault, and in particular his celebrated text, "Nietzsche, genealogy, history"[24] which could well be taken as a manifesto for the historical and comparative sociology of the political.

At this point in our discussion, one should keep in mind that the elective affinities between this form of sociology and a foucauldian problematization do not stem from mere strategic opportunism, pure intellectual snobbery or a fortuitous conjunction of scientific stars. They reflect, to a greater or lesser degree, a shared experience: that of foreign societies. Foucault has sometimes been criticized for his provincialism, his French-focused ethnocentrism. But this is to ignore his adventures in Sweden, Poland, North and South America, throughout his career. It means seeing his curiosity for the Iranian Revolution as of interest only through the specious indignation it aroused—and people forget that on this occasion he could count on an excellent specialist in Shiite critical philosophy, in the person of Christian Jambet, a pupil of Henry Corbin. Above all, it means discounting the fact that he wrote *The Archaeology of Knowledge* in Tunisia, in the middle of the student revolution, that radical and courageous protest against the almost unanimously respected single-party regime that, in Foucault's own view, would make May 1968 seem insipid and petit bourgeois. Foucault's concern for historicity seems to me inseparable from his ability to face up to other places and other ways of engaging in the political—the very focus of the historical and comparative sociology of the political, something which he encountered in real life, during his time as an expatriate or on his travels, and not just through his dialogue with the historians of Antiquity or the modern period.

## FOUCAULT, BUT DELEUZE TOO

In my view however, the appropriation of Foucault's thought by the historical and comparative sociology of the political will yield its full harvest only if we take seriously the philosophical friendship that linked him to Gilles Deleuze. In relation to Deleuze, Foucault's advantage is that he continues to think about the state, even if he does not make it his central focus—far from it. And the state is crucial in the contemporary process of globalization, since the universalization of the state is just one of the dimensions of globalization, rather than its antagonistic principle or its victim, whatever the currently fashionable but illusory view of the matter may be.[25] From the political analysis point of view, this is where "deterritorialization" reaches its limit: in contemporary globalization, there is not just a "multitude," and the "empire" still has a centre, or in any case, a framework, namely, the hierarchical system of nation-states, contrary to what Michael Hardt and Toni Negri[26] may claim.

On the other hand, Deleuze's problematic helps us to extend and refine the analysis of foucauldian subjectivation, taken in a quite Weberian sense as the "production of modes of existence or styles of life,"[27] but also as a process of "nonsubjective individuations."[28] This process can be grasped only through the "molar or rigid lines of segmentarity" (the so-called break lines), the "lines of molecular or supple segmentation" ("crack lines") and the "line of flight" or "rupture lines" that form it.[29] In other words, we need to identify social actors no longer as subjects, but as "assemblages," in the shape of a "multiplicity of dimensions, of lines and directions"[30] that compose them, and that are all positions that the latter can occupy, successively or simultaneously, with regard to domination. Deleuze writes,

> Here, there are no longer any forms or developments of forms; nor are there subjects or the formation of subjects. There is no structure, any more than there is genesis. There are only relations of movement and rest, speed and slowness between unformed elements, or at least between elements that are relatively unformed, molecules and particles of all kinds. There are only haecceities, affects, subjectless individuations that constitute collective assemblages. Nothing develops, but things arrive late or early, and form this or that assemblage depending on their compositions of speed. Nothing subjectifies, but haecceities form according to compositions of nonsubjectified powers or affects.[31]

This means that the political scientist has a new object of study: the "planes of consistency or of composition,"[32] the "planes of immanence"[33] which are experienced in a given society. Viewed this way, through the prism of such fragments, this society follows a logic of imbrication, of recessing (*encastrement*). There is an imbrication of planes; there is an imbrication of differing lengths of life and historical periods, in accordance with each of those planes; there is also an imbrication of objects and images in the way the planes of immanence unfold. This leads to a less anthropocentric interpretation of the social, a clearer perception of the diversity of the space-times from which it is woven, a more precise definition of obedience, dissidence or mere "looking after your own interests" (*Eigensinn*) than in the dichotomies of a certain sociology of domination made entirely of power and resistance (or submission). This quickly brings us to the regime of truth that Foucault prized so much. But it also means we can point out its incompleteness and ambiguity.[34]

Coming at the problem via Deleuze is especially productive as he allows us both to get beyond an unequivocal view of globalization, our contemporary regime of historicity, made of "difference" *because* it is made of "repetition."[35] For two centuries, the universalization of the nation-state, of the capitalist mode of production, of its material culture and of the techniques of the body linked with it may have been coercive, for example, in the context of colonialization, but it is neither an identical reproduction nor a pure alienation. It merges into a process of appropriation, in the Marxist sense of the term, that is, a process of creation—something which culturalism refuses to accept, though the historical and comparative sociology of the political understands it perfectly well.[36] Nonetheless, the relevant unit of analysis cannot be society postulated in its totality, but rather the dispersal of the planes of immanence that can be observed in it. This means that the relation between a given historical society and globalization can be seen as various complex points of connection between human beings and their material or immaterial works as produced by their personal or professional relations, the trading in which they engage with each other, the circulation of cultural models and images and even military occupation—multiple points of connection that do not necessarily form a system and may be contradictory between one domain and another, and also lie at the heart of processes of subjectivation, of "subjectless individuations." This results in various disjunctions, or even forms of schizophrenia, something that is particularly clear in France, a country where McDonald's restaurants are trashed yet France represents the biggest European market for this chain. The foucauldian concept of heterotopia—as used by Thomas Fouquet,[37] for example, in a fine unpublished thesis, to refer to the "social elsewhere" of night, in the dimension of which the young "women adventurers of the city" of Dakar affirm their independence while mobilizing the resources of cultural and material extraversion, and "deterritorializing" themselves—can also display its full measure (see Shapiro in this volume).

In order to problematize the so-called governmentality of the belly south of the Sahara, from the perspective of the historical and comparative sociology of the political, I used the term "rhizome-state."[38] It now strikes me that the concept can be broadened in this direction. The colonial state ensures "subjection" in both the senses Foucault gives this word (*assujettissement*—also a process of "making something a subject"—*Trans.*). It is at once a place of political obedience and a place where a moral subject can be constituted. Political subjectivation, however, is not inevitably consistent. It forms a dispersal, a "multiplicity"[39] that creates the discontinuous character or the false bottom of social life and the processes whereby moral subjects are constituted. The latter exist as compositions rather than as identities, as rhizomes rather than linearities, as "events" rather than as "essences," through an interplay of the Plenum and the Void.[40] In Africa, the rhizome-state cannot be reduced to a network of political relations at the interface of institutions, social relations of locality (*terroir*), economic exchanges, alliances of lineage and the interplay of factions. It also assumes a moral dimension, or one that is ethical or, if you prefer, imaginary: that of the "politics of the belly," full of contradiction and conflict. In short, it takes on the dimension of subjectivation, which is definitely inseparable from extraversion on the level of globalization, as Thomas Fouquet[41] points out in connection with Senegal.

Nonetheless, the concept cannot be restricted to a neo-orientalist, Africanist sense. It has a universal and comparative application, once we have made allowances for historicity. We all live in rhizome-states, in accordance with disparate and fleeting planes of immediacy. And, like Deleuze, Foucault recommends—in a very Weberian fashion—that we grasp its concrete dispositifs by drawing on *wirkliche Historie*, (effective history). We should guard against the various avatars of "universal history," the "kind of Esperanto" that, just like the language of that name, initially expresses a "hope," and we should keep in mind the variety of "histories" (*Historien*).[42] We should formulate the differentiated speeds of social transformations so as to escape the linear and teleological ways in which the different avatars of historicism and the ideology of progress inevitably grasp them, and we should definitely leave behind the hackneyed problematics of causality and intentionality. The categories of the social sciences of the political are still finding it difficult to understand how societies are unfinished and the structures and practices that underlie them are incomplete, the coexistence within them of a plurality of space-times, the ambiguity of relations of domination and the synergy between coercion and hegemony. But a society draws its strength from its dispersal, its discontinuity, its heterogeneity and its blind spots rather than from its consistency. This is the subject matter of *wirkliche Historie* when it pays attention not to the "origin" (*Ursprung*) but to the "descent" (*Herkunft*) and "emergence" (*Entstehung*) of things, the polar opposite of any preoccupation with identity:

> The purpose of history, guided by genealogy, is not to discover the roots of our identity, but to commit itself to its dissipation. It does not seek to define our unique threshold of emergence, the homeland to which metaphysicians promise a return; it seeks to make visible all of those discontinuities that cross us. [...] If genealogy in its own turn gives right to questions concerning our native land, native language, or the laws that govern us, its intention is to reveal the heterogeneous systems that, masked by the self, inhibit the formation of any form of identity.[43]

Thus, the monadology of political science needs to be replaced by a "nomadology"[44] of the political that no longer argues in the strategic terms of methodological individualism, or the holistic terms of cultural-ism, or the identitarian terms of the political problematics of native exis-tence (*autochtonie*), or the binary terms of class struggle, but rather in those of "multiplicity" of "assemblages" and "dispositifs"[45] that produce the historicity of rhizome-states.

If we are to do this, Foucault, 30 years after his death, can still provide us with valuable help, over and above any effect of reverence and any theoretical fetishism, and in spite of the irritation that his academic beati-fication in a certain tradition of the study of "cultural areas" may arouse, especially when this is postmodern in temper. Not that he is any greater than, or all that different from, the other leading lights of the histori-cal and comparative sociology of the political. We should learn from him precisely because he is in many ways close to them, encourages us to read them anew (even when he himself rarely quotes them), and painstakingly questions and refines their findings.

*Translated by Andrew Brown*

## NOTES

1. Jean-François Bayart, "Foucault au Congo," in *Penser avec Michel Foucault. Théorie critique et pratiques politiques,* ed. Marie-Christine Granjon, (Paris: Karthala, 2005), pp. 183–222; Jean-François Bayart, *Global Subjects: A Political Critique of Globalization*, transl. Andrew Brown (Cambridge: Polity, 2007).
2. Jean-François Bayart, "Comparer en France: petit essai d'autobiographie disciplinaire," *Politix*, 21(83) (2008): 201–228.
3. Paul Veyne writes that Foucault's idea of Weber was "incorrect" and that Foucault had failed to see that Weber was "just as nominalist as he himself was." Paul Veyne, *Foucault: His Thought, his Character* (Cambridge: Polity, 2010), p. 35.
4. Michel Foucault, "Questions of Method," in G. Burchel, C. Gordon and P. Miller (eds.), *The Foucault Effect: Studies in Governmentality* (London: Harvester Wheatsheaf, 1991 (1981)), p. 76.
5. Max Weber, *The Protestant Ethic and the Spirit of Capitalism* (Chicago and London: Fitzroy Dearborn, 2001), p. 77.
6. See the commentary by Béatrice Hibou, "De l'intérêt de lire *La Domination* de Max Weber aujourd'hui," *Liens socio* (2014). Available at http://lec-tures.revues.org/14098 (verified October 6, 2015). Paul Veyne compares the "discourse" of Foucault to the "ideal type" of Weber. See Veyne,

*Foucault: His Thought, his Character*, pp. 34–35. And it is permissible to see in Weber's notion an "individualization operator" in Paul Veyne's sense. On all these points, see Weber, Max, *The Protestant ethic and the spirit of capitalism.*

7. Weber, *The Protestant Ethic and the Spirit of Capitalism*, p. 156.

8. Ibid., p. 156 – Weber's emphasis.

9. Foucault Michel, "Technologies of the self," in Martin H. Luther, Huck Gutman et Patrick H. Hutton (eds.), *Technologies of the Self. A Seminar with Michel Foucault* (Amherst: the University of Massachusetts Press, 1988), pp. 16–49. See Weber, Ibid., pp. 176–79, 223–26 and 269–71.

10. Ibid., pp. 325–26 n. 29.

11. Béatrice Hibou, *The Force of Obedience: The Political Economy of Repression in Tunisia* (Cambridge: Polity, 2011); *The Bureaucratization of the World in the Neoliberal Era: An International and Comparative Perspective* (New York: Palgrave Macmillan, The Sciences Po Series in International Relations and Political Economy, 2015); and *Anatomie politique de la domination* (Paris: La Découverte, 2015).

12. Jean-François Bayart, *Global Subjects*, pp. 126–30.

13. Jean-François Bayart, *The Illusion of Cultural Identity* (London: Hurst, Chicago: The University of Chicago Press, 2005); "Foucault au Congo," in Marie-Christine Granjon (ed.), *Penser avec Michel Foucault. Théorie critique et pratiques politiques,* (Paris: Karthala, 2005b), pp. 183–222; *Global Subjects: A Political Critique of Globalization*, 2007, and *The State in Africa: The Politics of the Belly*, 2nd ed. (Cambridge; Malden, MA: Polity, 2009).

14. Jean-François Bayart, Achille Mbembe, and Comi Toulabor, *Le Politique par le bas en Afrique noire. Contributions à une problématique de la démocratie* (Paris: Karthala, 1992); "L'énonciation du politique," *Revue française de science politique* 35 no. 3 (1985): 343–373.

15. Jean-François Bayart, *Les Etudes postcoloniales, un carnaval académique* (Paris: Karthala, 2010); Jean-François Bayart and Romain Bertrand, "De quel 'legs colonial' parle-t-on?" *Esprit*, December (2006): 134–160. For an authentic foucauldian reading of a colonial situation, see Bertrand, Romain, *Etat colonial, noblesse et nationalisme à Java. La Tradition parfaite* (Paris: Karthala, 2005); Romain Betrand, "Penser le Java mystique de l'âge moderne avec Foucault: peut-on écrire une histoire 'non intentionnaliste' du politique?", *Sociétés politiques comparées* 2, February (2008a); and "Habermas au Bengale, ou comment 'provincialiser l'Europe' avec Dipesh Chakrabarty," Université de Lausanne: *Political Science Working Paper Series*, no. 24 (2008b).

16. Yves Chevrier, "L'empire distendu: esquisse du politique en Chine des Qing à Deng Xiaoping," in *La Greffe de l'Etat. Les Trajectoires du politique,* ed. Jean-François Bayart (Paris: Karthala, 1996), pp. 263–395; Jean-Louis Rocca, *La Condition chinoise. La mise au travail capitaliste à l'âge des*

*réformes (1978–2004)* (Paris: Karthala, 2006); Séverine Arsène, *Internet et politique en Chine* (Paris: Karthala, 2011); Françoise Mengin, *Fragments of an Unfinished War: Taiwanese Entrepreneurs and the Partition of China* (London: C. Hurst and Co. and New York: Oxford University Press, 2015).

17. Hibou, *The Force of Obedience.*
18. Fariba Adelkhah, *Being Modern in Iran* (London: Hurst & Co, 1999).
19. See the excellent account in Olivier Roy, "'L'énigme du soulèvement.' Foucault et l'Iran," *Vacarmes*, 29 (2004).
20. See also Jean-François Bayart, "Around *Political Spiritualities: The Pentecostal Revolution in Nigeria*, by Ruth Marshall," *Religion and Society*, 2 (2011): 145–150 and, for a very foucauldian analysis, in terms of civic subjectivation, of a trend in the Murid confraternity in Senegal, Audrain, Xavier, *Des 'punks de Dieu' aux 'taalibe-citoyens'. Jeunesse, citoyenneté et mobilisation religieuse au Sénégal. Le mouvement mouride de Cheikh Modou Kara (1980–2007)*, Paris: Université de Paris 1 Panthéon Sorbonne, 2013.
21. Jean-François Bayart, "Another look at the Arab Springs," *Sociétés politiques comparées*, 35 (2013): 1–34.
22. Jean-François Bayart, "Hors de la 'vallée heureuse' de l'africanisme. Note bibliographique," *Revue française de science politique* 44 no. 1 (1994): 136–139.
23. Jean-François Bayart, "Comparing from bellow," english version of "Comparer en France: petit essai d'autobiographie disciplinaire," *Politix*, 21, no. 83 (2008): 201–228 available at: http://www.fasopo.org/sites/default/files/papier1_eng_n1.pdf
24. Michel Foucault, "Nietzsche, genealogy, history," in *Essential Works of Michel Foucault*, ed. James Faubion, vol. 2 *Aesthetics* (London: Penguin, 1998), pp. 369–391.
25. This is why I feel it is preferable to talk in terms of national-liberalism, rather than neo-liberalism. See *Sortir du national-libéralisme. Croquis politiques des années 2004–2012* (Paris: Karthala, 2012). See also *Global Subjects: A Political Critique of Globalization.*
26. Michael Hardt and Toni Negri, *Empire* (Cambridge, Mass. and London: Harvard University Press, 2000).
27. Gilles Deleuze, *Negotiations, 1972–1990* (New York and Chichester: Columbia University Press, 1995), p. 98.
28. Deleuze, *Negotiations*, p. 144.
29. Gilles Deleuze and Félix Guattari, *A Thousand Plateaus: Capitalism and Schizophreni* (London: Athlone, 1987), pp. 212–228, especially 221; Gilles Deleuze and Claire Parnet, *Dialogues* (New York: Columbia University Press, 1987), p. 124ff.
30. Deleuze and Parnet, *Dialogues*, pp. 212–28, especially 217; Deleuze and Guattari. *A Thousand Plateaus*, p. 100. Remember that *Alltagsgeschichte*

also insists, in a different vocabulary, on the "multidimensional experiences" (*Mehrschichtigkeiten*) of actors and on the "interaction" (*Vermittlung*) and "overlapping" or "imbrication" (*Gemengelagen*) of the latter. See Alf Lüdtke, *Des ouvriers dans l'Allemagne du XXe siècle. Le quotidien des dictatures* (Paris: L'Harmattan, 2000), pp. 68ff.

31. Deleuze, and Guattari. *A Thousand Plateaus*, pp. 293–4.

32. Ibid., p. 558.

33. Gilles Deleuze, "Immanence: A life" in Jean Khalfa, ed., *An Introduction to the Philosophy of Gilles Deleuze* (London: Continuum, 2002), p. 170 ; Deleuze and Guattari, *What is philosophy?* (London: Verso, 1994), chapter 2.

34. Jean-François Bayart, *Le Plan cul. Ethnologie d'une pratique sexuelle* (Paris: Fayard, 2014).

35. Gilles Deleuze, "*Difference and repetition* (London: Bloomsbury Academic, 2014).

36. Bayart, *Global Subjects: A Political Critique of Globalization.*

37. Thomas Fouquet, *Filles de la nuit, aventurières de la cité. Arts de la citadinité et désirs de l'Ailleurs à Dakar* (Paris: Ecole des hautes études en sciences sociales, 2011).

38. Jean-François Bayart, *The state in Africa: The Politics of the Belly*, 2nd ed. (Cambridge; Malden, MA: Polity, 2009).

39. Gilles Deleuze, *Bergsonism* (New York: Zone, 1988).

40. "The plane of consistency or of immanence, the body without organs, includes voids and deserts. But these are 'fully' part of desire, far from accentuating some kind of lack in it" (Deleuze and Parnet, *Dialogues*, p. 90). And, "the voids which form part of the plane, as a silence forms part of a plane of sound [*plan sonore*], without it being possible to say 'something is missing'" (ibid., p. 94). See also Michel Foucault, *Subjectivité et vérité. Cours au Collège de France. 1980–1981* (Paris: Seuil, Gallimard, 2014), p. 247.

41. Fouquet, *Filles de la nuit, aventurières de la cité.*

42. Walter Benjamin, *Ecrits français* (Paris: Gallimard, 2003), p. 447 and pp. 452–55. See also Walter Benjamin (ed.), *Illuminations* (London: Fontana, 1973: 253–64); and Michel Foucault, *Archaeology of Knowledge* (London and New York: Routledge, 2002), p. 14.

43. Michel Foucault, "Nietzsche, genealogy, history," in *Essential Works of Michel Foucault*, ed. James Faubion, vol. 2 *Aesthetics* (London: Penguin, 1998), pp. 386–87.

44. Gilles Deleuze, *The Fold: Leibniz and the Baroque* (Minneapolis: University of Minnesota Press, 1993); Deleuze, Gilles and Félix Guattari. *A Thousand Plateaus*, p. 21.

45. Gilles Deleuze, "What is a Dispositif?" In *Michel Foucault Philosopher*, edited and translated by Timothy J. Armstrong, (Hemel Hempstead: Harvester Wheatsheaf, 1992), pp. 159–168.

# PART IV

# (Neo-)liberal?

# CHAPTER 11

# On Liberalism: Limits, the Market and the Subject

## Frédéric Gros

Between January and early April 1979, Foucault delivered a course entitled *The Birth of Biopolitics* at the Collège de France. Michel Senellart provided an accurate, rigorously annotated transcription for its publication in French in 2004 and in English in 2008.[1] The course is part of a set covering 13 years of packed, creative teaching at the Collège de France from 1971 to 1984. Yet the lecture delivered in 1979 contains a number of features that distinguish it from the rest. On the one hand, it is the only one that refers directly and at length not only to historical sequences from the twentieth century, but also to burning issues of the day, since the "liberal" policy of President Valéry Giscard d'Estaing and his Prime Minister Raymond Barre are evoked, as well as the 1974 Stoffaës report on "negative tax." Such an explicit, structured incursion into the immediate present is unique in the history of Foucault's lectures at the Collège de France. On the other hand, a certain discrepancy must be highlighted between course title (*The Birth of Biopolitics*) and content, as signaled by Michael Dillon among others.[2] Indeed, Foucault states that he "thought [he] could do a course on biopolitics this year,"[3] in the sense that he wanted to show how

F. Gros (✉)
Sciences Po, Paris, France
e-mail: fredu@club-internet.fr

© The Author(s) 2017
P. Bonditti et al. (eds.), *Foucault and the Modern International*,
The Sciences Po Series in International Relations and Political
Economy, DOI 10.1057/978-1-137-56153-4_11

191

a new style of government was articulated with an equally original object: population.[4] However, biopolitics did not figure in it, and it dealt with liberalism in its classical and more contemporary versions. The two problems are certainly linked and Foucault himself remarks that what he calls liberal governmentality ultimately represents something like the "general regime" on the basis of which the biopolitics of populations makes sense and takes shape.[5]

Publication of the course occasioned some very intense debates in France and elsewhere, which soon assumed a caricatural form, in the media at any rate: did Foucault venture a severe critique or a captivated praise of neo-liberalism in 1979?[6] For us the point is not to intervene in this debate, which, when cast in these terms at least, is skewed from the outset. On the one hand, Foucault's course is situated in a historical and descriptive perspective that short-circuits any value judgments. Expressing an ideological choice for or against liberalism never arises. But we would be ill-advised to think that Foucault displays and defends an easy, rather a cowardly, neutrality throughout his lectures.

It must be acknowledged that liberalism is at one and the same time regarded as a tool critical of government "excesses," as a call for the state to withdraw,[7] and as a system of government involving the constant control of individuals and uncircumscribed legal interventionism in social relations.[8] Above all, however, the debate over Foucault's "(neo-) liberal temptation" is slanted by the fact that, while perceived by all as extremely fresh, the course was delivered half a century ago and in the interval the meaning of "neo-liberalism" has changed profoundly. Foucault gave his lectures before the arrival in power of Margaret Thatcher in Britain and Ronald Reagan in the United States, and prior to the implementation of the Washington Consensus, which imposed nonsensical budgetary austerity on many "developing" countries. To put it in a nutshell, when Foucault referred to neo-liberalism, he was not thinking directly of the dismantling of public services, challenges to social gains, the introduction of "corporate governance" into the management of public services—what would today be called the new public management—to economic relocation, or to the pressure of financial markets on state policy. Even so, in his analyses of a "new" German and American liberalism, he clearly describes secular fault lines whose identification is highly illuminating today, because it makes it possible for us, taking the long view, to get a better grasp of our differences vis-à-vis the late 1970s, when Foucault gave his lecture.

My intention here is therefore not to resolve the debate about whether Foucault was attracted by the critical virtues of neo-liberalism or whether, as early as 1979, he offered a theoretically grounded condemnation of it. Instead, I would like to fix upon some of the principal concepts employed by him as vectors of identity for what he calls "liberal governmentality," as well as for their neo-liberal reconfiguration in our immediate present.

Roughly speaking, the structure of the course is as follows: initial definitions of liberalism in January; a characterization of "German" neo-liberalism in February and of "American" neo-liberalism in March; return to proto-liberalism in the last two sessions. However, this description is superficial, for it is in and through precise conceptualizations that differentiated styles of governmentality and liberalism are defined. In this course, then, "governmentality" is the most generic concept. Foucault generally defines it as a technique for conducting the conduct of human beings (see Bigo and Walters in this volume). Here it assumes the more specific sense of a technique, practiced by a sovereign power, for informing the conduct of its subjects and managing its objects.[9] Liberal governmentality in the late eighteenth century was defined on the basis of three main conceptual expressions: the proposition of an "internal limitation" to governmentalities;[10] the formation of the market as an instance of "veridiction";[11] and the invention of new modalities of subjectivation.[12] Once I will have clarified these three notions, I shall show how neo-liberalism proposes transformed versions of them.

Foucault initially seeks to characterize liberalism by differentiating it (either through rupture or simple inflection) from raison d'état. By the latter is meant a governmentality that endeavors to intensify the state, which creates more and more of it, exhausts itself enhancing its power (natural resources, population, material forces, etc.). This "classical" governmentality, whose most emblematic representative is doubtless Richelieu, encountered a so-called external principle of limitation that arrests political action. It takes the form, for example, of a number of "fundamental laws" of divine, natural, cosmic essence, or of "imprescriptible rights" attached to individuals, that represent *external* impediments to a state power whose extension partakes of a logic of perpetual, constant, infinite reinforcement.[13] Such limitations were also bound up with the system of sovereign states as developed in the modern age and in so far as it operated as a historical, contingent system of limits within which each of its constitutive units (modern territorial states) operated as a limit on the others.[14]

For Foucault, liberal governmentality, by contrast, will be characterized by the introduction of principles of "an *internal* limitation of governmental rationality."[15] This entails the sovereign power declining to intervene in certain specific areas of reality, without this renunciation being attributable to it encountering external stumbling blocks: it is the result of a deliberate abandonment. Infringement of an external limitation by a state power was an *illegitimate transgression*. Infringement of an internal limitation represents a *counter-productive error*. The "internal" character of the limitation derives from the fact that what is at issue is allowing the unfolding of immanent natural entities in accordance with their own dynamic truth, rather than in conformity with some transcendent external order. If Foucault makes liberal government a governmentality that operates via systematic reference to "truth" and "nature," such truth is obviously not that of revealed dogma; and the naturalness is not that of Creation. Liberalism builds on the spontaneity of processes in the face of which any state voluntarism proves at once pointless and harmful. The putative spontaneity of certain processes, such as the process of exchange, means that they are constituted as surfaces of objectivity (re-codifiable in true discourses) and networks of necessities (which grounds their naturalness). Once a number of domains of reality (of which the market is the paradigmatic example) are established as a "process," specifically liberal governmentality is one which, in and through an internal critique, obliges itself not to intervene unduly. The transition from a governmentality of raison d'état to a liberal governmentality is therefore one from prestige of the law as an expression of the sovereign will (the major question then being: upon what right is a political decision founded?) to recognition of immanent truth as the compass of any political decision (the major question then being: is the decision effective?).

   In the secular history of governmentalities, liberalism therefore represents for Foucault the moment when the reference point for assessing the "good" conduct of the sovereign is no longer to be sought in an analysis of the Prince's virtues (politico-pastoral governmentality), or in an estimate of the means employed to augment the power of the state (governmentality of raison d'état), but in a critical assessment of the manner in which immanent processes are allowed to unfold properly, in accordance with their own truth. Following the reign of spiritual counselors and great strategic guides, liberalism promoted that of experts on naturalness.[16] After the scandal of the vices of the corrupt monarch, or of abuses of power by an authoritarian state, liberalism introduces the scandal of incompetence.[17] Liberal recognition of a process as a principle of self-limitation also operates internationally:[18] the liberal promise is one of a possible regulation once the old Westphalian system of the mutual exteriority of states, defending incompatible interests, fades before the self-evident fact of the identity of Nations, recognizing one another as partners in a single market whose (putative) dynamic is one of collective enrichment. This enrichment, however, can only come from the conquest of markets *external* to Europe: the imperialism of conquest and exploitation is found at the heart of liberal logic[19] (see Esteves and Fernández in this volume). At bottom, this liberal practice merges with a third major idea of Europe. Foucault's intuitions here can in fact be extended to indicate the three European projects, the three historical modalities in which Europe has been conceived as a unit. A mystical unit in a shared faith in the Middle Ages: for the last Emperor to reign, ushering in a thousand years of happiness and plenty, millenarian hopes require the disappearance of borders and the advent of a unified Christian republic. A political unit in the seventeenth and eighteenth centuries: sovereign states are ultimately sustained by means of constant adversity and an endless search for an equilibrium that has always to be recreated. Finally, a commercial unit: liberalism succeeds political realism, proposing to transform Europe into a single market that will regulate the relations between peoples in accord with a genuine harmony of interests, gradually bringing about the disappearance of national rivalries.

At bottom, whether externally or internally, it is by taking the "market" into account that liberalism ventures a form of governmentality qua the art of governing less—the replacement of the model of the law imposed on wills vertically by a model of immanent regulation reconfiguring interests horizontally. The market is at the heart of liberal governmentality, both as a mandatory interpretative framework and as a privileged content. Foucault formulates an important thesis, which nevertheless retains an esoteric aspect in his formulation. It consists in stating that the market is advanced by liberalism as an instance of "veridiction," of the "formation of truth."[20] The idea is at once simple and fundamental. It involves saying that, as long as an absence of monopoly and transparency of information prevail, the price which emerges exclusively from the operation of supply and demand in an economic space of exchange is a true price, a "natural price"[21] corresponding to the real value of the goods exchanged. The truth of prices therefore emerges from a deregulated market, a truth ideally benefiting everyone, ideally contributing to general prosperity. We are aware that this theme of "market efficiency" is a very powerful neo-liberal dogma today, facilitating an ideological synthesis between truth (understood as objective necessity) and justice (construed as optimal situation).

Prices are true if they are determined by the logic of a transparent market. They are just *because they are true* (the governmentality of raison d'état argued from the converse deduction: *it is true because it is just*). Our age is marked—one might also say fissured or torn—by this opposition between a dogmatic justice of markets and a de facto social injustice, which can only figure in liberal discourse as derivative, inessential, temporary, with the dogma of market efficiency roughly playing the role of divine Providence, whose ways are inscrutable, and which cannot be challenged.

The point of emergence and the origin of this formation of the market as the site of veridiction are easily situated. It is the late eighteenth century, when the state fixed corn prices in authoritarian fashion and prohibited corn imports, and food shortages and famines occurred. If there is a shortage, claimed the economists, it is because excessive regulation is jamming the mechanisms that would allow supply to coincide harmoniously with demand. It is the state's authoritarian price-fixing that distorts determination of the true price of corn.[22] It should be added that the logic of the market as an instance of veridiction has since been extended to other types of goods, traditionally regarded as having to be fixed by a political will—for example, health, justice, security, education. These are so many "common goods" or "public services" that come under new kinds of so-called governance, that work by objectives and are applied indifferently to individuals, firms, the state or a group of states.[23] It is therefore proposed to make hospitals compete to create a "genuine" health service or to make universities compete to obtain "genuine" research; and users of public services are regarded as "customers." The extension of the market sphere to realities other than "produced" goods is at the heart of the liberal project (see Hibou in this volume).

Foucault's reflections make it possible to denounce this commodification of the world and individuals in a way that differs from the Marxist manner of doing so, on the basis of a dialectic of labor and as a process of reification. It is a determinate governmental practice which, for all that it is self-limiting and rejects any *dirigisme*, makes the market the instance where the value of things and human beings is *verified*.

A second major thesis concerns subjectivity—what liberalism presupposes by way of subjective modality. Foucault centers his analysis on the ultimately highly ambiguous notion of "subject of interest."[24] Liberalism believes that the individuals making up society must be regarded and treated less as citizens than as subjects of interests. A type of governmentality is deduced that is obviously distinct from a republican governmentality requiring everyone to sacrifice themselves for the common good, or a politico-pastoral governmentality requiring everyone to submit to their Prince in that recognition of the sovereign's authority is conducive to their salvation. Liberalism believes that political subjects are not dependent either on a sovereign, general will or on a transcendent, redemptive order. Subjects calculate their immanent interests and behave by guiding themselves toward their own preferences.

These things are well-known, but Foucault makes an important point that represents something like the structural ambivalence of liberal governmentality. In fact, we can basically venture two theses. First, we can say: the subject of interest is the subject of irreducible, non-transferable preferences.[25] However, it is not a question of denouncing moral egotism, but of registering the fact that every subject actually and inevitably pursues his or her own interests, and that it is therefore pointless and counter-productive for government to seek to impose external political will on them (even if allegedly in the public interest). On the contrary, it must limit itself in its pretensions and ultimately simply assume the role of arbiter in the conflict of interests, thus confining itself to the function of *Rechtsstaat* (Etat de droit). Unlike in the republican model, however, it cannot claim to inform the will of its subjects, because the composition of a general interest cannot as such be aimed at by a political will—even if it is generated spontaneously—because the process is too opaque and we shall remain utterly blind to it (reinterpretation of Smith's invisible hand in terms of blindness).[26] But it can also be said that the subject of interest rationally calculates his or her preferences as so many profits, and such calculability of interests is precisely what a form of governmentality can rely on to incentivize, encourage, induce one form of behavior rather than another. After all, if the liberal subject is a subject of calculation, who adapts interests to reality, who chooses in accordance with what seems most profitable, it suffices to modify the environment in such a way as to stimulate one desire, to prompt one choice, rather than another.[27] The whole problem, obviously, is whether what is meant by "interest" is an irreducible, ultimately irrational preference or a calculable profit. Hence the fact that an ambiguity unquestionably runs through the 1979 course, attaching to this notion of interest, which is liberalism's identity card: liberal governmentality is successively (but never dialectically) presented in terms of either intrusion and total control or restraint and self-limitation.

On the basis of this initial conceptual elaboration, neo-liberalism in Foucault's work is to be understood as a decisive inflection of the concept of market with German neo-liberalism and of the modality of subjectivation with American neo-liberalism. As regards German neo-liberalism, the most striking thesis revolves around the idea that the environment of economic competition (the market is perceived from the angle of competition as opposed to exchange) is not a spontaneous natural entity, but an artificial order of reality, which is ultimately fragile and unstable unless constantly supported politically (on the concept of environment, see Taylan in this volume). This neo-liberalism is therefore intent on countering a certain naivety about the postulate of a market as a site of veridiction, which consists in regarding market deregulation as reversion to its natural state: abolish artificial fetters, arbitrary impediments and you will set in motion profound mechanisms of spontaneous self-regulation! For Foucault the peculiarity of German ordo-liberalism is that it appreciates that a useful, efficient space of economic competition, where prices can express their truth, is an artificial environment that needs to be maintained by rules and vigilance; it is a game that depends on introducing rules, a game that benefits all players provided continuous pressure is exerted to avoid the creation of monopolies or to control the undesirable social effects (impoverishment, unemployment, etc.) of overly fierce competition. The problem West Germany faced in the immediate post-war period was roughly as follows: to hit upon a principle of legitimacy and agreement, of consensus, for the new state, which did not have any political content, which did involve adherence to a *national* idea, to a desire for the union of the German people, for that was how Nazism had made itself the master of Germany's fate with horrific consequences. Ordo-liberalism thus proposed establishing a consensus based on support for, and adherence to the market. We witness something very strange and paradoxical around this neo-liberalism: the state is the political instance that simply establishes, protects, demarcates, arbitrates a space of economic competition void of any public content, which at the same time makes it possible to save us from the monstrosity of the political.[28] A complex arrangement, then, and a paradoxical one, because it involves saying simultaneously "the state is what saves us from politics by maintaining a competitive market" and "individuals' consumption, investments and their participation in the market will count as direct support for the state and, ultimately, as legitimation of the latter." Neo-liberalism therefore brings state and market into a relationship of dialectical neutralization/foundation, far removed from classical liberalism, where the market featured as the natural phenomenon [*plage de naturalité*] that imposed restraints on governmentality. With American neo-liberalism, a redefinition of subjectivity is at work in the works of the theoreticians of human capital (Thomas Schultz, Gary Becker, and others; see Paltrinieri in this volume). It is a question not so much of the market in itself as of the calculations that bring it into being in a subject—one might even say the ethical conditions of its development. The concept of human capital makes it possible to examine the neo-liberal construction of the relationship to oneself. The calculation (cost of investment divided by profits) partakes of the rationality of the entrepreneur, who projects it onto his enterprise. The enterprise becomes a mode of intelligibility that can be endlessly extended to human relationships (friendship, marriage, etc., are so many investment calculations) or to public action.[29] Everyone is therefore enjoined to become an "entrepreneur of himself,"[30] the manager of his or her existence; and the state must learn to re-model its public policy (Foucault takes the example of penal policy)[31] through the filter of economic calculation, and replace investigation of the justice of its action by investigation of its profitability.

In his 1979 course, Foucault's problem was therefore not deciding his own relationship to liberalism, but describing the way in which what he called liberal and neo-liberal governmentality effects a break with older governmentalities (pastorate and raison d'état), and introducing the concept of an "internal limitation" of the market as "instance of veridiction," and proposing modalities of subjectivation irreducible to the classical political subject.

I would like to conclude with a theme—one should even say a stress—that has been little noticed in the numerous readings of this course: the idea of "political life." After all, is politics not also that—a set of public debates about too much or too little government, bad government or good government? On at least two occasions, in the first lecture and in his "Course Summary," Foucault underscored what a certain idea of politics as critical debate owes to liberalism. Here we may offer two quotations in full: "political economy[32] (...) establishes, in its most important features, not of course the reign of truth in politics, but the particular regime of truth which is a characteristic feature of what could be called the age of politics";[33] "The question of liberalism, understood as a question of 'too much government,' has been one of the constant dimensions of that European phenomenon which seems to have emerged first of all in England, namely: 'political life.' It is even one of its constituent elements, if it is true that political life exists when the possible excess of governmental practice is limited by the fact that it is the object of public debate regarding its 'good or bad,' its 'too much or too little.'"[34]

The aim here is not to say that Foucault declared his support to liberalism, but that he affirmed his loyalty to an issue (one might say a suspicion) formulated by early liberalism[35]—that of "governing too much"—in so far as it can always be divided into the question of "why should it be necessary to govern?" Liberalism, by installing civil society and the state in a fractious relationship of exteriority, reverses the traditional front of political thought, since it starts out not from the issue of the state, in order to establish its *right* to govern subjects, but from society in as much as it questions the very *fact* of being governed.

*Translated by Gregory Elliott*

## NOTES

1. Michel Foucault, *Naissance de la biopolitique. Cours au Collège de France, 1978–79*, ed. Michel Senellart (Paris: Hautes Etudes/Gallimard & Seuil, 2004); *The Birth of Biopolitics: Lectures at the Collège de France 1978–79*, transl. Graham Burchell (Basingstoke and New York: Palgrave Macmillan, 2008).
2. Michael Dillon, "Gouvernement, économie et biopolique," *Cultures & Conflits*, no. 78 (2010): 11–37.
3. Foucault, *The Birth of Biopolitics*, p. 21.
4. Foucault, *The Birth of Biopolitics*, p. 21.
5. Foucault, *The Birth of Biopolitics*, p. 22.
6. See, for example, the books by Christian Laval and Pierre Dardot, *The New Way of the World: On Neoliberal Society*, transl. Gregory Elliott (London and New York Verso, 2014) and, conversely, Geoffroy de Lagnaserie, *La dernière leçon de Michel Foucault sur le néolibéralisme, la théorie et la politique* (Paris: Fayard, 2012). For a precise re-contextualization, Serge Audier's *Penser le néolibéralisme. Le moment néolibéral* (Bordeaux: Le Bord de l'eau, 2015) may be read with profit.
7. For example, Foucault, *The Birth of Biopolitics*, pp. 20–21.
8. Foucault, *The Birth of Biopolitics*, pp. 66–7, 178–9.
9. Foucault, *The Birth of Biopolitics*, p. 2.
10. Foucault, *The Birth of Biopolitics*, p. 10.
11. Foucault, *The Birth of Biopolitics*, p. 32.
12. The term itself does not figure, but the lectures of 14 and 28 March are precisely concerned with describing styles of subjectivity bound up with liberal governmentality.
13. Foucault, *The Birth of Biopolitics*, pp. 8–10.
14. Readers are referred to the works of R.B.J. Walker—in particular, *Inside/Outside: International Relations as Political Theory* (Cambridge: Cambridge University Press, 1993) and *After the Globe, Before the World* (London and New York: Routledge, 2010). See also his contribution to this volume.

15. Foucault, *The Birth of Biopolitics*, p. 10; my emphasis.
16. Foucault, *The Birth of Biopolitics*, pp. 17–18.
17. Foucault, *The Birth of Biopolitics*, p. 16.
18. See the entire course of 24 January.
19. This important point only occurs in the manuscript: *The Birth of Biopolitics*, p. 21.
20. Foucault, *The Birth of Biopolitics*, pp. 30–34.
21. Foucault, *The Birth of Biopolitics*, p. 32.
22. This analysis was conducted in a course from the previous year, on 18 January 1978 (*Security, Territory, Population: Lectures at the Collège de France 1977–78*, ed. Michel Senellart and transl. Graham Burchell (New York and London: Palgrave Macmillan, 2007), pp. 29–54. In the sphere of consumer goods, this schema remains credible. But the truth generated by a deregulated market becomes hallucinatory when it comes to speculative goods or goods liable to give rise to speculation.
23. See Alain Supiot, *La Gouvernance par les nombres. Cours au Collège de France (2012–2014)*, (Paris: Fayard, 2015), pp. 215–44.
24. See the lecture of 28 March, in *The Birth of Biopolitics*, pp. 267–89; and see *The Birth of Biopolitics*, p. 46 for the theme of the "phenomenal republic of interests."
25. Foucault, *The Birth of Biopolitics*, p. 272.
26. Foucault, *The Birth of Biopolitics*, p. 280.
27. Foucault, *The Birth of Biopolitics*, pp. 269–70.
28. Foucault, *The Birth of Biopolitics*, pp. 86–7.
29. Foucault, *The Birth of Biopolitics*, pp. 226–33.
30. Foucault, *The Birth of Biopolitics*, p. 230; and see Dardot and Laval, *The New Way of the World*.
31. Dardot and Laval, *The New Way of the World*, pp. 248–60.
32. It is itself defined as the "form of rationality" of liberal governmentality: Dardot and Laval, *The New Way of the World*, p. 13.
33. Dardot and Laval, *The New Way of the World*, pp. 17–18.
34. Dardot and Laval, *The New Way of the World*, pp. 321–2.
35. To the end, Foucault focuses his analysis on "economic" liberalism. At bottom, "political" liberalism (which he also calls a "revolutionary approach": p. 39) starts out from the state to found liberty and individual rights, whereas liberalism in its more "radical" version starts from society and poses to government the question of its relevance and effectiveness.

# CHAPTER 12

# On Bureaucratic Formalization: The Reality-Like Fiction of Neoliberal Abstractions

## *Béatrice Hibou*

Neoliberalism has been over-analyzed, often—though not exclusively—along the lines of Foucault's analysis in *The Birth of Biopolitics*.[1] My aim in this chapter is not to make additional comments on these debates, rather to shift the glance to a very peculiar feature—both fundamental and under-studied—of the current situation: the bureaucratic dimension of neoliberalism. I have been able to pursue this way by crossing Foucault's analysis of neoliberalism with the work of Weber on bureaucracy, also drawing on Weber's methodological approach. This has enabled me to shed a new light on a particular dimension of neoliberalism which Michel Foucault seems to have slightly neglected in his work: the *specific process of abstraction* every act of formalization implies (be they operated by numbers, categories, procedures, or thinking).

While depicting the neoliberal narrative as the story of bureaucratization, my intention is not to tell a true story, the true story of neoliberalism. Rather, it is a way of interpreting and problematizing our very contemporary situation in which the neoliberal narrative—and its

B. Hibou (✉)
CNRS, CERI/Sciences Po, Paris, France and
CRESC, UM6P, Rabat, Morocco
e-mail: beatrice.hibou@sciencespo.fr

© The Author(s) 2017
P. Bonditti et al. (eds.), *Foucault and the Modern International*,
The Sciences Po Series in International Relations and Political
Economy, DOI 10.1057/978-1-137-56153-4_12

abstractions—transforms the relation to reality, to the world, and to us, and installs its own fiction(s), which play(s) a fundamental role in perpetuating its own criteria and formal procedures as a mode of government.

## WHAT IS NEOLIBERAL BUREAUCRATIZATION?

The growth in the number of norms has long been noticed with, over the past few years, an increasing number of studies that have emphasized the extension and diversification in the use of norms[2] behind a technicization that often conceals the breadth and the spread of the phenomenon.[3] As a result, the ubiquity of rules, norms, and procedures seems to "go without saying." Yet this is precisely what has to be questioned. In my most recent work, both personal and collective, I have come to problematize this situation in terms of a "neoliberal bureaucratization," understood as the spread of bureaucratic practices produced by the market and by managerial "big business" all over, and, so, as formalities becoming abstractions since they are universalized.[4]

A set of normative and procedural arrangements, the bureaucratization I analyze here is diffuse, dispersed, and often elusive. It is not an administrative arrangement, nor is it an institution or an administration, let alone an organizational structure. It is a social form of power, a "social movement"[5] in the sense that it does not lie outside society. Far from it: bureaucratization unfolds across all the actors whom it targets and who, wittingly or not, carry out this process by furthering it or combatting it. As a place in which the political sphere finds utterance, neoliberal bureaucratization is one of the forms of expression of domination in contemporary societies, whose shape is defined by the rise to power of a technical rationality, the increasing ubiquity of market and business norms, the formalization of a government at a distance, and the intensification of a specific kind of operations of abstraction.

This bureaucratic dimension of neoliberalism, even though it may appear paradoxical or indeed shocking from the point of view of neoliberal hegemony, is familiar to specialists in the historical sociology of politics and to readers of the great classics of this discipline. When, in his 1978–1979 Lectures at the Collège de France, Michel Foucault pointed out that "the market (…) was (…) invested with extremely prolific and strict regulations," also stating that government "must produce" freedom, and that the production and management of freedom came to constitute "the conditions for the creation of a formidable body of legislation and an incredible range of governmental interventions to guarantee production of the freedom needed in order to govern"[6]; when he pointed out that an art of governing based on the market cannot be embodied in laissez-faire, but rather in a "framework policy"[7] paving the way for an "active" governmentality necessary to ensure that society as a whole conforms to the principles of enterprise, competition and the market, Michel Foucault was writing within this tradition.

The above-mentioned analysis of the craze for rules and norms now goes back over a century, to when Max Weber showed that, historically speaking, liberalism had created an expansion in the number of economic institutions, and that the development of bureaucracy was closely linked with the development of capitalism. Karl Polanyi furthered this tradition when he pointed out that "there was nothing natural about laissez-faire," and highlighted the way liberalism triggered an unprecedented growth in legislative and administrative measures, precisely so as to facilitate the dismantling of obstacles to the commodification of land, money, and labor.[8] Historians have shown that markets were created by human interventions, especially on the part of the state.[9] I interpret this as a bureaucratic process because, in order for it to be accomplished, rules have had to be invented and procedures put in place.

With all this in mind, the bureaucratic dimension of neoliberalism should seem at least as paradoxical as the expression "neoliberal bureaucratization" might itself sound ironical. The irony comes from the fact that a whole part of neoliberal rhetoric takes wing from a critique of state bureaucracy and of direct government intervention in the economy. One of the key arguments of neoliberals (the well-known slogan "cut the red tape") turns on the necessary and radical limitation of state interventions. As suggested above however, neoliberalism can certainly not be equated with laissez-faire, and has been diversely interpreted as an "intervening liberalism,"[10] a "government at a distance,"[11] an "entrepreneurial government,"[12] a "normative state,"[13] or a "redeployment" of the state via its "privatization."[14] Neoliberalism is the art of governing by compartmentalizing and shaping interventions in accordance with market and managerial norms. From the world of big business, these bureaucratic modalities of government spread all over, within the state especially and in the name of the fight against bureaucracy! A whole series of measures is advocated, from the privatization of public businesses and services to new public management, via the development of various public-private partnerships, the implementation of rules that either favor business and market mechanisms or fit in with the demands of the private sector. The two inseparable aspects of the neoliberal art of governing—namely the critique of state administration and government practices on the one hand, and, on the other, the development of practices designed to foster an interventionism that respects the framework, and conforms to the market and to enterprise—both engender this specific form of bureaucracy.

This paradoxical and ironic dimension of the "bureaucratization thesis" can only be understood if "state administration" is not being confused with "bureaucracy": as Weber analyzed it, bureaucracy also characterizes business and private companies, the market economy as much as organizations that see themselves as being part of civil society.... In fact, anyone who lives, produces, or consumes, anyone who seeks relaxation, education, or health these days, is well aware of one thing: bureaucratic practices, arrangements, or procedures cannot be escaped. For how else are we to describe the ever-increasing demand for paperwork? We need papers to travel, to register at an institution, to cash an insurance policy (including for private insurance). We are increasingly confronted to formal procedures, be it when trying to rent a flat, to access to credit and electricity, to connect to a computer network, to go to law, or for a private business' accounts to be certified, a vegetable to be authenticated as "organic," and even an article to be accepted for publication in an academic journal. We are constantly required to conform to all set of norms and rules.

## BUREAUCRATIZATION AS ABSTRACTION

Its formal and abstract character has always characterized bureaucracy. The process of rationalization, just like the establishment of impersonal rules, is inherent to bureaucracy, and a great part of Weber's analysis focuses on the spirit of impersonality proper to formalism.[15] The argument is well known: formalism alone makes formal equality of treatment possible by enabling us to free ourselves from personal considerations. Laws, rules, norms, and codifications also provide us with the possibility of predicting life and overcoming resistances more easily: this is also why bureaucracy, as a mode of governing human beings, rests largely on such laws and norms. Weber does not use the argument of abstraction as such and yet, what are laws, rules, norms, and codifications, if not the product of operations of abstraction? This interpretation, faithfully couched in the consistent vocabulary and modes of argument deployed by Weber, is not often developed in studies on bureaucracy and bureaucratization which tend to focus on rationalization and formalism only.

The work of Arthur Stinchcombe certainly is an exception in this respect.[16] Stinchcombe reflects on bureaucracy as a set of formalities, tools, and modes of action that are effective so long as certain conditions are respected. His analysis of bureaucratic formalization as the development of an abstraction of burgeoning data shows a process that makes it possible to govern social action without having to go back to the original data. He points out that this development essentially consists in making things easier: when things and behaviors are formalized, there is no need to keep having to go "behind" them, to understand what underlies them, in order to act and to govern. It is this principle of formalization as abstraction that ensures social flexibility, the ability to respond to problems, and ultimately the day to day running of the government. In Stinchcombe's deeply Weberian interpretation, formalities are not the expression or the cause of rigid practices but a "vector of adaptations."

On the other hand, works inspired by the sociology of quantification, by critical sociology, by the theory of conventions and of regulation, or by political philosophy and the philosophy of science have made abstraction and formalization a key aspect of their arguments. In these works, abstraction is understood as a mental representation of real life, and not a reproduction of reality. It is rooted into, and emerges from the details of everyday life, while also being the product of a process of elaboration. The famous words of Alfred North Whitehead, "We think in generalities, but we live in details" are often quoted in this context, by Stinchcombe among others, who transforms it for the purposes of his own argument into "We think in abstraction but live in details"[17] (on abstraction, see Bonditti in this volume). These works take the opposite view to analyses that consider formalities as rituals, as the absence of rationality or even as unambiguous instruments of control and discipline. Instead, Stinchcombe and his peers focus on the modes and meaning of the processes of abstraction.

Laurent Thévenot, for example, speaks about the way a power, of whatever kind, needs to "give form" to the relations it seeks to govern; in his view, "power in forms" and "investment in form" are central features of the social order.[18] In particular, he shows that "formalized information" constitutes "forms of knowledge that can be abstracted from things, persons, and situations," and can thus become general and go into circulation.[19] Luc Boltanski sets out from the—commonplace—perception that reality is constructed, then highlights the original uncertainties on the qualifications and questions of knowledge to suggest that formats, rules, and tests enable us to organize reality.[20] Together, Thévenot and

Boltanski emphasize the tensions that spring from this very process of abstraction, an operation that equates different things and marks a rise in the level of generality.[21] These authors—and the same could be said of Alain Desrosières or Theodore Porter in the sociology of quantification, or François Fourquet in the historical sociology of accountancy— analyze the process whereby information is grasped in terms of coding and abstraction.[22] They show that economic aggregates impose a single form on heterogeneous data and behaviors, making it difficult to know what they are supposedly measuring, and even more tricky to define the macroeconomic phenomena they reflect and link them to economic realities. Following a quite different tradition, they meet Michel de Certeau who suggested that abstraction as a process can only reduce everything: the heterogeneous, the *bricolages*, and the straddling of different repertoires—and not reproduce the multiple.[23]

Yet, however rich and subtle they may be, these studies do not really analyze bureaucracy as such. They are mainly devoted to the analysis of quantification, of management, and of the world of business or of economic production. Here, I propose to combine these works and the different intellectual traditions they rely on, and to read *neoliberal bureaucratization as a process of abstraction aimed at bringing a complex reality within general and formal categories, norms, and rules as they emerge from a way of thinking that rationalizes society and the government of goods, human beings, and territories on the basis of market and managerial big enterprise mechanisms.*[24]

These formalities are abstractions since they are avowedly not reality itself, but an *elaboration*, a *mental representation* of real life. Although stemming from a particular world (the market with its competitional logic, and large-scale industrial and managerial companies), the abstractions I consider in these pages are deemed to be universal and, therefore, to be relevant for life in society as a whole. This way of thinking needs to be further analyzed if we are to understand what is specific to neoliberal bureaucracy and its abstractions.

As abstraction is a way of "knowing things from their destination,"[25] we need to grasp this "destination" if we are to understand the nature of bureaucracy. With this in mind, abstraction needs to be analyzed from the perspective of the processes through which it comes about—how, and under what conditions, it becomes effective. Even more importantly, we need to emphasize the concrete historical problems that the process of abstraction, or the set of abstractions, was meant to solve.[26] This is the (classic) question of "genealogy" if put in foucauldian terms, and of "the social conditions of genesis" if put in weberian.

## NEOLIBERAL BUREAUCRATIZATION: ABSTRACTION AS REALITY ERECTED INTO A SYSTEM

Analyzing *bureaucratization as a process of abstraction* is a necessary step for grasping the specificity of neoliberal bureaucratization. Three overlapping considerations strike me as being of particular importance. The first one lies in the nature of the process of formal elaboration which can merely be understood genealogically: at present, codes, norms, rules, and procedures that govern social life as a whole emerge from a process of abstraction that starts out from the entrepreneurial world, and more specifically from the big management industrial world. There is no need to repeat this, though it is worth remembering what problems these norms are deemed to conceptualize and solve. These are, of course, problems of efficiency and cost-effectiveness, and the quest for a scientific and rational organization of the cheapest mode of production, but also problems of unhampered control as symbolized by the principles of participation, of individual responsibility, and of self-discipline, or by the quest for modes of operation that will make things and human beings manageable in terms of risk, precaution, and prevention.

The second characteristic relates to the spread of these norms, codes, and procedures beyond the business world, and beyond economic affairs and modes of government, to the point where they affect not just the state but society as a whole. The ever-more pervasive processes of formalization and the universalization of the specific type of abstractions these processes are attached to, are quite specific to the current situation. Instead of talking—as Stinchcombe did—of formalities "that work" and those that "do not work," and to escape this kind of utilitarian, functionalist and somehow normative claims, I rely on Foucault's genealogical approach to better grasp and understand (the element of) the unexpected, (of) the contingent and (of) the unpredictable in the life of concepts and abstractions. In the tradition of historical sociology, many in this volume defend (see especially Bayart and Mattelart in this volume), as I do myself, this understanding that abstraction does enable broadening the analysis of the tensions between the logics of profession and bureaucratic logics, and more broadly, of the tensions between the many different logics of life in society and bureaucratic logics.

These tensions are all the greater and more perceptible because abstractions have migrated, have been transposed and extended into contexts and areas that are quite foreign to those that gave them birth. In other words, abstractions need not to be understood as effective representations of reality (as Stinchcombe advocates), but as historically situated social constructions. No concept is an empirical given. A concept is constructed from processes of recording that are, on the one hand, inevitably guided by the process of archiving, rationalizing and categorizing—a process that selects the qualities and kinds of relations—and, on the other hand, bring information to the awareness of the observer via success transmissions that themselves proceed from abstraction. Abstraction thus appears as a tool for knowledge: it is constructed in such a way as to be inevitably guided by some aim, in the service of something.[27]

Norms, rules, figures, the coding of procedures, and the formalization of behaviors—in short, what constitutes neoliberal bureaucratization—must be understood in the same way: as a process of abstraction that guides life in society. What needs to be questioned is not the credibility of these abstractions or their conformity with reality, but their uniqueness, the homogeneity thus constructed and the meaning of this construction. One very concrete example will make this more precise: figures are indices that impoverish reality insofar as they emerge from a process of aggregation (thousands of words, relationships, and languages are translated into a few words and a few categories in a nomenclature) that is simultaneously a certain exercise in reduction. The information "behind" these figures, that has made it possible for them to be constructed, is much richer, more variegated, disparate, and non-homogeneous. In these conditions, using figures and indexes is simultaneously a loss of information and a transformation of the way information is being shaped and highlighted. This does not mean that we cannot manage without these figures and these indexes, but that we need to be aware of what is constructed (regularity, uniqueness, certainty) and what is lost (diversity, plurality, ambiguity, and uncertainty) with the new regime of abstraction that develops: the neoliberal abstraction.[28]

The argument about figures and the categories of national accountancy or macroeconomics needs to be extended to the set of formalities that comprise bureaucratization. The essential thing is not merely to understand the abstractions that norms, rules, codes, and procedure formalities represent through their effectiveness, but rather to grasp how they have emerged and by what processes the abstraction has thus been created, bringing to light the particular kind of conceptualizations that made it possible, therefore the strategies and the interplay of power underlying it. In this respect, the so-called norm of excellence is a perfect example. It took shape in industry around questions of quality/price, and the efficient allocation of resources and evaluation, and now applies to the world of knowledge, of information, and research as much as to that of public health. It has taken concrete shape in the calculation of ratios and indicators, the use of audits and benchmarks,[29] and the definition of strategies in a world made up of competition, but also of alliances and tactical games, and political ambitions driven by the desire for profit. Being ignorant of their genealogy, the worlds of knowledge or public health take these norms—here the norm of excellence—as a guarantee of reform and improvement of the quality of their *own* professional practices thereby forced to change and mutate.[30] My argument here is of course not that we do not need abstractions, concepts, or categories, since there is neither thought, nor concrete practices outside of these forms (see Bonditti in this volume). Rather, it is to affirm the urgent necessity to understand that abstractions are social forms, that have their own history/trajectory, and that while migrating from a domain of practice to another they bring along conceptualizations, strategies, and ways of thinking and problematizing that shape our understanding of situations and practices themselves.

Finally, the third characteristic is proper to neoliberalism only in its intensity, and it stems directly from the previous one. With the transformation of bureaucratic forms—which are thus passed on less by direct intervention and the involvement of institutions and administrations than by the use of norms, rules, and formalities—the hierarchical exercise of authority, and the obligation to comply with orders coming from a certain outside (that are given as if from on high) is, to a great extent, replaced by *incentives*. These are presented as being voluntarily accepted and guide people's behavior all the more easily as these norms, rules, and formalities are abstracted from a conceptualization of reality presented as rational and reasonable. The intensification and spread of government by neoliberal abstraction imply that the meaning of this process of conceptualization is lost and leads us to take abstraction as a self-evident, neutral, and objective representation of reality—in short, as reality itself. Neoliberal abstraction as a mode of government is no longer in the realm of the legislator and of rational, technical government alone. These days, abstraction is also the way in which power is expressed and exercised by regulators and normalizers, by jurists and other actors, all involved in the processes whereby society is made judicial, by economic and financial actors, and by bureaucrats of thought, among so many others.

One emblematic illustration of this movement is definitely provided by the increasing importance of mathematization in knowledge—in scientific knowledge, of course, but also in economic knowledge and even in the social sciences. While theorists point out that theories and hypotheses are never real-istic by nature, it is an established fact that economic and financial mathemati-cal formalization is constantly taken to be a *representation* of reality—enabling the possibility not only to explain but also reproduce and even anticipate the constitutive events of social life. Ratings agencies are especially interesting to analyze in this respect. Such agencies are regularly criticized for their lack of independence, their methods of assessment, as much as for their active role in financial speculation and even their reluctance to grasp, characterize, and describe given economic and financial situations in their very concreteness. Yet this criticism will remain quite ineffective as long as it keeps focusing on the criteria of assessment and the rating grids of these agencies, that are the product of a process of abstraction based on very specific preoccupations, in fact limited to the management of financial risk. The most challenging problem lies elsewhere—less in these criteria than, first in the way an increas-ingly diverse number of actors (businesses, banks, financial actors, as well as governments, collectives of investors, etc.) come to resort to these agencies in an ever-more systematic way; second, in the exaggerated importance given to such ratings and the spread of norms that arise from American financial practices. People gradually forget that these agencies are merely measuring a financial risk at a time $t$, and in a given institutional configuration. The temp-tation exists to take their ratings as the faithful representation of the health of the entity under scrutiny and the image of its real situation.[31] The abstrac-tion (the figure calculated from financial criteria, measured almost exclusively quantitatively in accordance with a pre-existing grid) becomes the reality. It is thought pointless to take into account other factors and other modes of assessment, and the comparison of contradictory information and assessments is viewed as superfluous. This is the intellectual risk of abstraction, as high-lighted by François Fourquet in his remarks on national accountancy: it can always "close down minds."[32] As bureaucratic abstractions, norms, categories, rules, and formal procedures certainly are very useful tools, that also function as codes on which people have agreed at a given moment in order to exchange information, to act, and to guide people's behavior—in short, to govern.

The language of neoliberal formalization (with its endless formalities) proves to be an anti-historical, anti-localized, anti-specific language since, a product of an abstraction with universal pretensions, it actually neglects the radical heterogeneity of the realities it abstracts. It's in this sense that one can speak of neoliberal bureaucratization as a *fiction*.

## FICTION AT THE HEART OF NEOLIBERAL
## BUREAUCRATIZATION

Now, what does that mean to claim, as I do in these pages, that abstraction is taken as reality. This is no innocent "confusion." What does it mean when respect for ISO norm 9001 is taken as a proof of quality, and norm 26,000 as evidence of social responsibility? The notion of fiction enables to move toward a deeper understanding of the implications of this "confusion." Reality cannot be grasped outside categories, concepts, and other principles of ordering the sensible world. As Weber's interpretative sociology suggests, reality is inevitably transcribed and elaborated. This explains why there is no single truth, but merely truths—truths constructed by means of the norms and values proper to the society in which they are uttered.[33] This is also why, as Michel Foucault suggests in his latest Lectures at the Collège de France, *Le gouvernement de soi et des autres*, every discourse that presents itself as a discourse of veridiction (*discours de véridiction*) and transforms its own truth into a norm can be interpreted as a fiction.[34] "Reality" and "rationality" are shaped by social actions and also by this discourse of truth. Neoliberalism must be understood as a "game of veridiction" and analyzed as a particular moment when "singular inventions"[35] emerged. When grasped, the real cannot be represented outside this fiction, insofar as it is a "dimension in which the symbols are elaborated and through which we sum up our inscription in the world."[36] When studies in the social sciences, beginning with Weber, state that what is specific to the modern world, and comprises its reality, is rationality, they are implicitly highlighting the fiction at the heart of these societies. Another way to say this is to underline, with Weber, the work of interpreting, understanding, meaning proper to each specific historical and cultural situation or, with Foucault, the work of elaboration, of transformation that this discourse as practice operates.

Approaching this "confusion"—or, to say it with Gilles Deleuze, this "indiscernibility"—in terms of a fiction does not condemn the analysis to build along the true/false or real/imaginary divisions to which fiction is often associated: it means taking this confusion at face value, as a truth, and giving ourselves a chance to understand what it corresponds to and what effects follow. This narrative and the particular truth it carries appears as a fiction, if fiction is understood not as a pure and simple illusion deprived of historical effects, but as a fabrication that entails important consequences. The fictive dimension of the exercise of power, and of its interpretation, appears fundamental within this frame of analysis. Fiction lies at the intersection of two overlapping traditions. First, the legal tradition, with the figure of the *persona ficta* and the intensive use of "as if."[37] Resorting to legal fictions enables certain facts to be concealed, so as to consolidate a status quo and foster a development (e.g., the superiority of private over public management) and to assert certain truths ("to quantify is a proof of rationality and efficiency"; "there is no alternative"; "the economic consensus is a reality"). This fiction obviously has significant effects on institutions and behavior, as Michel Foucault already pointed out.[38] The second tradition is the literary tradition that Michel Foucault introduced into the social sciences following Roland Barthes and Herbert Marcuse among others (see Shapiro in this volume). Here, fiction belongs properly to subjective experience, the experience you make for yourself, which creates something that did not exist before but exists afterward, which names things.[39] Fiction is the object of which you are "completely master and which no shadow can hide from your gaze." It is "language which is, by definition, distance. It is the aspect of a fable."[40]

In so doing—and because it rests on supports, on perceptions, on the reproduction of prior analyses and understandings, and on rewritings of history—fiction is a crucial aspect of personal and historical experiences.[41] It expresses a reality, a gray zone between the real and the unreal: and only if this zone is taken into account can the position of anyone or anything within society be grasped.[42] The construction of indicators, the definition and implementation of norms, the principle of a close similarity between public and private, are integrated into modes of government, with the result that fiction must be considered as a practice producing a political and social reality, and not as a belief. In this way, bureaucratic fictions do not appear disconnected from the concrete details and the everyday realities of social life, but—like all abstractions—they are embodied in structures, techniques, and concrete practices.

If, as I have argued, neoliberal bureaucratization is one of, even possibly *the* crucial dimension of neoliberalism, then one can understand how this social action constructs the real in a singular manner, based on the fiction that elaborates as universal a very specific, socially and historically situated rationality, that of the market and business, and even more particularly that of management. In other words, like the so-called impoverished person or the jobseeker viewed as a potential entrepreneur, the head of a police department or of a hospital seen as a company boss, or norm 9001 taken as quality, there is a "bureaucratic production of the real,"[43] with specific and particular abstractions (bureaucratic abstractions) made reality. To conceptualize reality through the very process of formalization is a fiction because it "travesties facts" by "declaring them as something different from what they were actually": it reduces or transforms them by forcing them to fit the logic of this bizarre rationality and draws "the consequences of this adulteration" by taking them to be reality.[44] This "detour" makes it possible to bring in new norms that end up governing the facts and thus also govern human beings, with real effects. For this same reason, this fiction needs to be taken seriously, all the more seriously, indeed, as it alone guarantees the coherence of neoliberal bureaucratization: it makes it possible for various different logics to be brought together under the banner of a definite form of rationality. With Weber, we could say that, "irrational elements (are nested with)in the rationalization of reality." The "as if"—one of the expressions of fiction—means we can go beyond the contradictions and inconsistencies between "irrational presuppositions which have been accepted simply as 'given'"[45] and the rationality of formalities comprised in neoliberal bureaucracy.

## Notes

1. Michel Foucault, *The Birth of Biopolitics. Lectures at the Collège de France, 1978–9*, ed. by Michel Senellart; transl. by Graham Burchell (Basingstoke: Palgrave Macmillan, 2008).
2. See especially Laurent Thévenot, "Un gouvernement par les normes" in Bernard Conein, Laurent Thévenot (eds), *Cognition et information en société* (Paris: Editions de l'Ecole des Hautes Etudes en Sciences Sociales, 1997), pp. 204–242; Elizabeth C. Dunn, "Standards and Person-Making in East Central Europe," in Aihwa Ong and Stephen J. Collier (eds.), *Global Assemblages. Technology, Politics and Ethics as Anthropological Problems* (Oxford: Blackwell, 2005), pp. 173–93.
3. Amy Slaton, Janet Abbate, "The Hidden Lives of Standards. Technical Prescriptions and the Transformation of Work in America," in *Technologies of Power*, ed. Michael T. Allen and Gabrielle Hecht (Cambridge, MA: MIT Press, 2001), pp. 95–144; Martha Lampland and Leigh Star (eds.), *Standards and Their Stories. How Quantifying, Classifying and Formalizing Practices Shape Everyday Life* (Ithaca: Cornell University Press, 2008).
4. Béatrice Hibou, *The Bureaucratization of the World in the Neoliberal Era* transl. by Andrew Brown (New York: Palgrave Macmillan, 2015) and Béatrice Hibou (ed), *La Bureaucratisation néolibérale* (Paris : La Découverte, 2013).
5. Jean-François Bayart, "La revanche des sociétés africaines," in *Politique Africaine*, n°11, September 1983, pp. 95–127, and also, by the same

author: "L'énonciation du politique," *Revue Française de Science Politique*, 35(3), 1985, pp. 343–73 and " La Cité bureaucratique en Afrique subsaharienne" in *La Bureaucratisation néolibérale*, ed. Béatrice Hibou (Paris, La Découverte, 2013), pp. 291–313.

6.  Foucault, *The Birth of Biopolitics*, p. 30, p. 63 and pp. 64–65.
7.  Foucault, *The Birth of Biopolitics*, Lecture of 14 February, p. 140.
8.  Karl Polanyi, *The Great Transformation. The political and economic origins of our time* (Boston, Beacon Press, 1957).
9.  Fernand Braudel, *Capitalism and Material Life, 1400–1800*, transl. by Miriam Kochan (London, Weidenfeld and Nicolson, 1973); Pierre Rosanvallon, *Le capitalisme utopique. Histoire de l'idée de marché* (Paris, Le Seuil, 1999 [1979]).
10. Foucault, *The Birth of Biopolitics*, p. 133.
11. Andrew Barry, Thomas Osborne, Nicolas Rose (eds), *Foucault and Political Reason. Liberalism, Neo-Liberalism and Rationalities of Government* (Chicago: The University of Chicago Press, 1996); Nicolas Rose, *Powers of Freedom. Reframing Political Thought* (Cambridge, Cambridge University Press, 1999).
12. Pierre Dardot, Christian Laval, *The New Way of the World: on Neoliberal Society*, transl. by Gregory Elliot (London, Verso, 2014).
13. Dunn, "Standards and person-making in East Central Europe."
14. Béatrice Hibou, "Retrait ou redéploiement de l'État?," *Critique internationale*, n°1, October 1998: 151–68; Béatrice Hibou, "Preface to the English Edition," in *Privatising the State*, transl. by Jonathan Derrick (London: Hurst and New York, Columbia University Press, 2004), pp. vii–xvi.
15. Especially Max Weber, *Economy and Society, An Outline of Interpretive Sociology*, vol. 1 (Berkeley: University of California Press, 1978), pp. 225–6.
16. Arthur L. Stinchcombe, *When Formality Works. Authority and Abstraction in Law and Organizations* (Chicago, University of Chicago Press, 2001).
17. Ibid., p. 184. See also Andrew Barry, *Political Machines. Governing a Technological Society* (London, The Athlone Press, 2001).
18. A recurrent theme in the work of Laurent Thévenot: Laurent Thévenot, "Jugement ordinaire et jugement de droit," *Annales ESC*, 6, 1992, pp. 1279–99; "L'autorité à l'épreuve de la critique. Jusqu'aux oppressions du 'gouvernement par l'objectif'," in *Quel présent pour la critique sociale?*, ed. Bruno Frère (Brussels, Desclée de Brouwer, 2012).
19. Thévenot, "Un gouvernement par les normes," p. 208.
20. Luc Boltanksi, *On Critique. A Sociology of Emancipation*, transl. by Gregory Elliot (Cambridge, Polity Press, 2011).
21. Luc Boltanski and Laurent Thévenot, *On Justification: Economies of Worth*, transl. by Catherine Porter (Princeton, Princeton University Press, 2006).

22. Alain Desrosières, *Politics of Large Numbers: A History of Statistical Reasoning*, transl. by Camille Naish (Cambridge, Harvard University Press, 1998); Theodore Porter, *Trust in Numbers. The Pursuit of Objectivity in Science and Public Life* (Princeton, Princeton University Press, 1996); François Fourquet, *Les Comptes de la puissance. Histoire de la comptabilité nationale et du plan* (Paris, Éditions Encres, 1980).

23. Michel de Certeau, *The Practice of Everyday Life*, transl. by Steven Rendall (Berkeley, University of California Press, 1988).

24. An argument I developed elsewhere with Boris Samuel: Béatrice Hibou and Boris Samuel, "Macroéconomie et politique en Afrique," *Politique Africaine*, n°124, (2012): 5–27.

25. Fourquet, *Les comptes de la puissance*, p. 358 (our translation).

26. Ibid; Michel Foucault, "Nietzsche, genealogy, history," in Paul Rabinow (general ed.), *Essential Works of Foucault, 1954–84*, vol. 2, *Aesthetics, Method, and Epistemology*, ed. by James Faubion, transl. by Robert Hurley et al. (London: Penguin, 2000), pp. 369–391.

27. On the way the concepts of "national accountancy," "forecasting," and "planning" spring from a will to power and have come to be used as tools in its service to achieve prosperity and well-being, see Fourquet, *Les comptes de la puissance*. Herbert Marcuse developed a similar argument when he noted that norms are "externalized": they are defined by a collective and institutional system of abstractions produced by society as a whole. See Herbert Marcuse, "Some social implications of modern technology," in *The Essential Frankfurt School Reader*, eds. Andrew Arato and Eike Gebhardt (London, Continuum, 1982 [1941]), pp. 138–62.

28. I thank Philippe Bonditti for making me think more deeply about this process. See his analysis of abstraction in "Les concepts, parent pauvre des études (critiques) de sécurité? Proposition pour une archéologie des savoirs de la sécurité," *Etudes internationales*, 46(2–3), 2015: 167–188.

29. Isabelle Bruno, Emmanuel Didier, *Benchmarking. L'État sous pression statistique* (Paris, La Découverte, 2013).

30. Henri Audier, "Les 'ex' négligent les profils scientifiques des candidats," *CAES du CNRS, Le Magazine*, no. 97, (2011), pp. 12–13.

31. Christian Walter (ed.), *Nouvelles normes financières. S'organiser face à la crise* (Paris: Springer-Verlag France, 2010); Grégory Vanel, "La normalisation financière internationale face à l'émergence de nouvelles autorités épistémiques américaines. Le cas de la filière des chiffres," *Revue de la régulation*, 3(4), 2008, online journal available at http://regulation.revues.org/4443 (verified on October 26, 2015).

32. Fourquet, *Les comptes de la puissance*, p. 367.

33. See Paul Veyne in *Did the Greeks Believe in their Myths? An Essay on the Constitutive Imagination*, transl. by Paula Wissing (Chicago, University of Chicago Press, 1988).

34. Michel Foucault, *The Government of Self and Others. Lectures at the Collège de France 1982–1983.* transl. by Graham Burchell (Basingstoke, Palgrave Macmillan, 2010), (Lecture of March 2, 1983).

35. Ibid. p. 310.

36. Jean-François Bayart, "Historicité de l'État importé," in Bayart (ed.), *La Greffe de l'État* (Paris, Karthala, 1996), pp. 35–36, partially translated as "Finishing with the idea of the Third World: the concept of the political trajectory" in *Rethinking Third World Politics,* ed. James Manor (London: Longman, 1991), pp. 51–71.

37. Here, I have been influenced by two very different lines of research. Firstly, that of Étienne Balibar on fictive ethnicity and the imaginary social community: see in particular Etienne Balibar and Immanuel Wallerstein, *Race, Nation, Class: Ambiguous Identities,* transl. (of Balibar) by Chris Turner (London, Verso, 1991). Secondly, that of Françoise Mengin in a very specific context: Taiwan and the fiction of a non-State which does not lead to the "non-recognition" of a State, but to the recognition of a "non-State' (Françoise Mengin, "A Pretence of Privatisation. Taiwan's External Relations" in *Privatising the State,* ed. Béatrice Hibou, transl. Jonathan Derrick (London, Hurst and New York, Columbia University Press, 2004), pp. 147–167.

38. Michel Foucault, "Foucault étudie la raison d'Etat," *Dits et Ecrits,* n° 280 (Paris, Gallimard – Quarto, 1980), pp. 856–860.

39. Foucault, *Dits et Ecrits,* no.281, pp. 860–914.

40. Michel Foucault, "Introduction," in *Dits et Écrits, I. 1954–1969* (Paris, Gallimard, 1994), no. 7, p. 186.

41. See Michel Foucault's early writings, especially "Distance, aspect, origin," in *The Tel Quel Reader,* ed. Patrick French and Roland-François Lack (London, Routledge, 1998), pp. 97–108, and "Behind the Fable," transl. Pierre A. Walker, *Critical Texts* 5.2, 1988, pp. 1–5. See also Roland Barthes, *Mythologies,* transl. by Richard Howard and Annette Lavers (New York, Hill & Wang, 2012), and *Writing Degree Zero,* transl. by Annette Lavers and Colin Smith (New York, Hill & Wang, 2012); Marcuse, *One Dimensional Man;* and Veyne, *Did the Greeks Believe in their Myths?*

42. Gilles Deleuze, *Negotiations 1972–1990,* transl. Martin Joughin (New York: Columbia University Press, 1995); Jean-François Bayart, *The Illusion of Cultural Identity* (London, C. Hurst & Co., 2005).

43. Boris Samuel, "L'Education pour tous'. La production bureaucratique du réel," in Béatrice Hibou (ed.), *La bureaucratisation néolibérale* (Paris: La Découverte, 2013), pp. 263–90.

44. This analysis of fiction is proposed by Yan Thomas in "Fictio legis. L'empire de la fiction romaine et ses limites médiévales" in *Les Opérations du droit* (Paris, Le Seuil/Gallimard, 2011), pp. 133–186 (p. 135). Our translation.

45. Both quotes are from Max Weber, *From Max Weber: Essays in Sociology,* transl., ed., by H.H. Gerth and C. Wright Mills (New York: Oxford University Press, 1946), p. 281.

# CHAPTER 13

# Too-Late Liberalism: From Promised Prosperity to Permanent Austerity

*Laurence McFalls and Mariella Pandolfi*

In a celebrated scene of Luchino Visconti's classic film set in the Risorgimento, *The Leopard* (1963), the protagonist, the Sicilian Prince of Salina, engages in a dialog with a Piedmontese functionary sent to recruit him for the Senate of the newly established liberal Kingdom of Italy. The dignified representative of the old aristocracy mockingly declines the invitation, ironically dismissing the bourgeois opportunism of the new order of "jackals and hyenas" that has replaced a world of "lions and leopards": "I am utterly without illusions. What would the Senate do with an inexperienced legislator who lacks the faculty of self-deception, essential requisite for those who wish to guide others?" More than self-interested nostalgia, the prince's melancholy inspires Gilles Deleuze's concept of the "too-late," a concept that describes, we contend, the impossibility of fulfilling the promise of political redemption.[1] The prince recognizes not only that it is too late to save the old world but also, and more importantly, that it is always already too late for a new order to realize its self-deceiving emancipatory claims. Visconti's and/or Deleuze's political pessimism goes well beyond the classic interpretations of the Risorgimento and its discontents. It applies to liberalism as a whole.

L. McFalls (✉) • M. Pandolfi
University of Montréal, Montréal, QC, Canada
e-mail: laurence.mcfalls@umontreal.ca; pandolfi.mariella@gmail.com

P. Bonditti et al. (eds.), *Foucault and the Modern International*,
The Sciences Po Series in International Relations and Political
Economy, DOI 10.1057/978-1-137-56153-4_13

As we shall argue here, liberalism proposes a politics of human freedom that comes *too late*, not historically but inherently. Inspired by Deleuze's idea that "history [whether that of fascism, capitalism or childhood] always arrives too late *dynamically*,"[2] we posit that it is already too late to speak of post-liberalism. To be sure, liberalism is temporally bounded: following Michel Foucault, one can construct a genealogy of its rise (as a critique of absolutist reason of state), of its renewal (through the neo-liberal critique of its naturalist assumptions), and maybe even of its latter-day fall into what we have elsewhere theorized as post-liberal non-order. The prefix "post," however, does not fit, not because it is premature but because liberalism's eclipse had already happened even as it was articulated and implemented. Similarly, "neo"-liberalism merely describes a qualitative and temporal moment of the "programmation libérale"[3] in which its aporias become particularly evident. In introducing the concept of too-late liberalism, we wish to expose the already-always present impasse of contemporary "democratic capitalist" societies and to show that liberalism's truth claims as well as its practices and techniques have simultaneously realized and negated their premises, or whose limits have supplanted its promise.

In stepping back from the claim that we have already moved into a post-liberal era, we do not wish to deny that epochal changes in the relations between knowledge, truth, power, technology and subjectivity are underway or that understanding them requires new conceptual tools. Instead, with the "too-late" label, we want to argue that these changes mark less of a rupture than a realization of liberalism's illiberal potential. To make this argument, we must go beyond the neoliberal dystopia that Foucault anticipated in *Naissance de la biopolitique* and that actually seemed to be emergent in the 1990s and 2000s but still draw on the genealogical method that Foucault deployed in his analysis of the liberal order to expose the re-assemblage of power relations under too-late liberalism. Foucault's recognition of the inseparability of power and truth (regimes), moreover, compels us to examine how the fragile truths upon which (neo)liberal government rested have given way to even less certain truth criteria and to more arbitrary forms of knowledge-power and of diffuse subjectivity under the too-late moment of liberalism. Reason of state, as Foucault shows in *Naissance de la biopolitique*, overcame the problem of the uncertainty of knowledge by attributing to the law-giving sovereign the gift of abstract pure reason with its ability to deduce natural law. Liberalism, by contrast, confronted the crisis of knowledge through probabilistic empirical calculations and techniques of government that respectively either sought to prevent or to manage uncertainty/risk. We wish to pursue this foucauldian reflection and argue here that contemporary liberalism fully reveals liberalism's too-late quality as its problematic relationship between power and knowledge becomes evident with the emergence of practices and techniques of government that rest on creative, plausibilistic, even illusory truth criteria. Under the *dispositif* of too-late liberalism, the uncertainty of crisis becomes not that which must be foreseen, prevented or even managed but that by which government itself occurs. The meaning of government by crisis, moreover, is not only epistemological but also economic and political: whereas liberalism and neoliberalism literally grew their way out of crisis both by "producing and consuming freedoms" and by producing and consuming ever greater quantities of goods in the futile quest for permanent prosperity, too-late liberalism governs both by producing and consuming uncertainty and fear,[4] replacing liberalism's promise of prosperity with the threat of permanent austerity.

## LIBERAL GOVERNMENT: ON THE VERGE OF CRISIS

In order to make our argument that liberal government cannot realize its redemptive promise, we must briefly recall Foucault's account of the origins of liberalism as the political reason concomitant to the episteme of the human sciences. That is, we wish to underscore that liberalism is a form of knowledge-power in the strong epistemic sense: it is not merely a technique of government but a truth regime and discursive formation providing the conditions of possibility for a total form of human life. Foucault's critical analysis of liberalism in his work of the late 1970s is implicit or pre-programmed in his seminal *Order of Things* of 1966, in which he explores, from the Renaissance to the early nineteenth century, Western European civilization's three epistemes—of the Renaissance which was the age of resemblance and similitude, of the classical age which was that of representation, and of modernity with the gradual emergence of the science of wealth and human sciences—stressing the ruptures between them (see Onuf in this volume). Although the book's success propelled Foucault toward his chair at the Collège de France in "the history of systems of thought," his intentions were also clearly political. Thus, he begins the work with an analysis of Diego Velazquez's *Las meninas* (1642), whose subject, despite the centrality in the painting of the princess Infanta, is the monarchic sovereign: the Spanish king and queen, reflected in a distant mirror, occupy the spot of the painting's viewer, while the portraitist, Velazquez himself, occupies the painting's left hand foreground. Foucault's purpose is to illustrate the classical age's episteme of representation in contradistinction with the preceding epoch of resemblance. Viewers' ideational representation of the sovereign and their ability to project themselves rationally into the place of the sovereign matter more than the suzerain's resemblance with divinity or descent from tradition. Authority derives from the purity of abstract reason, of which the painting's viewers partake, and not from the concrete person of the monarch. We witness here the desubstantialization of power. With this illustration of the ideational infrastructure of legitimate authority, Foucault announces that his interest in epistemic truth regimes is first and foremost political. Moreover, Foucault may very well have had this mental image in mind when, in his lecture course of 1976 *Society Must be Defended* he invoked the need to "decapitate the king in our heads."[5]

Foucault's regicidal injunction arrives in the context of his genealogy of liberalism, which he presents, not unlike Montesquieu, Tocqueville and others before him, as the paradoxical fruit of the feudal reaction to absolutist reason of state's rise in seventeenth- and eighteenth-century Britain and France. With greater originality, however, in *Society Must be Defended*, Foucault exposes the common agonistic, historicist conception of politics under liberalism, racist fascism and the Marxist theory of class struggle. Common to these discourses are of course their critique of pure reason and their recourse to empirical truth criteria. Much more successfully than communism and fascism, which clung to reason of state's absolutist pretensions of rationalist omniscience, liberalism offers its own, entirely autonomous form of political reason in line with the modern episteme from which human sciences came to emerge, according to Foucault,[6] with the Kantian revolution of the late eighteenth century. As the late nineteenth century neo- and post-Kantians in particular emphasized, Kant's critique of pure reason opened the door to epistemological pluralism, if not relativism, as truth depended not only on the historicity of the knowing subject but also on the unfathomable diversity of knowable phenomena each subject to its own criteria of intelligibility. Such potential relativism also introduced epistemological pragmatism: the validity of each form of knowledge depended on its efficacy. In keeping with this epistemic rupture, liberalism's critique of the absolutely rational sovereign was in the first instance pragmatic: Reason of state was doomed to failure since the ambition of deductive legal reason dogmatism to regulate everyone and everything could hardly stand up to the contingencies of real life. Thus, when the veridiction—or capacity to speak relativistic, empirical, pragmatic truth—of the human sciences replaced the jurisdiction—or capacity to articulate absolute, ideal, dogmatic truth—of the episteme of representation, liberalism dealt a not-quite fatal blow to reason of state.[7]

Theoretically, liberalism with its deferral of authority to empirical veridiction, notably but not exclusively that of the market, did make possible the beheading of the king in our minds, that ideal fountainhead of law and justice, but empirically it did not. In practice, liberalism never did away with the sovereign authority of the state whose arbitrary legal authority it required to establish the veridiction of the market based on the sacrosanct legal right to property. More abstractly, however, liberalism transposed the pure reason of the sovereign upon the liberal subject, whence its democratic potential. This projection of transcendence onto the liberal subject, as Foucault among many others showed, was the Hobbesian legacy of absolutist natural law to liberal theory. Whereas Hobbes derived absolute monarchical authority from natural law's dictate that each subject cede his right to everything in the overriding interest of survival, liberalism made each rational subject's interest in obtaining everything from the mechanism not only for assuring survival and endless self-aggrandizement but for guaranteeing social peace, prosperity and order as well, all with a minimum of authoritative external intervention. Because the liberal "conduct of conduct" relied on the rational autonomous subject's pursuit of (material) (self-)interest to govern cost-effectively, liberalism, in Foucault's memorable formulation, had to "produce and consume freedoms." In doing so, liberalism paradoxically expanded almost infinitely the field of government in the name of restricting the powers of the state. Through the manipulation of incentives for autonomous self-interested action, liberal governmentality not only got "more bang for its buck" than did absolutist reason of state but expanded governmental imagination. As Foucault's celebrated formulation opposing absolutism's "let-live-and-make-die" to liberalism's "make-live-and-let-die" suggests, cajoling has endless potential whereas threatening stops with death; that is, there are more ways to live than to die.

The genius and measure of success of liberalism thus reside in its ability to walk the fine line between anarchy and control or, in Foucault's formulation, to strike a balance between freedom and security. Liberalism promises to deliver a safe and orderly society that maximizes individual freedom, but to do so it must recommend, or rather require, that we "live dangerously."[8] To accomplish such squaring the circle, it may also require that we develop our "faculty of self-deception," as the Prince of Salina might say. Inasmuch as liberalism depends on a political culture of danger, it domesticates uncertainty and insecurity, making them part of the repertoire of government itself. And it is precisely this paradoxical internalization of uncertainty and insecurity, previously understood as external to politics and to knowledge, that lies at the crux of liberalism's too-late quality and raises a whole series of questions: for example, when does a culture of danger tip into a culture of fear? Or: if reason of state ultimately depended on the rational subject's mortal fear of the sovereign, on what does liberal government depend if not on liberal subjects' fear of themselves?

To strike its precarious balance between freedom and fear, liberalism must ideally always be on the verge of governmental crisis. It must provide security by biopolitically normalizing populations so that rational, autonomous liberal subjects can pursue their self-interest with calculable predictability but without losing the pragmatic cost efficiency of relatively uncoordinated self-directed, self-sustaining social action. To be sure, in practice liberal governmentality succumbs to recurrent crises as either market mechanisms fail or run amok, social security schemes overinflate, or illiberal subjects refuse to respect the anthropological assumptions of the knowledge-power-truth regime. Yet such challenges are not insurmountable under the intrinsic logics of liberalism: dogmatic rationalist discourse can always re-assert the immutability of market laws; empiricist trial-and-error techniques can tweak or jolt markets and mechanisms of social protection back into equilibrium; and normalizing practices and pressures can always discipline and dress recalcitrant liberal subjects. Still, as Foucault foresaw in 1979, liberal biopolitics faced natural as well as geopolitical limits. The juggernaut of global market capitalism may not yet have hit the walls of peak oil and climate meltdown but it has reached its geopolitical frontiers.

In *The Birth of Biopolitics*, Foucault identifies three defining traits of liberalism: (1) the market as a locus of empirical veridiction; (2) the limitation of government through the calculation of its utility; and (3) "the positioning of Europe as a region of unlimited economic development in relation to a global market."[9] Whereas the first two traits are abstract and logical, the third is concrete and historical, for liberalism offered a plausible solution to the impasse of the eighteenth-century European state system's mercantilist zero-sum logic of competition (a single market and polity, that is, the victory of one imperial power, might already then have been another solution). Only external expansion toward a global market, that is, imperialism, made it possible for one European power's territorial or economic gain in market(-like) competition *not* to come at the expense of another's. What would happen to liberalism and the European state system when market/imperial expansion had reached the natural, geopolitical limits of a global economy and state system remained an open question to which the crises of the first half of the twentieth century offered chilling responses. Following the Cold War imperial stand-off, the widening and deepening of economic integration sought to reposition Europe on the globalized market, but as the current crises of the European Union in particular make abundantly clear, liberal expansion has proven itself unable to outrun the crisis of knowledge, power and economic growth always already a potentiality within liberalism.

## NEOLIBERAL GOVERNMENT: IN CRISIS

Liberalism's on-going twentieth-century agony did not go unnoticed among its defenders. Already as early as the 1930s, neoliberalism emerged as a fundamental but friendly critique not only of liberalism's aberrant practices but of its epistemological underpinnings. Commonly but erroneously dismissed as a dogmatic restatement of liberalism's faith in the spontaneous efficacy of market mechanisms, neoliberalism merits the serious attention that Foucault was among the first to give it[10] (see Gros in this volume). Foucault saw that neoliberalism was more than a restatement of liberalism's critique of reason of state, which had survived the First World War in the modernized form of Nazism and more insidiously in Keynesian interventionism.[11] Critiquing reason of state's rationalist omniscient pretentions from a relativist perspective, neoliberal skepticism could not leave liberalism's empiricist naturalism unscathed.[12] As a product of human society and history, the market, the neoliberal critique acknowledged, can have no existence independent from society and social (scientific) knowledge about it. Without spontaneous, natural origins, the market can exist only as an effect of constant political action.[13]

If the market is an effect of historically contingent forms of knowledge and practices, then so too is the liberal subject. Under neoliberalism, according to Foucault's formulation[14], the liberal subject becomes an "entrepreneur of the self" ("entrepreneur de lui-même"). This neoliberal subject remains a rational actor—indeed its theoretical elaboration occurs within the framework of American anarcho-liberalism's rational-choice theory such as that of Gary Becker[15]—but not one simply driven by immanent interests and the rational quest for their maximization. Rather, just as neoliberalism as a doctrine seeks to enhance competitiveness so that the market can function efficiently, the neoliberal subject constructs itself as an enterprise with the greatest possible competitive potential. The entrepreneur of the self must therefore adopt a self-reflective, self-critical stance, understanding itself as a moving target always in need of repositioning and improvement, that is, as being always not entirely (if at all) adequate for the task at hand. To be sure, this auto-entrepreneurial stance lends neoliberalism its dynamism, but it also illustrates how and why neoliberal government stands no longer, like classic liberalism, on the verge of crisis, but rather thrives in the context of crisis. Crisis does not necessarily entail disorder or systemic collapse. It describes a situation of uncertainty, contingency or indeterminacy. In popular psychological language, we might say that the neoliberal subject suffers from a permanent identity crisis; more philosophically, we can posit that it abandons (some of?) its empirical immanence and becomes self-referential, though its transcendent rationality renders it imminently governable. Thus, an explosion of technologies of the self accompanies neoliberalism, a plethora of techniques for the constant, rational quest for improvement of the self—and of others, to boot. This care for oneself and for others lends neoliberalism more than just an air of benevolence: its mode of government is therapeutic.[16] It saves neoliberal subjects from themselves, but to do so it must continually throw them into a state of crisis. This claim does not derive from a theoretical deduction from neoliberalism's relativist epistemology and ontology, but from our concrete observation of neoliberal governmental practice, evident already in the postwar era but particularly obvious during the post-Cold War 1990s and 2000s (see Hibou in this volume).

Foucault's critical analysis of neoliberalism in the late 1970s was visionary because at the time the techniques and conditions of neoliberal government were still in gestation. In *The Birth of Biopolitics*, Foucault devoted particular attention to West Germany, showing already then that its "social market economy" was not an exemplar of what contemporary observers thought to be the postwar settlement of social democratic consensus that decommodified social relations but rather a vector of neoliberal marketization of society. Retrospectively we can interpret the whole period of postwar capitalism, and not just in West Germany, as one of neoliberalism in the sense that what might then have appeared to be a social democratic mitigation of market logic was in fact an expansion of market freedom to all spheres of life. To be sure, classic liberalism expanded, notably through the analogy of the marketplace of ideas, the freedom of economic exchange to the freedom of religion, of association, of political participation and of the press. The postwar period, however, witnessed an undeniable and truly massive expansion of claims and gains of liberal rights well beyond classic bourgeois freedoms. It would be difficult to contest the argument that the expansion of civic, political, cultural, sexual, reproductive and other rights as well as of access to higher education, to social and geographic mobility, and to traditional and new forms of communication and other media in the decades following the Second World War gave liberal subjects unprecedented possibilities for individual self-determination. At the same time, however, the widening and deepening of the welfare state and other instruments of collective rights and social security massively extended the biopolitical government of populations. Foucault[17] developed the concept of "pastoral power" to describe this double movement of liberal governmentality in which individual's liberty and personal responsibility, on the one hand, and the state's responsibility for security, on the other, are intimately linked if not indistinguishable. The persona of the good shepherd vacillates between the responsible (auto-entrepreneurial) subject and the dispositive of social control since power under the liberal art of government has no identifiable source.

Liberalism's "victory" with the end of the Cold War marked the decline of the libertarian side of liberal discourse and the rise of securitarian discourse and policies even as the deconstruction of the welfare state's provision of social security moved into full swing. Mark Duffield has no doubt been the most perspicacious observer of this trend at the level of international politics, his critical studies of development politics having shown their convergence and (con)fusion with humanitarian aid and security strategies.[18] The liberal promise of prosperity and security through market-based economic development has given way to a minimalist agenda of survival as (neo)liberal interventionism seems to breed insecurity even as it claims to combat it in on-going global war.[19] In an aptly entitled article referring to Foucault's[20] analysis of the figure of the naturally self-reliant savage in the eighteenth-century origins of liberal thought, "Getting Savages to Fight Barbarians,"[21] Duffield exposes how contemporary aid/development/security reproduces the indirect rule of nineteenth-century liberal colonial government by promoting the natural "resilience" of traditional societies. In the place of the catch-up modernizing development schemes of the 1960s and 1970s and with the benediction of politically correct discourses of sustainability, the uninsured populations of the global South in the 1990s and 2000s were invited to draw on indigenous models of development that did not rely on costly social welfare schemes and bureaucracies. In their natural state of resilience, these peoples were to stay at home and provide a buffer against terrorist, or barbarian, attacks on northern privilege. Meanwhile, the insured populations of the global North had to accept a reduction of social welfare in the name of sustainability but also to prevent attracting savage migration. The concept and tool of "resilience," however, did migrate north as the removal of social protection was to eliminate welfare dependency just as excessive development aid blocked indigenous growth.

Indeed, the migration of the concept of resilience from psychology, where it describes the capacity to overcome trauma, into social and political discourse at large signals not only an insidious naturalization of social catastrophes but also practically invites their production as a technique of government. The entrepreneurial subject is now called upon to cultivate this capacity to rebound from ever-tougher blows. The liberal principle of governmental efficiency thus slides into one of precariousness by design: making more for less in search of profit turns to making do with less in search of survival.[22] An extreme example of such planned penury can be seen in the administration of resources in refugee camps, where food provision, for example, is based on minimum caloric requirements. The multiplication of techniques, procedures and organizations for efficiently saving lives leaves the refugee camp as an emblematic life-saving institution almost indistinguishable in its bureaucratic impersonality as the death camp. This resemblance has led Giorgio Agamben[23] to conclude that the camp, as an institution of ultimate social triage at the margins of legality, is the paradigm of modern biopolitics. Although we would agree that the sovereign or Leviathan's right to decide over life and death ultimately still lurks behind liberalism's claim to carve out spaces of individual freedom, we contend that we lose analytic traction and nuance if we affirm that the liberal subject has lost all the transcendent qualities that endow it with certain universal rights. Whether understood legally, theologically or zoologically, the "bare life"[24] that erupts to the surface of the liberal subject in the face of the sovereign does not efface the subject's claim to transcendence. The violent core of liberalism is exposed, however, when the flipside of security is no longer freedom but insecurity, when liberalism no longer produces and consumes freedoms but promotes and profits from insecurity, or when the culture of danger becomes a culture of fear. And this, we shall argue, has become the case since the practices and technologies of (neo)liberal government in the exceptional context of crisis, in particular as developed on sites of humanitarian intervention on the global periphery, have become the governmental norm at the global center.

## TOO-LATE LIBERAL GOVERNMENT: BY CRISIS

Our research group's work on humanitarian interventions in crisis zones from the postcommunist Balkans to West Africa and Haiti has led us to conclude that these sites of biopolitical crisis management in the 1990s and 2000s were in fact laboratories for the development of practices and technologies initially of crisis management but ultimately of government by crisis.[25] We can here only briefly summarize our anthropological and political analysis of the international community of interveners including a host of governmental, intergovernmental and non-governmental organizations (NGOs) and actors from armies and churches to various corps of experts "without borders." Our work does not necessarily call into question the need for, or the sincerity of, massive humanitarian intervention into societies in the wake of conflict or catastrophe. Nor does it seek foremost to criticize the legality or the efficiency of these operations.[26] Instead, our ethnographic observations of relations between interveners and target populations allowed us to uncover the particular power relations that emerge in the context of acute crisis. We have observed how the circumstances of emergency lead to a suspension of temporal, spatial and cultural contexts. The urgency of crisis both freezes and accelerates time, calling on the unreflected application of standard operating procedures and presumably universally valid expert knowledge. In a cross-reading of Foucault's concept of biopolitics with Max Weber's sociology of domination, we have labeled the mode of authority exercised on sites of humanitarian intervention "therapeutic domination."[27] Like bureaucratic authority, but unlike charismatic authority, therapeutic domination, which can be understood metonymically like the doctor-patient relationship, rests on impersonal authority, notably treatment protocols. Like charisma, but unlike bureaucracy, however, therapeusis is ideal-typically extraordinary, a fleeting response to crisis, but in practice it slides into routinization, whether traditional or bureaucratic in form. We cannot here elaborate on the institutional forms that therapeutic authority adopts but mention only that the NGO best typifies the tensions between flexibility and bureaucracy as well as between (charismatic) appeals to absolute values and (bureaucratic) recourse to instrumental procedures.[28]

Despite its claims to be temporary or provisional, therapeutic domination in practice proves enduring and reveals, in fact, the authoritarian core of liberal benevolence. Interveners insist on their passing presence, working either to restore or introduce the proven techniques of liberal government: the market, organized civil society, representative democracy, and so on. Empirically, however, in places like Bosnia and Kosovo or in Palestinian refugee camps so-called transitions and temporary measures lasted decades or became permanent. Haiti, for example, has come to be called the "Republic of NGOs." To be sure, NGOs and the cosmopolitan corps of experts that circulate between them and other humanitarian/ securitarian/developmental organizations from consultancy to consultancy and from disaster site to disaster site have a material (as well as ideal) interest in perpetuating their practices and power. Independently of interests and ideals, therapeutic government by crisis has generated practices and techniques that perpetuate themselves. On the one hand, the benevolence of intervention makes resistance difficult, and when beneficiaries do resist they generate a spiral of what we call iatrogenic violence that further pathologizes them and prompts further therapeutic domination. On the other hand, the prolongation and even provocation of crisis, sometimes even willfully, has emerged as a successful tactic of neoliberal reform. From just-in-time delivery to tight budgeting, the importation of "new management" techniques into public policy has not merely sought to heighten governmental efficiency but to stimulate creative disorder, if not destruction.

Although the new techniques of government by crisis were already detectable 20 years ago on the peripheral sites of humanitarian intervention that we studied, they have meanwhile come to full fruition at the erstwhile global center. As epitomized now in the Greek tragedy, Europe has clearly slid into therapeutic government by crisis since 2008 as expert institutions above and beyond any putatively democratic determination exercise the therapeutic tutelage that they developed in the preceding decades, notably in the western Balkans. We do not wish to succumb to the polemics of blame (and hence moralism) at work in the current European crisis, nor for that matter in Canada, where we have witnessed the discursive and technical fabrication of budgetary crises as a pretext for austerity and the further dismantling of the welfare state. We would argue, however, that these phenomena are symptomatic of something more than a neoliberal refinement of the conduct of conduct through (self-)inflicted hardship as a means to attaining greater competitive health. Beyond the empirical validity of the dubious benefits of austerity, for example, what has come to a head in the current (post)humanitarian (neo)liberal moment is in fact the relationship between liberalism and truth.

Liberalism is not, of course, a lie, but rather a truth regime, or framework of veridiction that provides the conditions of possibility for speaking truth. As we have seen with Foucault, liberal truths, in keeping with the (Kantian) revolution of the human sciences, rest on empirical probabilities consistent with the presuppositions and perspectives of different sciences' delimitation of reality's infinite complexity.[29] Liberalism's epistemology is thus relativistic, but it is also tempered by pragmatism. Truths hold as long as they are effective, especially if their effectiveness reinforces the belief in their truth. The market thus can effectively yield the "true" value of goods and services when market agents act as if and believe that it does. In recasting the liberal subject as an entrepreneur of the self, as we saw, neoliberalism rendered the subjective foundations of market truth explicit. To be sure, the subjectivity of the market was always evident (even Locke admitted the purely imaginary value of money), notably during speculative bubbles and panic runs. To this day, the concept of "market corrections" suggests that such irrationalities of the market are subject to the empirical checks of the "real economy." Yet in an age when the nominal value of virtual, speculative and derivative markets outstrips that of real exchanges by several orders of magnitude, few people actually believe in the fairy tale of the empirical truth of market prices.[30]

Indeed, the too-late liberal present exposes the self-deception at the heart of liberalism's promise of freedom and prosperity. It suggests that liberal veridiction rests not only on empirical truths, but also upon verisimilitude, the appearance of what might be true. This replacement of empirical probability by subjective plausibility has become particularly acute under contemporary neo-/too-late-liberalism's mobilization of insecurity and austerity instead of freedom and prosperity. This is especially the case when the liberal culture of danger slips into a culture of fear and worst-case scenario planning according to the precautionary principle supplants policy planning based on (statistical) extrapolations from the past. Beyond the obvious sacrifice of classic liberal freedoms to the cause of the "war on terror" despite the objective decline in deaths due to terrorism, verisimilitude in conjunction with fear has become the epistemological premise of today's political (non)reason (see Bonditti in this volume). The arbitrary violence of contemporary politics does not mark the death of liberalism but rather its apotheosis. This realization of what was already inherent to liberalism arrives of course too late. Even worse, the liberal imposture is double. The impossibility of its promise of redemption is not only always already there from the beginning but repeats itself, doubles back on itself continually. Every attempt to realize freedom comes too late as each inevitable crisis asks us to try again, placing our hopes if not in the market, then in legal rights, in the welfare state, in humanitarian compassion, or now in the resilience spurred by permanent austerity.[31] The genealogy of liberalism thus shows us that each of its manifestations, each of its faces draws on and generates a lie of coming freedom.[32] It is no wonder, then, that the "last" Foucault[33] turned to the cynicism of Antiquity after his prescient analysis of contemporary liberalism.

## NOTES

1. *"La rédemption vient trop tard [...], elle survient quand l'information s'est déjà emparée des actes de parole [...]. Mais le trop-tard n'est pas que négatif, il est le signe de l'image-temps, là où le temps fait voir la stratigraphie de l'espace et entendre la fabulation de l'acte de parole."* ["Redemption comes too late (...), it arrives when information has already appropriated the speech-act (...). But the too-late is not negative only, it is the sign of image-time, the moment when time exposes the stratigraphy of space as well as the confabulation of the speech-act." Gilles Deleuze, *Cinéma 2: L'image-temps* (Paris: Editions de Minuit, 1985), p. 354.
2. Ibid., p. 127.
3. Michel Foucault, *Naissance de la biopolitique* (Paris: Seuil/Gallimard, 2004), p. 80.
4. Our argument about the role of fear in too-late liberal government is similar to Dillon's identification of the fear of "'life' understood as constant non-linear adaptation and change" as being at the heart of contemporary western security practices. Dillon's understanding of "life," however, situates it within liberalism's ontology whereas our conception of the too-late liberal biopolitics of fear sees fear as inherent to liberalism's relativist epistemology, or in Deleuze's terms in the disjuncture between "information" and the "confabulation of the speech act" (see note 1). See Mick Dillon, "Governing Terror: The State of Emergency of Biopolitical Emergence," *International Political Sociology*, 1, 7–28.
5. Michel Foucault, *Il faut défendre la société. Cours au Collège de France (1975–1976)* (Paris: Seuil/Gallimard, 1997), p. 117.

6. We do not wish to address here debates surrounding Foucault's (mis) interpretation of Kant in his thesis on Kant's *Anthropology* or in his chapter 9 of *The Order of Things*. An exegesis of Foucault's historicizing appropriation of Kant and his transgressive reading of the *a priori* of the Kantian subject for the purposes of his genealogy of the modern subject goes beyond the scope of this chapter.

7. Indeed, we might even go so far as to argue that liberalism requires the preservation of the sovereign state, the autonomy of the liberal subject depending always on its tension with the figure of the sovereign, which the liberal subject can oppose but also on which it can impose itself.

8. Foucault, *Naissance de la biopolitique*, p. 68.

9. Ibid., p. 62.

10. Laurent Jeanpierre, "Une sociologie foucaldiennne du néo-libéralisme est-elle possible?" *Sociologie et societies* 38(2) (2006): 87–111.

11. Foucault, *Naissance de la biopolitique*, pp. 80–1.

12. For an in-depth analysis of neoliberalism's "epistemological recoding" of liberalism from naturalism to constructivism and a friendly critique of Foucault's reading of it, see Martin Beddeleem, "Le projet scientifique d'un renouvellement du libéralisme: le néolibéralisme de 1933 à 1973," doctoral dissertation, Université de Montréal (in progress, forthcoming 2016).

13. Foucault, *Naissance de la biopolitique*, p. 124.

14. Ibid., p. 232. Our treatment of Foucault's treatment of neoliberalism shares the same perspective as, among others, Pierre Dardot and Christian Laval, *The New Way of the World: On Neoliberal Society* (New York: Verso, 2014).

15. Ibid., pp. 221ff.

16. Laurence MacFalls, "Benevolent Dictatorship: The Formal Logic of Humanitarian Government," in *Contemporary States of Emergency: The Politics of Military and Humanitarian Interventions*, eds. Didier Fassin and Mariella Pandolfi (New York: Zone Books, 2010); Laurence McFalls and Marielle Pandolfi, "L'intervento come ordine terapeutico" in *Il corpo e lo stato*, eds. Giovani Pizza and Helle Johannessen (Perugia: Morlacchi editore, 2014).

17. Michel Foucault, *Histoire de la sexualité, I. La volonté de savoir* (Paris: Seuil/Gallimard, 1976); and "Omnes et Singulatim: Towards a Critique of 'Political Reason,'" Tanner Lectures, Stanford University, 1979.

18. Mark Duffield, *Global Governance and the New Wars* (London: Z Books, 2001); Mark Duffield, *Development, Security and Unending War* (Cambridge, UK: Polity Press, 2007).

19. Mark Duffield, "Liberal Interventionism and Fragile States: Linked by Design," in *Development and Colonialism: The Past in the Present*, ed. Mark Duffield and Vernon Hewitt (Suffolk: James Currey, 2009), pp. 116–129.

20. Foucault, *Il faut défendre la société*, p. 174.
21. Mark Duffield, "Getting savages to fight barbarians: development, security and the colonial present," *Conflict, Security and Development* 5(2) (2005): 141–159.
22. Marc Abélès, *The Politics of Survival* (Durham, NC: Duke University Press, 2010).
23. Giorgio Agamben, *Homo Sacer: Il potere soverano e la vita nuda* (Giulio Einaudi, 1995).
24. Ibid.
25. Mariella Pandolfi, "Contract of Mutual (In)Difference: Governance and Humanitarian Apparatus in Albania and Kosovo," *Indiana Journal of Global Legal Studies* 10(1) (2003): 369–381; "Humanitarianism and its Discontents." In *Forces of Compassion between Ethics and Politics*, ed. Erica Bornstein and Peter Redfield (Santa Fe, NM: School for Advanced Research Press, 2011).
26. A huge literature exists on these topics, see Didier Fassin and Mariella Pandolfi, eds. *Contemporary States of Emergency: The Politics of Military and Humanitarian Interventions* (New York: Zone Books, 2010).
27. McFalls, Laurence, "Les fondements rationnels et sociaux des passions politiques: vers une sociologie de la violence contemporaine avec Weber et Foucault," *Anthropologie et Sociétés* 32(3) (2008): 155–172; McFalls, "Benevolent Dictatorship: The Formal Logic of Humanitarian Government"; Pandolfi & McFalls "L'intervento come ordine terapeutico."
28. McFalls "Benevolent Dictatorship: The Formal Logic of Humanitarian Government."
29. The best statement of this liberal epistemological position, as informed by neo-Kantianism and the German historical school, probably remains Max Weber's 1904 essay "'Objectivity' of Knowledge in the Social Sciences and Policy," in Max Weber, *Wissenschaftslehre* (Tübingen: Mohr, 1988). See also Laurence McFalls, ed. *Max Weber's 'Objectivity' Reconsidered* (Toronto: University of Toronto Press, 2007).
30. Few observers have the candor of George W. Bush's strategist Karl Rove, who in an interview with journalist Ron Suskind mocked those who believe in empirical truths: "The aide [subsequently identified as Karl Rove] said that guys like me were 'in what we call the reality-based community,' which he defined as people who 'believe that solutions emerge from your judicious study of discernible reality.' I nodded and murmured something about enlightenment principles and empiricism. He cut me off. 'That's not the way the world really works anymore,' he continued. 'We're an empire now, and when we act, we create our own reality. And while you're studying that reality—judiciously, as you will—we'll act again, creating other new realities, which you can study too, and that's

how things will sort out. We're history's actors . . . and you, all of you, will be left to just study what we do.'" Suskind, Ron, "Without a Doubt," *New York Times*, 17 October 2004. Unfortunately we do not have the space here to explore the relation between the new forms of empire and of epistemology that Rove evokes.

31. More optimistically, Jay Lampert, "Theory of Delay in Balibar, Freud, and Deleuze," in *Deleuze and History* ed. Jeffrey A. Bell and Claire Colebrook (Edinburgh: University of Edinburgh Press, 2009), p. 90 concludes: "It may be an accident that the too-late was discovered too late, but it is not too late to discover it now, it is not too late to make history [...] though of course, hopefully, in time." He places his thin hopes in the Deleuzian diachronic analysis.

32. As we write these lines, another new, promising face of liberalism seems to be emerging in Europe in response to the growing migration crisis of 2015. Overcome with humane (not to say humanitarian) concern for the lives and transcendent rights of refugees and in light of the breakdown of the legal-technical dispositive for managing these migratory flows, individuals, in an act that we might call self-pastoralization, have undertaken spectacular, perhaps even heroic rescue operations outside of all regular channels. We might again ask if this latest liberal redemptive promise comes too late.

33. Michel Foucault, *Le gouvernement de soi et des autres* (Paris: Seuil/ Gallimard, 2008, first ed 1983); *Le courage de la vérité* (Paris: Seuil/ Gallimard, 2009, first ed. 1984).

# PART V

# Biopolitical?

# CHAPTER 14

# Biopolitics in the Twenty-First Century: The Malthus–Marx Debate and the Human Capital Issue

## Luca Paltrinieri

In his article "The Malthus Effect: Population and the Liberal Government of Life,"[1] Mitchell Dean highlights a strange paradox: around the mid-1970s, at a time when Foucault was concerned with the emergent figure of "population" in pre-Malthusian economic thought, Malthus's thinking enjoyed a worldwide revival of interest thanks to the work of the Club of Rome, the 1974 Bucharest conference on global population and other circumstances which resulted in enduring fears of over-population.[2] Yet Foucault seems to have remained blind to the political consequences of this "Malthusian moment."[3] Rather bizarrely, his analysis in the lecture series on *Security, Territory, Population* ends in the late eighteenth century without broaching either Malthus's thought or contemporary political demographics. Not only did the following year's lectures' focus on a subject seemingly far removed from research into population—neo-liberalism[4]—but it still seems to leave the possibility of neo-liberal biopolitics without a genuine theoretical foundation. That is why Dean can claim that

L. Paltrinieri (✉)
University Rennes 1, Rennes, France
e-mail: l.paltrinieri@gmail.com

© The Author(s) 2017
P. Bonditti et al. (eds.), *Foucault and the Modern International*,
The Sciences Po Series in International Relations and Political
Economy, DOI 10.1057/978-1-137-56153-4_14

"by neglecting the paradigm of Malthus and his concept of population, Foucault missed the opportunity for placing the government of life at the heart of not only classical but also contemporary liberal government."[5]

Dean's reading is all the more pertinent in that it roots this lacuna in a certain narrowness of Foucault's reading of early liberalism: "Foucault fails to reach an understanding of the *contemporary* government of life precisely because he neglects its paradigmatic case in the formation of the early *liberal* arts of government."[6] Liberal government did not develop exclusively in connection with those collective entities, the market and civil society. For Dean, the constant threat of demographic disaster heralded by Malthus prompted a different paradigm of the government of self and others in the liberal and neo-liberal age, "which has the government of life at its very core." Alongside the individual who pursues his interests in the market, and his desire for liberty in civil society, we find another individual who must govern his procreative capacity in the face of an impending catastrophe affecting the whole species.

In this chapter, we shall draw upon Dean's reading and, more particularly, his critique of Foucault to try to understand how a neo-liberal "politics of life" was able to take shape. In this purpose, and more specifically, I propose to analyze the transformations of the economic concept of "population" from the moment it appeared in the work of Malthus to its most recent specification by the contemporary theorists of human capital. In this way, I hope to sketch out what could possibly be understood as an intellectual history of the economic valuation of human life.

## MALTHUS OR THE BIO-ECONOMIC POPULATION PROBLEM

Malthus's *Essay on the Principle of Population*, published in 1798, opens with the two fixed inviolable laws of human nature: "First, that food is necessary to the existence of man. Secondly, that the passion between the sexes is necessary and will remain nearly in its present state."[7] These two laws inscribe a catastrophic contradiction in natural necessity between the geometrical progression of population and the arithmetical progression of animal and vegetable resources: "I say, that the power of population is indefinitely greater than the power in the earth to produce subsistence for man."[8] The law of diminishing returns, formulated by Ricardo in 1821 but already foreshadowed by Turgot in 1768, provided this limit with an economic justification. Ricardo based his analysis on the principle of the scarcity of the source of value: land. Because population increases, less fertile and, consequently, less productive land has to be exploited, leading to a fall in production for every unit of land exploited. Since laborers buy essential goods, the price of food supplies increases. But profits can only rise at the expense of wages, and hence, supply and demand balance and the profit rate tend toward zero. As Malthus explains,

> Man is necessarily confined in room. When acre has been added to acre till all the fertile land is occupied, the yearly increase of food must depend upon the amelioration of the land already in possession. This is a stream which, from the nature of all soils, instead of increasing, must be gradually diminishing. But population, could it be supplied with food, would go on with unexhausted vigour; and the increase of one period would furnish the power of a greater increase the next, and this without any limit.[9]

Human existence thus takes the form of a permanent struggle waged on one side against the scarcity of resources and on the other against the reproductive instinct. This struggle for survival in a context of scarcity had been highlighted by Foucault himself in *The Order of Things* when dealing with the analysis of wealth in economics. For the Physiocrats as for the Utilitarians, "population" was an element in the creation of value, which depended on the twofold role of the attribution/articulation of wealth in the circuit of exchange but within the temporal horizon of a radiant future where multiplication of human beings was a consequence of an expansion of agricultural production.[10]

The role of population in the political economy inaugurated by Ricardo and Malthus is quite different. Here the horizon is no longer unlimited progress but the "analytic of finitude"—the fundamental limit which the new figure of man encounters in the "quasi-transcendentals" of life, labor and language.[11] Political economy replaces generous abundance of the land—prolific inexhaustible source of value—by the principle of scarcity as a source of valorization—the reflection of a "fundamental insufficiency."[12] Awareness that man has a limited place in the world is then inscribed in an anthropology of catastrophe: the "natural" progression of population is subject to the "positive check" of the shortages and famines that shorten human beings' natural lifespan.

As we know, Malthus prescribed continence, moral compulsion or the deferment of marrying age ("preventive check") as means for a non-catastrophic regulation of population. The idea of regulation through compulsion targeted the optimism expressed by Condorcet or Godwin for which social and political self-organization would make it possible to control demographic forces thanks, in particular, to political action on environments, trade, work, public hygiene and everything that Foucault dubbed "dispositifs of security."[13] To this mythology of progress, Malthus counter-posed a theological and eschatological perspective: the world and existence are an "imposing process established by God not to test, but to create and fashion the mind, a process that is necessary to awaken the mind from inert, chaotic matter."[14] Unfortunately, man is by nature "inert, sluggish, and averse from labour, unless compelled by necessity."[15] So how can he fashion a mind for himself if not impelled by the two great laws of human nature—the need for nourishment and the impulse to procreation? For Malthus, demographic pressure imparts tension and meaning to social existence, the essence of social existence precisely consisting in this endeavor to control the terrible power of reproduction. The "natural and eternal" law of population is thus a divine instrument that explains the existence of evil and impels men to seek moral perfection and the kingdom of the spirit, the sole veritable metaphysical principle which explains human progress: "Had population and food increased in the same ratio, it is probable that man might never have emerged from the savage state."[16] The goal of the contradiction between the unbalanced ratios of population and resources is to impel "man to further the gracious designs of Providence by the full cultivation of the earth."[17]

But this progressive detachment from the instincts via moral improvement is not uniform: it occurs differently as between higher classes, which, conscious of the difficulty of raising a family, adopt the preventive check, and "extreme" classes exposed to poverty and, as a result, the animality of vice. This is precisely where the economic dimension of the law of population comes in: to circumvent positive checks by finding one's place socially also means recognizing that it is demand for labor which governs supply—that is, production must be governed through existing income and spending power. But the only social groups capable of creating strong, sustained demand are unproductive consumers (or higher classes). So if the aim is to regulate population with respect to the supply of food, the best way is unquestionably to defend the interests of unproductive classes and increase unproductive consumption. In this regard, the issue is also an economic issue. In particular, over-population must be limited by altering the price structure—by encouraging, for example, the market in manufactured products—which means lowering the price of goods that are only available to the bourgeois classes and raising the price of staple items. This will serve simply to exacerbate the poverty of proletarians still further. In Malthus's construct, the state of poverty combined with moralization should impel the proletarian classes to limit procreation, for "our best-grounded expectations of an increase in the happiness of the mass of human society are founded in the prospect of an increase in the relative proportions of the middle parts."[18]

Thus, starting with Malthus, the concept of population is lodged in a kind of enduring contradiction. On the one hand, the law of population is a metaphysical, even theological, principle rooted in a conflictual nature that always risks ending up in a catastrophic event. On the other, the only way humanity can dispel the threat is inextricably bound up with the appropriation of land, space and the economic securitization of territory. In Dean's words, we can affirm that the Malthusian law of population inaugurated a "bio-economics of scarcity." This new bio-economics had consequences for the international policies of European states. The technology of pre-modern classical government was characterized by an enormous circulation of things and human beings, which states sought to encourage rather than prevent.[19] "What is the best means of weakening neighboring states whose power and industry overshadow us?" asked Tucker in connection with Protestants emigrating to America. "Should we force them to remain in their countries, by refusing to welcome them and integrate them into our society, or should we try and attract them by according them the same privileges as all other citizens?"[20] In a governmental regime where the strength of the state lies in numbers, states competed to tap flows of migrants, "persuading" laborers to leave their native country by various measures. A positive balance in the immigration/emigration ratio indicated a country's well-being. The concept of the "number of people" in a territory was conceived as the effect less of an endogenous dynamic than of population movements between the borders of states; the internal–external distinction—asserted at juridical and economic levels—did not as yet refer to the idea of a "national population." Belonging to a state was conceived in terms less of "birth" in a territory than of more or less voluntary adhesion to a political community.[21] Thus, in the pre-Malthusian view of population, the importance of number outweighed any consideration of the origin of members of the population.

By contrast, in the bio-economics of scarcity that developed from Malthus and Ricardo onward, population was conceptualized as an aggregate of finite individuals in a territory, whose regularities, means and variations over time could be calculated. The anchorage of the population in a territory resulted in its biologization and "naturalization": it was now conceived as a stable homogeneous collective in isolation from any migration. Whereas the population policies of the previous century sought to tap flows of migrants, the new models referred to a closed territory defined by national boundaries and exclusively to the lever of the birth rate to promote demographic growth.[22] The secret of economic growth now became maintaining a balance between endogenous population and landed capital, as demonstrated by Malthusian economic theory. Thus we witness a decline in major migratory flows and the emergence of a silent war against those—Negroes, the abnormal, the internal enemy—who threaten the very source of wealth and value from within. One of the sources of modern racism in its biologizing and biopolitical form precisely consists in the dual nature of population, as a metaphysical principle and an "organism" rooted in a national territory.[23]

As Dean shows, the "Malthus effect" exhibited "a remarkable persistence over more than two centuries [...] In the nineteenth century, Malthus's principle was a paradigm for both political economy and evolutionary biology; in the twentieth, for bio-demography and systems ecology."[24] In fact, not only did the metaphysical principle of a population permanently out of kilter with resources become a global problem in the twentieth century but the demographic argument unquestionably played a role in the justification of US power politics, in the imposition of family planning in developing countries[25] and in the formation of the environmentalist movement throughout the twentieth century.[26]

An especially interesting chapter in the history of the "Malthus effect" is the relationship between neo-liberalism and demography. On the one hand, the neo-liberal wave of the 1980s resulted in a serried critique of any form of state control of the economic mechanism (see Gros and Hibou in this volume) and hence also of interventionism in procreation. On the other, it was precisely the internationalization of labor and capital that led to the formulation of the demographic problematic in welfare policies once again, to the theorization of sustainable development and, above all, to the regulation of immigration.[27] All these typical problematics of neo-liberal governmentality on a world scale thus remain haunted (according to Dean) by the issue of limits—not only those placed by the market on government, as stressed by Foucault, but also the limits to development posited by scarce resources, lifestyles, lack of space and, more generally, by the "catastrophic" conflict between population and resources.

## MARX: UNDERLYING POPULATION, CLASSES

Dean notes that what prevented Foucault from spotting the importance of the Malthus effect was both abandonment of the problem of scarcity and dissociation of the problem of population from that of occupation of territory, both of which were theorized in *The Order of Things*. In the 1978 lectures, the sole mention of the latter occurs precisely when Foucault cites Malthus to claim that the figure of man as subject and object of knowledge in the 1966 book is actually "nothing other than a figure of population."[28] The new subject/object whose emergence was described in 1978—population—is therefore a historical and political operator of transformation of forms of knowledge, which enabled the transformation of analysis of wealth into political economy, of natural history into biology and of general grammar into linguistics. The "man" of the human sciences is no longer simply a figure of knowledge but also a correlate of liberal governmentality. The human sciences are supposed to reveal the most intimate aspects, as well as the external ones, of the consciousness of this governable man in order for him to be governable. The following passage seems to restore a major role to the Malthusian paradigm, but it must be said—and this is another major difference compared with *The Order of Things*—that mention of Malthus is inseparable from another name, Marx's:

> For Malthus, the problem of population basically has to be thought as a bio-economic problem, whereas Marx tried to circumvent the problem and get rid of the very notion of population, but only to rediscover it in the no longer bio-economic form, but in the specifically historical-political form of class, of class confrontation and class struggle. This is the source of their disagreement: either population or classes, that is where the split occurs, on the basis of an economic thought, a political economic thought, that was only possible as such with the introduction of the subject-population.[29]

Whereas in 1966, Foucault had asserted that from the standpoint of economic knowledge Marx and Malthus pertained to the same (Ricardian) horizon, in 1978, regarding governmentality, the Marx–Malthus duo indicates an alternative, a rupture internal to the paradigm of political economy. And in my view, it is around this alternative—either population or classes—that a different genealogy of neo-liberal biopolitics can be traced, a genealogy where not only Malthus but also Marx function both as a source of inspiration and as a foil. Marx's critique of Malthus is well-known: "The Malthusian theory is but the economic expression of the religious dogma of the contradiction of nature and spirit"[30]; his "natural man" abstracted from historically determinate humanity "exists only in his brain; hence also the geometric method of reproduction corresponding to this natural Malthusian man."[31] The violence of this argument is explicable: the "shameless sychophant" and "plagiarist by profession" bore intellectual responsibility for the 1833 Poor Law, whose impact Engels was able to measure from his Manchester observatory.[32] The impoverishment of the popular classes preached by Malthus prompted not limitation of the population but the creation of a surplus population because workers increased their fertility to enjoy the benefits of an extra wage. This example alone served to indicate that the poverty of the working classes was the result of a particular situation where the employment of children in manufacturing was not only possible but also normal. Whereas Malthus "regards overpopulation as being of the same kind in all the different historic phases of economic development"[33] and thinks that "pauperism was held to be an *eternal laws of nature*,"[34] for Marx it was a question of showing that "In different modes of social production there are different laws of the increase of population and of overpopulation; the latter identical with pauperism."[35] The "law of population" was simply an expression of the way that each mode of production, in reproducing the dominant social relations of production, creates and reproduces a certain demographic regime.[36] Consequently, there is no such thing as a law of population but several laws of population, and limits to it, depending on the elasticity of a determinate form of production, the ability to render labor productive and increase productivity rates. Marx completely inverts Malthus's approach. Rather than starting from an inflexible law of population to deduce its consequences for economic regulation, he starts with economic analysis in order to bring out the conditions of production and the mechanisms for adjusting supply and demand of labor that determine over-population, subsequently pauperism "appear as the result of labor itself, of the development of the productive force of labor."[37]

   In the capitalist system, over-population is not merely a supplementary mass of human beings but above all a mass of men who can be exploited by capital: "The invention of surplus laborers, i.e. of propertyless people who work, belongs to the period of capital."[38] The first precondition of capitalist accumulation involves the specificity of the labor commodity, which, unlike other commodities, has the capacity to reproduce itself indefinitely. Secondly, unlike the slave, the worker is not sold once but continues to sell himself precisely because he owns nothing but his labor power. This is a point already highlighted by Engels in *The Condition of the Working Class in England*, which indicated that capital ultimately had an interest in exploiting precarious mobile labor power because it proves less expensive than slavery. Thus, capital not only reproduces the conditions of labor but also produces the wage-labor and productive workers it requires, that is, it eternalizes the social relationship between capitalist and wage-laborer.

Furthermore, the social dynamic of the reproduction of labor power itself has a history—that of the historical stages of capital accumulation. In the initial phase of capitalist production, capital sought to increase the population so as to increase labor time and, as a result, surplus labor, that is, exchange value. Taking up Ricardo and John Barton, however, Marx saw that the process of capital accumulation was not homogeneous because the proportion of constant capital (i.e. machines) gradually increases at the expense of variable capital (the share of wages). In a phase of powerful economic acceleration, variable capital and, consequently, demand for labor and job creation can go on increasing in absolute value while declining in proportion to constant capital.[39] But such demand is destined to fall dramatically when the growth rate of capital slows and the increase in constant capital translates into net erosion of the capital earmarked for wages. Furthermore, slow-downs are implicit in the very nature of the capitalist process of production, for when a society achieves "full employment," the price of labor and average wages necessarily rise—something that will accelerate recourse to machinery, an increase in the proportion of constant capital and a consequent constriction of variable capital because a smaller working class population will be needed to supply the same amount of labor. Thus, machinery on the one hand transforms circulating capital into fixed capital, while on the other, it facilitates the ejection of growing masses of workers from production. At one and the same time, capital creates the conditions for employment and for its destruction, that is, for the creation of a "reserve army" of laborers who, remaining unemployed, represent a stock of manpower on which capital can draw when necessary and in accordance with its phases of development, subsequently expelling surplus workers during crisis periods.[40]

Marx and Engels thus showed that over-population is neither the fatal effect of a natural law—on the contrary, it is an integral part of capitalist technological development, which facilitates expansion of constant capital at the expense of variable capital—nor an unpredictable subsidiary effect of capitalist accumulation. According to Ricardo himself, "it is therefore the means of employment and not of subsistence which put the worker into the category of surplus population."[41] Therefore, the creation of a floating population in an urban milieu and of latent over-population in the rural milieu introduces competition between workers, making it possible to compress wages and render them compatible with super-exploitation: "The constant generation of a relative surplus-population keeps the law of supply and demand of labor, and therefore keeps wages, in a rut that corresponds with the wants of capital. The dull compulsion of economic relations completes the subjection of the laborer to the capitalist."[42] A stagnant surplus population is thereby created—an active population whose conditions of employment are so episodic and irregular that its reproduction resembles "the boundless reproduction of animals individually weak and constantly hunted down,"[43] whose inclusion in the labor market is possible but eternally deferred.[44] The process of expanded reproduction of capital is so indissolubly bound up with the creation of a relative surplus population, included in the labor market but excluded from work itself, that Marx can assert: "The laboring population therefore produces, along with the accumulation of capital produced by it, the means by which it itself is made relatively superfluous, is turned into a relative surplus population."[45]

While the Malthusian population principle is a "chimera" without "scientific value," it continues to play an important role as an ideological construct in the service of the private interests of the landed aristocracy.[46] Recourse to compulsion or force to compel the worker to enter into the wage-labor relationship is, in fact, exceptional: it is enough for this state of affairs to be presented as "natural" and "obvious" for the worker to be abandoned to the logic of competition and the divisions between active, floating, latent and stagnant populations. Thus, once workers discover that the intensity of competition depends on the pressure exercised by supernumeraries, once they seek to overcome this division by creating solidarity between employed and unemployed, the liberal economist cries sacrilege, claiming that the law of supply and demand in the labor market is being violated.[47] Symmetrically, Malthus on the one hand defended the ideal of a middle class responsible for its procreative behavior, while on the other he believed that the precondition for humanity's gradual moral improvement was the preservation of social stratification:

[I]t is evident that all cannot be in the middle. Superior and inferior parts are, in the nature of things, absolutely necessary; and not only necessary, but strikingly beneficial. If no man could hope to rise or fear to fall in society; if industry did not bring with it its reward and indolence its punishment; we could not expect to see that animated activity in bettering our condition that now forms the master-spring of public prosperity.[48]

That is why, according to Marx and Engels, the law of the tendency for the population to increase and the consequent prices policy are to be regarded as an open declaration of war on the proletariat: "that the earth is perennially over-populated, whence poverty, misery, distress, and immorality must prevail; that it is the lot, the eternal destiny of mankind, to exist in too great numbers, and therefore in diverse classes, of which some are rich, educated, and moral, and others more or less poor, distressed, ignorant, and immoral."[49] Against Malthusian ideological naturalism, it is necessary to bring out the historical dynamic of capitalism and the class struggle underlying it: "The population is an abstraction if I leave out, for example, the classes of which it is composed. These classes in turn are an empty phrase if I am not familiar with the elements on which they rest. E.g. wage labor, capital, etc. These latter in turn presuppose exchange, division of labor, prices, etc."[50]

This integration of the law of population into a historical dynamic of struggle also inscribes it in a broader context, involving capitalist development as a global phenomenon. While the concept of over-population simply expresses the subordination of demographic development to the reproduction of social labor power, the functioning of capitalism is international and is characterized primarily by a new international division of labor. Thus, the import of mechanically manufactured English calico led to the ruination of the Indian cotton industry, creating a surplus population in another part of the world.[51] More generally, in a context where the power of expansion of capital grows, "because the technical conditions of the process of production themselves—machinery, means of transport, &c.—now admit of the rapidest transformation of masses of surplus-product into additional means of production,"[52] market stagnation, trade crises and even financial speculation are global phenomena that dictate thinking crises of over-population and the circulation of labor power at an international level. Whereas Malthus elevated the law of population into a timeless metaphysical principle while territorializing the economic policies that would make it possible to halt the infernal mechanism of demographic catastrophe, Marx historicized the law of population by showing that the mechanism of social production of a surplus population depends upon a global capitalist dynamic. Rather than dissolving the very notion of population in that of "class," it is the concept of "national population" that Marx dissolves, showing that problems of over-population are in fact never national but depend upon a global conflict pitting capitalists against the international working class.

## NEO-LIBERALISM AND THEORIES OF HUMAN CAPITAL: NEITHER POPULATION, NOR CLASS

We may now return to the alternative sketched by Foucault: "either population or classes." It is clear that this involves choosing not only between a metaphysical principle and the historical dynamic peculiar to capitalism but also between a territorialized conception of population/nation and an economic analysis of the demographic phenomenon whose horizon is now global.[53] More precisely, it involves reformulating Malthus's question about limits to growth on a global scale that Marx alone had hitherto proved capable of imagining. As I have shown elsewhere, Foucault was probably not unaware of the debates between "Malthusians" and "Marxists" about the "limits of the planet." But it is likely that rather than participating in them, he chose to engage in a kind of archaeology of the "Malthusian moment."[54]

That is why the definition of population given by him in 1978 in the *Security, Territory, Population* lecture series reads more like an attempt to reveal the conceptions of his own time than those of the eighteenth century. In his interpretation, population is neither a kind of biological organism that regulates itself automatically in terms of resources nor an ideological "construct", but a set of various *forms of behavior*, multiple, non-totalizable *habits*, which can nevertheless be grasped thanks to a behavioral invariant—*interest*: "Desire is the pursuit of the individual's interest (...) The production of the collective interest through the play of desire is what distinguishes (...) the naturalness of population."[55] This talk of interest which "tames" society's destructive passions actually has its roots in the eighteenth century, in the political economy of enjoyment that subverts the juridical discourse of the "transfer of rights" to the sovereign, of obligation and obedience.[56] But the originality of Foucault's reading consists in presenting the immediate political reality of population, whose appearance attests to a new political semantics displacing the level of pertinence of government action from obedience to interest as an individual, atomistic, and non-transferable choice by the subject in the form of an immediate subjective volition.[57] The new political rationality, acting on the "social" as well as on the biological existence of human beings, must now respect a set of natural givens that are resistant to complete manipulation: morbidity, birth rates, migration and so on. Governing will mean acting on a whole series of variables that condition demographic changes (surroundings, material conditions, habits and customs) through calculated judicious techniques: acting on the conditions of possibility of action by men and women. Government action will be more effective to the extent that it restrains itself, thus allowing a certain freedom of action to individual or collective subjects and permitting the operation of the principle of free competition between interests and the "natural self-regulation" of the price system. It is clear that in Foucault's interpretation, the "nature" of population consists neither in its "catastrophic" geometrical progression nor in the effects of the international division of labor: it is a kind of matrix of government action on the environment of individuals driven by their interests (see Taylan in this volume).[58]

That is why, in fashioning a kind of archaeology of the Marx–Malthus debate, Foucault in fact discloses the characteristics of a new art of governing which rejects that alternative: neo-liberalism (the 1978 lecture series might almost be read as an introduction to that of 1979 on *The Birth of Biopolitics*). In the vast contemporary debate on the legacy of neo-liberalism and Foucault's interpretation,[59] the new economic approach to population by the neo-liberals, and their critique of the classical model, has not been sufficiently registered.[60]

The key point of Thomas Schultz's analysis is that the enormous stock of physical capital in the rich countries in the post-war years prompted neither significant diminishing returns, as Malthus would have it, nor wage compression under the pressure of the reserve army of the unemployed, as Marx had it. Quite the reverse, encouragement to undertake remunerated work and the existence of significant manpower requirements in Europe and the USA translated into an increase in real hourly wages, which depended on improvements in labor productivity. In its turn, this result derived from a particular type of economic growth, which, in contrast to classical economics, was now based not on the exploitation of natural resources but on investment in human capital, that is, treated as "attributes of acquired population quality, which are valuable and can be augmented by appropriate investment."[61] The increase in the stock of skills, and hence of human capital, through education or experience translated into an increase in the "quality" of the population—for example, a less numerous population but one more qualified to perform certain tasks or jobs. The growth in population quality in its turn implies an increase in labor productivity and the economic value of labor time, translating into higher income. According to Schultz, this virtuous circle demonstrates that "increases in the acquired abilities of people throughout the world and advances in useful knowledge hold the key to future economic productivity and to its contributions to human well-being."[62]

In other words, classical economic theory supposedly did not take into account the fact that the human being is a form of constantly expandable capital, a source of value which is almost infinitely renewable, making it possible to reject the idea of an economy condemned to the exploitation of scarce, disputed resources. Thus, it is no accident if criticism of Malthus is a leitmotif of neo-liberal analyses. In a "quantitative theory of population," he reduced quality of life to "the subsistence of the rank and file of the population"[63] without realizing the importance of acquired aptitudes, skills and forms of competence that can be improved.

Gary Becker's micro-economic approach is often presented as an example of the "new demographic economics."[64] In fact, the Malthusian approach was incapable of explaining the negative relationship between fertility and income characteristic of higher and average households in the USA at the end of the baby boom. Becker shows that couples' fertility is subject to economic variables and can be studied within the same framework as analysis of demand for consumer durables. Demand for children exists in just the same way as there can be a demand for real estate, and a child has a price, which depends on investment in education. Like other goods, a child produces a utility for the parents, more particularly, a "psychic income." In other words, the number of children is subject to a choice about the way to allocate resources: "The demand for children would depend on the relative price of children and full income. An increase in the relative price of children (...) reduces the demand for children and increases the demand for other commodities (if real income is held constant)."[65] The greater the rise in household incomes, and the higher the price of children in terms of investment in time, education and so on, the greater their "utility" for parents and for the labor market. This is the case until the point when parents have to arbitrate between income impact and price impact, which can have negative consequences for fertility, especially if, in order to preserve optimal conditions of equilibrium between different kinds of goods, parents choose to reduce the number of children, either in order to increase their consumption of different goods or so as to increase the utility of the children they have already had. Through this micro-economic tour de force, Becker arrives at a causal explanation of the relationship between the increase in human capital and the drop in fertility but, above all, at an economic measure of human capital based upon the relationship between investment in children, returns on investment (salary benefits) and "population quality." This theory proves decisive when it makes it possible to interpret spending on education, health and training as so many forms of investment in human capital, whose purchase costs are covered by past remuneration.[66] It shows that the Malthusian error consists in interpreting such expenditure as non-recoverable consumption, whereas it involves "roundaboutness" generating economic benefits.[67]

While this theorization recalls Marx's concept of "expanded reproduction," neo-liberal theoreticians obviously also attack the other pole of the alternative. Where Marx conceives the wage as reproduction of the labor power, which is a source of profit to the capitalist, Schultz interprets wages as a source of "self-investment." The neo-liberal individual who is the bearer of a non-liquid human capital, which he therefore cannot alienate, but whose services he can only sell is a capitalist: "Laborers have become capitalists not from a diffusion of the ownership of corporation stocks, as folklore would have it, but from the acquisition of knowledge and skills that have economic value."[68] Foucault's analysis discloses a figure of subjectification whose complexity is much greater than that of the emblematic figure of the "capitalist": an individual who constructs himself by continually assessing his skills in order to enhance or augment them by making life itself a constant test of his human capital.[69] In any event, the objective of the neo-liberal economic analysis that defines each individual as the owner of their human capital is to dissolve the very concept of class, making generalized competition the only economically *justifiable* reality in which social actors move.

The stroke of genius by theoreticians of "human capital" is to have created a tool for assessing the value of existence which is without a scale, measurement of the cost of investments in human capital equally applying to the "skills portfolio" of an individual and the human resources of a firm, nation or continent. A unit of measurement perfectly suited to the knowledge society, the concept of "human capital" makes it possible to circumvent the population/class alternative, challenging both the quantitative rigidity of the first category and the explanatory relevance of the second in the era of the "entrepreneur of the self."[70]

CONCLUSION

If we read the lectures given by Foucault at the Collège de France in 1978 and 1979 together, we can reconstruct a developing line of economic and political thought about population. Before the nineteenth century, the key government problem was achieving a large population, by all possible means, and, in particular, migration: population became a sign and pertinent indicator of good government. With Malthus, by contrast, the question of an uncontrollable increase in the biological population in a confined territory was raised—a question to which Marx counter-posed class as a result of the international division of labor and as an entity that could be politicized in the struggle against capitalism. For Marx, the fact that population is structured in classes is not innocent for its reproduction. But it is not inevitable either, given that over-population is an effect of the dynamic of capitalist accumulation. Yet Malthus and Marx's starting point remained a Ricardian idea—namely, that the economic game is limited. Thus, in both cases, the population's relationship to the source of wealth (food supply or labor) assumes a conflictual form: a natural conflict between geometrical progression of the population and arithmetical progression of resources, compelling human beings to struggle against nature and themselves in Malthus—a class struggle that represents the truth of the historical development of capital in Marx. Above all, in both instances, conflict is the motor of history.

This conflictual form is precisely what neo-liberalism has sought to circumvent. In the post-war years, a "qualitative" figure of population became established, in which the "value" of individuals is measured by their degree of skill ("soft and hard skills") and proves itself in the competitive dynamic. Above all, human capital presents itself as a potentially infinitely renewable resource whose very existence contradicts classical economics' scarcity principle. In fact, it has been able to develop as the main instrument of a neo-liberal government of life that simultaneously challenges the "bio-economics of scarcity" and the "catastrophist" horizon that irreducibly command the idea of a proclivity to over-population.

The genealogical sketch of the economic valuation of human life I have proposed in this contribution eventually shows that this neo-liberal credo in human capital as an inexhaustible resource can today be challenged precisely at the international level where Marx criticized Malthusianism. In the first place, the syndrome of "burn out" of professional exhaustion and of suffering at work are transnational phenomena, revealing, with the speculative and financial crisis, a crisis of the human resource that is affecting the world economy on a long-term basis. Secondly, generalization of the principle of human capital as a key criterion for defining optimum mobility in the neo-liberal set-up implies that individual mobility now depends less on racial and national affiliation than on the stock of skills possessed by the individual. Thus, if neo-liberal economics subscribes to the inter-mingling of populations and develops, via NGOs and international agencies, human capital implementation programs in developing countries, elements of the old anthropological and biological racism will continue to circulate in the form of a kind of "skills racism". In effect, the market in the skills that make up human capital is based, like any other market, on rising and falling prices and on the exclusion of those unable to play the game. The new "danger" threatening the social body is the individual incapable of engaging in the mechanism of competition, incapable of developing their skills and appraising themselves. Thus, the differential inclusion of workers in the labor market depending on nation-states' human capital requirements recasts migratory flows, creating both a new lumpen-proletariat bereft of basic civil rights, but supposed to live and work on the national soil, and a new surplus population of the unskilled, whose life itself now seems "superfluous" by evaluative criteria based on "human capital."[71]

If the old Malthusian question of energy limits and excess population is posed even more sharply today, in a context of ecological crisis, it is in a global economic order reconfigured by the doctrines of human capital, with their effects on the labor market and the transnational mobility of labor power. That is why Foucault's interpretation of neo-liberalism, re-read in an international perspective and from the standpoint of the gradual globalization of demographic problematics, rather than distancing us from Marx, should persuade us to re-read Marx and Foucault together.

*Translated by Gregory Elliott*

## NOTES

1. Mitchell Dean, "The Malthus Effect: population and the liberal government of life," *Economy and Society*, 44(1) (2015): 18–39.
2. See Paul R. Ehlrich, *The Population Bomb*, (Ballantine Books, 1968). About the relationship between the overpopulation theories and biopower, see Paltrinieri Luca, "Biopouvoir, les sources historiennes d'une fiction

politique," *Revue d'histoire moderne et contemporaine*, 60(4) (2013): 49–75.

3. Thomas Robertson, *The Malthusian Moment: Global Population Growth and the Birth of American Environmentalism* (Rutgers University Press, 2012).

4. Michel Foucault, *The Birth of Biopolitics. Lectures at the Collège de France 1978–1979* (New York: Palgrave-MacMillan, 2008).

5. Dean, "The Malthus Effect: population and the liberal government of life": 19.

6. Ibid: 36.

7. Thomas Malthus, *An Essay on the Principle of Population*, 1$^{st}$ edn, ed. Antony Flew, (Harmondsworth: Penguin, 1970), ch. 1, p. 70.

8. Ibid., p. 71.

9. Thomas Malthus, *An Essay on the Principle of Population*, variorum edn, ed. Donald Winch, (Cambridge: Cambridge University Press, 1992), Bk. 1, ch. i, p. 17.

10. Michel Foucault, *The Order of Things: An Archaeology of the Human Sciences*, transl. A.M. Sheridan Smith (London: Tavistock, 1970), pp. 166–200.

11. Etienne Balibar, "Foucault's Point of Heresy: 'Quasi-Transcendentals' and the Transdisciplinary Function of the Episteme," *Theory, Culture & Society*, 32 (5–6) (2015): 45–77.

12. Ibid.: 256.

13. Michel Foucault, *Security, Territory, Population, Lectures at the Collège de France 1977–1978* (New York: Palgrave-MacMillan 2009), pp. 25–39.

14. Hervé Le Bras, *Les Limites de la planète* (Paris: Flammarion, 1994), p. 292.

15. Malthus, *An Essay on the Principle of Population*, 1st edn, ch. 19, p. 205.

16. Ibid., p. 206.

17. Ibid., p. 205.

18. Malthus, *An Essay on the Principle of Population*, variorum edn, Bk. IV, ch. xiii, p. 322.

19. Laurent Jeanpierre, "Capitalisme et gouvernement des circulations," in Christian Laval, Luca Paltrinieri, Fehrat Taylan, *Marx & Foucault. Lectures, usages, confrontations*, (Paris: La Découverte, 2015), pp. 213–227.

20. Quoted in Michel Foucault, *History of Madness*, transl. Jonathan Murphy and Jean Khalfa (Abingdon: Routledge, 2006), p. 409.

21. Philip Kreager, "Early modern population theory: A reassessment," *Population and Development Review*, 17(2) (1991): 207–227.

22. Hervé Le Bras (ed.), *L'invention des populations. Biologie, idéologie et politique* (Paris: Editions Odile Jacob, 2000), p. 7–54.

23. Michel Foucault, *Society must be defended: Lectures at Collège de France, 1975–1976*, (New York, Picador, 2003).

24. Dean, "The Malthus Effect...", p. 34.

25. Betsy Hartmann, *Reproductive Rights and Wrongs: The Global Politics of Population Control* (Boston, South End Press, 1995).
26. Robertson, *The Malthusian Moment.*
27. Matthew Connelly, *Fatal Misconception: The Struggle to Control World Population* (Cambridge and London: Harvard University Press, 2008).
28. Michel Foucault, *Security, Territory, Population: Lectures at the Collège de France, 1977–1978* (New York: Palgrave Macmillan, 2007), p. 79.
29. Ibid., p. 77.
30. Karl Marx and Frederick Engels, *Collected Works*, Vol. 3, (London: Lawrence and Wishart, 1975), p. 439.
31. Karl Marx, *Outlines of the Critique of the Political Economy* (London: Penguin, 1973), p. 540.
32. Friedrich Engels, *Condition of the Working Class in England* (London: Panther Edition, 1969), p. 224–231.
33. Marx, *Outlines of the Critique of the Political Economy*, p. 539.
34. Karl Marx, "Critical Notes on the Article: The King of Prussia and social reform," in Karl Marx & Friedrich Engels, *Collected Works*, Vol. 3 (London: Lawrence and Wishart), 1975: 202.
35. Marx, *Outlines of the Critique of the Political Economy*, p. 538.
36. See Karl Marx & Friedrich Engels, *Capital. A Critique of Political Economy* (London, Penguin Classics, 1990), vol I, part 7, chap. 25, pp. 434–449; see Lazar Behar, "Loi de population et science démographique. Pour une problématique matérialiste en démographie (II)," *La Pensée*, 186, (March-April 1976): 3–27.
37. Marx, *Outlines of the Critique of the Political Economy*, p. 538.
38. Ibid., p. 541.
39. Karl Marx & Friedrich Engels, *Capital. A Critique of Political Economy*, vol I, part 7, chap. 25, section 5, pp. 453–464.
40. Cf. Karl Marx & Friedrich Engels, *Capital. A Critique of Political Economy*, vol I, part 7, chap. 25, section 3 and 4, pp. 442–453; see also Suzanne de Brunhoff, *Etat et capital* (Paris, PUF, 1973); and Lazar Behar, "Surpopulation relative et reproduction de la force de travail. Pour une problématique matérialiste en démographie," *La Pensée*, 176 (August 1974): 9–29.
41. Marx, *Outlines of the Critique of the Political Economy*, p. 540.
42. Marx & Engels, *Capital. A Critique of Political Economy*, vol. I, p. 523.
43. *Ibid.*, p. 450.
44. Guillaume Sibertin-Blanc, "Loi de population du capital, biopolitique d'État, hétéronomie de la politique de classe," in Franck Fischbach (ed.), *Relire Le Capital* (Paris, PUF, 2009) and "Race, population, classe : discours historico-politique et biopolitique du capital de Foucault à Marx," in

Laval, Paltrinieri, Taylan, *Marx & Foucault. Lectures, usages, confronta-tions*, pp. 228–243.

45. Marx & Engels, *Capital. A Critique of Political Economy*, vol. I, p. 443.
46. Armand Mattelart, "Une lecture idéologique de l'essai sur le principe de population," *L'Homme et la société, Marxisme et sciences humaines* 15(1970): 183–219.
47. Marx & Engels, *Capital. A Critique of Political Economy*, vol. I, p. 448.
48. Malthus, *An Essay on the Principle of Population*, variorum edn, Bk. IV, ch. 13, p. 322.
49. Engels, *Condition of the Working Class in England*, p. 224.
50. Marx, *Outlines of the Critique of the Political Economy*, p. 41.
51. Marx & Engels, *Capital. A Critique of Political Economy*, vol I, part 4, chap. 15, section 5, pp. 287–292.
52. Ibid., p. 444.
53. See Dennis Hodgson, "Demography as social science and policy science," *Population and Development Review*, 9(1) (1983): 1–34; Matthew Connelly, *Fatal Misconception*; Saul Halfon, *The Cairo Consensus: Demographic Survey, Women's Empowerment and Regime Change in Population Policy* (Plymouth (UK), Lexington Book, 2007).
54. Paltrinieri Luca, "Biopouvoir, les sources historiennes d'une fiction politique."
55. Foucault, *Security, Territory, Population*, p. 73.
56. Albert O. Hirschman, *The Passions and the Interests: Political Arguments For Capitalism Before Its Triumph* (Princeton, Princeton University Press, 1977); and Catherine Larrère, *L'invention de l'économie au XVIIIᵉ siècle. Du droit naturel à la physiocratie* (Paris, PUF, 1992).
57. Foucault, *The Birth of Biopolitics*, pp. 270–271.
58. Ferhat Taylan, "Environmental Interventionism: A Neoliberal Strategy," *Raisons politiques*, 52(4) (2013): 77–87.
59. See Daniel Zamora & Michael C. Berhent, *Foucault and Neoliberalism* (Cambridge, Polity Press, 2016); Serge Audier, *Penser le 'néolibéralisme.' Le moment néolibéral, Foucault, et la crise du socialisme* (Lormont: Le Bord de l'eau, 2015) and above all Mitchell Dean, "Michel Foucault's 'apology' for neoliberalism," *Journal of Political Power*, 7(3)(2014): 433–442.
60. As I suggest in Luca Paltrinieri, "Quantifier la qualité: Le 'capital humain' entre économie, démographie et éducation," *Raisons politiques*, 52(4) (2013): 89–107.
61. Theodore W. Schultz, *Investing in People: The Economics of Population Quality*, (Berkeley: University of California Press, 1981), p. 21.
62. Ibid., p. xi.
63. Ibid., p. 21.
64. Marc Nerlove, "Toward a New Theory of Population and Economic Growth," in Theodore W. Schultz, *Economics of the Family, Marriage,*

*Children and Human Capital*, (Chicago/London: University of Chicago Press, 1974), pp. 527–545; see in particular Gary S. Becker, *A Treatise on the Family* (Cambridge/London, Harvard University Press, 1981).

65. Gary S. Becker, "An Economic Analysis of Fertility," in Ansley J. Coale (ed.), Demographic and Economic Changes in Developed Countries (New Jersey, Princeton University Press, 1960), p. 210.

66. Theodore W. Schultz, *Investing in People*, pp. 14–15, 31–34, 40–56; and Gary S. Becker, *Human Capital. A Theoretical and Empirical Analysis with Special Reference to Education* (Chicago/London: The University of Chicago Press, 1975 [sec. ed. 1983]), chap. 2 and 3, pp. 15–81.

67. Eugen v. Böhm-Bawerk, *Capital and Interest: A Critical History of Economical Theory*, (London: MacMillan & Co., 1890).

68. Theodore W. Schultz, "Investment in Human Capital," *The American Economic Review*, 51(1) (1961): 3.

69. Michel Fehrer, "Self-Appreciation; or, The Aspirations of Human Capital," *Public Culture* 21(1) (2009): 21–41.

70. Michel Foucault, *The Birth of Biopolitics*, pp. 215–237.

71. Alessandro dal Lago, *Non-persons. The Exclusion of Migrant in a Global Society* (Milano: Ipoc Press, 2009).

# CHAPTER 15

# Mesopolitics: Foucault, Environmental Governmentality and the History of the Anthropocene

## Ferhat Taylan

It seems increasingly undeniable that no "world politics" (or what is referred to by this concept) can ignore the new problems posed by the ecological crisis, which (according to the Pentagon) is a major national security issue for the USA.[1] We know how far geostrategic considerations have asserted their own logic in ways of tackling the effects of climate change. Thus, the melting of the Arctic sea ice seems to be problematized predominantly from the perspective of the new opportunities for exploiting natural resources it opens up for the countries that seize them and the tensions this may cause between them. A whole new field of knowledge is in the process of being created under the rubric of "Climate Governance and Environmental Policy," conveying a new "global raison d'État," that is, a form of rationality that approaches the environment exclusively via actors' strategic and economic interests. Not surprisingly, this geostrategic and economic approach to the environment by states frequently seems to be in contradiction with the prerequisites for the recovery of the ecosystem, such as a sustained reduction

F. Taylan (✉)
University Paris Ouest Nanterre, Paris, France
e-mail: ferhattaylan@gmail.com

© The Author(s) 2017                                                                                  261
P. Bonditti et al. (eds.), *Foucault and the Modern International*,
The Sciences Po Series in International Relations and Political
Economy, DOI 10.1057/978-1-137-56153-4_15

in $CO_2$ rates. Since the publication, in 1972, of *The Limits To Growth* Report, which undermined how exponential growth was incompatible with finite resources of the Earth, these contradictions have regularly been exposed in major inter-governmental summits since the Rio Conference in 1992, and this was the case once again with the UN Climate Change Conference held in Paris in December 2015 (COP 21).

In this context, "global environmental politics" may legitimately be regarded as apparently suffering from certain impasses and blind spots and doubtless requires new analytical grids to pose the questions differently.

For a decade, the social sciences have sought to furnish a multiplicity of perspectives on what it now seems appropriate to call the "Anthropocene," that is, the new epoch when the impact of human activity on nature is said to have become a geological factor. If a significant number of political scientists are rushing to become inventors of superior forms of "governance" in the Anthropocene,[2] we also find initiatives examining the significance of this transformation for modern thought itself.[3] In short, the West's entry into the Anthropocene in the eighteenth century entails rethinking political and scientific modernity from the standpoint of the ways in which it has posed the problem of human beings' natural and social environment. Is it correct to think that the relationship between environment and politics started with the recent ecological crisis? Did the environment become an object to be governed, a domain of political problematization, once the impact of human action on it became patent? In fact, as long as the modern relations between politics and environment remain obscure, as long as they are not the object of a political philosophy informed of their history, discoursing on the optimal forms of "governance" of the environment seems futile—as if it were enough to develop management techniques to escape an ecological crisis so profoundly rooted in our ways of acting and thinking.

This article will be concerned with the modern history of "environmental governmentality," that is, a modern political rationality which tends to "conduct the conduct" of human beings by planning their surroundings. Michel Foucault unexpectedly provides us with some pointers for this alternative way of conceiving the history of the relations between politics and the environment, which includes the issue of governing human beings by planning their environment in the vast problematic of government. In fact, Foucault's works[4] clearly flag up the environment as a problem of *government* for the Moderns. Alluding to the science of milieux, which the positivist doctor Bertillon called "mesology" in the 1870s, we might dub this ensemble of knowledge and techniques geared to governing human beings by planning their environment "mesopolitics."

Before proceeding to the lectures by Foucault where the premises of this mesopolitics are to be found, I would like to rapidly invoke some aspects of the environmental issue as posed today. We may start with a very simple observation: the environmental problem is often treated as requiring exclusively technical or technocratic solutions—and urgently. To the question "What can philosophy, or anthropology, or sociology or history do when confronted with the urgency of the environmental issue?" the usual answer is that, in view of the slow pace of such research, the right approach is to give the floor to the experts, climatologists and technocrats who participate in international summits and hope that politicians will prove responsive to their suggestions. In other words, the urgency of the environmental issue is often coupled with expectations of miraculous technical solutions when not consigned exclusively to government decisions.

However, there is another way of posing the problem: from the standpoint not of the urgency of the ecological crisis but of its historical and philosophical profundity. In the event, we discover that what is called the "ecological crisis," and the imperatives people seek to associate with it, is actually part of a largely ignored and unknown modern environmental history where the fundamental problem is our way of relating to what is around us. Broached thus, the issue assumes a historical–ontological dimension because it involves conducting a series of investigations into the relations between the Moderns and their surroundings, into the way they have problematized these surroundings, prioritizing some aspects at the expense of others. Obviously, the idea of the historical and ontological profundity of the "environmental crisis" is today articulated primarily by anthropologists or sociologists of nature.[5] Such work suggests that the ecological crisis goes hand in hand with a crisis of the modern forms of knowledge and concepts in which it originates. This applies to concepts of nature, culture, environment and even ecology that pertain to ways of dividing up reality, which we are precisely beginning to problematize. In my view, in registering the crisis of modern environmental categories, anthropology and the sociology of nature do not take exploration of the governmental reason that accompanied the emergence of these environmental categories far enough. Accordingly, this is the direction, still under-explored, I propose to proceed in here.

Furthermore, recent environmental historiography has demonstrated that the Moderns developed their own "environmental reflexivity"[6]: the environmental question was posed and discussed during modernity, contrary to the idea of a kind of ecological awakening that supposedly occurred only in the second half of the twentieth century. According to the new environmental history, entry into the Anthropocene in the late eighteenth century and early nineteenth century did not transpire in the absence of analyses, theoretical debates and political resistance that have been too quickly forgotten, and which should therefore be "unearthed" to understand how we have got to where we are. By attending to the ideas, debates and resistance of the time, these historians contribute— positively—to a politicization of the Anthropocene. Rather than being consigned to the status of a geological epoch that "humanity" entered largely unawares, the Anthropocene emerges in these critical studies as a moment of political and scientific tensions regarding the natural and social environment. The Moderns have been worried about their environment since at least the eighteenth century, and the forms in which these anxieties were expressed and institutionalized are often fundamental for the way that we interact with the environment today.

Reference to Michel Foucault's work assumes its significance in the context of this ferment of the environmental humanities, of which I have given a brief indication. In his lecture courses at the Collège de France from 1976 to 1978, he furnishes us with pointers as to the way in which the environment was posed as a problem by the Moderns from the standpoint of the government of human beings. The first occurs in his lecture of 17 March 1976 when he formulated the hypothesis of a biopower, that is, "the acquisition of power over man insofar as man is a living being" or, more simply, "state control of the biological."[7] Foucault listed the main areas for investigation—among them, "control over the relations between the human race, or human beings insofar as they are a species, insofar as they are living beings, and their environment, the milieu in which they live."[8]

This initial indication obviously refers to the theme, already old in Foucault, of medicalization. This involved a problematization, in the late eighteenth century, of endemic illnesses in connection with the living environment of populations. The problem had already been studied in lectures on social medicine, which became "a medicine of the living conditions of the existential milieu," and public hygiene, a politico-scientific technique to control this environment.[9] Given that social medicine was predominantly an urban medicine, Foucault soon extended the scope of his analysis to urbanization. Thus, at the end of the first lecture in the lecture series on *Security, Territory, Population*, the practices of urban planning in the late eighteenth century were treated as a problem of the government of environments. According to Foucault, the concept of environment had not yet emerged, but the practical schemas heralding it were already present in the form of a politics geared towards the environment, which planned it to act on human behaviour. Foucault foreshadowed this in the context of his analysis of liberal governmentality, that is, a way of governing human beings through action at a distance, which does not act directly on bodies like the disciplines but acts on the population by planning its living environments. Mainly at stake was the urban environment whose planning, as early as the *ancien régime*, began to be posed as a simultaneous medical and political problem, prior to becoming an important means of social action after the revolution.

Finally, in *The Birth of Biopolitics*, the theme of governing environments recurred, presented by Foucault this time as one of the neo-liberal Chicago School's government apparatuses, which "act on the environment and systematically modify its variables".[10] In particular, studying Gary Becker's economic analyses of criminality, Foucault concluded in his lecture of 28 March that the economic subject is regarded as being responsive to environmental action, and economics is consequently defined as "the science of the systematic nature of responses to environmental variables."[11] Foucault's argument is that for classical liberalism, economic man was a subject of interest to be left to his own devices, whereas with the neo-liberalism theorized by the Chicago School, he becomes an agent who will respond systematically to alterations in his environment and, as such, is "eminently governable." He thus emerges as a figure whose economic conduct can be altered through what Foucault calls "environmental action." This term is to be taken in the sense not of the "study of public action"—that is, the public policy which an ecology ministry, for example, is likely to implement—but of interventions by an economic actor in the environment to induce specific effects on it. Thus, "[f]rom being the intangible partner of laissez-faire, homo oeconomicus now becomes the correlate of a governmentality which will act on the environment and systematically modify its variables."[12] On the basis of Foucault's analysis, we can formulate a form of "environmental interventionism" at work both in the "framework politics" of German ordo-liberals and in American neo-liberals like Becker.[13]

This idea of environmental governmentality, whose continuity from 1976 to 1978 is clear, seems like a promising working hypothesis, even if it was not further explored by Foucault. In an extended time frame—from the eighteenth century to the twentieth—it underscores a continuity in ways of regarding human beings' natural and social environment as a means of economic action on them. This environmental governmentality does not act directly on bodies or individuals, unlike the disciplinary techniques that mark bodies, but acts indirectly on those individuals' surroundings in order to conduct their conduct. For Foucault, this general schema of action at a distance seems to be one of the essential matrices of liberal and neo-liberal governmentality insofar as such public intervention can act efficaciously on the context of human action while appearing sufficiently discreet. More profoundly, following the guiding threat of the concept of *milieu*—synthesized in French by Lamarck and Comte in the early nineteenth century—rather than the English concept of *environment*— systematized by Spencer in the 1860s—makes it possible to explore the prehistory of an environmental politics from the late eighteenth century. In other words, there was indeed an environmental politics prior to the emergence of the concept of environment, and tracking the history of the concepts of climate, recently ventured by Fressoz,[14] or of *milieu*, as I have done,[15] helps to reveal a much older, much more explicit problematization of environment than is usually credited.

Mesopolitics therewith emerges as a modern procedure with its roots in the eighteenth century when human beings' relations to the environment were invested as objects of scientific knowledge, philosophical reflection and political intervention. Let us take the example of the second half of the eighteenth century. As regards the life sciences, these years were marked by the emergence of the concepts of irritability and sensibility in Haller, Bordeu and other doctors of the Montpellier School, and these concepts stamp the image of a living being profoundly sensitive to its material surroundings. All the medicine of the time, and soon its philosophy and literature, was marked by this discovery of sensibility, a human being sensitive to its surroundings, alterable and governable by the planning of the entities around it.[16] Gradually replacing the mechanistic regime opposing soul and body, the new duo of organism and milieu resulted in unprecedented attention being paid to the environment. The latter was a threatening environment, which might be pathogenic, like the miasmatic air of towns or workshops that was such a source of anxiety to doctors. What is called the climate question was thus transformed in the eighteenth century, predominantly becoming the object of a medical research programme.

It should not be thought that this was solely the domain of social medicine since philosophical re-workings of these themes clearly formulated the perspective of an environment that must be governed in order to govern men themselves. There are several possible cases, but here I shall confine myself to mentioning Rousseau. We are familiar with Rousseau's project of a "sensitive morality"—a way of governing the influence of the outside world on human beings.[17] According to Rousseau, we are naturally sensitive to the objects around us, which impress us and normally lead us into vice, whereas if we succeed in controlling the effects of this environment, we might conduct it in such a way as to create positive effects. The principal terrain of this sensitive morality is education: if it is necessary to "form an enclosure around [the] child's soul," to "draw its circumference,"[18] it is precisely to try to protect it from the unpredictable effects that might hail from its environment. The principle of negative education thus goes hand in hand with that of sensitive morality, both of them seeking to "control the effects of external influences on an originally pure individual." However, this negative aspect of the operation soon proves inadequate, in as much as the governor cannot make do with preventing, proscribing or containing the effects of the environment. He must also act *positively* on the child's surroundings by creating an artificial universe around him so that his attention is channelled in the desired direction. Thus, rather than penning in sensibility, which will operate in any event, it is a question of *adjusting* it. Education precisely becomes action on actions when it is assigned the task of acting on the child's will by means of a prudent organization of its surroundings. A famous passage in *Emile* clearly indicates that government by freedom is principally a form of government by the environment. Rousseau writes that "[t]here is no subjection so perfect as that which keeps the appearance of freedom. Thus the will itself is made captive. The poor child who knows nothing, who can do nothing, who has no learning, is he not at your mercy? Do you not dispose, with respect to him, of everything which surrounds him? Are you not the master of affecting him as you please?"[19]

These ideas of Rousseau found an echo in Bentham, who opens his famous work on the panopticon with a little-noticed sentence, which advises governments "to utilize a highly dynamic, very useful instrument, which involves controlling what happens to a certain number of men, in arranging everything around them, so as to create in them the desired impression."[20] Foucault manifestly prioritizes the strictly disciplinary aspect of the panopticon apparatus. But it should not be forgotten that behind it in Bentham, there is a whole argument involving the idea of action at a distance, acting on the environment in order to act on individual behaviour. Individual self-interest is not impervious to government action once the latter is directed at the context in which the interest emerges. In other words, the variables that make up the playing field of individual interests can be inflected by indirect action. In Rousseau and Bentham alike, government by freedom is thus clearly formulated as action on the environment, understood as action on the very conditions of the will or interest.

We find the same configuration in Cabanis, who precisely dubs a politics seen at work in public assistance "government by freedom" involving the regulation of surroundings so that men can govern themselves.[21] Cabanis was a "doctor-philosopher," who was highly active in the bodies of the new republic, concerned to reform the circumstances in which people lived. Thus, around 1800, in a context pervasively marked by the revolution, there was increased attention to the social environment and a new consistency was achieved. Rival projects for a "science of man" began to emerge from doctors, geographers or naturalists, composing a panoply of forms of knowledge about man as he existed in the midst of circumstances. A plan of republican action against isolationism existed, which sought to create a republican environment to combat degeneration and dislocation. For Cabanis, the point was to regulate social existence by discovering the *correct distance* between human beings so that solidarity might be obtained without promiscuity having side effects. This correct distance allowed everyone to be positioned in "their own sphere" in such a way that they could operate self-interest—the great lever of social existence. For example, in order to banish begging, individuals must be encouraged to act not with the disciplinary methods of the workshop but with the "felicitous influence of freedom": "the felicitous influence of freedom will end up almost completely freeing the legislator from the task of providing for the subsistence of a large number of needy persons … All these moral dispositions, and all these circumstances, exercise such sway that the government seems to have almost nothing to do about begging."[22]

In short, in the late eighteenth century, mesopolitics emerged as a form of government by freedom at the intersection of bio-medical knowledge of the environment, philosophical investigation of this knowledge and the forms of political action it inaugurated. In effect, Foucault had sensed this when he proposed to interpret the idea as an essentially liberal one, as a technique of liberal governmentality. As we progress towards the nineteenth century, especially in the exploration of sociological thought, the picture becomes more complicated, and it seems more difficult to reduce mesopolitics to an exclusively liberal form of governmentality. Governing human beings by planning their surroundings, by transforming their conditions of existence, emerged as one of the key ideas of sociological thought.

This is readily apparent when we study the way that the concept of *milieu* was formulated and treated in sociological thinking in France in the nineteenth century. It was above all the emergence of the concepts of conditions of existence and surrounding milieux in Cuvier and Lamarck, respectively, which marked the stabilization of a paradigm now confirmed by the nascent biology. As we know, Auguste Comte relied on this biology to develop his project for the pacification of post-revolutionary society—a project whose cornerstone was precisely the harmony between the organism and its milieu.[23] The social science elaborated by Comte involves a regulatory power whereby the social organism is to govern itself by regulating its living environment, by altering its own conditions of existence. To put it differently, society must govern itself by planning its environment, which is a simultaneous physical, chemical, biological and social milieu. Of all living beings, man is the only one who lives in the most complex milieu—the social milieu—knowledge of which pertains to the new science-dubbed sociology by Comte. We can therefore assert that at the point of its original formulation, sociology emerged as the science of man's relationship to the social milieu. Therewith, attention to the environment was channelled predominantly towards the social environment, which was regarded as the most decisive milieu for human beings.

Obviously, this was not an exclusively Comtean paradigm since at the century's close, Durkheim was to inscribe it in a much more pronounced divide between Nature and Society. When, in *The Division of Labour in Society*,[24] he proposed to study the way that societies react to their given conditions of existence, Durkheim defined social milieu as a set of constraints to which individuals are required to adapt. When this milieu becomes denser and more voluminous, as occurred in the West with urbanization, the division of labour emerges as a way of pacifying the struggle for existence waged by individuals in such a social milieu. Consequently, social facts or psychic facts cannot be reduced to the exclusively physical environmental causalities advanced by eighteenth-century materialism because they depend on the transformation of social milieux as irreducible entities. With Durkheim, the milieu that counts for human beings, the milieu to which they must adapt, definitively becomes the social milieu. Hence the concern with moral education, whose goal is to organize a moral milieu around the child, making him experience the reality of the milieu to which he must adapt.[25] Here too we find an argument that involves governing human beings in accordance with the external promptings of the social milieu and by planning or intensifying their moral milieu. Where the great divide between nature and society is instituted, human nature is defined as profoundly alterable by the milieu peculiar to it, which is the social milieu.

But it is not only in scholarly texts that we find mesopolitics at work. Mesology—the science of milieux—was defined by Bertillon in the 1870s as an applied science of milieux concerned with the acclimatization of colonists in Algeria as well as public hygiene or the treatment of criminals under the Third Republic. This, moreover, was the main difference between it and the ecology invented by Ernst Haeckel—the term, at least, if not the science itself—some years earlier in Germany, which was based on Darwinian conditions of possibility and did not have direct political applications. As to mesology, it was not only a scholarly idea but a set of political technologies and social practices, which were actually operative, especially in the second half of the nineteenth century in France, as is also remarked by Rabinow in a spirit that is more enthusiastic than critical.[26]

This brief excursion in nineteenth-century France suffices to demonstrate that mesopolitics is far from being an exclusively liberal configuration. On the contrary, it has also been systematized, theorized and articulated by scholars who identify with socialism—at least with a certain type of socialism, as in Durkheim—or a certain kind of republicanism, as in the case of Cabanis. Mesopolitics emerges as a more general configuration, irreducible to the opposition between liberalism and socialism, indicating a very widespread form of reflexivity among the Moderns.

We may now try to draw some conclusions from this exposition. While the term "environmental reflexivity" of the Moderns, recently proposed by Fressoz to refer to the various ways of conceiving the environmental consequences of human action, seems pertinent for pointing up the fact that modern societies entered the Anthropocene with a form of reflexivity and very real resistance, it does not enable us to grasp a fundamental dimension of the way in which the environment was conceived in the eighteenth and nineteenth centuries in Europe. On the one hand, from Montesquieu to Durkheim, via the Idéologues and Comte, the nascent social sciences never stopped problematizing human milieux as sites of a necessary political investment, as a lever of social action. On the other hand, a series of government apparatuses, whether urban planning, acclimatization techniques or pedagogical strategies, emerged as mesopolitical strategies, making the environment a means of governing. We might call this general problematization of human milieux, which one seeks to alter to govern human beings, "mesopolitics." Thus, mesopolitics seems to indicate another form of "environmental reflexivity," referring not only to realization of the human impact on the environment but, more generally, to a highly articulated body of thought about the need to intervene in the environment in order to intervene in society.

What of mesopolitics in the twentieth century? Was it a curiosity of nineteenth-century France, of a moral Lamarckism confined to the Third Republic? Following Foucault's indications, we are justified in thinking that environmental governmentality was in fact highly active in the twentieth century and doubtless remains so today. The main perspective introduced by this idea of environmental action consists today in a precise analysis of the connections between economics and other bodies of knowledge, demonstrating the emergence of unprecedented figures of economic man at the intersection of neurosciences and cognitive psychology. Recent analyses of "attention economics," involving the development of marketing strategies in a market where consumers agree to receive services in exchange for their attention, on the economic model of Google, proceed in precisely this direction. In a context where attention is becoming a scarce resource, the conduct of conduct does indeed take the form of planning milieux (numerical or other) so that some things attract more attention than others.

Thus, the relations between politics and environment are not confined today to international governance of the global environment. They also concern government of human beings' immediate environments, be they physical territories or numerical milieux, as attested by current political struggles for greater participation by citizens in decisions about the planning of their living environments.

The relatively unexpected contribution of Foucault's lectures to the current debate on the Anthropocene can now be summarized in a sentence: the history of the Anthropocene is not only the story of the brutal transformation of a nature gradually posited as "external" to human beings but also the strange history of a rationality that seeks knowledge of the environment in order to govern human beings better. Two conclusions follow. On the one hand, the Moderns, obsessed as they were by the issues of social pacification, competition and adaptation within their society, seem to have approached the environment as a problem internal to society, thus excluding the set of problems concerning non-humans from their mesopolitics. On the other hand, this mesopolitics internal to human societies makes the environment a pointedly political issue, whose planning is the object of increasingly vigorous democratic demands. Recent struggles around "commons"—such as the occupation of physical environments to oppose their transformation into financial values or shopping malls—can be thought of as much resistance to a government by the environment. At the intersection of these two domains, a form of political engagement may be emerging in which the environment of human beings will cease to be invested solely by the geostrategic considerations of a Raison d'État, however radically recast.

*Translated by Gregory Elliott*

## Notes

1. "Climate change will affect the Department of Defense's ability to defend the nation and poses immediate risks to U.S. national security." See the Defense Department's "Climate Change Adaptation Roadmap": www.acq. osd.mil/ie/download/CCARprint_wForward_e%202015.pdf (verified on November 4, 2015) On this subject, see also the proceedings of a conference organized by the US army in 2007: Carolyn Pumphrey (ed.), *Global Climate Change: National Security Implications*, US Strategic Studies Institute, 2014. Available to download at http://www.strategicstudiesinstitute.army.mil/pubs/display.cfm?pubID=862 (verified on November 4, 2015).
2. Frank Biermann, *Earth System Governance: World Politics in the Anthropocene* (Cambridge, Mass: MIT Press, 2014).
3. Christophe Bonneuil, Clive Hamilton and François Gemmenne, (eds), *The Anthropocene and the Global Environmental Crisis: Rethinking Modernity in a New Era*, (New York: Routledge, 2015).
4. Michel Foucault, *Security, Territory, Population: Lectures at the Collège de France, 1977–1978*, transl. Graham Burchell, New York: Palgrave Macmillan, 2009. Michel Foucault, *The Birth of Biopolitics: Lectures at the Collège de France, 1978–1979*, transl. Graham Burchell (New York: Palgrave Macmillan, 2008).
5. Latour, Bruno, *Politiques de la nature* (Paris: La Découverte, 2004).
6. Jean-Baptiste Fressoz and Fabien Locher, "Le climat fragile de la modernité. Petite histoire climatique de la réflexivité environnementale," *La Vie des idées*, 20 April 2010.
7. Michel Foucault, [1997], *"Society Must be Defended": Lectures at the Collège de France, 1975–76*, transl. David Macey (New York: Picador, 2003), pp. 239–40.
8. Foucault, *"Society Must be Defended,"* p. 245.
9. Michel Foucault, "La naissance de la médecine sociale," in *Dits et Écrits*, Vol. 2, (Paris: Gallimard, 2001), p. 222.

10. Foucault, *The Birth of Biopolitics, Lectures at the Collège de France*, 1978–1979, transl. Graham Burchell (New York: Palgrave Macmillan, 2004b), p. 271.
11. Foucault, Ibid., p. 269.
12. Foucault, Ibid., pp. 270–1.
13. Ferhat Taylan, "L'interventionnisme environnemental, une stratégie néolibérale," *Raisons politiques*, no. 52, November 2013, ed. F. Gros (Paris, Presses de SciencesPo, 2013), pp. 77–88.
14. Jean-Baptiste Fressoz, "Biopouvoir et désinhibitions modernes : la fabrication du consentement technologique au tournant des XVIIIème et XIXème siècles," *Revue d'Histoire Moderne et Contemporaine*, 60 (4/4bis) (2013): 122–138.
15. *La Rationalité mésologique. Connaissance et gouvernement des milieux de vie (1750– 1900)*, unpublished doctoral thesis, University of Bordeaux Montaigne, 2014.
16. Anne C. Vila, *Enlightenment and Pathology: Sensibility in the Literature and Medicine of Eighteenth-Century France* (Baltimore: Johns Hopkins University Press, 1998).
17. Jean-Jacques Rousseau, "Note sur le projet de la morale sensitive," *Oeuvres de Rousseau*, (Paris: Pléiade edition, Gallimard, 1966, Vol. 1), pp. 408–09.
18. Jean Jacques Rousseau, [1762] *Emile or On Education*, transl. Allan Bloom (New York: Basic Books, 1979), p. 38.
19. Jean Jacques Rousseau, *Emile or On Education*, p. 120.
20. Bentham, James, *Panoptique. Mémoire sur un nouveau principe pour construire des maions d'inspection, et nommément des maisons de force*, (Paris: Imprimerie Nationale, 1791).
21. Pierre Jean George Cabanis, *Rapports du physique et du moral de l'homme*, (Paris: Crapart, Caille et Ravier 1802).
22. Pierre Jean George Cabanis, *Quelques principes et quelques vues sur les secours publics*, in *Oeuvres philosophiques de Cabanis*, (Paris: PUF, 1956 [1793]), p. 27.
23. Auguste Comte, *Cours de philosophie positive*, leçons 46–51, (Paris: Hermann, 2012 (1832)).
24. Emile Durkheim, *De la division du travail social* (Paris: PUF, 2007 [1893]).
25. Emile Durkheim, *Education morale* (Paris: PUF, 2012 [1922]).
26. Paul Rabinow, *French Modern: Norms and Forms of the Social Environment* (Chicago: University of Chicago Press, 1995).

# PART VI

# Global?

# CHAPTER 16

# The Word and the Things: An Archaeology of an Amnesic Notion

*Armand Mattelart*

Globalization? Isn't it first of all the speed with which most languages have incorporated this term taken over from English, without it ever being subject to a preliminary inventory by citizens? Yet this word, which indisputably evokes the new modalities of interconnection between societies, economies and cultures, is part of a specific ideological configuration with a totalizing ambition—or, to use a foucauldian concept, it belongs to a particular "regime of truth" where it finds its meaning. This "'Truth' is linked in a circular relation with systems of power which produce and sustain it, and to effects of power which it induces and which extend it."[1] What is presumed to be true is therefore not merely "superstructural." It is the very condition for the formation and the development of what has come to be called the integrated world capitalism. Its very own vision of the world gradually turns into a universally shared belief.

The context of social atopy that presided over the dissemination of the "global" as a common belief accounting for the current and future state

A. Mattelart (✉)
University Paris VIII, Paris, France
e-mail: armand.mattelart@club-internet.fr

© The Author(s) 2017                                                           277
P. Bonditti et al. (eds.), *Foucault and the Modern International,*
The Sciences Po Series in International Relations and Political
Economy, DOI 10.1057/978-1-137-56153-4_16

of our planet largely contributes to the vagueness that surrounds such a notion. Hence the importance there is to unearth the archaeology of some of the expressions of this one-sided thinking.[2]

## THE NEGATION OF THE *LONGUE DURÉE*

Global integration is being achieved through a multi-secular movement divested of any memory of conflict and, hence, of any grasp of what is now at stake. The historian Marc Ferro, a disciple of Fernand Braudel, was right to warn us against repressing the historical view: "The end of this millennium is dominated by the idea that we have entered a new historical era, that of globalization. But isn't this simply an optical illusion? The movement in the direction of world unification appeared long ago, even though it has recently been extended and expanded at an accelerated pace."[3] During the 1950s, Fernand Braudel fought against a certain conception of history understood as a line of facts, or evolutions, and encouraged to revive the plurality of social time and the "dialectic of length."

Historians are not the only ones to remind us of the need to take a long-term view of this process. Some economists have expressed a similar concern. Robert Boyer, the leading economist of the so-called regulation school, insists on the fact that history seldom repeats itself in an identical fashion and that the contemporary situation of the global economy represents an original configuration. He speaks of "true" and "false" novelty with regard to globalization and argues that we must urgently transcend the "retrospective analyses of economists and of most researchers in social science which, at best, deal with a period of one or two decades" and that we should "take the long-term view of capitalism into account."[4] Pierre Bourdieu and Loïc Wacquant have expressed a similar need for caution: "The globalization of material and symbolic exchange, and the diversity of cultures are not products of the twentieth century, they are co-extensive with human history, as Emile Durkheim and Marcel Mauss already pointed out in their *Note on the notion of civilization*."[5] When insisting on the necessity to move away from the univocal vision of globalization, which he defines as our contemporary regime of historicity, Jean-François Bayart draws on this same heuristical concern.[6]

Amnesia provides the foundation for a modernity without substance. Instead of a genuine social project, techno-mercantile determinism has instituted endless, unlimited communication, the heir to the notion of ongoing limitless progress. In the process, the old scheme to westernize the world has been recycled along with the coming of the so-called information society. "The educated person of the future will have to expect to live in a globalized world, which will be a westernised world," proclaimed the management theoretician Peter Drucker in his book on "post-capitalist society," a society free from friction.[7] The diffusionist theory according to which progress can only reach the periphery through the radiation of values outwards from the centre, first formulated by nineteenth century classical ethnology and updated a century later by the sociologies of modernization and westernization in the fight against "under-development" of the 1960s and the first half of the 1970s (see especially Lerner's and Rostow's modernization theories)[8], has resurfaced with a new liberal Darwinist twist on the pretext that today's technology has made "universal knowledge" accessible to the whole world. Yet, the global age, which both *ingénues* and cynics seem so happy to view as the end of imperialism, has hardly put an end to the ethnocentrism of the age of empires.

Refusal to join historians in "seeing the future in the mirror of the past" means deliberately overlooking the underlying moments of conflict that have built up the imaginary we carry in our minds of planetary society and consciousness. Indeed, from the fifteenth century onwards, it is possible to track the dream of world unity as variously coming under the sign of a religion, an empire, an economic model or the struggle of the oppressed. There has been a profusion of plans and schemes for reorganizing and "pacifying" the planet. The "discovery" of a New World opened up the prospect of dialogue and, thanks to sixteenth-century Spanish scholastic theologians such as Francisco de Vitoria who justified the *jus communicationis* (the right to communicate), paved the way to modern international public law but ended in massacres and the negation of Native Amerindian cultures. The philosophy of the Enlightenment sketched out a plan for the joint control of nature and provided a justification for the great colonial enterprises. The international thrust of true socialism was diluted as it gave way to nationalism. Free trade turned into an imperialist nightmare. To an unusual degree, the promise of redemption by building a universal community veered into damnation of the "wretched of the earth," to borrow the expression of the Martinique-born writer Frantz Fanon (see Fernández and Esteves in this volume).[9]

Each of these historical moments has contributed successive notions of universality and of our relationship to others, which in turn were reflected in utopias that emphasized either technological networks or social networks in the service of building a "supranational social bond" or both.[10]

To exorcise the techno-global representation of the world's destiny that forces us to adopt the short-term view, we might well go back and read through some of the essays by Jorge Luis Borges on the Holy Grail of the "universal library," "Babel" or "The Congress" on the impossible quest for a "planet-wide organization":

> To set up a worldwide organisation is no trifling enterprise ... Twirl, who had a farseeing mind, remarked that the Congress involved a problem of a philosophical nature. Planning an assembly to represent all men was like fixing the exact number of Platonic types—a puzzle that had taxed the imagination of thinkers for centuries. Twirl suggested that, without going farther afield, Don Alejandro Glencoe might represent not only cattlemen but also Uruguayans, and also humanity's great forerunners and also men with red beards, and also those who seated in armchairs. Nora Erfjord was Norwegian. Would she represent secretaries, Norwegian womanhood, or—more obviously—all beautiful women? Would a single engineer be enough to represent all engineers—including those of New Zealand?[11]

Or yet again, another text from Borges on "The Analytical Language of John Wilkins,"[12] which recounts the equally quixotic quest for the "principles of a world language," undertaken at the time of the great intellectual restoration, which translate into a "thought chart" enabling all creatures to be ordered and classified, the same utopian scheme at work in all the ensuing projects to develop a "universal language," including the new language of "computerese." Michel Foucault acknowledged that this text was the "place of birth" of his "archeology of human sciences": *The order of things* (*Les mots et les choses*).[13]

Let us shift our gaze from this brief look at the founding moments of the project for world integration and unification and take up a vantage point in the more recent past. This angle is just as essential, for it has resulted in the one-dimensional discourse announcing the entry of human societies into the global age and the development of the "end-of" thesis responsible for the insidious infiltration of an ideology that prefers to remain nameless.

## THE PREMISES OF A GLOBALIST REPRESENTATION

The Pentagon's strategic thinkers were among the first ones to use global semantics. This occurred in the context of the Cold War and served to designate their new enemy and the cybernetic apparatus set up to monitor each and every one of its movements (*Global Positioning System*). In 1955, the Strategic Air Command inaugurated the first defence system prefiguring the large system of real-time connection between computers: the Semi-Automatic Ground Environment network, the touchstone of the future Worldwide Military Command and Control System. This gigantic spider web became a metaphor—andmyth—of "total defense."[14]

The conquest of space and the first satellite system with a planetary reach served as backdrop for the launch of the techno-determinist myth of the "global village," quickly becoming a widely shared cliché.[15]

In his late 1960s' analyses of the worldwide consequences of the convergence of data processing and telecommunications, Zbigniew Brzezinski— at that time director of the Columbia University Research Institute on Communist Affairs, a faculty member of the University's Russian Institute and counsellor to the US President Lyndon B. Johnson—was explicitly presenting a geopolitical grid that lent legitimacy to the notion of the information society as a global society.[16] In fact, his book on technetronic revolution can be read as the final outcome of "end-of" discourse expressed as a strategy for worldwide hegemony. His central thesis went as follows: President John F. Kennedy was the first president of a global era because he viewed the entire world as a domestic policy problem; since the United States controlled world networks, it was the "first global society in history," the one that "communicates the most"; the "global society" model represented by the United States foreshadows the destiny of the other nations; the new universal values flowing from the United States will inevitably captivate the imagination of humanity as a whole, which will then imitate them. The moral of the story: the time of gunboat diplomacy was over; the notions of imperialism, Americanization and a *Pax Americana* were obsolete; and long live the new "network diplomacy." In 1974, two years before his appointment as national security advisor to the US President James Carter, Zbigniew Brzezinski proposed to set up a special inter-agency body to manage the "economic-political-international machinery" or "global system," which would report to the Vice-President and be in charge of "global matters."[17] The plan did not materialize, however, until the Clinton administration created an ad hoc Under-Secretary of State position.

At the same period, the business community was furbishing its weapons against the nation-state perceived as the "nationalist monster," the final pitfall hindering the deployment of the *Global Shopping Center* rationality.[18] The triumphalist vision noticeable in the *global leaders* or *World Managers'* discourses during the 1970s is nevertheless not sufficient to hide the intensive medication used against the growth model of great industrial nations, all confronted with a crisis of energy, the malfunction of the regulatory financial institutions established by the United Nations and the claims for a new economic order backed by the movement of the non-aligned. It is a "crisis of civilization" according to the Trilateral Commission, in as much as it affects the "governability of western democracies."[19] The technologies of information are promoted as a way to get out of the crisis.

## TOWARDS THE MANAGERIAL INTEROPERABILITY

The enthronement of the concept of globalization and its popularization did, however, occur in the 1980s only. Years 1984–1985 are pivotal. A fantastic opportunity was offered by the deregulation of geo-finance. Partitioned as they were in the past, financial markets became part of a global market liquefied by widespread real-time interconnection. The communication sphere was not lagging behind: following up on the deregulation of telecommunications initiated by his Democrat predecessor, Republican President Ronald Reagan lifted the ban on international competition for satellite systems.

A global market requires a global culture. In 1983, Theodore Levitt, professor at the Harvard Business School and director of the *Harvard Business Review,* gave the outline of this new age that strived after upsetting all frontiers: everywhere on earth, desires and individual behaviours had changed in a mimetic fashion, be it in terms of soda drinks, microprocessors, jeans, films or TV shows. This *converging commonality* was the product of the "Republic of Technology."[20] This abrupt thesis is widely echoed by those who call for mega-fusions of transnational companies, starting with the media, advertising and marketing industry. An instrumental vision of culture imposed itself and made sense in the managerial discourse.[21]

Just as it had in the previous phases of internationalization of the communication networks and mass culture, the advertising industry appeared as a laboratory of avant-garde at a time when new projects of satellite pan-television with a planetary or a continental reach were being launched. Empirically, the notion of global culture was born in the marketing domain around the issue of global product policies. Is it possible to make brands profitable in several countries by using the same lines, by basing the strategic approach to targets on the same arguments and similar emotional registers? Defenders of an outrageous globalization answered this question bluntly. The key to the operation of international markets is in the launch of products and global brands, that is, in the marketing of products and standardized brands around the world. This strategy of "universal standardization" is the only adequate response to the homogenization of global needs and the need for economies of scale in production and marketing. It does not deny the existence of segmented markets, namely, markets composed of groups that are socially, economically and demographically different. It does, however, assume that these segments respond more to a global logic than to national thinking. Similar groups of people living in different countries may have the same needs and the same requests for the same products. There are more similarities between groups living in certain areas of Milan, Paris, Sao Paulo and New York than between a resident of Manhattan and the Bronx. The decision to elaborate transborder typologies of lifestyles came from there. These typologies regroup and sort individuals into *consumption communities* on the basis of their values, their priorities, their tastes or norms, and above all, their solvency. Segmentation and globalization therefore appear as the two sides of a similar process leading the world towards *commonality*. This form of segmentation is in fact the patent confession that there is no global society but rather an "archipelago" due to the growing dichotomies within it—dichotomies that are also found, in their own way, inside the rich countries themselves.

The global grid integrates in a relational conception of corporate business. The network-centric company is presumed to prevail over the Fordist hierarchical model. Any default of "interoperability" between the parties of this organic whole, any lack within the free exchange of flows, risks seizing up the system. Communication, which guarantees fluidity, needs to be omnipresent. This cybernetic vision leads the managers in their aim of functional integration of conception, production and consumption within the perspective of a great planetary whole. The consumer loses his status of passive actor and is promoted as a "co-producer," a "prosumer." In the same way, the necessity of integration makes the sedimentation of geographical spaces obsolete.[22] The local, the national and the international are no longer compartmentalized but rather put into interaction and thought of in a synchronic manner. This imperative bears its neologism: *glocalisation*, born from the hybridization of global/local, a term invented by Japanese management theorists. In this scheme of pragmatic relation to the world/global space, there is none but a space for an operatory notion of culture. Are particular cultures pitfalls for performance and standardization of products and behaviours? This is the only relevant question.

The ideology of corporate globalization is indissolubly linked to the ideology of pan-communication. Together, they form the matrix both for the symbolic management of the worldwide scheme and for the further unacknowledgement reality of a world ruled by the logic of socio-economic segregation and relations of force. The "universals of communication" thoroughly permeated the techno-global newspeak. "The most shameful moment came, wrote Deleuze and Guattari, when computer science, marketing, design, and advertising, all the disciplines of communication, seized hold of the word *concept* itself and said: this is our concern, we are the creative ones, we are the *ideas men!* ... We are the friend of the concept, we put it in our computers [...] Certainly, it is painful to learn that *Concepts* indicates a society of information services and engineering."[23]

For more than 25 years, the techno-global regime of truth has gone hand in hand with hubris. The global business community has continually claimed playing the messianic role of "shaping the world." Yet in 2008, the economic and financial crisis showed, live, the damages of a globalized economy abandoned to the mathematical models of traders taking advantage of reticular tools without measuring the external effects of their operations. Frantic speculation appeared even more disconnected from the basic human needs that this systemic crisis goes together with a crisis of the ecosystem, the energetic crisis and food crisis, the centres for social crises. The neoliberal model as the unsurpassable horizon of human evolution lost part of its credit, just as the belief in the capacity of the all-market and all-technology alliance to dissolve inequalities and to "reunite the great human family."

## THE "GLOBAL INFORMATION DOMINANCE"

As the processes of deregulation and privatization were stepped up, the image of the information age encountered that of the "global age." In March 1994 in Buenos Aires, Vice-President of the United States Albert Gore announced his plan for a *Global Information Infrastructure*, holding out to the "great human family" the prospect of a new Athenian agora on a planetary scale.[24] In February 1995, the G7 countries met in Brussels where they ratified the notion of the Global Information Society along with the decision to speed up the pace of telecom market deregulation.

We had come full circle, ending the long conceptual journey during which—bearing the stamp of determinism—the field of ideas about technological change was formed.

For the United States, the implosion of the communist regimes in Eastern Europe raised the issue of preserving its status as the sole super-power, a power resting on four pillars: technological, economic, military and cultural. The control over information and communication networks in wartime as well as peace time—known as "global information domi-nance" in the strategic jargon of the so-called Revolution in military affairs and revolution in diplomatic affairs—became the principle of a new doctrine of hegemony. The expression "network diplomacy," coined by Zbigniew Brzezinski during the 1960s, had become operational.

In 1996, political analyst Joseph S. Nye and Admiral William A. Owens, both advisors to the Clinton administration, said the same thing exactly when they introduced the notion of soft power as the basis of the new doctrine of "global security":

> Knowledge, more than ever before, is power. The one country that can best lead the information revolution will be more powerful than any other. For the foreseeable future, that country is the United States ... The infor-mation edge is equally important as a force multiplier of American diplo-macy, including soft power—the attraction of American democracy and free markets.[25]

Conclusion: only modern communications, first and foremost the Web, can "encourage the expansion of a peaceful community of democracies, which will be the best guarantee of a safe, free, prosperous world." The same Joseph Nye, in a book published a year after the fall of the Berlin wall and bearing the telling title *Bound to Lead: The Changing Nature of American Power*, had launched the notion of "soft power" defined as,

> the ability to achieve desired outcomes in international affairs through attraction rather than coercion. It works by convincing others to follow, or getting them to agree to, norms and institutions that produce the desired behavior. Soft power can rest on the appeal of one's ideas or on the ability to set the agenda in ways that shape the preferences of others. If a state can make its power legitimate in the perception of others and establish interna-tional institutions that encourage them to channel or limit their activities, it may not need to expend as many of its costly traditional economic and military resources.[26]

The novelty lied in the military starting to use the geo-economic criteria for their decision making. It was promoting an offensive strategy of peaceful enlargement of the world market as a paradigm in place of the defensive strategy of containment adopted during the polar opposition of the Cold War years. Hence, the revolution in military affairs assigned prime importance to extending the realm of free trade, revealing the close connections it was developing among the control of information networks, the universalist model of market democracy and the so-called global security strategy intended to ensure the stability of the planet viewed strictly through the prism of the new liberalism. The concentration of geopolitical power in the hands of the lonely superpower was the logical counterpart to economic globalization, defined as nothing less than decentralization at the planetary level.

The concept of soft power reflects the hidden side of globalization doctrines, namely, the thinking of the military establishment. A new doctrine arose in connection with the Gulf War and was later consolidated with regard to the war in Bosnia and the implosion of Africa. The doctrinal revision aimed at redesigning "military control in an uncontrollable world" where the players in the "global system" have increased in number, along with their modes of action. According to its proponents, wars of agrarian and industrial civilization in the era of information war were a relic of the past, requiring careful doses of intervention and abstention. War, which acquired legitimacy in the name of humanitarian universalism, thus had a number of targets, from which America's overriding national interests would choose. The United States should avoid intervening in local wars in which belligerents solved their problems by hacking each other to death. In any case, when intervention did occur, it should have been limited to the commitment of bringing into play the resources of cyberwar, namely, control of the skies.

Since the fall of the Berlin Wall, experts in the military establishment have delighted in celebrating the so-called Revolution in military affairs. The antiseptic wars in the Gulf and Kosovo seemed to confirm this vision, with its traces of technological determinism. Yet, the technological option ("Techint"), which substituted for the techniques of human information gathering ("humint" as they call it in intelligence circles), was invalidated a decade later only by the attacks on September 11, 2001. The latter proved the macro systems of remote surveillance—based on spy satellites and planetary eavesdropping—to be incapable of anticipating terrorist actions. Similarly, the doctrine of zero casualties from among their own ranks appeared totally outdated when formulating a counterattack on a faceless enemy.

## SECURITY DYNAMICS

With the so-called global war on terror, the project for the construction of a "global information society" showed its hidden dystopia: the expansion of security dispositifs with the increased resort to techniques of surveillance, identification and tracking of people[27] as well as, always, their intensification, especially after each new surge of violence such as in the United States following the twin towers attacks; in Spain after the Madrid attacks on March 11, 2004; in the United Kingdom after the London attacks on July 7, 2005; and in France after the January 7, and November 13 2015, Paris attacks. The repercussions of these security logics have never ceased.

Infringements of the rule of law accepted by Western governments in their fight against terrorism reveal existing links between concepts, institutional logics and technological developments that appeared isolated until then. The new socio-historical depth combined with the foucauldian archaeological investigation helps to illuminate in a harsh light the sense of the long gestation of the art of governing the people by the trace (see Bonditti in this volume) in peacetime as in wartime. What has become clear is that several parallel developments suddenly displayed their articulations and their convergences by designing new power configurations, new modes of governing people and things, and new modes of controlling bodies, hearts and minds.

The fragile democratic balance wavers between the rule and the exception, liberty and security, consent and coercion, and transparency and secrecy. The imperative of "national security" comes at the heart of the project of reorganization of society and the world required by a mode of accumulation of transnational capital consistent with the neoliberal hegemony. It magnetizes the various sectors of the State apparatus, establishing itself as a link between law enforcement and national defence, domestic and civil security, on the one hand, and foreign affairs and the economy, on the other. Synergies that had proved their worth during the Cold War by bringing closer industry, defence and academic research are rekindling with stronger connections with the entertainment industry.[28] The national security doctrine formulated by the US government at the threshold of the Cold War goes global, which legitimates exceptions to the separation of powers and the guarantee of rights, the two pillars of the rule of law.

The control of the flows constitutive of the algorithmic mode of communication and circulation of people, goods and messages tightens, justified by alarming discourses on the "new threats." This tightening around the "security project"—which had intrigued Foucault in the late 1970s—consecrates the new strategic orientation based on anticipation and knowledge. This commands the quest for intelligence and data as instruments for watching and monitoring, the so-called dataveillance now applied to massive databanks ("BigData"), and the establishment of ever increasing files on an ever growing number of people, as well as the remodelling of the architecture and the functions of all intelligence services, be they civil or military. New links are forged between national territory and the global space, between the internal and external realms of security,[29] between the police and the military and between secret services and open source intelligence. The American experience is paradigmatic in this regard: agencies whose official mission used to be confined to the national territory install relays abroad. Agencies that could act abroad only, have widened their field of intervention to national territories.

The fight against terrorism has accelerated the integration of information systems, the fluidity and interoperability of technical networks, and the normalization of procedures and protocols. Passports and ID cards have become biometric, transatlantic flights' passengers are recorded and their data are internationally exchanged between intelligence services, codes define the scale of threats, targets of national and international phone tapping systems are more and more numerous, the data collected is kept for longer periods, and phone and Internet (services) providers are requested to record and keep the metadata generated at each connection. In the United States and several countries in Europe, laws are passed by national parliaments to make these data legally available for police, justice and intelligence services. These are some of the most visible indicators of the global boost/expansion of what Michel Foucault had tentatively called "security dispositifs" in the late 1970s.

In such dispositifs, normalization has a crucial importance as evidenced by the establishment by the US Administration of the *Homeland Security Standards Panel* when the new department for Homeland Security was established in 2003 and a new anti-terrorist legislation (the *Patriot Act*) promulgated. The mission of that Panel was to reach agreements on the technical standards for security industries—both civil and military—that could serve as world references. Just as a history of surveillance techniques tells us, the innovation dynamic moves towards the diffusion of technologies initially designed for military applications to the civilian domain. A telling example is that of the conversion of drones from the military cyberwar arsenal to police surveillance tasks, maybe the most actual expression of the military dream of society Michel Foucault had pointed in *Discipline and Punish*?

## The Hybridization of Profiling

The argument of the war on terror has come to justify the enlargement and the increasing of the number of categories of people and groups likely to cause "breach of the peace." Repeated reforms of the penal code, of the code of criminal procedure and of law concerning intelligence signal how multifaceted the listing and classification of sentences, suspects and real or perceived enemies from within are.

Here the positivistic notion of dangerousness is at the very heart of this justice–police dispositif. Such a notion entails a memory of repression that is also a memory of class. It has taken part in the development of the dispositifs of surveillance that, since the invention of anthropometry during the second half of the nineteenth century, fuelled the old technocratic dream of an actuarial society fully governed by the statistical reason and capable of controlling/disciplining the "dangerous classes." This may explain why the imaginary that feeds the contemporary executive powers' security obsession for civil disobedience and deviance is so close to the imaginary distilled by Gustave LeBon's psychology of the crowd, inevitably delinquent;[30] Cesare Lombroso's thesis on the born criminal biotype; and the prophylactic philosophy of "social defense" of the pioneers of fingerprinting.[31] Incidentally, the old demons of the genetic management of populations are never too far.

Testing, sorting, compiling files and building biological indicators aiming to grasp people's behaviours in order to determine the probability of a particular conduct is an approach that reduces the citizen-subject to a measure-individual and that goes beyond the traditional limits of the field of justice and spreads through other sectors such as health, education or immigration. What is visible today is a mode of government built on traceability—of all and in all sectors (see Bonditti in this volume). Keeping everyone and everything on file has become the norm so that anyone who escapes the field of vision of tracking systems is potentially guilty.

Additionally, any prospective on the evolutions of the modes of control in a digital environment cannot spare itself the trouble of also isolating their commercial objectives in addition to their security purposes. Although profiling has long been the states' domain, it certainly is no longer. Actors of the so-called global market, whose economic model is based on marketing logics (see Hibou in this volume), never cease to track their customers and multiply data banks filled with personal information. Private companies have indeed emerged as monopoles based on the capitation and commercial exploitation of personal data by offering free services and encouraging people to participate in social networks. It is becoming increasingly clear that the innovations that they never cease to introduce in the tracking of customers directly impact on the limits of what we have come to understand as privacy. Recent revelations by Edward Snowden regarding the collaborations between private (Internet) companies and the (military) agency in charge of electronic and signal intelligence within the US Administration (the famous NSA) remind us that the state and its apparatuses are never too far from the ultraliberal logics at play, especially when they govern the global trade of personal data in the contemporary context of a highly integrated global capitalism.

## FROM VISIBLE TO INVISIBLE CONTROL

The paradigm of a surveillance society that prevailed in the understanding/perception of the "new domestic order" (*nouvel ordre intérieur*) during the 1970s was strongly influenced by Michel Foucault's work on the panopticon and prisons in his book *Discipline and Punish*. When Gilles Deleuze introduced the concept of "society of control" later in the 1990s,[32] there is little doubt that he tried to capture the shift—resting on deregulations and privatizations—from disciplinary societies to an art of government in which the managerial rationality was gaining centrality. Deleuze's society of control would be that in which flexible control mechanisms, leaning on computer systems, would multiply based on the model of the network-centric company of a post-Fordist era characterized by short-term controls, speedily operating through continual and illimited flows. By the time Gilles Deleuze coined the term "societies of control," this entrepreneurial management became a tutelar reference and was exported towards all institutions with its load of new instruments of result assessment and measure as well as of modalities of citizens' observation.

What is new compared to when Michel Foucault built his archaeology of the disciplinary society is that compared to the disciplines and their *visible* dispositifs, the efficiency and acceptability of technologies of control now rest on their invisibility. "Whereas the 'disciplinary relation' requires the participation of the one who is monitored, technologies transform the individual into an object of information only. An illustration of this is that while through discipline the individual participated to his own normalization through self-coercion and self-control, he is now liberated from this task thanks to the information that have been collected on him, without him knowing."[33] This being said, some new technologies sometimes perpetuate disciplines. With the electronic bracelet, prison walls and prison guards seem to vanish since the virtual character of intangible limits and internalized obligations suffices. But convicts who do not comply with the constraints will return to confinement.

What has changed since Gilles Deleuze forged the concept of societies of control is that traceability techniques kept becoming more sophisticated, entering all the interstices of society. The collection of traces has become consubstantial with a mode of organization of social relations that needs to anticipate behaviours, identify the probability of certain conducts and build categories based on statistical frequencies. Not only is this collection of trace invisible but it is also mobile and automatic with a deterritorialized treatment of the data collected. The real risk is that automatization goes hand in hand with the autonomy of technique, as Jacques Ellul had warned early on, long before computer science had deployed its full potential.[34]

The overbid on security and protection that governments maintain in an alarming way remind us of those dystopic worlds of a totalitarian social control imagined by Evgueni Zamiatine and Aldous Huxley in the interwar period, or by George Orwell just after WWII. The difference with these imaginary worlds is that contemporary democratic societies and their social control mechanisms have little to do with the age of industrial, Fordist or totalitarian society. Contemporary societies live at the pace of apparent transparency and fluidity of digital technologies, whereas the other existed at the age of machines, symbol of the ideology of never-ending progress. Contemporary societies drink the ideology of communication, which are deemed limitless. The faith in the power of redemption of communication and of its networks that has accompanied the processes of wild deregulation and toxic speculation is the one that legitimated the dissemination and painless introduction of techniques of intrusion into society. If the exception tends to become the rule and manages to convert to normality and become one with everyday life, it is because there is a firmly rooted belief—in the collective mentality—that technology has the power to solve the fundamental problems of society.

# NOTES

1. Michel Foucault, "Truth and Power" [1977], in Colin Gordon (ed.), *Power/Knowledge: Selected Interviews & Other Writings by Michel Foucault. 1972–1977*, transl. by Colin Gordon, (New York: Pantheon Books, 1980), p. 133.

2. In this contribution, I address issues that I have been researching on since the early 1990s and about which I have extensively written, especially in Armand Mattelart, *Mapping World Communication. War, Progress, Culture*. Translated by Susan Emanuel and James A. Cohen, Minneapolis (Mineapolis: University of Minnesota Press, 1994) and *Histoire de l'utopie planétaire: de la cité prophétique à la société globale*, Paris, La Découverte, 1999 (new ed. 2011). I thank Miriam Périer who accepted to translate to English a few sections initially written in French and Philippe Bonditti for the revision of the translation.

3. Marc Ferro, "Le futur au miroir du passé," *Le Monde diplomatique*, September 1999, p. 28.

4. Robert Boyer, "Les mots et la réalité," in Serge Cordellier (ed.), *Mondialisation au-delà des mythes* (Paris: La Découverte, 2000), p. 32.

5. Pierre Bourdieu, Loïc Wacquant, "La nouvelle vulgate planétaire", *Le Monde diplomatique*, March 2000, p. 7. Emile Durkheim, Marcel Mauss, Benjamin Nelson, "Note on the notion of civilization," *Social Research*, 38(4), 1971: 808–813.

6. Jean-François Bayart, *Le gouvernement du monde. Une critique politique de la mondialisation* (Paris: Fayard, 2004).

7. Peter Drucker, *Post-capitalist Society* (New York: Harper Business, 1990), p. 215.

8. Daniel Lerner, *The Passing of Traditional Society: Modernizing the Middle East* (Glencoe, Ill, Free Press, 1958) and Walt W. Rostow. *The Stages of Economic Growth: A Non-Communist Manifesto* (Cambridge: Cambridge University Press, 1960).

9. Frantz Fanon, *The Wretched of the Earth* (New York: T. Grove Press, 1961).

10. Armand Mattelart, *Mapping World Communication* and *Histoire de l'utopie planétaire: de la cité prophétique à la société globale*.

11. Jorge Luis Borges, "The Congress," *The Book of Sand* (London, Penguin 2001 (first ed 1975)), pp. 21–22.

12. Jorge Luis Borges, *Other Inquisitions 1937–1952* (University of Texas Press, 1993).

13. Michel Foucault, *The Order of Things. An archaeology of human sciences* (London and New York, Routledge, 2005 (first translated in 1970)), p. XVI.

14. Paul N. Edward, "The Closed World. Systems, Discourses, Military Policy and Post-World War II US Historical Consciousness," in Les Levidow and Kevin Robins ed. *Cyborg Worlds, The Military Information Society* (London: Free Association Books, 1988), p. 49.
15. Marshall McLuhan, *The Gutenberg Galaxy* (London-New York: Ark Paperbacks, 1962).
16. Zbigniew Brzezinski, *Between Two Ages. America's Role in the Technetronic Era* (New York, Viking Press, 1969).
17. Zbigniew Brzezinski, "Recognizing the Crisis," *Foreign Policy*, 1974, n. 17.
18. Peter F. Drucker, *The Age of Discontent* (London: Pan Book's, 1970).
19. Michel Crozier, Samuel P. Huntington, Joji Watanuki, *The Crisis of Democracy. Report on the Governability of Democracies to the Trilateral Commission*, Preface by Z. Brzezinski (New York: New York University, 1975).
20. Theodore Levitt, "The Globalization of Markets," *Harvard Business Review*, May–June, 1983.
21. Armand Mattelart, *Advertising International. The Privatisation of Public Space*, Translated by Michaël Chanan (London, Routledge, 1991).
22. Kenichi Ohmae, *The Triad Power* (New York: Free Press, 1985), and *The End of the Nation State* (London: Harper-Collins, 1995).
23. Gilles Deleuze, Félix Guattari, *What is Philosophy?* (New York: Columbia university Press, 1994), pp. 10–11.
24. Albert Gore, *Remarks Prepared for Delivery by Vice-President Al Gore to the International Telecommunications Union (Buenos Aires, March 21, 1994)*, Washington: Department of State, 1994.
25. Joseph S. Nye, William A. Owens, "America's Information Edge," *Foreign Affairs* 75(2) (1996): 20.
26. Joseph S. Nye, *Bound to Lead: The Changing Nature of American Power* (New York, Basic Books, 1990).
27. Didier Bigo, Laurent Bonelli, Thomas Deltombe (ed.), *Au nom du 11 septembre* (Paris, La Découverte, 2008).
28. James Der Derian, *Virtuous War: Mapping the Military-Industrial-Media-Entertainment Network* (Boulder, Co: Westview Press, 2001).
29. Didier Bigo, "The Möbius Ribbon of Internal and External Security(ies)" in Mathias Albert, David Jacobson, and Yosef Lapid (eds), *Identity, Borders, Orders* (Minneapolis, University of Minnesota Press, 2001), pp. 91–116.
30. Gustave Le Bon, *The Crowd. A Study of the Popular Mind* (Southampton: Sparkling books, 2009).
31. Armand Mattelart, *The Invention of Communication*, transl. Susan Emanuel (Minneapolis, MN: University of Minnesota Press, 1996) and

*The Globalization of Surveillance. The Origin of the Securitarian Order* transl. Susan Taponier and James A. Cohen (Oxford: Polity Press, 2010).

32. Gilles Deleuze, "Control and Becoming," *Negotiations 1972–1990* (New York, Columbia University Press, 1995).

33. Armand Mattelart, André Vitalis, *Le profilage des populations* (Paris, La Découverte, 2014), pp. 290–291.

34. Jacques Ellul, *The Technological Society*. transl. John Wilkinson (New York, Knopf, 1964. London: Jonathan Cape, 1965. Rev. ed.: New York: Knopf/ Vintage, 1967).

# CHAPTER 17

# Foucault and Geometrics

## Stuart Elden

Foucault's work on biopolitics and biopower has received an enormous amount of attention in recent years, and been developed in a range of different, and not always complementary, ways. This was initially taking up and developing some fairly brief comments in his published books, but is now supplemented by a range of analyses in his lecture courses. With the courses between the 1974 Rio lectures on medicine through *"Society Must be Defended"* (1975–76) to *On the Government of the Living* (1979–80), we can trace his interest and its development.[1] The purpose of this chapter is not to trace his inquiry in this register,[2] nor to track those multiple appropriations, extensions and critiques. Instead, it is to think about how his work can be useful in a parallel and related inquiry, not looking at biopolitics, but at *geopolitics*.

S. Elden (✉)
University of Warwick, Coventry, UK
e-mail: stuart.elden@warwick.ac.uk

© The Author(s) 2017
P. Bonditti et al. (eds.), *Foucault and the Modern International*,
The Sciences Po Series in International Relations and Political
Economy, DOI 10.1057/978-1-137-56153-4_17

## POPULATION-TERRITORY; BIOPOLITICS-GEOPOLITICS

I have argued elsewhere that Foucault is misguided in suggesting that population came to displace territory as the principal object of government.[3] Nonetheless, I think that his work examining the emergence of population is enormously helpful in tracing the related emergence of territory. Just as the relation between these two developments needs to be rebalanced historically, I think the same today is true if we are to look at the relation between biopolitics and geopolitics. A contemporary concentration on biopolitics at the expense of geopolitics would, I think be flawed, in just the same way that a neglect of biopolitics would be. Rather, as I've suggested historically with the parallel developments of population and territory out of earlier, vaguer notions of the people or land, respectively, work today needs to interrogate the relation between these two registers, rather than privilege one over the other.

Amy Swiffen, for example, suggests that "biopolitical sovereignty is less invested in the efficacy of the rule of law in a specified territory than in the capacity to control and change the life of population in a territory."[4] This is a helpful orientation, provided that we continue to understand that the question of territory remains crucial in both determinations. We cannot imagine, as has been done all-too-often in the past, that territory is a simple container for these complicated and contested processes. As Swiffen underlines, "biopolitics is a term that applies when biopower comes into contact with territorial sovereignty as conventionally conceived."[5] As I've argued at length elsewhere, territory and sovereignty are not straightforward concepts, and the conventional conception masks a great deal of complicated interrelations.[6] Strategies turned toward the object and constitution of population are similarly directed toward the object and constitution of territory, which should be understood more as a process than an outcome, more as a political technology than a container for political action (see also Bigo in this volume). Indeed, the very same techniques directed toward population are also those that are central to the idea of territory—calculative techniques, modes of measuring and controlling—that find their expression in land surveying, terrain analysis, cartographic practices, administrative strategies, statistical surveys, legal codes, financial techniques and military technologies.

One of the most productive developments of Foucault's work has been in thinking about biometrics, studying how calculative measures of life and its component parts can be analyzed and utilized. Louise Amoore, for example, has written powerfully about the "biometric border."[7] Matthew Hannah has noted that we should think biopower rather than biopolitics, with the latter understood as a particular, and narrower, set of questions within the former.[8] This is a helpful distinction, but there is a threefold relation that needs explication—Biopower, Biopolitics and Biometrics. While the literature on the first two can be related to writings by Agamben, Esposito, Hardt and Negri and Dillon and Reid,[9] biometrics has found its most able exponent in the work of people like Louise Amoore and Joseph Pugliese.[10]

How then might that threefold relation be helpful in understanding geopolitics? Foucault's work on biopolitics, governmentality and the politics of calculation can, as I have argued elsewhere,[11] be very helpful in understanding transformations of political space and the concept of territory. How can this be extended to look at the world, the global? The first shift is in thinking about geopower as a broader category within which geopolitics operates. The work here, obliquely, relates to the project of Gilles Deleuze and Félix Guattari, whose interrogation of the relation between deterritorialization and reterritorialization, especially as outlined in their book *A Thousand Plateaus*, requires much more careful interrogation if we are to use it to understand contemporary political-geographical relations, or a new world Imperium.[12] Reterritorialization is a term with especial potential: spatial relations are not just unmade by processes such as globalization, but remade. They take these ideas forward in *What is Philosophy?* which, building on Nietzsche discusses the idea of geophilosophy.[13] Deleuze and Guattari describe this by suggesting that "thinking is neither a line drawn between subject and object nor a revolving of one around the other. Rather, thinking takes place in the relationship of territory and the earth."[14]

One of the most productive developments of this work has been in the writings of Elizabeth Grosz's *Chaos, Territory, Art: Deleuze and the Framing of the Earth* is a useful initial point of reference.[15] In it, Grosz suggests a fundamental distinction between earth and territory. The territory has something added to the earth, it is framed, it has qualities, it is ordered and constructed.

> The frame is what establishes territory out of the chaos that is the earth. The frame is thus the first construction, the corners, of the plane of composition. With no frame or boundary there can be no territory, and without territory there may be objects or things but not qualities that can become expressive, that can intensify and transform living bodies. Territory here may

be understood as surfaces of variable curvature or inflection that bear upon them, singularities, eruptions or events. Territory is that which is produced by the elaborate, if apparently useless, activity of construction, attention grabbing, and display that mark most sexual selection.[16]

For Grosz, then, there is a vitalist element to this, a vibrancy. Territory and body go together in this sense, as both are framed, ordered: "Territory and body only emerge as such to the extent that such qualities can be extracted."[17] While I have some doubts concerning this element of her thinking, which comes very close to work on *territoriality*, it can none-theless be another way of approaching the idea that territory is a process, a tangled multiplicity of a range of relations—political, economic, strategic, technical and legal.[18] An important caution here is that it is not at all clear that Deleuze and Guattari use the term "territory" to mean the same as political geographers, and as yet no-one has worked through those complexities with sufficient care and detail. Nonetheless, we can turn back from that inquiry and see how it helps us to make some sense of the earth. Grosz declares that,

> There is only earth rather than territory until qualities are let loose in the world. Qualities and territory coexist, and thus both are the condition for sexual selection and for art making—or perhaps for the art of sexual selection and equally the sexuality of art production.[19]

This relates to her earlier claim about how "framing" is a way of structuring and making sense of the inchoate,

> The earth can be infinitely divided, territorialized, framed. But unless it is in some way demarcated, nature itself is incapable of sexualizing life, making life alluring, lifting life above mere survival. Framing is how chaos becomes territory. Framing is the means by which objects are delimited, qualities unleashed and art made possible.[20]

This work has only recently begun to be analyzed by geographers, but it offers some powerful resources for thinking what might be understood as a more active "geo" in geopolitics, and perhaps, by extension, geometrics.[21] In her opening comments to a discussion of her work at the Association of American Geographers in 2012, Grosz suggests that,

The relations between the earth and its various forces, and living beings and their not always distinguishable forces, are forms of geopower, if power is to be conceived as the engagement of clashing, competing forces... Power— the relations between humans, or perhaps even between living things—is a certain, historically locatable capitalisation on the forces of geopower.[22]

At its best, such a politics of the earth would take into account the power of natural processes, or resources; the dynamics of human and environment; the interrelation of objects outside of human intervention; the relation between the biosphere, atmosphere and lithosphere; and the complex interrelations that produce, continually transform and rework the question of territory and state spatial strategies. There are a number of resources that can be drawn upon in such an inquiry. Manuel de Landa has begun to sketch some of the ways that this could be understood in his *A Thousand Years of Nonlinear History*;[23] literary theorist Jonathan Bate looks at the way poetry can retrieve a connection to the earth.[24] John Protevi has suggested the hybrid multiplicity of "geo-hydro-solar-bio-techno-politics" to make sense of the connections.[25] In a related inquiry, Jane Bennett similarly wants to retrieve an active, earthy sense to what she calls vibrant matter.[26] Within a wider rethinking of geopower, we can then resituate what we mean by geopolitics, as a politics of the earth.

Geopolitics has, today, become effectively a synonym for global politics. Armchair strategists still come up with grand plans for understanding and changing the world;[27] critical geopolitics scholars offer broad analyses of such strategies and the interlinked relations of capital, state power, nationalism and territory. Robert Kaplan's recent *The Revenge of Geography* seems destined to be all that many people learn of Geography, especially in policy circles, as if exhuming Mackinder were the way forward;[28] or they read Harm de Blij's last offering of *Why Geography Matters*.[29] But even the critical geopolitics work tends to think of this as global or world politics— new ways for understanding and making sense of that particular scale.[30] In these terms, we risk losing the element of the "geo," as earth, and replacing it with other ideas. So geopolitics is being re-conceived as global politics; geometry is a branch of mathematics, abstract and detached; geography is no longer earth-writing but a loose spatial sensibility to work that could equally have been done in other disciplines. Perhaps it is in geology that we find the true inheritor of the etymological sense of the term, the *logos* of the *geo*. Yet as Robert Frodeman notes, even there, "geology," while "once identified exclusively with the study of the solid Earth (...) has lost ground to 'Earth sciences' (...) meant to highlight the need for an integrated study of air, water, soil, rock, ice, and biota."[31] In the light of the work by Grosz and others, we can begin to see how geopolitics could be rethought in a way that was closer to the etymological roots of the word, as earth-politics, yet for progressive political purpose. Geopolitics literally means politics of the "geo," the earth, land, planet or world. Each of those terms would need to be thought carefully, both in relation to and in differentiation from each other, and from a notion of the global. But in broad terms, this geopolitics would sit alongside, rather than replace, the attention given to biopolitics in recent years. Here I particularly want to retrieve the sense of geopolitics and geometrics as, respectively, a politics of the earth and earth-measuring.

## GEOMETRICS

This is the second key point. Just as with biopower, biometrics and biopolitics, there is a threefold relation between geopower, geometrics and geopolitics. Geometrics can be understood in the traditional sense of the term, a measuring of the earth, as geometry. In Herodotus there is a description of the original earth-measurers, the Egyptians sent to remark the boundaries of fields after the Nile's floodwaters had subsided.[32] Heidegger claims that Thales is crucial here, as the first scientific philosopher and first mathematician. He took the Egyptian geometry of empirical measurement, and turned it into an abstract and deductive process.[33] This originary, fundamental, sense became increasingly abstract in Aristotle and Euclid, and especially when fully mathematicized in the sixteenth and seventeenth centuries.[34]

An understanding of the politics of calculation in relation to the way the world is constructed might help us to track how mechanistic ways of rendering have become increasingly technocratic. These are something that we might call regimes of global calculation.[35] To think the world of globalization forces us to realize that this is not a transcending of spatial or territorial problematics, but rather their reconfiguration. Territory— understood as the political corollary of calculative space, as a political technology—offers us insight into the world scale or the notion of the worldwide. In Henri Lefebvre's terms, *l'échelle mondiale* is not the same as *le niveau global*; the world scale is distinct from the global or general level.[36] The process of globalization is an acceleration of the understanding of space and time as coordinates on a three- and four-dimensional grid. The understanding of space and time as calculative, and extension as the primary characteristic of material nature, is to make it amenable to science through geometry and measure more generally. A difference of degree rather than an ontological transformation is thus the way to grasp the spatiality of globalization.

But there are traces in the tradition too—in my work on territory, I think about some of this in the argument that we can conceive of territory as a *political technology*. This, again following Foucault, thinks about the techniques used for measuring land and controlling terrain, rather than just territory as land or terrain. While recognizing that the material, the geophysical, is important, particular political strategies directed toward that are equally significant. In other words, looking at measure and control, as markers for the technical and the legal, is significant alongside economic and strategic concerns. Territory is a *political* question, but the political needs to be understood in multiple registers, as economic, strategic, legal and technical.

In the historical account of the emergence of the concept and practice of territory, I put some stress on what I called "the geometry of the political." In this I looked at writings including those of the Roman land surveyors in the *Corpus Agrimensorum Romanorum*—literally, the work of the Roman field measurers, as well as the work of the 14th legal scholar Bartolus of Sassoferrato, who as well as writing legal texts that I think are crucial in the emergence of the relation between law and place, jurisdiction and territory, also wrote a text on the issues relating to rivers. There were three key questions for Bartolus: what happens to the possession of land if the river changes course? What about an island that emerges from a river? Who owns the land of a dried up riverbed? These legal questions can be traced back to Justinian's *Institutes* in relation to property of farms on either side of the river, and are the same kinds of issues that concern international river boundaries today. But Bartolus is interesting because he makes use of a fairly rudimentary geometry to legislate on such cases—a founding text of legal geography, or legal geometry. So we might be able to retrieve the Egyptian sense of geometry to make sense of measures of the earth. But there are also a range of other ways geometrics might be thought today beyond the applied sense of land surveying; looking at the measuring of the yields of oil and gas, soil fertility and air quality.

## THE GEOMETRICS OF GEOPOLITICS

There is substantial potential in this. One aspect would be to relate this to questions being raised by Phil Steinberg's work on the ocean, and especially in his emerging interest in ice, with its dynamic properties and blurred status between sea and solid land. Following the UN Convention on the Law of the Sea, and long-standing laws concerning "solid land" territory, Steinberg has suggested we need to produce a "law of ice" to make sense of resource politics and borders in, especially, the Arctic. Similarly, work on river boundaries is complicated by the dynamics of rivers. While the political may want to remain static, the geophysical is dynamic. This forces us to understand the geomaterial, the geophysical, rather than just the geopolitical in a narrowly conceived way.

In a somewhat different register, Shiloh Krupar's 2013 genre-disrupting *Hot Spotter's Report* examines the legacies of military toxic waste on landscapes and bodies,[37] in a related way to how Rachel Woodward turned military geographies from the impact of geographical considerations on the military to the impact of the military presence and militarism on the environment and landscape.[38] Or, again, Matthew Huber's book on the everyday politics of oil in the United States—*Lifeblood: Oil, Freedom and the Forces of Capital*—talks of a "historical ecology of neoliberalism."[39] He sees this as a challenge to work thinking oil as "a strategic object amid the absolute spaces of national territories, pipelines, oceans, and military bases."[40] In part, his approach is directed toward Timothy Mitchell's *Carbon Democracy*.[41] Nonetheless, Mitchell is helpful in the wider project too. He suggests, for example, that "governing the global supply of oil, like most things that we call 'global', rested on the control of a comparatively small number of sites—a few dozen major oilfields, pipelines and terminals, and the handful of bulk tanker fleets that journeyed between them."[42]

Another instance would be in political ecology, or on the geopolitics of food. One example would be John Perkins's book *Geopolitics and the Green Revolution*, subtitled "wheat, genes and the Cold War."[43] This book explores how four countries, the United States, Britain, India and Mexico all tried to increase agricultural production through genetic breeding of plants during the Cold War, as a measure of national security. Simon Dalby notes that, "Cold War scholars will remember the importance of satellite-based estimates of the Soviet harvest. North Korea watchers do similar calculations today."[44] Another would be the work Saskia Sassen is doing on land grabs, feeding, she suggests, "the disassembling of national territory."[45] There is also the question of population density—which is interesting as a function of the relation of number to area, bridging bio-politics and geopolitics.[46] In other words, we need to think about these calculative techniques, in both biopolitical and geopolitical registers, as biometrics and geometrics, measuring life and the earth. So, following Foucault, just as those calculative techniques were crucial to modern statecraft, so too are these techniques, these regimes of global calculation, crucial today in thinking about the world, earth and geopolitics.

## THE GEOPOLITICS OF CLIMATE CHANGE

In his 2013 *Political Geography* lecture at the Association of American Geographers annual conference, Simon Dalby generously engaged with my essay "Secure the Volume: Vertical Geopolitics and the Depth of Power," the previous year's *Political Geography* lecture, given at the Royal Geographical Society annual conference in July 2012. In that essay, I suggested that the spaces of geography were often thought of as areas, as flat, as planes or surfaces rather than as volumes. Taking the practices of security as my inspiration, I looked at what happened if we seriously considered height and depth. In doing so I linked work on vertical geopolitics—an emerging field that looks at aerial bombardment, drone warfare, visual surveillance and so on—with work on urban exploration and the security issues raised by the subsoil, tunnels, infrastructure and foundations. In recent work, Eyal Weizman has begun to propose an idea of forensic architecture, a means to understand and comprehend "the deep surface of the earth."[47] This too would contribute to that work of rethinking a politics of the earth.[48]

A renewed politics of the earth would be appropriate to the complexi-ties of space and territory in three dimensions, rather than the tendency to imagine political space as a surface, an area. My examples in "Secure the Volume" were drawn from the West Bank—developing claims made by Weizman in the book *Hollow Land*—and Israel's border with Lebanon at Rosh Hanikra. I juxtaposed Peter Sloterdijk's work on spheres with Paul Virilio's early work on bunker architecture and his own architectural prac-tice with Claude Parent which emphasized the function of the oblique, angles and surfaces, the question of volume. I suggested that thinking vol-ume—about volume, through volume, with volume—rather than simply the vertical was essential if we were to make sense of the complexities of territory, today certainly, but I think the same holds true for the relation between place and power in all historical and geographical contexts.

How would our thinking of geopower, geopolitics and geometrics work if we took the earth; the air and the subsoil; questions of land, terrain, territory; earth processes and understandings of the world as the central terms at stake, rather than a looser sense of the "global"? There would be, I think, a need for a greater concentration on the question of terrain, a geophysical element within geopolitics, is a theme that Gastón Gordillo has begun to examine in some detail.[49] There is little on this question, aside from some work in military geography, but it pervades, in a perhaps uncritical way, work taking a political-strategic approach to questions of territory.[50] But there is a beginning of a move to take this notion more seriously. While he eschews use of the term "terrain," I would see Derek Gregory's work on the "natures of war" as sympathetic to this project. Equally, some volumes in Polity Press's "Resources" series, take the geophysical very seriously. Derek Hall's book on land is one example, but the series also includes volumes on water, oil, timber and so on.[51]

In the "Secure the Volume" essay, I suggested that both biopolitics and geopolitics could be "understood through processes and technologies of bio-metrics and geo-metrics, means of comprehending and compelling, organizing and ordering."[52] I closed by suggesting the idea of the volumetric,

Work in this register equally needs to think in terms of the volumetric. The Oxford English Dictionary suggests this word dates from 1862, is formed from Volume and Metric, and means 'Of, pertaining to, or noting measurement by volume.' While the term is used in cartography and physics, there is real potential in working out in detail its two aspects: the dimensionality implied by 'volume' and the calculability implied by 'metric.' The political technology of territory comprises a whole number of mechanisms of weighing, calculating, measuring, surveying, managing, controlling and ordering. These calculative techniques— similarly to those employed in biometrics and geo-metrics—impact on the complexities of volume. In terms of the question of security, volume matters because of the concerns of power and circulation. Circulation does not simply happen, nor does it need to be contained, controlled and regulated, on a plane. Thinking about power and circulation in terms of volume opens up new ways to think of the geographies of security.[53]

Picking up on and developing some of these ideas, Simon Dalby provides a number of examples of ways of tracking and measuring the global impact of changing climates. One of the most striking is the previously mentioned satellite images of drought in the former Soviet Union, North Korea and Arab countries. He notes that, "these technologies are also modes of knowing, charting, measuring and calculating the earth as it is transformed."[54] Dalby suggests that "How all this is to be measured and surveilled is a matter of geometrics in Elden's terms."[55]

Dalby notes that at the same time as my "Secure the Volume" lecture "prominent climate activist Bill McKibben published an article in *Rolling Stone* magazine that suggested that the most important geometrics of our time relate to basic aspects of the climate system."[56] This is not the language used by McKibben himself, even if the questions he is posing fit neatly into these proposed categories. Dalby argued, entirely rightly, that "the materialities of spaces matter, not just the volume," drawing on the work of Neil Smith.[57] Perhaps the work on terrain might be an element within a multi-dimensional material geopolitics. But most importantly for my argument here he puts forward the term "Neoliberal geometrics," suggesting that "the logic of his [i.e. my] argument fits into the new mathematics of global security, and the market logics of carbon measurement."[58]

> Extending that argument to suggest that the volume that matters most now are some of the key geometrics related to the atmosphere and the ocean, and the struggles to secure them are the next phase of geopolitics, also emphasizes both the continuity of climate as a matter in geopolitical thinking and the importance of taking seriously the reversal of the assumed relationship between climate and humanity in the most recent stage of the Anthropocene.[59]

## 'ANTHROPOCENE GEOPOLITICS'

And it is with the Anthropocene that I want to conclude (see also Taylan in this volume). If we think of a range of questions such as risk, security, prediction; aid, sustainability, development; finance, the economy, populations, many of these would fit within the broad range of what Foucault called biopolitics. This would be to take politics of calculation and situate it in relation to the politics of life. That is an invaluable inquiry, and what is being proposed here is in no sense an attempt to marginalize that work. What is being suggested is that alongside those registers we need to think about earth, land, the world and the global, recognizing that these are not simply frames within which regimes of calculation take place.

The spaces within which, between which, over which, the regimes operate, shape and calculate is a crucial element; but it is what is being done to those, made possible by those, these as the objects of transformation and possibility. Alongside biopolitics attention then to geopolitics, not in the loose sense of global or international politics, but a politics of the earth. Alongside the broad realm of biopower attention to what Elizabeth Grosz calls geopower, of "the engagement of clashing, competing forces"—some of which are human, more of which are living, many of which are what Jane Bennett calls vibrant matter, or what might be called animate objects. That last term is the best I can imagine make sense of Ben Marcus's wonderful little novel *The Age of Wire and String*.[60] Recall Grosz's suggestion of the relation between geopower and human power,[61] which can be usefully paired with William Connolly's argument in *The Fragility of Things*:

> One theme of this book is that the planet, and indeed the cosmos, is replete with self-organizing, spatiotemporal systems flowing at different speeds, levels of sophistication, and degrees of self-sustaining power. These impersonal systems are open to some degree and never in perfect equilibrium; they interact, with each having a degree of entanglement with several others.[62]

Alongside the crucial emphasis on the types of calculation, of reduction to number, of modes of measure, that can be understood under the term of biometrics, what about the techniques of calculation, operations of measure and control, which are directed toward the earth, the geo? This broader, retrieved sense of geometrics, that would include but not be reducible to the abstract or applied arts of geometry, would, I think, help us to make sense of "regimes of calculation" in their relation to *global* governance.

Such a politics of the earth ultimately aims to be appropriate to the anthropocene. Especially so in what Simon Dalby has called "Anthropocene Geopolitics."[63] In that, at least, we should insist on a serious, critical, focus on the notion of the "Geo," more than there has been in the past, even in *critical* geopolitics. To put this another way, why is Simon Dalby *not* Anthony Giddens or John Urry, both of whom have written about the politics of climate change?[64] There is a real importance to a geographical perspective to this most geographical of political questions.

This is what I mean by a rethinking of geopolitics—a renewed emphasis on the material, the earth, the geo element of these political questions. William Connolly has talked of the need for thinking through the relation between political economy and environmental issues, especially in the light of a philosophy of becoming. He suggests that,

To come to terms with looping relations between capitalist production, carbon and methane emissions, state policy, consumption practices, glacier movements, and climate change sets the stage to link political economy regularly to the behavior of non-human force fields.[65]

So, our thinking about the Anthropocene and geopolitics would benefit from thinking more carefully about earth and metrics. Foucault's contribution to world politics can then be positioned as a genuine thinking about the politics of the world, the politics of the "geo." If political geography, geopolitics, is to live up to the promise of its names, then it is crucial that it is at the very forefront of such debates.

## NOTES

1. Michel Foucault, *'Society Must Be Defended,'* transl. David Macey (London: Penguin, 2003); *On the Government of the Living: Course at the Collège de France (1979–1980)*, edited by Michel Senellart, transl. Graham Burchell, (London: Palgrave, 2014).
2. Some of the work of tracing Foucault's concerns in this period is undertaken in my book *Foucault's Last Decade* (Cambridge: Polity, 2016).
3. See Stuart Elden, "Governmentality, Calculation, Territory," *Environment and Planning D: Society and Space* 25(3) (2007): 562–580; and "How should we do the History of Territory?" *Territory, Politics, Governance* 1, no 1 (2013): 5–20.
4. Amy Swiffen, *Law, Ethics and the Biopolitical* (London: Routledge, 2011), p. 93.
5. Ibid., p. 63.
6. See Stuart Elden, *The Birth of Territory* (Chicago: University of Chicago Press, 2013).
7. Louise Amoore, "Biometric Borders: Governing Mobilities in the War on Terror," *Political Geography* 25(3) (2006): 336–51.
8. Matthew G. Hannah, "Biopower, Life and Left Politics," *Antipode* 43(4) (2011): 1034–55.
9. Giorgio Agamben, *Homo Sacer: Sovereign Power and Bare Life*, transl. Daniel Heller-Roazen (Stanford: Stanford University Press, 1998); *The Open: Man and Animal*, transl. Kevin Attell (Stanford: Stanford University Press, 2004); Michael Hardt and Antonio Negri, *Empire* (Cambridge: Harvard University Press, 2000); *Multitude: War and Democracy in the Age of Empire* (New York: The Penguin Press, 2004); *Commonwealth* (Cambridge: Harvard University Press, 2009); Julian Reid, *The Biopolitics of the War on Terror: Life struggles, liberal modernity and the defence of*

*logistical societies* (Manchester: Manchester University Press, 2006); Michael Dillon, *Biopolitics of Security: A Political Analysis of Finitude* (London: Routledge, 2015).

10. Joseph Pugliese, *Biometrics: Bodies, Technologies, Biopolitics* (London: Routledge, 2010); Louise Amoore, *The Politics of Possibility: Risk and Security beyond Probability* (Durham, NC: Duke University Press, 2013); and see also Philippe Bonditti, "From Territorial Space to Networks: A Foucaldian Approach to the Implementation of Biometry," *Alternatives* 29 (2004): 465–82, and his contribution to this volume.

11. See Elden, *The Birth of Territory*.

12. Gilles Deleuze and Félix Guattari, *A Thousand Plateaus: Capitalism and Schizophrenia*, transl. Brian Massumi (London: Athlone, 1988).

13. See Mark Bonta and John Protevi, *Deleuze and Geophilosophy: A Guide and Glossary* (Edinburgh: Edinburgh University Press, 2004); and Ben Woodard, *On an Ungrounded Earth: Towards a New Geophilosophy* (Brooklyn, NY: Punctum Books, 2013).

14. Gilles Deleuze and Félix Guattari, *What is Philosophy?* transl. Hugh Thompson and Graham Burchell (New York: Columbia University Press, 1994), p. 84. See Roberto Esposito, *Living Thought: The Origins and Actuality of Italian Philosophy*, transl. Zakiya Hanafi (Stanford: Stanford University Press, 2012), p. 12.

15. Elizabeth Grosz, *Chaos, Territory, Art: Deleuze and the Framing of the Earth* (Durham, NC: Duke University Press, 2008).

16. Grosz, *Chaos, Territory, Art*, pp. 11–12. On the understanding of territory, deriving from Deleuze and Guattari, *A Thousand Plateaus*, see p. 47.

17. Grosz, *Chaos, Territory, Art*, p. 102.

18. See Stuart Elden "Land, Terrain, Territory," *Progress in Human Geography*, vol 34 (2010): 799–817.

19. Grosz, *Chaos, Territory, Art*, p. 102.

20. Ibid., p. 17.

21. See Kathryn Yusoff, Elizabeth Grosz, Arun Saldanha, Catherine Nash and Nigel Clark, "Geopower: A Panel on Elizabeth Grosz's *Chaos, Territory, Art: Deleuze and the Framing of the Earth*," *Environment and Planning D: Society and Space* 30(6) (2012): 971–88, p. 971.

22. Grosz in Yusoff et al. "Geopower," p. 975. Grosz has worked some of these questions through in relation to Darwin in *The Nick of Time: Politics, Evolution, and the Untimely* (Durham, NC: Duke University Press, 2004); *Time Travels: Feminism, Nature and Power* (Durham, NC: Duke University Press, 2005); and *Becoming Undone: Darwinian Reflections on Life, Politics and Art* (Durham, NC: Duke University Press, 2011).

23. Manuel de Landa, *A Thousand Years of Nonlinear History* (New York: Zone Books, 1997).

24. Jonathan Bate, *The Song of the Earth* (London: Picador, 2000).
25. John Protevi, *Life, War, Earth: Deleuze and the Sciences* (Minneapolis: University of Minnesota Press, 2013).
26. Jane Bennett, *Vibrant Matter: A Political Ecology of Things* (Durham, NC: Duke University Press, 2010), p. 3.
27. See, for example Thomas P. Barnett, *The Pentagon's New Map: War and Peace in the Twenty-First Century* (G.P. Putnam's Sons, 2004).
28. Robert D. Kaplan, *The Revenge of Geography: What the Map Tells Us About Coming Conflicts and the Battle Against Fate* (New York: Random House, 2012).
29. Harm de Blij, *Why Geography Matters: More than Ever* (New York: Oxford University Press, second edition, 2012).
30. Classic texts include Gearóid Ó Tuathail, *Critical Geopolitics: The Politics of Writing Global Space* (Minneapolis: University of Minnesota Press, 1996); and John Agnew, *Geopolitics: Re-visioning World Politics* (London: Routledge, 1998 (second edition 2003)).
31. Robert Frodeman, *Geo-logic: Breaking Ground between Philosophy and the Earth Sciences* (Albany, NY: SUNY Press, 2003), p. 3.
32. Herodotus, *The Histories*, transl. Robin Waterfield (Oxford: Oxford University Press, 1998), p. 109.
33. Martin Heidegger, *Die Grundbegriffe der Antiken Philosophie* (Frankfurt am Main: Vittorio Klostermann, 1993), pp. 40, 51–2. See Edward A. Maziarz & Thomas Greenwood, *Greek Mathematical Philosophy* (New York: Frederick Ungar, 1968), p. 7.
34. On the conception of space and its underpinning in calculation that has dominated our conceptions of modern political life see my *Speaking Against Number: Heidegger, Language and the Politics of Calculation* (Edinburgh: Edinburgh University Press, 2006) and *The Birth of Territory*, as well as R.B.J. Walker, "Gulliver and the territorial state", in *Inside/Outside. International Relations as Political Theory* (Cambridge: Cambridge University Press, 1993), pp. 125–140.
35. A preliminary version of some of these arguments was first presented as a keynote to a workshop on "Regimes of Calculation and Global Governance," at the Balsillie School of International Affairs, Waterloo, Ontario. The phrase "Regimes of Global Calculation" was developed as a way of engaging with the themes of that event and the other papers presented there. Subsequent versions were given at the University of Basel, Zurich and Groningen. I am grateful to audiences in each place for comments.
36. See Henri Lefebvre, *De l'État* (Paris: UGE, Four Volumes, 1976–78); *State, Space, World: Selected Essays*, edited by Neil Brenner and Stuart Elden (Minneapolis: University of Minnesota Press, 2009).

37. Shiloh R. Krupar, *Hot Spotter's Report: Military Fables of Toxic Waste* (Minneapolis: University of Minnesota Press, 2013).
38. Rachel Woodward, *Military Geographies* (Oxford: Wiley-Blackwell, 2004).
39. Matthew T. Huber, *Lifeblood: Oil, Freedom and the Forces of Capital* (Minneapolis: University of Minnesota Press, 2013), p. xv.
40. Ibid., p. 2.
41. Timothy Mitchell, *Carbon Democracy: Political Power in the Age of Oil* (London: Verso, paperback edition, 2013).
42. Ibid., p. 67.
43. John H. Perkins, *Geopolitics and the Green Revolution: Wheat, Genes, and the Cold War* (New York: Oxford University Press, 1998).
44. Simon Dalby, "The Geopolitics of Climate Change," *Political Geography* 37(1) (2013): 38–47, 39.
45. Saskia Sassen, "Land Grabs Today: Feeding the Disassembling of National Territory," *Globalizations* 10(1) (2013): 25–46. See also her book *Expulsions: Brutality and Complexity in the Global Economy* (Cambridge, MA: Harvard University Press, 2014).
46. This work could be related to Mark Whitehead's study *State, Science and the Skies: Environmental Governmentality and the British* Atmosphere (Oxford: Wiley-Blackwell, 2009) and Gavin Bridge's work on the subsoil and natural resources, for example "The Hole World: Scales and Spaces of Extraction," *New Geographies*, no 2 (2009): 43–49.
47. Eyal Weizman, "Forensic Architecture: The Deep Surface of the Earth," Society and Space 30th Anniversary Lecture, 3rd July 2012, available at http://societyandspace.com/2012/08/22/eyal-weizman-society-and-space-30th-anniversary-lecture/ (site verified on October 15, 2015); see also *Forensic Architecture: Notes from Fields and Forums* (English-German edition, Kassel: dOCUMENTA, 2012) and *The Least of All Possible Evils: Humanitarian Violence from Arendt to Gaza* (London: Verso, 2012).
48. See Stuart Elden, "Secure the Volume: Vertical Geopolitics and the Depth of Power," *Political Geography* 32(2) (2013): 35–51; and the references within that piece. On tunnels, see additionally Nicolas Pelham, "Gaza's Tunnel Phenomenon: The Unintended Dynamics of Israel's Siege," *Journal of Palestine Studies* 41, no 4, 2012, http://palestine-studies.org/jps/fulltext/42605 (verified on October 15, 2015).
49. To date these have largely been on his blog: http://spaceandpolitics.blogspot.co.uk (website verified on October 15, 2015).
50. See also Bernard Cache, *Earth Moves: The Furnishing of Territories*, transl. Anne Boyman (Cambridge, MA: MIT Press, 1995), Ch. 1. The book is dedicated to Gilles Deleuze.
51. Derek Hall, *Land* (Cambridge: Polity, 2013).
52. Elden, "Secure the Volume," p. 49.

53. Ibid.
54. Dalby, "The Geopolitics of Climate Change," p. 39.
55. Ibid., p. 40.
56. Ibid., p. 42. See Bill McKibben, "Global Warming's Terrifying New Math", *Rolling Stone*, July 19 2012. Available at http://www.rolling-stone.com/politics/news/global-warmings-terrifying-new-math-20120719 (verified on October 15, 2015).
57. Dalby, "The Geopolitics of Climate Change," p. 43. Neil Smith, *Uneven Development: Nature, Capital and the Production of Space* (Atlanta: University of Georgia Press, third edition, 2008).
58. Dalby, "The Geopolitics of Climate Change," p. 43.
59. Ibid., p. 45.
60. Ben Marcus, *The Age of Wire and String* (Illinois: Dalkey Archive Press, 1995).
61. Grosz, in Yusoff et al., "Geopower," p. 975.
62. William E. Connolly, *The Fragility of Things: Self-Organizing Processes, Neoliberal Fantasies, and Democratic Capitalism* (Durham, NC: Duke University Press, 2013), p. 81.
63. Simon Dalby, "Recontextualising Violence, Power and Nature: The Next Twenty Years of Critical Geopolitics," *Political Geography* 29(5) (2010): 280–88; Simon Dalby, "Biopolitics and Climate Security in the Anthropocene," *Geoforum* 49 (2013): 184–92.
64. Anthony Giddens, *The Politics of Climate Change* (Cambridge: Polity, second edition, 2011); John Urry, *Climate Change and Society* (Cambridge: Polity, 2011).
65. Connolly, *The Fragility of Things*, pp. 30–1.

# CHAPTER 18

# Conclusion: Which Foucault? Which International?

*R.B.J. Walker*

## PROBLEMATIZATIONS

So many Foucaults! Perhaps too many; perhaps not enough. In either case, his name proliferates, in this book as in many other settings. Each proliferation evokes ample scholarly possibilities in diverse intellectual, institutional and political contexts, sometimes demanding close attention to the available sources and sometimes not, sometimes driven by the overall shape of a shifting body of work and sometimes driven by specific texts, concepts or intuitions.

Nick Onuf begins the present sequence of essays by responding to the elusive figuration of Foucault when his name is deployed in the analysis of what we have come to call international relations or international politics. I feel compelled to start in a complementary manner toward the end of this sequence, though not with any intention of resolving some mystery behind the proliferating name. Foucault clearly celebrated pluralistic possibilities, not least in his own life, which nevertheless expressed considerable integrity. We might even honor this among his greatest achievements.

R.B.J. Walker (✉)
University of Victoria, Victoria, Canada
e-mail: rwalker@uvic.ca

© The Author(s) 2017
P. Bonditti et al. (eds.), *Foucault and the Modern International,*
The Sciences Po Series in International Relations and Political
Economy, DOI 10.1057/978-1-137-56153-4_18

313

Indeed, in what follows here, I want to turn what may be an irritating absence of a manageably consistent voice behind the texts circulated under Foucault's name, as well as an equally irritating desire to impose a singular voice so as to appropriate that name, into a concern with the problems that provoked him. I especially want to pursue problems involved in resisting fixed identities and reified concepts, the art in which he was one of the great masters.

Thus, my present concern is directed less to some specific use of Foucault in the analysis of international relations/politics, or to an explicit evaluation of how others have used him to productive effect, than to note some important commonalities and discontinuities between the problems that have engaged both Foucault and those struggling to make sense of some kind of international. This is not least because my own inclination is to presume that the term international refers to a problem (or set of interrelated and quite profound problems, even a problematization, as Foucault, reworking Kant's understanding of the possibilities of critique, may have preferred) before it can be understood as anything else.

It is because I understand the terms of international relations and international politics as an expression of a problem that I tend to refer to the modern international and sometimes even to the sovereign international. I do so in both cases to both parallel and invoke contradictory relations with the modern/sovereign state. On the one hand, it is a term that, like the term state, affirms an historically and culturally specific understanding of what it must mean to speak about humanity in the sense of a generically modern "man" defined against the prior authority of some natural or theological order, and thus as a creature in need of its own authorization in secular political terms. This is the context in which figures like Machiavelli and Hobbes have been (mis)appropriated as canonical, foundational and originary sources defining what it must mean to invoke an international. On the other hand, and again like the term state, it is a term that seeks to explain the organization, practices and consequences of a spatiotemporal "order" grounded in that affirmation of what it means to speak about a specific version of humanity and its political qualifications: that is, to speak both about humanity in general and about citizenship in particular, in both cases as a coming into the world of man, into modern subjectivity, in ways that leave all other worlds somewhere beyond, or behind.

We know well enough that the organization and practices of that supposed order together with ordering capacities predicated on a figure of man split both from all its others and within itself are supposed to have had both positive and negative consequences: some kind of liberty, equality, subjectivity, self-determination and subjectivization perhaps, but also wars, colonial subordinations and objectivizations of less than fully human others. We have been a bit slower to acknowledge that these positives and negatives are intimately connected. Thus far, too many conventions of contemporary political analysis still work on the untenable assumption that "liberalism" is somehow the conceptual and historical opposite of both "realism" in some spatial or geopolitical framing and "colonialism" in a closely related temporal or historical framing. Relations between the politics of liberal subjectivities and their spatiotemporal exteriorities, and thus limits, may be very complex, but they are precisely relations rather than ontological, axiological, epistemological and political solitudes, both in principle and in practice. Whatever one means by this conveniently slippery term, liberalism works on the basis of claims to legitimate violence on both spatial and temporal trajectories, which makes its use in the context of an international, or indeed a colonial, especially tricky.

Nevertheless, there are increasing suspicions that the negative consequences pose very serious questions about the most basic assumptions about humanity and its political qualifications that are expressed in and constantly affirmed by the modern international, as well as by the scholarly traditions informing us about its organization, practices and consequences. Something like this suspicion might be identifiable in at least some of Foucault's texts, mainly in relation to the state, though sometimes also in terms of the external and thus in some vague sense international aspects of states, and especially of their practices of security and colonialism as relations of internality and externality.

One might say that the problems generated by a double affirmation of a specific understanding of humanity in general and sites of political citizenship within specific states that are themselves organized within a constellation of states have been at stake in most or even all forms of modern politics; as indeed they have. If it is possible to assign some specificity to modern forms of politics—a significant conditionality—it would presumably involve both an affirmation of self-constituting forms of human subjectivity and consequent attempts to reconcile humanity in some general sense with particular versions of humanity, both as individuals and as collectivities. Yet while closely related, indeed mutually constitutive, attempts to reconcile competing claims to humanity and citizenship have taken different forms within states than between states. All modern forms of politics are organized both internally and externally, though most forms of political analysis prefer to divide internalities and externalities into distinctive fields of knowledge, thereby leaving the crucial relation of internal and external—crucial to what we call modern man and modern subjectivity—in some kind of no-man's-land within sites of indeterminacy and determination at the boundaries, borders and limits of modern political life.[1]

Foucault, like almost all social and political theorists, was also concerned with the figure of "man" and its political qualifications, but very largely in relation to an internalized arena, to a statist polity of some kind, even while he was explicitly (even if unsuccessfully) resisting at least some statist conceptions of politics; Foucault's treatment of the state was never a straightforward matter. Consequently, to bring the figures of Foucault and the modern international into conjunction cannot be just a matter of applying theorizations from one domain to another on a common and comparable field of domains. It must be to apply such theorizations from one domain to another that has been distinguished sharply from it in order to both divide and correlate their common problem, "man," into distinct political orders: not just as citizens and/or humans but also as friends and/or enemies. Modern forms of politics affirm many very sharp distinctions, some between "man" and just about everything else, and some within that "man," understood sometimes as the singular individual, sometimes as a singular collectivity and sometimes as an expression of humanity itself contained within a grand structure of states/nations and individualized/collectivized citizens. In effect, the modern international expresses our standard account of how modern "man," that fateful name we have learnt to give both to the human species and to particular versions of that species, both is and should be organized, spatially and temporally, internally and externally, pluralistically and universally. It also expresses our standard—hegemonic—account of a political order that must struggle to reconcile claims to individualized subjectivity, to statist/national citizenship and to an internationally specified humanity: three sites of potential but never absolute sovereignty distributed on a scale from small to large but articulated as if on a flat plane of territorialized spatiality; and also distributed on a scale from backward to advanced as if on a straight line of developmental history.

It is in relation to this broad context that I would say that the problems that provoked Foucault are most obviously but also most obscurely related to the problems that have provoked people studying the modern international. Both are responding to historically and culturally specific claims about the status, both generic and political, of modern "man," of human subjectivity and humanity as such. Nevertheless, it is not always easy to translate engagements with such questions in relation to domestic or statist settings into engagements with them in external or international settings.

There are some familiar ways through which this difficulty can be and has been made to seem relatively trivial, or, more positively, at least made to seem open to negotiation and diplomatic appreciation. Some of these are at work, as well as in question, both in Foucault's own texts and in various attempts to use Foucault to analyze international relations.

Both the modern state and the modern international might be treated as subsidiary parts of a more encompassing totality, a universalizing capitalism and/or modernity, for example; as if one can speak coherently of a singular and universalizing capitalism, or a modernity, that has not also been articulated as a multiplicity and at least in part as an international. Or one can simply insist that the state is the only significant political reality, that international relations is consequently only a matter of relations between states and that the structural or systematic organization of relations between states is of little or no consequence either for specific states or for relations between them; this option might be traced to the radically nationalist and/or statist formulations of Max Weber and Carl Schmitt and the forms of "political realism" they enabled, but also to the tacit nationalism/statism affirmed by most traditions of social and political theory, which would nevertheless prefer to resist any idea that they share very much with the nationalistic traditions of political realism. Or, conversely, one can insist that the systemic organization of relations between states is the only significant reality, and that the structural configuration or polarity of these relations is the ultimate determinant of political life, including the possibilities open to supposedly sovereign states. This is an option that has appealed especially to scholars attracted to patterns of continuity that might be explained in some socio-scientific manner. It is much less attractive to scholars more attuned to historical practices and contingencies, among whom one might include both Weberian/Schmittean realists and Foucault, although he clearly has a very different understanding of what it means to engage with history and histories, part of his attraction in this context.

Alternatively, one can simply assume a common ground on which states can be compared, so that the modern international can indeed be treated as a comparative politics in which conceptions of an international order of radical difference disappear in favor of claims about convergence; or the universality of rational or some other kind of behavior; or something like a Kantian perpetual peace that has already become manifest despite Kant's own acute analysis of its impossibility. Precisely which common ground is to be assumed is of some consequence when examining phenomena that are usually characterized as having minimal degrees of commonality. Not least, this is the contestable presumption that permits social and political theorists to appeal to general or even universal principles in their analyses of sociopolitical formations that work precisely through negotiations of relations between universality and particularity, humanity in general and citizenships in particular. Or, in a common variation on this theme, one might admit a sharp distinction between state and international as an historical condition that has now passed, perhaps even insist that "we have never been international" despite appearances, in much the same way as Bruno Latour has claimed that we have never been as modern as the prevailing narratives have presumed.[2]

Moreover, even if some sharp ontological or axiological difference between internality and externality is affirmed, tacitly or implicitly, one can nevertheless assume a common ground for epistemology and methodology; this has been the general stance of attempts to shape the study of international relations as part of a generalizing social science: a stance that once generated sharp differences between "the American science of international relations" and the more historically and interpretively inclined "English School."[3] Add a privileging of a comparative politics to a universalizing philosophy of history, and then confirm the conjunction through pretensions to a universalist conception of a scientific method, and one can perhaps understand much of the hegemonic character of the scholarly discipline claiming to know how the politics of the modern international *must* work.

Rather more persuasively, I would say, one might argue that the modern state and the modern international have together articulated antagonistic but mutually constitutive claims to sovereign authority that are also implicated in antagonistic relations with other practices of power and authority, especially those framed under the rubrics of capitalism and modernity. Here, at least, one might come to appreciate what is at stake in the contradictory character of modern forms of politics, and in the practices through which distinctions between internality and externality, citizenship and humanity, liberalism and political realism, or peace and war also affirm complementarities rather than alternatives, in ways the prevailing structures of scholarly life predicated on sharp and even essentializing distinctions would prefer us to forget. Here also one might appreciate what Foucault was up against when introducing concepts of governmentality in order to understand the increasingly extensive instruments necessary to understand temporal practices and specific techniques of governing without relying on spatialized claims about state sovereignty, as well as to extend concepts of governing into increasingly influential challenges to sovereign states from de facto claims to sovereignty by capitalist markets. It is in this sense, for example, that Foucault might be read less in the context of statist forms of international relations than to forms of international political economy under conditions of post-Keynesian neo-liberalisms, rightly the concern of the preceding essays by Frederic Gros, Lawrence McFalls and Mariella Pandolfi, and Beatrice Hibou. While it is not clear that the term neo-liberalism ultimately gets us very far in understanding phenomena once so easily named as markets and states, Foucault seems to have had a good sense of what might be required to pursue multiple relations between phenomena so named so as to elude the chronic reductionisms that treat each of these as ultimate sites of value or essentialized regimes of truth.

Also more persuasively, and in ways about which Foucault clearly had much more to say, one might argue, with Didier Bigo, William Walters, Michael Shapiro and others here, that, as with concepts of the state, or civil society, or sovereignty, or modernity or capital, we all need to try much harder to resist the over-determining force of generalizing and reifying categories that make it so difficult to identify specificities, processes and relations and that constantly impose a dubious metaphysics shaping what we must find when we examine phenomena we all too easily call an international ; even or perhaps especially when those categories insist on a need to appreciate the constitutive contradictions expressed by a politics of modern man.

All these options have long found at least some minimal expression within even the most conventional parts of the scholarly discipline of international relations. Some have even been portrayed, implausibly in scholarly terms but very effectively in disciplinary terms, as the essential core of international relations theory. Still, while some of these moves may be more persuasive than others, none of them offer a convincing claim that an internal/external articulation of the doubled claim to humanity in general and citizenships in particular has yet given way to something else: to some kind of singular empire, for example, or a highway to globalization, to take the two most recently popular alternatives, though I would certainly say, in ways that speak to the different analytical explorations advanced here by Philippe Bonditti, McFalls and Pandolfi, Armand Mattelart, Jean-François Bayart, and Stuart Elden, that the spatiotemporal articulation of political life has been changing quite dramatically for a considerable time. Following these lines of thought, and in thinking about the preceding sequence of essays, I want to play out a double argument. In one register, I want to appreciate how the many Foucaults at work in this book do indeed have much to say about the modern international. In another register, I also want to suggest that the modern international may also have a lot to say to figures like Foucault who ultimately presume an international quite as much as they show us how it might be understood, engaged and challenged. Despite the proliferation of Foucault's name, and despite highly suggestive comments in some of his lectures, Foucault tended to follow a fairly familiar path among the traditions of social and political theory in his relative silence about an international. This is especially so in his systematic texts, perhaps less so in his lectures and more informal texts,[4] but even there he tends to affirm much of the statist traditions he was hoping to avoid. The degree to which he offers something more provocative in this respect depends, I would say, on the extent to which the conventional account of a fairly sharp distinction between the modern state and the modern international is still deemed to be significant or not, the extent to which his specific concepts and analytical procedures are deemed to be applicable to both the state and the international in ways that speak to changing relations between them, and the extent to which his analysis engages with practices of subjectivity that challenge assumptions about humanity in general and citizenship in particular that are affirmed by both the modern state and the modern international. My argument moves toward an ambivalent conclusion in all three cases.

## ON THE POLITICS OF CONCEPTS

The elusiveness of particular authors is unsurprising. Readers respond to authors, and authors are always vulnerable to re-authorizations that elude their control because authors and readers are only moments among complex transactions shaping both authors and readers. Even so, Foucault was strikingly reluctant to hold onto a consistent self-authorization and refreshingly open to the authorial responsibilities of reading. He seems to have been an unusually generous thinker, and many of us are indebted to his generosity. In the present context, part of the complex transactionality of author and reader has been generated by the practices and authorizations of the specific scholarly discipline (or subdisciplinary field) of international relations/politics. This is a discipline or field that is itself often reduced to a lazy shorthand, to "IR," in ways that affirm a dubious distinction between an arena of scholarly authority and an object of analysis from which it is set apart. Even engagements with this discipline cast in the name of critique are sometimes drawn to affirm this reification of a depoliticizing academic convention and to worry excessively about the integrity of the discipline. As I have already intimated, I am not so sure that the discipline, that which the discipline claims to know, or the relations between them, are quite so easy to identify.

In fact, neither Foucault nor the modern international are likely to be of much interest if we presume that either name has a clear and unambiguous referent, even though this presumption has had many compelling attractions that are themselves very interesting politically. The essays in this volume work very effectively to affirm the productive legacies of many Foucaults. We come across his provocations, prodigious scholarship, innovative conceptualizations and critical strategies, but no single program of research of the kind endorsed by some accounts of a properly scientific project. As both Bayart and Hibou demonstrate here, this is only one of many ways in which Foucault invites comparison with Max Weber as well as an appreciation of very sharp divergences between them. The modern international, by contrast, remains a figure in the shadows: also a singular name that seems to have many possible referents, though only a few of them come into sharp or sustained focus here.

Foucault's name is rightly held in great respect in many quarters precisely because it identifies a source of resistance not only to static and universalizing concepts but also, and more substantively, to notions of human freedom resting on a capacity to ground a sovereign law in prior sovereign acts of precise definition. The younger Foucault had clearly thought a lot about Kant, but it was scarcely a surprise to see that Hobbes would eventually attract his attention as a significant foil. Though often read as sharply dismissive of claims to sovereignty, he clearly thought a lot about how sovereignties work. As a disciplined form of scholarship, by contrast, international relations has been enabled by persistent attempts to fix meanings, maintain classifications and affirm the necessary consequences of a sovereign law that is only rarely interrogated. It is a discipline famously known for unembarrassed appeals to a political realism (sometimes historicist, sometimes structural, often at the same time and without much sense of what is at stake in the conflation of spatialities and temporalities, or necessities and contingencies), as well as to a very tightly constrained understanding of methodological orthodoxies; as if claims about and idealizations of reality are somehow irrelevant to political contestation, and as if claims about methodology are never strategies deployed to shore up highly contentious claims about realities and ideals, and thus about political necessities/contingencies and the delimitation of normative ambitions.

Oddly enough, international relations is a form of scholarship that is explicitly concerned with often radically disorderly conduct, and with extraordinary violence, yet which has been constructed as a form of disciplined scholarship through an almost puritanical repertoire of concepts, great debates and permissible modes of enquiry. This is presumably because it is a discipline that has worked very closely with concepts like sovereignty, state, nation and security that have attained the status of conditions of possibility for modern politics, and are thereby especially difficult to challenge in principle let alone in practice. It is also because it is so closely associated with a small handful of very powerful states and has been gradually absorbed into specific conceptions of social science honoring generalization and replication more than they do the contingency, mutability and spatiotemporal specificities of human affairs. Thus, while Hobbes had relatively little to say about international relations despite his canonical place in so many claims about it (though, and to foreshadow some subsequent remarks, he did say many important things about the spatiotemporal externality of the state), the more Platonist and Galilean aspects of his thought are strongly felt in structural accounts of some unchanging laws of political motion in a system that may be dynamic in some senses but nonetheless retains much the same structural form of considerable diversity and minimal commonality. Consequently, while all scholarly disciplines rely on reifications and dogmas of many kinds, international relations has perhaps become more reliant than most. The authorizations of the modern state and the modern international are never very far removed from the authorizations of the categories through which we are encouraged to examine the modern state and the modern international.

However, it should also be said immediately that the standard self-portraits of this discipline tend to tell a homogeneous story that has often been exaggerated precisely so as to restore discipline to a discipline that in many contexts has become quite fractured and diffuse, spread across many fields of enquiry and increasingly across many societies. What has become known as "IR" has become a powerful cliché that coexists uneasily with more complex and more fluid patterns of scholarship even while many of its practices impose an over-determining conceptual frame on phenomena that have become ever more puzzling. Moreover, it should also be said that something like Foucault's resistance to dogmas and reified concepts is not entirely foreign to this discipline, even in its most entrenched forms; perhaps to the contrary. Precisely because international relations has been counter-posed as a negative externality to a positive internality,[5] it has often worked as a kind of critique by negation of the received wisdom of an internalized politics; the opposition by many "political realists" to imperializing policies toward Vietnam and Iraq or to claims about a "liberal peace" come to mind in this respect. Moreover, at various times and places, particularistic modes of history and skepticism about conceptual analysis of any kind have been fairly commonplace, and not only within the English School. Older forms of historically oriented empiricism tended to affirm very conservative tendencies, not least in the strong colonial heritage of the English School's complaints about the more imperializing ambitions of its American counterpart. Nevertheless, it is probably worth noting that Foucault may offer some potential for radicalizing forms of critique that arise from the least expected places.

If there are common threads running through the essays collected here, I would say that the most important even if least explicit involves this underlying attitude of the various Foucaults who have made an appearances in the work of some scholars working on the modern international toward very tightly constrained disciplinary accounts of what this term is supposed to mean: accounts of the phenomena to which the term refers, the procedures through which they must be known, and the practices through which claims about the status of phenomena and claims to knowledge about them have become authoritative.

In some respects, this attitude may have been more important than any of the substantive claims made in any of Foucault's texts and underlies the various attempts here and elsewhere to say something inspired by those texts about the substantive practices of the modern international. After all, as with Hobbes, those texts say relatively little about international relations or international politics in any direct way, even if the posthumously published lectures of the late 1970s mark some provocative exceptions. As with any thinker focused on the internal life of states and societies, however, with Hobbes being an exemplary figure in this respect, it is always possible to sense the limits within which, and enabling which, analyses of internal affairs have become thinkable, even and sometimes especially when those limits are treated with a resounding silence. Foucault himself was of course one of the most perceptive of the many people of his generation who have had important things to say about political limits.

Beyond this, however, we necessarily confront all those different Foucaults. In part, this is the consequence of the rich diversity of texts, but the range of interpretations of these texts is especially bewildering. Specialists engage with a large archive and may well be able to make sense of the relations between its contents. The rest of us are caught in a daunting array of practices in which Foucault has become a flag, a weapon, a symbolic ally and a caricature as well as a guide to various ways we might think differently about politics and political analysis. Various fields of reception have produced figures who may bear a resemblance to written texts, or not, and may be somehow in line with the spirit of Foucault's preoccupations, or not. Again, Foucault is far from being alone in this respect.

Moreover, I would say that the struggles in which Foucault is engaged are precisely of the kind that permits much earnest rewriting so as to ensure that Foucault's attempts to articulate and explore very complex problems are converted back into fairly safe answers; perhaps, given prevailing political conditions, that *must* be converted into answers that defang his most provocative insights. This is because he is to some extent reengaging with problems that have had a long and contentious life within post-Kantian philosophy and politics. Specifically, I would say, he was especially up against a long history of attempts to make sense of claims about freedom, on the one hand, and, perhaps in an even more fundamental way, up against the difficulty of thinking possibilities of heterogeneity beyond the conventional understandings of pluralism and difference, on the other hand. These twin concerns, whatever the details of his response to them, are arguably sufficient to make Foucault's work of central importance for thinking about the modern international, which works to reproduce very specific accounts of freedom within a very specific orchestration of relations between universality and diversity. This is why I think it is necessary to appreciate a conceptual problem shared by both Foucault and the modern international before engaging with specific applications of his analysis, or his failure to think much beyond the state, or even his attempts to resist the over-determining effects of specific conceptual inheritances.

Much of the force of his engagement with prevailing accounts of politics comes from his deep but also ambivalent commitment to specificity and detail, a commitment that seems to threaten the very idea that there can be something so generalized as a modern politics characterized by an identifiable field of polarized principles. Read as a kind of historian, or perhaps as a critic of historians, Foucault joins many others in the struggle against overgeneralization, reification, anachronism, myths of tradition and so on. As Paul Veyne puts it, "the task of a historian who follows Foucault is to detect those ruptures that are concealed by misleading continuities.... Furthermore, Foucault the philosopher simply practices the method adopted by all historians, that of tackling every historical question on its own merits and never as a particular case of a general problem, let alone a philosophical question."[6] Still, it is not entirely clear that all historians are in methodological solidarity, or even that every historical question has its own merits. Nor is it clear that Foucault was simply an historian, or that he ever fully escaped from philosophy and political theory through his appeals to history and his meticulous attention to detail. Moreover, although it is easy enough to admire the force of complaints about excessive generalization and presumptions of continuity, many have made similar complaints before; it used to be a specialty of the English speakers, in the manner of David Hume or R. G. Collingwood. There is also clearly more to the wider concern for heterogeneity, which Foucault also shared with many of his generation, than a revival of an ordinary empiricism. Perhaps the easiest response to make about whether Foucault has something to say about an internationalized political order is simply that yes, he is a useful ally in the struggle against the determined presentism grounded in a pernicious myth of an eternal tradition that sustains a very limited understanding of what it means to speak about a modern international. One does not need Foucault in particular to engage in this struggle, but as Machiavelli might say, the reproductive capacities of the conventional narratives suggest that one needs the strongest possible allies for the task.

While it is important to keep stressing the degree to which Foucault participates in the desire to resist universals, it is equally necessary, especially in Anglo-American contexts, to stress the way he does so while maintaining the Kantian distinction between *phenomena* and *noumena*, and thus a longer inheritance of nominalism. He may have called himself a happy positivist, but this description works more in relation to the many precursors and inheritances of logical positivism than of the simplistic empiricisms that have become more firmly attached to this label. This is, of course, why some commentators[7] are much taken with his analyses of historical forms of *a priori*. He wants to pay attention to precise empirical details but keeps something of the Kantian account of the constitutive role of categories in making sense of phenomena. He may be clearly and radically anti-Kantian in the sense that he refuses the abstract and universalizing account of the *a priori* offered in Kant's first Critique. He is nevertheless one of those who insists on the historical and socially produced character of all *a priori* categories (in line with Hacking and others, but also with tendencies that were already visible in the nineteenth century). Moreover, unlike many who also move from universalist to historical accounts of the *a priori* (the neo-Kantians/neo-Hegelians down through Ernest Cassirer, and those trying to identify a progressivist subject of history from Marx to Weber to György Lukacs to Karl Mannheim and so on), he sometimes tries to resist the teleological readings of history given in both Kant and Hegel, famously preferring genealogical and archaeological understandings of historical trajectories—contrast Bonditti and Mattelart here—not least so as to resist conventional narratives about origins. Hibou's discussion of acts of formalization producing the "reality-like fiction of neoliberal abstractions" makes this heritage especially clear.

This, at least, is how I make sense of the background against which one can understand Foucault's various attempts to work out ways of thinking about forms of analysis that are sensitive simultaneously to specific experiences and diverse historical/social categories: through his archaeological and genealogical phases and his complex understanding of "discourse" on to his conceptions of a *dispositif* and problematization as ways of understanding heterogeneous constitutive practices as some kind of de-centered singularity without falling back into transcendental categories or playing out the usual binaries of rationalism and empiricism, or statism and anti-statism. This thinking was clearly a struggle that produced a range of what have come to be called methods of analysis, though I prefer to think more in terms of his analytical tactics. Still, unlike most people who draw on Foucault, I am stimulated less by any of his specific concepts or methods than by the ways in which he is driven to create them. Two sets of questions arise here.

One concerns the coherence of Foucault's specific formulations, especially about what happens when concepts are historicized and sociologized in ways that try to finally break from transcendentalism in the name of immanence, or break from ontotheology in the name of governmentality, or break from decisionism in the name of a micropolitics and so on. It is one thing to refuse transcendence and choose immanence, but quite another to resist the effects of a presumed choice between immanence and transcendence. Old debates about the status of secularism remain relevant in this respect, in ways that find many echoes in Michael Dillon's engagement with the truths of rule and the rule of truths. At stake here, most obviously, is the status of claims about sovereignty, but also the place of claims about equality in formulations driven more by claims about freedom. Or at least, these stakes remain active to the extent that one wants to hold on to the account of "man" that is affirmed by the modern international and modern state, or wants to try to perfect the options available for us to reconcile that concept of man in general with politically qualified citizens in particular. Or perhaps one should say that these possibilities are ultimately what is at stake when it is said that someone like Foucault should be brought into conjunction with international relations.

Another set of questions concerns the use of Foucault's methodologies or tools by others. As the preceding essays demonstrate, this is clearly a context in which Foucault has had a very productive effect. Foucault's advice seems to recommend engagements with problems wherever they arise, following dispersals of phenomena, applying methods and techniques wherever they prove useful and paying close attention to how concepts and classifications work rather than naively submit to the work they perform. Many of the preceding essays demonstrate the productivity of his recommendations in this respect. Nevertheless, we also confront the danger of converting procedures cultivated in the spirit of heterogeneity into generalizable methods applicable across homogenized fields of scholarship, with all the promises of normalization and institution building this implies. This is a challenge confronted not only by studies of governmentality (especially when attached to the mega-reification of something global) but also by attempts to establish a field of critical security studies, where Foucault's influence has also been both extensive and productive. Here we might say that it will be necessary to ensure that Foucault's instincts for heterogeneity prevail over the reification of either his specific concepts or techniques, and that his insistence that security and liberty must be understood as a relation prevails over the usual statist tendency to distinguish "security studies" from "liberty studies," which tend to be generously funded and underfunded (or just abandoned) respectively, to the point of illiberalism in both cases.

## So Which International?

Onuf responds to the indeterminacy of Foucault as a figure who has had some influence on scholars working on the modern international in a way that intentionally tells us much more about how Onuf wants to read Foucault than about how Foucault's more committed followers might have wanted him to be read. Moreover, while most of the essays that follow try to stay more closely in touch with some of the better-established accounts of what Foucault's legacy must be, they also express the distinctive voice and interpretation of each commentator. Again, I take this to be a positive virtue. Just as an expansive reading of Foucault has enabled many different scholars to converge on a shared attitude that is clearly needed in any serious engagement with the phenomena of international relations that increasingly elude established modes of analysis, so Foucault has been unusually productive in generating novel ways of thinking and doing research. In a discipline in which the meaning of methodology has often narrowed to a mean and dogmatic catechism, Foucault has inspired productive re-engagements with what is involved in the production of knowledge as well as with questions about the relation between knowledge and politics. Purists might quibble that this inspiration has often come at the cost of invocations of Foucault's name that legitimize distinctly non-foucauldian options. His name has certainly become a slogan, a "perspective", a vessel into which it has been possible to pour many things, and the history of his reception is itself an instructive arena for political analysis. Even so, a second underlying commonality among these essays is a sense of gratitude toward a thinker who has been able to provoke imagination at a time when so much scholarly work tends to confuse creativity with nostalgia and knowledge with reliable technique.

As one might expect from one of the most perceptive historically inclined theorists of international relations, Onuf wants to rescript Foucault's reading of the history of modernity, build on his account of normalization, and enhance what he thinks is a limited engagement with normativity and law. Others in this volume also urge a reconsideration of Foucault's reading of history, rightly in my view, and impressive as it is in many respects, and as reflective as it is about the perils of all historical analysis. Marta Fernández and Paulo Esteves, for example, point to worrying parallels between Foucault's reading of the history of the international and that given by the English School, with both neglecting much consideration of the colonial character of international relations. Indeed, as I have long argued, the most important thing to know about the modern international concerns its affirmation of a clear distinction between the international and everything that lies outside, both spatially and temporally: colonies, premodern societies and natural/theological authorities most obviously.[8] It affirms the famous story about modern "man" and the practices of internalization and subjectivization, of a coming into the modern world of modern subjects and subjectivities as well as the expansion of that world out into some broader world that nevertheless stops just before the world as such, whether as Kantian noumenon or Planet Earth. This is not a story that fits comfortably into Foucault's famous tripartite periodization, which struggled mainly with and against already established (Kantian, Hegelian) narratives about Europe's own internalizing trajectories. In a sense, international relations expresses patterns of inclusion and exclusion that already enabled Foucault to begin his rereading of the histories of modern subjectivity; at least this is how it may be seen in retrospect.

My own view here is that it is especially instructive to understand Foucault's engagement with these histories through not only his major dissertation on the *History of Madness* and his subsequent and often quite brilliant attempts to resist its procedures but also his dissertation on Kant's anthropology.[9] In the latter, Foucault rightly stresses Kant's anthropological grounding of philosophical possibility with an eye on Kant's later shift to the "Copernican Revolution" of his Critiques. Whatever the virtues of his reading of this shift, he devotes surprisingly little attention to the conditionality that is embedded in this possibility, a distinction between those deemed capable of what Kant would later call a universal history with a cosmopolitan intent and those who are not.

It is arguably not too much to say that the modern international works largely within limits set out in Kant's *Idea of a Universal History with a Cosmopolitan Aim*[10] and his *Perpetual Peace*.[11] The former marks a turning from a view of man understood in relation to a then novel sense of the past to a now familiar sense of the linear path from present to future. The latter affirms the necessity for incessant war driving us to ever more perfect but never perfectible subjectivities, the vaunted ambition for self-determination simultaneously within individuals, states and a system of states. The conjunction between a specific philosophy of history and a spatialized, scalar and antinomian understanding of human/political subjectivities is crucial in this respect. In this context, it is telling that while Foucault does famously engage with Kant's question about the meaning of Enlightenment he pays much less attention to the implications of Kantian texts that are even more explicit about the "developmental" framing of questions about what it means to think for oneself. Many exclusions have been at work to enable an international order that is itself constructed as a structure of inclusions and exclusions within and between states, and it is certainly striking that Foucault turns mainly to the figure of "man" that emerges within Europe rather than to the radical splits within humanity that are effected by the practices of internalization, subjectivization and the teleological realization of the "hidden plan of nature" shaping the rise of the modern international. It is not difficult to read Foucault as an entirely conventional European political thinker in this respect.

So I would say that Onuf, Fernandez and Esteves, along with Barry Hindess and others, have put their finger on one of the key difficulties that must be negotiated in bringing Foucault and international relations into conjunction. I would also say that this points to one of the reasons why Onuf might be right to lament Foucault's desire to resist any obsession with law, which certainly works as a key practice effecting distinctions between that which is included within the modern international and that which is not, as well as the practices of sovereignty that are enacted quite as much by the modern international as by those states that both constitute and are constituted by the modern international.

Onuf retains a (critical) commitment to at least some of the scholarly conventions of international relations theory. Bigo is considerably more antagonistic, in ways that enable his sympathetic account of Foucault's own resistance to disciplinary conventions in the specific French context of the 1970s. The details he offers of the situation in which Foucault found himself are very important and instructive in their own right, but they also raise broader questions about the relation between scholarly disciplines and the phenomena they seek to engage. Let me mention three very briefly.

First, we might wonder about the often highly variable character and also restricted geographical range of international relations as a discipline. Bigo himself is responding to what he sees as the highly constrained character of options available within a predominantly Americanized political science. It is a perfectly reasonable concern. Yet I would also say that the forms of constraint have changed considerably over time. There is, for example, some difference between hegemonies premised on nationalistic and/or Cold War claims about political realism as a criterion for excluding the supposedly naïve and radical, and those predicated on universalizing claims about epistemology and method as a criterion for evaluating scholarly authority. Despite many continuities, there was a significant shift from the one to the other of these positions toward the very end of the late 1970s, a shift that perhaps parallels the shift from liberalism to neo-liberalism, if one can still resort to such oversimplified terms. But in neither era was there an uncontested homogeneity. Many other disciplines managed to have substantial voices in what counted as serious claims about international relations. What is striking is that despite a fair degree of empirical diversity, a more or less caricatured version of a disciplinary mainstream has been both reproduced and constantly affirmed, to the point that many critics keep urging a move to greener pastures. The dogmatization of disciplines like political science certainly must be challenged, but it would be a mistake to see the discipline itself as the primary problem rather than as a telling expression and reproduction of many other and broader forces.

Second, however one characterizes the situation in the USA in recent years, it stands in marked contrast with the situation in which Foucault found himself in the 1970s. I find it striking that Foucault found it so easy to avoid such disciplinary constraints and to work with and even invent a broad range of other concepts through which to recast the phenomena claimed by theorists of international relations in very different terms. In the Anglo-American world this would have required—and did require— many energetic interdisciplinary circumventions, through geography, or law, or history, or political and social theory, or literature, or postcolonial studies, and so on, as well as some appreciation of the capacity for disciplines to close ranks and undermine all relationalities.

Third, and my main point in this context, the relative ease with which Foucault was able to engage with political analysis by eluding established forms of political science brought both advantages and disadvantages. The advantages are clear. But sometimes he comes close to reinventing the wheel. Sometimes he runs into predictable dead-ends. Very often, the terms and stakes of his analyses remain veiled. Almost all of the time one can almost feel him thinking through positions and refusing to follow the established tramlines. It is, it must be said, quite exhausting even if exhilarating to follow his creative shifts. But sometimes the established forms of disciplinary knowledge are not the problem. Disciplines, after all, tend to become normalized in ways that render their initial provocation more or less uninteresting, banal, a mere presupposition. And in escaping so easily from rather rickety forms of political science that relied on transparently political presuppositions, one must worry about the degree to which Foucault never had much chance to worry about international relations as a problem in anything but the narrowly constrained terms given by figures like Aron and the importation of fairly simplistic versions of political science.

Let me take this observation in two opposing directions in order to come closer to my ambivalent conclusions. First, some quick comments about Foucault's engagement with Hobbes in order to tease out what version of an international he had in mind in that context and what escaped his analysis. Then some comments about Foucault's capacity to mobilize other ways of thinking, which I take to be the animating spirit of this volume of essays as a whole.

Foucault's reading of Hobbes is striking in many respects. For a start, he understands that it is not helpful to think about Hobbes primarily as driven by claims about what is now fetishized as "security." This is consistent with both Hobbes's text and the standard interpretive convention that he was starting with claims about the "natural condition" of "man." That man was conceived abstractly, as Foucault also recognizes. In that abstraction, a condition of radical insecurity is a consequence of the specification of man that Hobbes establishes through an act of definition. That consequence of the definition of man as naturally free and equal, in a qualified sense in both cases, is then made the rationale for a subsequent moment of rebirth in which natural man is miraculously, contractually, turned into civil man, and the antagonism of man and the now politically qualified citizen is contained and mobilized within the legal jurisdiction of a sovereign law. In this respect, Foucault offers an appropriate but scarcely novel reprimand to all those analyses of international relations that simply reverse the relation between man and security in order to affirm, reify and discipline the kind of "man," the specifically modern (and perhaps liberal) subject that generates insecurity. It is clearly no accident that Hobbes is often deployed as a canonical theorist of security in that such a reading permits a systematic evasion of questions about who is being secured, and thus a switch from civil man as the always potential source of insecurity internally to other men somewhere beyond their domesticated sovereign jurisdiction. Thus, Foucault gets at the profound significance of Hobbes's move to abstractions, the use Hobbes makes of them in constituting an internalized political order, and thus the problematic relationship between that internality and that which lies outside, both in abstract principle and in spatiotemporal practice.

Difficulties begin to arise from the manner in which he sets up his engagement with Hobbes through his refusal of the Clausewitzian formulation of war as the continuation of politics by other means. Perhaps with Raymond Aron's version of this formulation in mind,[12] or perhaps thinking of other nationalist positions that link Clausewitz with Aron, he plays the reversibility card in order to read the relation between the violence inherent in Hobbes's account of a state of nature and Hobbes's account of a sovereign legal order as always subject to reversal. In effect, Hobbes is read as a theorist of peace rather than war, and Hobbes is shown to be a lot more interesting than Aron and company. This too is conventional, and again works as a reprimand to those analysts of international relations who default to an understanding of the relation between violence and peace as one of absolute opposition, as in the classification of theories as either realist or liberal, for example, or the deployment of Kant as the peaceful antithesis of Hobbes rather than a theorist of the violence necessary to move toward a peace that must be endlessly deferred. Still, the axis on which thinkers like Clausewitz and Aron imagined a relation between politics and war was characteristically articulated from an internality to an externality on a horizontal plane, from friend to enemy in a field of autonomous nation states. While Hobbes does have a place for externalities, the line of flight that may be subject to reversibility is not primarily about horizontal relations among nation states.

Hobbes was a thinker of sovereign states and not of any international order that was becoming thinkable by Clausewitz in the wake of the French Revolution and the Congress of Vienna. Foucault does identify the very close relation between war and some kind of politics in Hobbes, but this is a relation, I would prefer to say, that is played out not in terms of a horizontal line where war and politics is imagined as internality and externality but as overworld and underworld: the two surfaces of a flattened abstract space that Hobbes constructs as the necessary alternative to prevailing hierarchies, a relatively equalitarian remnant of older distinctions between higher and lower. The problem of internal rebellion is much more pressing for Hobbes than the problem of war. Peace is always likely to collapse down into the originary state of nature, even while that collapse is simultaneously open to an external projection in both space and time, precisely the projection that he deploys so as to establish the contractual act of constitution in the first place. So I would say that any simple horizontal axis that is assumed to be subject to a simple reversal is going to miss much of what is most interesting about the use Hobbes makes of his own out and back projections in order to construct a distinction between internality and externality as well as the strikingly minimalist account of relations between higher and lower that Hobbes uses to counter prevailing accounts of natural or theologically ordained hierarchies. While Foucault has some interesting insights about Hobbes, these only amplify the importance of questions about what is at stake in the way Foucault engages Hobbes by way of a singular axis along which one can imagine a point of reversal, a cut distinguishing one condition from another, whether as condition of politics or war, as a condition of internality or externality, or as a temporal relation of before and after. The state of civil society may be a continuation of a state of nature by other means, but that is not the relation that is at stake at the point of which the sovereign state meets its constitutive externality. Many important themes lie in the wings here: Hobbes's commitment to limited accounts of both freedom and equality; the practices through which he instanti-ates an account of what sovereignty must be, the precise relations that Hobbes contracts between force and consent, or power and authority, and unhappy parallels between the possibility of reversing Clausewitz's understanding of politics and war and claims about contemporary transi-tions from a statist condition of specific exceptions to some globalized condition of generalized exceptions.

Foucault doesn't really pursue such matters, perhaps wisely but per-haps not. He is more concerned to engage with the highly contested arena in which Hobbes is a figure of historical interpretation by offering a narrative about how Hobbes was struggling to eradicate the effects of various claims about histories of wars and invasions by turning all histo-ries into an abstract condition. This might be understood as a version of the again commonplace view that Hobbes the historically inclined translator of *The Peloponnesian War* had shifted to what we might call a structuralist or architectural mode in which history is effectively sub-dued. The basic insight is right, and helpful for the way it shifts attention to the various ways in which Hobbes's account of sovereignty hinges on an account of origins and limits, not on achieved centers of authority of the kind reified in Weberian accounts of the monopolistic state that are reproduced by figures like Aron.

Still, if Hobbes's concept of a state of nature is a response to an his-torically situated problem, it is not clear that Foucault has come close to resolving questions about what that problem was, and thus why Hobbes is misunderstood as a theorist of security. After all, Hobbes begins his text by talking about the physiology of perception and then mounting an entertaining nominalist attack on the corruptions of philosophical realism and the proper and improper use of language. The stakes of these early chapters are a lot greater than those involved in claims about histories of invasion in England, though one can see their potential relevance for many more parochial concerns. Foucault was clearly quite aware of these broader stakes, and of the dangers of falling into the conventional accounts of the history of modernity and so on. It is thus curious that he chose to load the great weight of concepts of politics and war as framed by a nineteenth-century thinker like Clausewitz, and its relations to a seventeenth-century thinker like Hobbes, onto a rather flimsy claim about English history.

More important, I would say, would be to understand Hobbes's account of an abstract state of nature as not only a solution to the effects of prevailing historical narratives, especially those grounded in naturalistic and theological authorizations, but also a crucial element in the construction of the abstract spatiotemporality that is later normalized in Kant's account of history and the ambitions of normalized subjects and subjectivities. This abstraction does indeed work through something like the horizontal line on which it is possible to imagine the reversible relation between politics and war, the projection of the negative reading of man out to America as both spatiotemporally distant in order to affirm the natural necessity of a space of a politics that is always likely to revert to the violence that is just below the surface but which is also simultaneously both out there and back then. As one of the great theorists of political founding, Hobbes is deeply implicated in shaping the linear accounts of history against which Foucault was clearly struggling when laboriously articulating his archaeological—and later genealogical—method(s) of historical inquiry. Even so, up to this point one can see how Foucault has many interesting insights into the ways Hobbes might speak to the modern international in terms that evade many disciplinary orthodoxies.

Nevertheless, despite the seemingly unbreakable appropriation of Hobbes by those who claim to speak about international relations, and also despite his crucial role in shaping our understanding what lies beyond the sovereign jurisdictions he sought to construct as abstract form, and thus of the relation of internality to externality as anything but a simple line of distinction, Hobbes himself says very little about politics beyond the state.[13] What he does say, right in the famous chapter 13 that theorists of international relations so love to quote, is that there is a radical difference between the state of nature and the state of war. The crucial difference is that states are not equal in the way he describes individuals, nor are they as vulnerable. On the contrary, wars are good for states. Moreover, the whole point of Hobbes's analysis is to constitute the sovereign state as a different ordering of being than its constituent parts, a different ordering that is expressed not least as a difference of scale. Inequality is reintroduced as a necessary consequence of the initial premise of equality domestically, and the inequality of states becomes available as a parallel principle of order internationally. It is true that many theorists of international relations blissfully ignore this distinction in order to arrive at claims about an international anarchy and so on, but many others recognize inequality, hegemony, great power responsibility and so on as a key principle of international order. It is a consequential difference, not least because it disrupts any notion that the kind of horizontal axis on which one can imagine reversals of politics and war once it is extended beyond the limits of Hobbes's account of statist jurisdiction, unless we understand it precisely as a practice of securing statist jurisdictions internally, a practice that is much more interesting than a simple point of reversal.

Hobbes himself says very little about the realm in which states big and small might circulate. Moreover, there is a big difference between claims about an international as simply a disordered realm in which states collide with each other and one in which such collisions constitute another kind of political ordering that might project its own version of an axis of politics and war back toward the states that constitute it. The historical conventions here work with the nineteenth and twentieth centuries. And the core problems that then arise according to these conventions concern the relations—contradictions, negotiations, politics, wars—not only among modern states but also between modern states and the modern international. It is in this context that one can see attempts to reconcile claims to a generic humanity with claims about politically qualified citizens, as well as questions about whether it is state law or international law that is the ultimate claimant to law and sovereign authority.

I would say that this is not the understanding in which Foucault was interested, although Mitchell Dean's contribution to this volume advances elements of a plausible case to the contrary. Hobbes is not obviously a theorist of international relations in this sense either, and it is not even clear that Foucault would be interested in him if he was. In my view, both are thinking about specific states and have only vaguely specified understandings of what lies beyond them. It might also be said that large parts of the disciplinary knowledge about the modern international displays a related disinterest. In all three cases, the singular state is heavily foregrounded. Externalities may be recognized in some fashion, but as I suggested at the outset, there are many ways in which that externality may be called international in some sense, and the precision of the sense is another case of the devil being in the details. I would certainly say that neither mere externality nor comparability adds up to a serious engagement with an international as it has now come to be institutionalized. I would also say that this is a matter that has significance far beyond the specific case of Michel Foucault, who at least has a grip on fundamental problems of human subjectivity that exceed the ordering capacities of established political jurisdictions, both statist and international.

For there is another story to be told, the one that is told in various ways throughout this book. This is the story of the Foucault who resists all the official categories and concepts, the Foucault of practices, techniques, the microphysics of power and the conduct of conduct, the Foucault who tries to mobilize dispersals while hanging on to patterns of intelligibility. But this may be a Foucault who is most useful for examining contemporary situations that are scarcely recognizable if we assume that we still live in the modern international; as I think we both do and do not.

In his later life, of course, Veyne directed Foucault's attention to more classical sources, though not to the standard texts about the Greek polis. The obvious temptation is to see that Foucault was shifting toward thinkers who were alive to the possibilities and constraints of empires rather than to states or their systematic relations. Perhaps, though this possibility seems to be of little interest to those who take his later work to be of interest for contemporary contexts. Nevertheless, concepts of empire are likely to over-determine our understanding of contemporary trajectories quite as easily as concepts of state and international. Foucault offers many resources for interrogating those trajectories, even while one must remain alive to the statism that persisted in his counterstatist thinking, to the Eurocentricism that constrained his many more cosmopolitan sympathies, and to the long history of failed attempts to escape from reified concepts through the pursuit of empirical details without attending to their multiple conditions of intelligibility and, most crucially, to those who might find them intelligible.

## NOTES

1. See R. B. J. Walker, *Inside/Outside: International Relations as Political Theory* (Cambridge: Cambridge University Press, 1993); *After the Globe, Before the World* (London and New York: Routledge, 2010); and *Out of Line: Essays on the Politics of Boundaries and the Limits of Modern Politics* (London and New York: Routledge, 2016).
2. Bruno Latour, *We Have Never Been Modern*, transl. Catherine Porter (Cambridge, MA.: Harvard University Press, 1993).
3. Stanley Hoffmann, "An American Social Science: International Relations," *Daedalus*, 106(3) (1977): 41–60; Klauss Knorr, and James N. Rosenau, *Contending Approaches to International Politics* (Princeton: Princeton University Press, 1969).
4. See Michel Foucault, *Society Must Be Defended: Lectures at the College De France, 1975–1976*, eds. Arnold Davidson, Mauro Bertani, Francois Ewald and Alessandro Fontana, transl. David Macey (New York: Picador, 2003); *Security, Territory, Population: Lectures at the College de France, 1997–1978*, ed. Arnold Davidson, Michel Senellart, Francois Ewald and Alessandro Fontana, transl. Graham Burchell (New York: Palgrave Macmillan, 2007); and *The Birth of Biopolitics, Lectures at the College de France, 1978–1979*, ed. Arnold Davidson, Michel Senellart, Francois Ewald and Alessandro Fontana, transl. Graham Burchell (New York: Palgrave Macmillan, 2008).
5. Martin Wight, "Why is There No International Theory?" in H. Butterfield and M. Wight (eds.), *Diplomatic Investigations* (London: Allen and Unwin, 1966), pp. 17–34; Walker, *Inside/Outside*.
6. Paul Veyne, *Foucault: His Thought, His Character*, transl. Janet Lloyd (Cambridge: Polity, 2008), pp. 20–21.
7. Ian Hacking, *Historical Ontology* (Cambridge MA.: Harvard University Press, 2002); Beatrice Han, *Foucault's Critical Project: Between the Transcendental and the Historical* (Stanford: Stanford University Press, 2002); Marc Djaballah, *Kant, Foucault and Forms of Experience* (New York: Routledge, 2008); Colin Koopman, *Genealogy as Critique: Foucault and the Problems of Modernity* (Bloomington: Indiana University Press, 2013).
8. R. B. J. Walker, "World Politics and Western Reason, Universalism, Pluralism, Hegemony," *Alternatives*, 7(2) (1981), reprinted in Walker, *Out of Line*, pp. 37–64.
9. Foucault, *Security, Territory, Population*; Michel Foucault, *The Order of Things: An Archeology of the Human Sciences* (1966) (New York: Pantheon, 1970).
10. Immanuel Kant, "Idea for a Universal History with a Cosmopolitan Aim" (1784), transl. Allen Wood, in Amelie Oskenberg Rorty and James Schmitt, eds., *Kant's Idea for a Universal History with a Cosmopolitan Aim: A Critical Guide* (Cambridge: Cambridge University Press, 2009), pp. 9–23.

11. Immanuel Kant, "Towards Perpetual Peace" (1795) in Mary J. Gregor, editor and translator, *Immanuel Kant: Practical Philosophy* (Cambridge: Cambridge University Press, 1996), pp. 311–352.

12. Raymond Aron, *Clausewitz: Philosopher of War*, transl. C. Booker and N. Stone (Routledge & Kegan Paul, 1983 [1976]); Claude Lefort, "Lectures de la guerre : le Clausewitz de Raymond Aron" *Annales. Économies, Sociétés, Civilisations*, 6 (1977): 1268–1279.

13. Walker, *After the Globe, Before the World*; R. B. J. Walker, "Hobbes, Origins, Limits" in Raia Prokhovik and Gabriella Stomp, eds., *International Political Theory after Hobbes: Analysis, Interpretation and Orientation* (Basingstoke: Palgrave, 2011), pp. 168–188; reprinted in Walker *Out of Line*, pp. 201–216.

# BIBLIOGRAPHY

## WORKS BY MICHEL FOUCAULT CITED IN THE VOLUME (BY CHRONOLOGICAL ORDER OF THE FIRST PUBLICATION/ PRONUNCIATION)

### Books

Michel Foucault, *Introduction to Kant's Anthropology*, transl. R. Nigro and K. Briggs (Los Angeles: Semiotext(e), 2008 [1964]).

Michel Foucault, *History of Madness*, transl. J. Murphy and J. Khalfa (Abingdon: Routledge, 2006 [1961]).

Michel Foucault, *The Order of Things: An Archaeology of the Human Sciences*, transl.. A.M. Sheridan Smith (London: Tavistock, 1970 [1966]).

Michel Foucault, *Archaeology of Knowledge & The Discourse on Language*, transl. A.M. Sheridan Smith (London and New York: Routledge, 2002 [1969 & 1970]).

Michel Foucault, "The Order of Discourse," in Michael Shapiro (ed.), *Language and Politics* (New York: New York University Press, 1984 [1970]), pp. 108–138

Michel Foucault. *Discipline and Punish: The Birth of the Prison* (London: Allen Lane; New York, Vintage Books, 1977 [1975]).

Michel Foucault, *History of Sexuality, Volume 1: An Introduction*, transl. R. Hurley (London: Allen Lane, 1979 [1976]).

Michel Foucault, *The Use of Pleasure. Volume 2 of the History of Sexuality*, transl. R. Hurley (New York: Pantheon, 1985 [1984]).

© The Author(s) 2017
P. Bonditti et al. (eds.), *Foucault and the Modern International*,
The Sciences Po Series in International Relations and Political
Economy, DOI 10.1057/978-1-137-56153-4

## Lectures at the *Collège de France*

Michel Foucault, *Lectures on the Will to Know. Lectures at the College de France 1970–1971, and Oedipal Knowledge,* ed. D. Defert and A. I. Davidson, transl. G. Burchell (London: Palgrave Macmillan, 2013).

Michel Foucault, *Society Must be Defended: Lectures at Collège de France, 1975–1976,* ed. M. Bertani, A. Fontana, transl. D. Macey (New York, Picador, 2003; London: Penguin, 2003).

Michel Foucault, *Security, Territory Population. Lectures at the Collège de France 1977–1978,* ed. F. F. Ewald, A. Fontana and A. I. Davidson, transl. G. Burchell (New York, Palgrave-MacMillan, 2008).

Michel Foucault, *The Birth of Biopolitics. Lectures at the Collège de France 1978–1979,* transl. G. Burchell (New York, Palgrave-MacMillan, 2008).

Michel Foucault, *On the Government of the Living. Lectures at the Collège de France 1979–1980,* ed. Michel Senellart, transl. G. Burchell (London: Palgrave, 2014).

Michel Foucault, *The Hermeneutics of the Subject: Lectures at the Collège de France 1981–82,* F. Ewald, A. Fontana and A. I. Davidson, transl. G. Burchell (Basingstoke and New York: Palgrave Macmillan, 2006).

Michel Foucault, *The Government of Self and Others, Lectures at the Collège de France 1982–1983,* ed. F. Gros and A. I. Davidson, transl. G. Burchell (London: Palgrave Macmillan, 2010).

Michel Foucault, *The Courage of Truth, The Government of Self and Others II, Lectures at the College de France 1983–1984,* ed. F. Gros and A. I. Davidson, transl. G. Burchell (London: Palgrave Macmillan, 2010).

Michel Foucault, *Subjectivité et vérité. Cours au Collège de France. 1980–1981,* ed. F. Gros, (Paris: Seuil, Gallimard, 2014). [Untranslated]


## Articles, Conferences, Interviews

Michel Foucault, "A Preface to Transgression," in *Language, Counter-Memory, Practice: Selected Essays and Interviews* (Ithaca: Cornell University Press, 1977 [1963]), pp. 34–5.

Michel Foucault, "Distance, aspect, origin," in *The Tel Quel Reader,* ed. P. French and R.-F. Lack (London, Routledge, 1998 [1968]), pp. 97–108.

Michel Foucault, "Nietzsche, genealogy, history, [1971]" in *Essential Works of Michel Foucault,* ed. James Faubion, transl. R. Hurley et al., vol. 2 *Aesthetics,* (London: Penguin, 1998), pp. 369–391.

Michel Foucault,"Truth and juridical forms, [1974]" in M. Foucault, *Power, The Essential Works,* Volume 3 (New York: The New Press, 2000), pp. 1–89.

Michel Foucault, "Entretien avec Roger-Pol Droit [1975]," *Le Point,* n°1659, July 1st 2004. [Untranslated]

Michel Foucault, "The Confession of the Flesh [1977]," in C. Gordon ed. *Power/ Knowledge: Selected Interviews and Other Writings 1972–1977* (Brighton: Harvester, 1980).

Michel Foucault, "About the Concept of the 'Dangerous Individual' in 19th-Century Psychiatry, [1977]" *International Journal of Law and Psychiatry,* 1(1) (1978).

Michel Foucault, "*Omnes et singulatim: towards a criticism of political reason* [1979]", in *The Tanner Lectures on Human Values,* vol. 2, ed. S. McMurrin (Salt Lake City, UT: University of Utah Press, 1981), pp. 223–254.

Michel Foucault, "Foucault Examines Reason in Service of State Power," Interview with M. Dillon in *The Three Penny Review,* n°1, 1980, pp. 4–5.

Michel Foucault, *Wrong-Doing Truth-Telling. The Function of Avowal in Justice* [1981], ed. F. Brion and B. E. Harcourt, transl. S. W. Sawyer, (Chicago: Chicago University Press and Presses Universitaires de Louvain, 2014).

Michel Foucault, "Technologies of the Self [1982,]" *in Technologies of the Self: A Seminar with Michel Foucault,* ed. L. H. Martin, H. Gutman and P. H. Hutton (London: Tavistock, 1988), pp. 16–49.

Michel Foucault, "On the Genealogy of Ethics: An Overview of Work in Progress," in H. Dreyfus and P. Rabinow, *Michel Foucault: Beyond Structuralism and Hermeneutics,* 2nd ed., (Chicago: University of Chicago Press, 1983), pp. 229–252.

Michel Foucault, "The Concern for Truth," in S. Lotringer, *Foucault Live,* transl. J. Johnston (New York: Semiotext(e), 1989 [1984]), pp. 465–464.

Michel Foucault, "The Birth of Social Medicine [1974]," transl. Robert Hurley, in James Faubion et al. (eds), *Power: The Essential Works of Michel Foucault. 1954–1984 vol. 2* (London: Allen Lane, 2000), pp. 134–56.

Michel Foucault, *Fearless Speech,* ed. Joseph Pearson (New York: Semiotext(e), 2001 [1983])

## Collection of Essays

Michel Foucault, *Dits et écrits,* Vol. 1&2, Quarto Gallimard, 2001.

Michel Foucault, *Power/Knowledge: Selected Interviews and Other Writings, 1972–1977, by Michel Foucault,* ed. C. Gordon (New York: Pantheon, 1980).

Michel Foucault, *The Foucault Reader,* ed. by Paul Rabinow (New York: Pantheon Book, 1984).

Michel Foucault, *The Politics of Truth,* transl. L. Hochroth and C. Porter (New York: Semiotext(e), 2007).

## GENERAL BIBLIOGRAPHY

Abélès, M., *The Politics of Survival* (Durham, NC: Duke University Press, 2010).

Adelkhah, F., *Being modern in Iran*, transl. J. Derrick (London: Hurst & Co, 1999).

Afary J. and K. B. Anderson, *Foucault and the Iranian Revolution. Gender and the Seductions of Isamism* (Chicago and London: University of Chicago Press, 2005).

Agamben, G., *Homo Sacer: Sovereign Power and Bare Life*, transl. D. Heller-Roazen (Stanford: Stanford University Press, 1998).

Agamben, G., *The Open: Man and Animal*, transl. K. Attell (Stanford: Stanford University Press, 2004).

Agamben, G., *What is an Apparatus?* transl. D. Kishik and S. Pedatella (Stanford, CA: Stanford University Press, 2009).

Agamben, G., *The Kingdom and the Glory: For a Theological Genealogy of Economy and Government*, transl. L. Chiesa with M. Mandarini (Stanford, CA: Stanford University Press, 2011).

Agnew, J., "The Territorial Trap: The Geographical Assumptions of International Relations Theory," *Review of international political economy* 1(1) (1994): 53–80.

Agnew, J., *Geopolitics: Re-visioning World Politics* (London: Routledge, 1998 (second edition 2003)).

Albert, M., Jacobson D., and Y. Lapid (eds), *Identity, Borders, Orders* (Minneapolis, University of Minnesota Press, 2001).

Allen, A. and R. Goddard, "The Domestication of Foucault: Government, Critique, War," *History of the Human Sciences* 27(5)(2014): 26–53.

Althusser, L., *Initiation à la philosophie pour les non-philosophes* (Paris: PUF, 2014).

Amoore, L. "Biometric Borders: Governing Mobilities in the War on Terror," *Political Geography* 25(3) (2006): 336–51.

Amoore, L., *The Politics of Possibility: Risk and Security beyond Probability* (Durham, NC: Duke University Press, 2013).

Andersen, A., *Discursive Analytical Strategies. Understanding Foucault, Koselleck, Laclau, Luhmann* (Chicago: University of Chicago Press, 2003).

Anderson, M., Bigo D., and E. Bort, "Frontiers, Identity and Security in Europe: An Agenda for Research," in Pratt M. and J. Brown (eds.), *Borderlands under Stress* (La Haye: Kluwer Law International, 2000), pp. 251–274.

Andersson, R., "Hunter and Prey: Patrolling Clandestine Migration in the Euro-African Borderlands," *Anthropological Quarterly* 87(1) (2014): 119–149.

Aron, R., *Clausewitz: Philosopher of War*, transl. by C. Booker and N. Stone (New York: Routledge & Kegan Paul, 1983 [1976]).

Aron, R., *Paix et Guerre entre les Nations* (Paris: Calman Levy, 1984 (1962)).

Arsène, S., *Internet et politique en Chine* (Paris: Karthala, 2011).

Ashley R., Walker R.B.J., "Speaking the Language of Exile: Dissident Thought in International Studies", *International Studies Quarterly* 34(3), pp. 259–268.

Audier, S., *Penser le 'néolibéralisme.' Le moment néolibéral, Foucault, et la crise du socialisme* (Lormont: Le Bord de l'eau, 2015).

Audrain, X., *Des 'punks de Dieu' aux 'taalibe-citoyens'. Jeunesse, citoyenneté et mobilisation religieuse au Sénégal. Le mouvement mouride de Cheikh Modou Kara (1980–2007)* (Paris: Université de Paris 1 Panthéon Sorbonne, multigr, 2013).

Bachelard, G., *Essai sur la connaissance approchée* (1927) (Paris: Vrin, 2000).

Balfour, I., *The Rhetoric of Romantic Prophecy* (Stanford: Stanford University Press, 2002).

Balibar E. and I. Wallerstein, *Race, Nation, Class: Ambiguous Identities*, transl. (of Balibar) by C. Turner, (London, Verso, 1991).

Balibar, E., "Foucault's Point of Heresy: 'Quasi-Transcendentals' and the Transdisciplinary Function of the Episteme," *Theory, Culture & Society*, 32 (5–6) (2015): 45–77.

Ball, K., Haggerty K., and D. Lyon, *Routledge Handbook of Surveillance Studies* (Abingdon: Routledge, 2012).

Barnett, T. P., *The Pentagon's New Map: War and Peace in the Twenty-First Century* (G.P. Putnam's Sons, 2004).

Barnett M., and R. Duvall, "Power in International Politics," *International Organization*, 59(1) (2005): 39–75.

Barry, A., *Political Machines. Governing a Technological Society* (London, The Athlone Press, 2001).

Barry, A., T. Osborne and N. Rose (eds), *Foucault and Political Reason. Liberalism, Neo-Liberalism and Rationalities of Government* (Chicago: The University of Chicago Press, 1996).

Bartelson J., *A Genealogy of Sovereignty* (Cambridge: Cambridge University Press, 1995).

Barthes, R., *Mythologies*, transl. R. Howard and A. Lavers (New York, Hill & Wang, 2012).

Barthes, R., *Writing degree zero*, transl. A. Lavers and C. Smith (New York, Hill & Wang, 2012).

Bate, J., *The Song of the Earth* (London: Picador, 2000).

Bauman, Z., *Globalization: The Human Consequences* (New York: Columbia University Press, 1998).

Bauman, Z., *Liquid Times* (Cambridge: Polity Press, 2007).

Baumann Z. and D. Lyon, *Liquid Surveillance: A Conversation* (Cambridge and Malden: Polity, 2013).

Bauman, Z. et al. "After Snowden: Rethinking the Impact of Surveillance," *International Political Sociology* 8(2)(2014): 121–144.

Bayart, J.-F., "La revanche des sociétés africaines," *Politique Africaine*, 11 (September 1983): 95–127.

Bayart, J.-F., "L'énonciation du politique," *Revue française de science politique* 35(3) (1985): 343–73.

Bayart, J.-F., *Le gouvernement du monde. Une critique politique de la mondialisation* (Paris, Fayard, 2004).

Bayart, J.-F., "Foucault au Congo," in M.-C. Granjon (ed.), *Penser avec Michel Foucault. Théorie critique et pratiques politiques*, (Paris: Karthala, 2005), pp. 183–222.

Bayart, J.-F., *The Illusion of Cultural Identity* (London: Hurst, Chicago: The University of Chicago Press, 2005).

Bayart, J.-F., *Global subjects: A Political Critique of Globalization*, transl. A. Brown. (Cambridge: Polity, 2007).

Bayart, J.-F., "Comparing from below," *Sociétés politiques comparées*, 1 (2008): 1–27.

Bayart, J.-F., *The state in Africa: The Politics of the Belly* (2nd ed. Cambridge; Malden, MA: Polity, 2009).

Bayart, J.-F., *Les Etudes postcoloniales, un carnaval académique* (Paris: Karthala, 2010).

Bayart, J.-F., "Around *Political Spiritualities: The Pentecostal Revolution in Nigeria*, by Ruth Marshall," *Religion and Society*, 2 (2011): 145–150.

Bayart, J.-F., *Sortir du national-libéralisme. Croquis politiques des années 2004–2012* (Paris: Karthala, 2012).

Bayart, J.-F., "Another look at the Arab Springs," *Sociétés politiques comparées*, 35 (2013): 1–34.

Bayart, J.-F. and R. Bertrand, "De quel 'legs colonial' parle-t-on?" *Esprit*, December (2006): 134–160.

Bayart, J.-F., Mbembe, A. and C. Toulabor, *Le Politique par le bas en Afrique noire. Contributions à une problématique de la démocratie* (Paris: Karthala, 1992 [revised and enlarged edition 2008]).

Beck, U., *Risk Society: Towards a new Modernity* (London: Sage, 1997 [1986]).

Becker, G. S., "An Economic Analysis of Fertility," in Ansley J. Coale (ed.), *Demographic and Economic Changes in Developed Countries* (New Jersey, Princeton University Press, 1960).

Becker, G. S., *A Treatise on the Family* (Cambridge/London: Harvard University Press, 1981).

Becker, G. S., *Human Capital. A Theoretical and Empirical Analysis with Special Reference to Education* (Chicago/London: The University of Chicago Press, 1975 [sec. ed. 1983]).

Becker, G. S., Ewald F., and B. Harcourt, "Becker on Ewald on Foucault on Becker: American Neoliberalism and Michel Foucault's 1979 'Birth of Biopolitics' lectures," Coase-Sandor Institute for Law and Economics Working Paper No. 614 (Chicago: University of Chicago Law School, 2012).

Beddeleem, M., "Le projet scientifique d'un renouvellement du libéralisme: le néolibéralisme de 1933 à 1973," PhD thesis, Université de Montréal (2016).

Bell, J. A. and C. Colebrook (eds), *Deleuze and History* (Edinburgh: University of Edinburgh Press, 2009).

Behar, L., "Surpopulation relative et reproduction de la force de travail. Pour une problématique matérialiste en démographie," *La Pensée*, 176 (August 1974): 9–29.

Behar, L.,"Loi de population et science démographique. Pour une problématique matérialiste en démographie (II)," *La Pensée*, 186, (March–April 1976): 3–27.

Benjamin W., *Illuminations*, transl. H. Zohn (London: Fontana, 1973).

Benjamin W., *The Arcades Project*, transl. H. Eiland and K. McLaughlin (Cambridge, MA; Harvard University Press, 2002)

Benjamin W., *Ecrits français* (Paris: Gallimard, 2003).

Bennett, J., "'How is it Then That We Still Remain Barbarians': Foucault, Schiller, and the Aestheticization of Ethics," *Political Theory* 24(4) (1996): 653–672.

Bennett, J., *Vibrant Matter: A Political Ecology of Things* (Durham, NC: Duke University Press, 2010).

Bentham, J., *Panoptique. Mémoire sur un nouveau principe pour construire des maions d'inspection, et nommément des maisons de force* (Imprimerie Nationale, Paris 1791).

Bertrand, R., *Etat colonial, noblesse et nationalisme à Java. La Tradition parfaite* (Paris: Karthala, 2005).

Bertrand, R., "Habermas au Bengale, ou comment 'provincialiser l'Europe' avec Dipesh Chakrabarty," Université de Lausanne: *Political Science Working Paper Series*, no. 24 (2008).

Bertrand, R., "Penser le Java mystique de l'âge moderne avec Foucault: peut-on écrire une histoire 'non intentionnaliste' du politique?" *Sociétés politiques comparées* 2, February (2008): 1–34.

Bhabha, H., "The Third Space: Interview with Homi Bhabha," in J. Rutherford (ed.), *Identity, Community, Culture, Difference*, (London: Lawrence & Wishart, 1990), pp. 207–221.

Bhabha, H., "A questão do 'Outro': diferença, discriminação e o discurso do colonialismo," in *Pós-Modernismo e Política* (Rio de Janeiro: Editora Rocco, 1991).

Bhabha, H., *The Location of Culture* (London: Routledge, 1994).

Biermann, F., *Earth System Governance: World Politics in the Anthropocene* (MIT Press, Cambridge, Mass. 2014).

Bigo, D., "The Moebius Ribbon of Internal and External Security(ies)," in M. Albert, D. Jacobson and Y. Lapid (eds.), *Identities, Borders, Orders: Rethinking International Relations Theory* (Minneapolis, London: University of Minnesota Press, 2001), pp. 91–116.

Bigo, D., "Gérer les transhumances. La surveillance à distance dans le champ transnational de la sécurité" in M. C. Granjon (ed.), *Penser avec Michel Foucault, Théorie critique et pratiques politiques* (Paris: Khartala and CERI, 2005), pp. 129–160.

Bigo, D., "Security: A Field Left Fallow," in M. Dillon and A. Neal (eds.), *Foucault on Politics, Security and War* (Basingstoke and New York: Palgrave Macmillan, 2011), pp. 93–114.

Bigo D. and E. Guild, "Schengen et la politique des visas," *Cultures&Conflits* 49 (2003): 5–21.

Bigo, D., Bonelli L., and T. Deltombe (ed.), *Au nom du 11 septembre* (Paris: La Découverte, 2008).

Bigo, D. and A. Tsoukala, *Terror, Insecurity and Liberty: Illiberal Practices of Liberal Regimes after 9/11* (London: Routledge, 2008).

Blanchot, M., *The Space of Literature* (Lincoln: University of Nebreaska Press, 1982).

Blij, H. de, *Why Geography Matters: More than Ever* (New York: Oxford University Press, second edition, 2012).

Böhm-Bawerk, E. v., *Capital and Interest: A Critical History of Economical Theory* (London: MacMillan & Co., 1890).

Boltanksi, L., *On Critique. A Sociology of Emancipation*, transl. G. Elliot (Cambridge: Polity Press, 2011).

Boltanski L. and L. Thévenot, *On Justification: Economies of Worth*, transl. C. Porter (Princeton: Princeton University Press, 2006).

Bonditti, P., "From Territorial Space to Networks: A Foucaldian Approach to the Implementation of Biometry," *Alternatives* 29 (2004): 465–82.

Bonditti, P., *Antiterrorism in the United States: A Foucauldian Analysis of the Transformation of the Practices of Sovereignty and of the Art of Government* (PhD Thesis, Sciences Po, Paris 2008).

Bonditti, P., "Violence, 'Terrorism', Otherness: Reshaping Enmity in Times of Terror," in Roderick Campbell (ed.), *Violence and Civilization* (New York: New York University Press, 2013), pp. 192–214.

Bonditti, P., "Les concepts, parent pauvre des études (critiques) de sécurité? Proposition pour une archéologie des savoirs de la sécurité," *Etudes internationales*, 46(2–3)(2015): 167–188.

Bonneuil, C., Hamilton, C. and F. Gemmenne, (eds), *The Anthropocene and the Global Environmental Crisis: Rethinking Modernity in a New Era* (New York: Routledge, 2015).

Bonta, M. and J. Protevi, *Deleuze and Geophilosophy: A Guide and Glossary* (Edinburgh: Edinburgh University Press, 2004).

Borges, J. L., *The Book of Sand* (London: Penguin, 2001 [first ed 1975]).

Borges, J. L., *Other Inquisitions 1937–1952* (University of Texas Press, 1993).

Bowden, C. and A. L. Briggs, *Dreamland: The Way out of Juarez* (Austin: University of Texas Press, 2010).

Bouchard, D. F. ed. *Language, Counter-Memory, Practice*, transl. Sherry Simons (Ithaca, NY: Cornell University Press, 1977).

Boucher, D., *Political Theories of International Relations. From Thucydides to the Present* (Oxford: Oxford University Press, 1998).

Bourdieu, P. and L. Wacquant, "La nouvelle vulgate planétaire," *Le Monde diplomatique*, March 2000.

Boyer, R., "Les mots et la réalité," in S. Cordellier (ed.), *Mondialisation au-delà des mythes* (Paris: La Découverte, 2000).

Braudel, F., *Capitalism and material life, 1400–1800*, transl. M. Kochan (London: Weidenfeld and Nicolson, 1973).

Bridge, G., "The Hole World: Scales and Spaces of Extraction," *New Geographies*, 2 (2009): 43–49.

Bröckling, U., Krasmann S. and T. Lemke, "From Foucault's Lectures at the College de France to Studies of Governmentality: An Introduction," in U. Bröckling, S. Krasmann and T. Lemke, *Governmentality: Current Issues and Future Challenges*, (New York: Routledge, 2011), pp. 1–33.

Bruce, B. and J. Lonsdale, *Unhappy Valley. Conflict in Kenya and Africa* (Portsmouth: James Currey, 1992).

Brunhoff, S. de, *Etat et capital* (Paris: PUF, 1973).

Bruno, I. and E. Didier, *Benchmarking. L'État sous pression statistique* (Paris: La Découverte, 2013).

Brzezinski, Z., *Between Two Ages. America's Role in the Technetronic Era* (New York: Viking Press, 1969).

Brzezinski, Z., "Recognizing the Crisis," *Foreign Policy*, n. 17, 1974.

Buck-Morss, S., "Hegel and Haiti," *Critical Inquiry*, 26(4) (2000): 821–865.

Bull, H., *The Anarchical Society: A Study of Order in World Politics* (NY: Columbia University Press, 1977).

Burchell, G., C. Gordon, and P. Miller (eds), *The Foucault Effect* (London: Harvester Wheatsheaf, 1991).

Butler, J., *Precarious Life: The Powers of Mourning and Violence* (London: Verso, 2004).

Buzan, B., *People, State and Fear. The National Security Problem in International Relations* (Brighton: Wheathsheaf Books Ltd, 1983).

Cabanis, P., *Quelques principes et quelques vues sur les secours publics*, in *Oeuvres philosophiques de Cabanis* (Paris: PUF, 1956 [1793]).

Cabanis, P., *Rapports du physique et du moral de l'homme* (Paris, 1802).

Cache, B., *Earth Moves: The Furnishing of Territories*, transl. A. Boyman (Cambridge, MA: MIT Press, 1995).

Campbell D., *Writing Security. United States Foreign Policy and the Politics of Identity* (Minneapolis: University of Minnesota Press, 1998).

Canguilhem G., "Qu'est-ce que la psychologie?," *Revue de Métaphysique et de Morale* (1) (1958): 12–25.

Cavaillès, J., *Philosophie mathématique* (Paris: Hermann, 1962).

Certeau, M. de, *The Practice of Everyday Life*, transl. S. Rendall (Berkeley: University of California Press, 1988).

Césaire, A., *Discourse on Colonialism* (New York University: Monthly Review Press, 2000).

Chakrabarty, D., *Provincializing Europe. Postcolonial Thought and Historical Difference* (Princeton: Princeton University Press, 2000).

Chamon, P., "Foucault crosses the English Channel: Interpreting the 'international politics' in *The Anarchical Society* and *Security Territory Population*," Presentation at the Doctoral Workshop *Foucault and International Politics*, IRI-PUC-Rio, September 25–27, 2013.

Chevrier, Y., "L'empire distendu: esquisse du politique en Chine des Qing à Deng Xiaoping," in Jean-François Bayart (ed.), *La Greffe de l'Etat. Les Trajectoires du politique*, (Paris: Karthala, 1996), pp. 263-395.

Connelly, M., *Fatal Misconception: The Struggle to Control World Population* (Cambridge and London: Harvard University Press, 2008).

Connolly, W. E., *The Fragility of Things: Self-Organizing Processes, Neoliberal Fantasies, and Democratic Capitalism* (Durham, NC: Duke University Press, 2013).

Coole, D., "Experiencing Discourse: Corporeal Communicators and the Embodiment of Power," *British Journal of Politics and International Relations* 9(3) (2006): 413–433.

Comte, A., *Cours de philosophie positive*, leçons 46–51 (Paris: Hermann, 2012 (1832)).

Crampton J. W. and S. Elden, *Space, Knowledge and Power. Foucault and Geography* (New York: Palgrave Macmillan 2007).

Crozier, M., S. P. Huntington, and J. Watanuki, *The Crisis of Democracy. Report on the Governability of Democracies to the Trilateral Commission* (New York: New York University, 1975).

Dalby, S., "Recontextualising Violence, Power and Nature: The Next Twenty Years of Critical Geopolitics," *Political Geography* 29(5) (2010): 280–88.

Dalby, S., "Biopolitics and Climate Security in the Anthropocene," *Geoforum* 49 (2013): 184–92.

Dalby, S., "The Geopolitics of Climate Change," *Political Geography* 37(1) (2013): 38–47.

dal Lago, A., *Polizia Globale. Guerra E Conflitti Dopo L'11 Settembre, Cartographie* (Verona: Ombre Corte, 2003).

dal Lago, A., "La Guerra-Mondo," *Conflitti globali*, 1 (2005): 11–31.

dal Lago, A., *Non-persons. The Exclusion of Migrant in a Global Society* (Milano, Ipoc Press 2009).

Danowski, D. and E. Viveiros de Castro, *L'arrêt du monde*, in Hache E. (ed.), *De l'Univers clos au monde infini* (Paris: Editions Dehors, 2014).

Dardot P. and C. Laval, *The New Way of the World: On Neoliberal Society*, transl. G. Elliott (New York: Verso, 2014).

Dean, M., "Powers of life and death beyond governmentality," *Cultural Values* 6(1) (2002): 117–136.

Dean, M., *Governmentality, Power and Rule in Modern Society* (London: Sage, 2010).

Dean, M., *The Signature of Power: Sovereignty, Governmentality and Biopolitics* (London: Sage, 2013).

Dean, M., "Michel Foucault's 'apology' for neoliberalism," *Journal of Political Power*, 7(3) (2014): 433–442.

Dean, M., "The Malthus Effect: population and the liberal government of life," *Economy and Society*, 44(1) (2015): 18–39.

Dean, M. and K. Villadsen, *State Phobia and Civil Society. The Political Legacy of Michel Foucault* (Stanford CA: Stanford University Press, 2016).

De Larrinaga, M. and M. G. Doucet, *Security and Global Governmentality: Globalization, Governance and the State* (London: Routledge, 2010).

Deleuze, G., *Cinéma 2: L'image-temps* (Paris: Editions de Minuit, 1985).

Deleuze, G., *Bergsonism*, transl. H. Tomlinson and B. Habberjam (New York: Zone, 1988).

Deleuze, G., *Foucault*, transl. S. Hand (Minneapolis, MN: University of Minnesota Press, 1988).

Deleuze, G."What Is a Dispositif?" in T. J. Armstrong (ed), *Michel Foucault Philosopher*, (Hemel Hempstead: Harvester Wheatsheaf, 1992), pp. 159–68.

Deleuze, G., *The Fold: Leibniz and the Baroque*, transl. T. Conley (Minneapolis: University of Minnesota Press, 1993).

Deleuze, G., *Negotiations, 1972–1990*, transl. M. Joughin (New York and Chichester: Columbia University Press, 1995).

Deleuze, G., "Immanence: A life," in J. Khalfa (ed.), *An Introduction to the Philosophy of Gilles Deleuze* (London: Continuum, 2003), pp. 170–73.

Deleuze, G., *Two Regimes of Madness*, transl. A. Hodges and M. Taormina (New York: Semiotext(e), 2006).

Deleuze, G., *Difference and Repetition*, transl. P. Patton (London: Bloomsbury Academic, 2014).

Deleuze, G. and F. Guattari, *A Thousand Plateaus: Capitalism and Schizophrenia*, transl. B. Massumi (London: Athlone, 1987).

Deleuze, G. and F. Guattari, *What is philosophy?*, transl. H. Tomlinson and G. Burchell (London: Verso, 1994).

Deleuze, G. and C. Parnet, *Dialogues*, transl. H. Tomlinson and B. Habberjam (New York: Columbia University Press, 1987).

Der Derian J., *On Diplomacy. A Genealogy of Western Estrangement* (Oxford: Basil Blackwell, 1987).

Der Derian J., *Virtuous War: Mapping the Military-Industrial-Media-Entertainment Network* (Boulder, Co: Westview Press, 2001).

Der Derian J., "Critical Encounters in IR," *International Social Science Journal*, 59(191), 2008, pp. 69–73.

Der Derian J., Shapiro M., *International/Intertextual Relations. Postmodern Readings of World Politics* (New York: Lexington Books, 1989).

Descola, P., *Beyond Nature and Culture*, transl. J. Lloyd (Chicago: The University of Chicago Press, 2013).

Desrosières, A., *Politics of Large Numbers: A History of Statistical Reasoning*, transl. C. Naish, (Cambridge: Harvard University Press, 1998).

Dijstelbloem H. and A. Meijer, *Migration and the New Technological Borders of Europe* (Houndmills: Palgrave Macmillan, 2011).

Dillon M., *Politics of Security. Towards a Political Philosophy of Continental Thought* (London/New York: Routledge, 1996).

Dillon M., "Governing Terror: The State of Emergency of Biopolitical Emergence," *International Political Sociology*, (1)1 (2007): 7–28.

Dillon M., "Gouvernement, économie et biopolique," *Cultures&Conflits*, no. 78 (2010): 11–37.

Dillon M., *Biopolitics of Security: A Political Analysis of Finitude* (London: Routledge, 2015).

Dillon, M. and A. Neal (eds.), *Foucault on Politics, Security and War* (Basingstoke and New York: Palgrave Macmillan, 2011).

Dilts, A., "From 'Entrepreneur of the Self' to 'Care of the Self': Neo-liberal Governmentality and Foucault's Ethics," *Foucault Studies* 12 (2011): 130–146.

Djaballah, M., *Kant, Foucault, and Forms of Experience* (New York: Routledge, 2008).

Donzelot J., "Michel Foucault and Liberal Intelligence," *Economy and Society* 37(1) (2008): 115–134.

Doty, R. L., *Imperial Encounters: The Politics of Representation in North-South Relations* (Minneapolis, MN: University of Minnesota Press, 1996).

Drucker, P. F., *The Age of Discontent* (London: Pan Books, 1970).

Drucker, P. F., *Post-capitalist Society* (New York: Harper Business, 1990).

Duara, P., *Rescuing History from the Nation. Questioning Narratives of Modern China* (Chicago: University of Chicago Press, 1995).

Duffield, M., *Global Governance and the New Wars* (London: Z Books, 2001).

Duffield, M., "Getting savages to fight barbarians: development, security and the colonial present," *Conflict, Security and Development* 5 (2) (2005): 141–159.

Duffield, M., *Development, Security and Unending War* (Cambridge, UK: Polity Press, 2007).

Duffield, M., "Liberal Interventionism and Fragile States: Linked by Design," in M. Duffield and V. Hewitt (eds.), *Development and Colonialism: The Past in the Present* (Suffolk: James Currey, 2009), pp. 116–129.

Dunn, E. C., "Standards and Person-Making in East Central Europe," in A. Ong and S. J. Collier (eds.), *Global Assemblages. Technology, Politics and Ethics as Anthropological Problems* (Oxford: Blackwell, 2005), pp. 173–93.

Durkheim, E., *De la division du travail social* (Paris: PUF, 2007 [1893]).

Durkheim, E., *Education morale* (Paris: PUF, 2012 [1922]).

Durkheim, E., M. Mauss, and B. Nelson, "Note on the notion of civilization," *Social Research*, 38(4), 1971: 808–813.

Edward, P. N., "The Closed World. Systems, Discourses, Military Policy and Post-World War II US Historical Consciousness," in Levidow, L. and Robins K. (ed.) *Cyborg Worlds, The Military Information Society* (London: Free Association Books, 1988).

Ehlrich, P. R., *The Population Bomb*, (New York: Ballantine Books, 1968).

Ellul, J., *The Technological Society*, transl. J. Wilkinson (New York: Knopf, 1964; London: Jonathan Cape, 1965. Rev. ed.: New York: Knopf/Vintage, 1967).

Elden, S., "Governmentality, Calculation, Territory," *Environment and Planning D: Society and Space* 25(3) (2007): 562–580.

Elden, S., "Land, Terrain, Territory," *Progress in Human Geography*, 34 (2010): 799–817.

Elden, S., "How should we do the History of Territory?" *Territory, Politics, Governance* 1(1) (2013): 5–20.

Elden, S., "Secure the Volume: Vertical Geopolitics and the Depth of Power," *Political Geography* 32 (2) (2013): 35–51.

Elden, S., *The Birth of Territory* (Chicago: University of Chicago Press, 2013).

Elden, S., *Foucault's Last Decade* (Cambridge: Polity Press, 2016).

Ellermann A., *States Against Migrants: Deportation in Germany and the United States*, (New York: Cambridge University Press, 2009).

Énard. M., *Zone*, transl. C. Mandell (Rochester, NY: Open Letter, 2010).

Engels, F., *Condition of the Working Class in England* (London: Panther Edition, 1969).

Esposito, R., *Living Thought: The Origins and Actuality of Italian Philosophy*, transl. Z. Hanafi (Stanford: Stanford University Press, 2012).

Fanon, F., *The Wretched of the Earth*, transl. R. Philcox (New York: Grove Press, 2004 [1963]).

Fasolt, C., *The Limits of History* (Chicago: University of Chicago Press, 2004).

Fassin D. and M. Pandolfi (eds.), *Contemporary States of Emergency: The Politics of Military and Humanitarian Interventions* (New York: Zone Books, 2010).

Fehrer, M., "Self-Appreciation; or, The Aspirations of Human Capital," *Public Culture* 21(1) (2009): 21–41.

Fekete L., "Accelerated Removals: The Human Cost of EU Deportation Policies," *Race & Class* 52(4) (2011): 89–97.

Felman, S., *The Juridical Unconscious: Trials and Traumas of the twentieth Century* (Cambridge, MA: Harvard University Press, 2002).

Ferguson, J., *Global Shadows. Africa in the Neoliberal World Order* (Durham and London: Duke University Press, 2006).

Ferro, M., "Le futur au miroir du passé," *Le Monde diplomatique*, September 1999.

Fontana A. and M. Bertani, "Situating the lectures," in M. Foucault, *Society Must be Defended* (New York: Picador, 2003), pp. 273–293.

Fouquet, T., *Filles de la nuit, aventurières de la cité. Arts de la citadinité et désirs de l'Ailleurs à Dakar* (Paris: EHESS, 2011).

Fourquet, F., *Les Comptes de la puissance. Histoire de la comptabilité nationale et du plan* (Paris: Éditions Encres, 1980).

Fressoz, J-B. and F. Locher, "Le climat fragile de la modernité. Petite histoire climatique de la réflexivité environnementale," *La Vie des idées*, 20 April 2010. URL: http://www.laviedesidees.fr/Le-climat-fragile-de-la-modernite.html

Fressoz, J.B., "Biopouvoir et désinhibitions modernes: la fabrication du consentement technologique au tournant des XVIIIème et XIXème siècles," *Revue d'Histoire Moderne et Contemporaine*, n°60-4/4bis (2013/4): 122–138.

Frodeman, R., *Geo-logic: Breaking Ground between Philosophy and the Earth Sciences* (Albany, NY: SUNY Press, 2003).

Giddens, A., *The Politics of Climate Change* (Cambridge: Polity, second edition, 2011).

Gordon, A., *Ghostly Matters: Haunting and the Sociological Imagination* (Minneapolis: University of Minnesota Press, 1997).

Gordon, C., "Governmental Rationality: An Introduction," in G. Burchell, C. Gordon and P. Miller (eds.), *The Foucault Effect: Studies in Governmentality* (Chicago: University of Chicago Press, 1991).

Gordon, C., "Le possible : alors et maintenant. Comment penser avec et sans Foucault autour du droit pénal et du droit public," *Cultures&Conflits*, 94-95-96 (2014): 111–134.

Granjon, M.-C., (ed.), *Penser avec Michel Foucault. Théorie critique et pratiques politiques* (Paris: Karthala, 2005).

Grovogui, S. N., "Regimes of Sovereignty: International Morality and the African Condition," *European Journal of International Relations* 8(3) (September 2002): 15–38.

Grosz, E., *The Nick of Time: Politics, Evolution, and the Untimely* (Durham, NC: Duke University Press, 2004).

Grosz, E., *Time Travels: Feminism, Nature and Power* (Durham, NC: Duke University Press, 2005).

Grosz, E., *Chaos, Territory, Art: Deleuze and the Framing of the Earth* (Durham, NC: Duke University Press, 2008).

Grosz, E., *Becoming Undone: Darwinian Reflections on Life, Politics and Art* (Durham, NC: Duke University Press, 2011).

Gutting, G., *Michel Foucault's Archeology of Scientific Reason* (Cambridge: Cambridge University Press, 1989).

Golder B. and P. Fitzpatrick, *Foucault's Law* (Abingdon: Routledge, 2009).

Hache E., (ed.), *De l'Univers clos au monde infini* (Paris: Editions Dehors, 2014).

Hacking, I., *Historical Ontology* (Cambridge, MA: Harvard University Press, 2002).

Halfon, S., *The Cairo Consensus: Demographic Survey, Women's Empowerment and Regime Change in Population Policy* (Plymouth (UK), Lexington Book, 2007).

Hall, D., *Land* (Cambridge: Polity, 2013).

Hall, P., *Exposed by the Mask* (London: Oberon Books, 2000).

Han, B., *Foucault's Critical Project: Between the Transcendental and the Historical* (Stanford: Stanford University Press, 2002).

Hall S., Held D., Hubert D., Thompson K. (eds.), *Modernity: An Introduction to Modern Societies* (Oxford: Open University, 1996).

Hannah, Matthew G. "Biopower, Life and Left Politics," *Antipode* 43 (4) (2011): 1034–55.

Harvey, D., *The Condition of Postmodernity: An Enquiry into the Origins of Cultural Change*, (New York: Wiley-Blackwell, 1991).

Held, D., *Global Convenant: The Social Democratic Alternative to the Washington Consensus* (Cambridge: Polity, 2004).

Herman, E. S. and G. O'Sullivan, *The Terrorism Industry: The Experts and Institutions that Shape our View of Terror* (New York: Pantheon Books, 1989).

Hardt, M. and T. Negri, *Empire* (Cambridge, Mass. and London: Harvard University Press, 2000).

Hardt, M. and T. Negri, *Multitude: War and Democracy in the Age of Empire* (New York: The Penguin Press, 2004).

Hardt, M. and T. Negri, *Commonwealth* (Cambridge: Harvard University Press, 2009).

Heidegger, M., *Die Grundbegriffe der Antiken Philosophie* (Frankfurt am Main: Vittorio Klostermann, 1993).

Herodotus, *The Histories*, transl. R. Waterfield (Oxford: Oxford University Press, 1998).

Hibou, B., "Retrait ou redéploiement de l'État?," *Critique internationale*, 1 (October 1998): 151–68.

Hibou, B., *Privatizing the State*, transl. J. Derrick (London: Hurst and New York: Columbia University Press, 2004).

Hibou, B., *The force of Obedience: The Political Economy of Repression in Tunisia.* (Cambridge: Polity, 2011).

Hibou, B., *The Bureaucratization of the World in the Neoliberal Era: An International and Comparative Perspective*, transl. A. Brown (New York: Palgrave Macmillan, 2015).

Hibou, B., *Anatomie politique de la domination* (Paris: La Découverte, 2015).

Hibou, B., "De l'intérêt de lire *La Domination* de Max Weber aujourd'hui," *Liens socio* (2014). Available at http://lectures.revues.org/14098 (accessed March 2, 2016).

Hibou B. and B. Samuel, "Macroéconomie et politique en Afrique," *Politique Africaine*, n°124, (2012): 5–27.

Hindess, B., "The Liberal Government of Unfreedom," *Alternatives* 26 (2001): 93–111.

Hintjens, H., Richa K. and A. Pouri., "Pro-Asylum Advocacy in the EU: Challenging the State of Exception," in T. Thanh-Dam and D. Gasper (eds) *Transnational Migration and Human Security* (Berlin: Springer-Verlag, 2011), pp. 209–223.

Hirschman, A. O. *The Passions and the Interests: Political Arguments For Capitalism Before Its Triumph* (Princeton : Princeton University Press, 1977).

Hobbes, T., *Leviathan. Or The Matter Form and Power of A Commonwealth Ecclesiastical and Civil*, Edited with an introduction by Michael Oakeshott (Oxford: Basil Blackwell, 1960).

Hoche, A., *De Freigabe der Vernichtung Lebensunwerten Lebens: Ihr Mass und ihre Form* (Leipzig, 1920).

Hodgson, D., "Demography as social science and policy science," *Population and Development Review*, 9(1) (1983): 1–34.

Houellebecq, M., *The Map and the Territory*, transl. Gavin Bowd (London: William Heinemann, 2011).

Hoffmann, S., "An American Social Science: International Relations," *Daedalus* 106(3) (1977): 41–60.

Inayatullah, N. and D. L. Blaney, *International Relations and the Problem of Difference* (New York: Routledge, 2004).

Jabri, V., "War, Security and the Liberal State," *Security Dialogue* 37(1) (2006): 47–64.

Jameson, F., *Brecht and Method* (New York: Verso, 2011).

Jeanpierre, L. "Une sociologie foucaldiennne du néo-libéralisme est-elle possible?" *Sociologie et societies* 38 (2) (2006): 87–111.

Jeanpierre, L., "Capitalisme et gouvernement des circulations," in C. Laval, L. Paltrinieri, F. Taylan, *Marx & Foucault. Lectures, usages, confrontations*, (Paris: La Découverte, 2015), pp. 213–227.

Johanes, F., *The Time and the Other: How Anthropology makes its Objet* (New York: Columbia University Press, 2002).

Kant, I., "Towards Perpetual Peace" (1795) in M. J. Gregor, ed. & transl., *Immanuel Kant: Practical Philosophy* (Cambridge: Cambridge University Press, 1996), pp. 311–352.

Kant, I., "Idea for a Universal History with a Cosmopolitan Aim" (1784), transl. A. Wood, in A. Oskenberg Rorty and J. Schmitt, eds., *Kant's Idea for a*

*Universal History with a Cosmopolitan Aim: A Critical Guide* (Cambridge: Cambridge University Press, 2009), pp. 9–23.

Kaplan, Robert D., *The Revenge of Geography: What the Map Tells Us About Coming Conflicts and the Battle Against Fate* (New York: Random House, 2012).

Kapoor, I., "Acting in a tight spot: Homi Bhabha's postcolonial politics," *New Political Science* 25(4) (2003): 561–577.

Keenan, T. "Getting the Dead to Tell Me What Happened: Justice, Prosopopoeia, and Forensic Afterlives," in Forensic Architecture (eds), *Forensis: The Architecture of Public Truth* (Oberhausen: Sternberg Press, 2014), pp. 35–55.

Keene, E., *Beyond the Anarchical Society: Grotius, Colonialism and Order in World Politics* (Cambridge: Cambridge University Press, 2002).

Kelley, R. D. G., "Introduction. A Poetics of Anticolonialism," in Césaire, A. *Discourse on Colonialism* (New York, Monthly Review Press, 2000).

Khalfa, J., ed., *Introduction to the philosophy of Gilles Deleuze* (London: Continuum, 2002).

Kiersey, N. J. Stokes D., and J. R. Weidner, "Introduction," in *Foucault and International Relations. New Critical Engagements* (Oxon, UK and New York, USA: Routledge, 2011), pp. xiii-xxi.

Knorr, K. and J. N. Rosenau, *Contending Approaches to International Politics* (Princeton: Princeton University Press, 1969).

Koopman, C., *Genealogy as Critique: Foucault and the Problems of Modernity* (Bloomington: Indiana University Press, 2013).

Koyré, A., *From the Closed world to the Infinite Universe* (Baltimore: John Hopkins University Press, 1957).

Kreager, P., "Early modern population theory: A reassessment," *Population and Development Review*, 17(2) (1991): 207–227.

Kriegel, B., *The State and the Rule of Law* (Princeton, NJ: Princeton University Press, 1996).

Krupar, S. R., *Hot Spotter's Report: Military Fables of Toxic Waste* (Minneapolis: University of Minnesota Press, 2013).

Kuttner, S., *History of Ideas and Doctrines of Canon Law in the Middle Ages* (Ashgate Variorum, 1980).

Lagnaserie, G. de. *La dernière leçon de Michel Foucault sur le néolibéralisme, la théorie et la politique* (Paris: Fayard, 2012).

Lampert, J., "Theory of Delay in Balibar, Freud, and Deleuze," in Bell, J. A. and C. Colebrook (eds). *Deleuze and History* (Edinburgh: University of Edinburgh Press, 2009).

Lampland M. and L. Star (eds.), *Standards and Their Stories. How Quantifying, Classifying and Formalizing Practices Shape Everyday Life* (Ithaca: Cornell University Press, 2008).

Landa, M. de, *A Thousand Years of Nonlinear History* (New York: Zone Books, 1997).

Larrère, C., *L'invention de l'économie au XVIII<sup>e</sup> siècle. Du droit naturel à la physiocratie* (Paris : PUF, 1992).

Latour, B., *We Have Never Been Modern*, transl. C. Porter (Cambridge, MA.: Harvard University Press, 1993).

Latour, B., *Politiques de la nature* (Paris La Découverte, 2004).

Latour, B., *Reassembling the Social: An Introduction to Actor-Network-Theory* (Oxford: Oxford University Press, 2005).

Latour, B., "L'anthropocène et la destruction de l'image du monde," in Emilie Hache (ed.), *De l'Univers clos au monde infini* (Paris: Editions Dehors, 2014), pp. 29–56.

Laval, C., L. Paltrinieri, and F. Taylan, *Marx & Foucault. Lectures, usages, confrontations*, (Paris: La Découverte, 2015).

Le Bon, G., *The Crowd. A Study of the Popular Mind* (Southampton: Sparkling books, 2009).

Le Bras, H., *Les Limites de la planète* (Paris: Flammarion, 1994).

Le Bras, H. (ed.), *L'invention des populations. Biologie, idéologie et politique* (Paris: Editions Odile Jacob, 2000).

Lefebvre, H., *De l'État* (Paris: UGE, Four Volumes, 1976–78).

Lefebvre, H., *State, Space, World: Selected Essays*, ed. N. Brenner and S. Elden (Minneapolis: University of Minnesota Press, 2009).

Lefort, C., "Lectures de la guerre : le Clausewitz de Raymond Aron," *Annales. Économies, Sociétés, Civilisations*, 6 (1977): 1268–1279.

Lemke, T., "An Indigestible Meal? Foucault, Governmentality and State Theory," *Distinktion: Scandinavian Journal of Social Theory* 8(2) (2007): 43–64.

Levitt, T., "The Globalization of Markets," *Harvard Business Review*, May–June, 1983.

Little, R., *Balance of Power in International Relations: Metaphors, Myths and Models* (Cambridge University Press, 2009).

Loader, I. and N. Walker, "Policing as a public good: Reconstituting the connections between policing and the state," *Theoretical Criminology* 5(1) (2001): 9–35.

Louis, W. R. and J. Stengers (eds.), *E. D. Morel's History of The Congo Reform Movement* (Oxford, UK: The Clarendon Press, 1968).

Löwith, K., *Meaning in History* (Chicago, IL: University of Chicago Press, 1949).

Hacking, I., "Michel Foucault's Immature Science," *Noûs*, 13(1) (1979): 39–51.

Hartmann, B., *Reproductive Rights and Wrongs: The Global Politics of Population Control* (Boston: South End Press, 1995).

Herbert M., "Some social implications of modern technology," in A. Arato and E. Gebhardt (eds.), *The Essential Frankfurt School Reader* (London, Continuum, 1982 [1941]), pp. 138–62.

Huber, M. T., *Lifeblood: Oil, Freedom and the Forces of Capital* (Minneapolis: University of Minnesota Press, 2013).

Lerner, D., *The Passing of Traditional Society: Modernizing the Middle East* (Glencoe, Ill.: Free Press, 1958).

Lipschutz R., *On Security* (New York: Columbia University Press, 1996).

Lüdtke, A., *Des ouvriers dans l'Allemagne du XXe siècle. Le quotidien des dictatures* (Paris: L'Harmattan, 2000).

Malthus, T., *An Essay on the Principle of Population*, 1st edn, ed. A. Flew, (Harmondsworth: Penguin, 1970).

Malthus, T., *An Essay on the Principle of Population*, variorum edn, ed. D. Winch, (Cambridge: Cambridge University Press, 1992).

Marcus, B., *The Age of Wire and String* (Illinois: Dalkey Archive Press, 1995).

Marshall, R., *Political Spiritualities. The Pentecostal Revolution in Nigeria* (Chicago: University of Chicago Press, 2009).

Marx, K., *Outlines of the Critique of the Political Economy* (London: Penguin, 1973).

Marx, K., *Capital. A Critique of Political Economy* (London: Penguin Classics, 1990).

Marx, K. and F. Engels, *Collected Works*, Vol. 3, (London: Lawrence and Wishart, 1975).

Mattelart, A., "Une lecture idéologique de l'essai sur le principe de population," *L'Homme et la société, Marxisme et sciences humaines* 15(1970): 183–219.

Mattelart, A., *Advertising International. The Privatisation of Public Space*, transl. M. Chanan (London: Routledge, 1991).

Mattelart, A., *Mapping World Communication. War, Progress, Culture*, transl. S. Emanuel and J. A. Cohen, Minneapolis (Mineapolis: University of Minnesota Press, 1994).

Mattelart, A., *The Invention of Communication*, transl. S. Emanuel (Minneapolis, MN: University of Minnesota Press, 1996).

Mattelart, A., *Histoire de l'utopie planétaire: de la cité prophétique à la société globale* (Paris, La Découverte, 1999 [new ed. 2011]).

Mattelart, A., *Networking the World 1794–2000* (Minneapolis: University of Minnesota Press, 2000).

Mattelart, A., *The Globalization of Surveillance. The Origin of the Securitarian Order*, transl. S. Taponier and J. A. Cohen (Oxford: Polity Press, 2010).

Mattelart, A. and A. Vitalis, *Le profilage des populations* (Paris: La Découverte, 2014).

Maziarz E. A. & T. Greenwood, *Greek Mathematical Philosophy* (New York: Frederick Ungar, 1968).

Mazrui, A. A., "From Social Darwinism to Current Theories of Mondernization. A Tradition of Analysis," *World Politics* 21(1) (1968): 69–83.

Mbembe, A., "Necropolitics," *Public Culture* 15(1) (2003): 11–40.

Mbembe, A., "What is Postcolonial Thinking: An Interview with Achille Mbembe," *Esprit*, 2008. Available at http://www.eurozine.com/articles/2008-01-09-mbembe-en.html

McLuhan, M., *The Gutenberg Galaxy* (London-New York: Ark Paperbacks, 1962).

McFalls, L. (ed.), *Max Weber's 'Objectivity' Reconsidered* (Toronto: University of Toronto Press, 2007).

McFalls, L., "Les fondements rationnels et sociaux des passions politiques: vers une sociologie de la violence contemporaine avec Weber et Foucault," *Anthropologie et Sociétés* 32 (3) (2008): 155–172.

McFalls, L., "Benevolent Dictatorship: The Formal Logic of Humanitarian Government," in Fassin, D. and M. Pandolfi (eds.) *Contemporary States of Emergency: The Politics of Military and Humanitarian Interventions* (New York: Zone Books, 2010).

McKibben, B., "Global Warming's Terrifying New Math," *Rolling Stone*, July 19 2012. Available at http://www.rollingstone.com/politics/news/global-warmings-terrifying-new-math-20120719 (accessed on October 15, 2015).

Mengin, F., "A Pretence of Privatisation. Taiwan's External Relations" in B. Hibou (ed.) *Privatising the State*, (London: Hurst and New York: Columbia University Press, 2004), pp. 147–167.

Mengin, F., *Fragments of an Unfinished War: Taiwanese Entrepreneurs and the Partition of China* (London: C. Hurst and Co. and New York: Oxford University Press, 2015).

Merlingen M., "Foucault and World Politics: Promises and Challenges of Extending Governmentality Theory to the European and Beyond," *Millennium* 35 (December 2006): 181–196.

Miller, P., and N. Rose, "Political Thought and the Limits of Orthodoxy: A Response to Curtis," *British Journal of Sociology* 46(4) (1995): 590–597.

Mitchell, T., "The Stage of Modernity," In *Questions of Modernity* (Minneapolis: University of Minnesota Press, 2000).

Mitchell, T., *Carbon Democracy: Political Power in the Age of Oil* (London: Verso, paperback edition, 2013).

Moreno, M. F., Braga, C. C. and M. S. Gomes, "Trapped Between Many Worlds: A Post-colonial Perspective on the UN Mission in Haiti (MINUSTAH)," *International Peacekeeping* 19(3) (2012): 377–392.

Munro, M. and R. Shilliam, "Alternative Sources of Cosmopolitanism: Nationalism, Universalism and Creolité in Francophone Caribbean Thought," in R. Shilliam (ed.), *International Relations and Non-Western Thought: Imperialism, Colonialism and Investigations of Global Modernity* (London: Routledge, 2011), pp. 159–77.

Negri, T., "Ruptures within Empire, the Power of Exodus: Interview with Toni Negri," *Theory* 19(4) (2002): 187–194.

Nerlove, M., "Toward a New Theory of Population and Economic Growth," in T. W. Schultz (ed.), *Economics of the Family, Marriage, Children and Human Capital*, (Chicago/London: University of Chicago Press, 1974), pp. 527–545.

Nicholls, B., "Disrupting time: Post-colonial politics in Homi Bhabha's The Location of Culture," *Southern Review* 30(1) (1997): 4–25.

Nunes, Z., *Cannibal Democracy* (Minneapolis, London: University of Minnesota Press, 2008).

Nye, J. S., *Bound to Lead: The Changing Nature of American Power* (New York: Basic Books, 1990).

Nye, J. S. and W. A. Owens, "America's Information Edge," *Foreign Affairs*, 75(2), 1996.

Oakely, F., *The Politics of Eternity: Studies in the History of Medieval and Early Modern Thought* (Amsterdam: Brill, 1999).

Ohmae, K., *The Triad Power* (New York: Free Press, 1985).

Ohmae, K., *The End of the Nation State* (London: Harper-Collins, 1995).

Onuf, N., "Escavando a 'comunidade internacional': por uma arqueologia do conhecimento metafórico," *Contexto Internacional* 32(2) (2010): 253–296.

Opitz S., "Government Unlimited: The Security Dispositif of Illiberal Governmentality," In *Governmentality: Current Issues and Future Challenges* edited by Ulrich Bröckling, Suzanne Krasmann and Thomas Lemke, (New York: Routledge, 2011), pp. 93–114.

Osborne P., "Modernity is a Qualitative, not a Chronological Concept," *New Left Review*, 1(192) (March-April 1992): 65–84.

Ó Tuathail, G., *Critical Geopolitics: The Politics of Writing Global Space* (Minneapolis: University of Minnesota Press, 1996).

Paltrinieri, L., *L'expérience du concept. Michel Foucault entre épistémologie et histoire* (Paris: Publications de la Sorbonne, 2012).

Paltrinieri, L., "Biopouvoir, les sources historiennes d'une fiction politique," *Revue d'histoire moderne et contemporaine*, 60(4) (2013): 49–75.

Paltrinieri, L., "Quantifier la qualité: Le 'capital humain' entre économie, démographie et éducation," *Raisons politiques*, 52(4) (2013): 89–107.

Pandolfi, M., "Contract of Mutual (In)Difference: Governance and Humanitarian Apparatus in Albania and Kosovo," *Indiana Journal of Global Legal Studies* 10(1) (2003): 369–381.

Pandolfi, M., "Humanitarianism and its Discontents," in Bornstein, E. and P. Redfield (eds.), *Forces of Compassion between Ethics and Politics* (Santa Fe, NM: School for Advanced Research Press, 2011).

Pandolfi, M. and L. McFalls. "Intervention as Therapeutic Order," *AM. Rivista della Società italiana di antropologia medica*, 27–28 (2009): 91–111.

Pandolfi, M. and L. McFalls, "L'intervento come ordine terapeutico" in G. Pizza and H. Johannessen (eds), *Il corpo e lo stato* (Perugia: Morlacchi editore, 2014).

Pasquino, P., "The Political Theory of War and Peace: Foucault and the History of Modern Political Theory," *Economy and Society* 22(1) (1993): 77–88.

Pelham, N., "Gaza's Tunnel Phenomenon: The Unintended Dynamics of Israel's Siege," *Journal of Palestine Studies* 41(4) (2012), available at http://palestinestudies.org/jps/fulltext/42605 (accessed on October 15, 2015).

Perkins, John H., *Geopolitics and the Green Revolution: Wheat, Genes, and the Cold War* (New York: Oxford University Press, 1998).

Petersen, A., "Risk, governance and the new public health," in Petersen A. and R. Bunton (eds.), *Foucault, Health and Medicine*, (London: Routledge, 1997), pp. 189–206.

Ploger, J., "Public participation and the art of governance," *Environment and Planning B*, 28(2) (2001): 219–242.

Poggi, G., *The State: Its Nature, Development, and Prospects* (Stanford: Stanford University Press, 1990).

Polanyi, K., *The Great Transformation. The Political and Economic Origins of our Time* (Boston: Beacon Press, 1957).

Porter, T., *Trust in Numbers. The Pursuit of Objectivity in Science and Public Life* (Princeton: Princeton University Press, 1996).

Protevi, J., *Life, War, Earth: Deleuze and the Sciences* (Minneapolis: University of Minnesota Press, 2013).

Pugliese, J., *Biometrics: Bodies, Technologies, Biopolitics* (London: Routledge, 2010).

Rabinow, P., *French Modern: Norms and Forms of the Social Environment* (Chicago: University of Chicago Press, 1995).

Rabinow, P., ed. *The Foucault Reader* (New York: Pantheon, 1984).

Reid, J., *The Biopolitics of the War on Terror: Life struggles, liberal modernity and the defence of logistical societies* (Manchester: Manchester University Press, 2006).

Robertson, T., *The Malthusian Moment: Global Population Growth and the Birth of American Environmentalism* (New Brunswick: Rutgers University Press, 2012).

Rocca, J-L., *La Condition chinoise. La mise au travail capitaliste à l'âge des réformes (1978–2004)* (Paris: Karthala, 2006).

Rosanvallon, P., *Le capitalisme utopique. Histoire de l'idée de marché* (Paris: Le Seuil, 1999 [1979]).

Rose, N., *Powers of Freedom. Reframing Political Thought* (Cambridge: Cambridge University Press, 1999).

Rose, N., O'Malley, P. and M. Valverde, "Governmentality," *Annual review of law and social science*, 2(2006): 83–104.

Rostow, W. W., *The Stages of Economic Growth: A Non-Communist Manifesto* (Cambridge: Cambridge University Press, 1960).

Rotman, B., *Ad Infinitum* (Stanford: Stanford University Press, 1993).

Rotman, B., *Mathematics as Sign* (Stanford: Stanford University Press, 2000).

Rousseau, J.-J., "Note sur le projet de la morale sensitive," *Oeuvres de Rousseau* Vol. 1 (Paris: Pléiade, Gallimard, 1966), pp. 408–09.

Rousseau, J.-J., [1762] *Emile or On Education*, transl. Allan Bloom (New York: Basic Books, 1979).

Roy, O., "'L'énigme du soulèvement.' Foucault et l'Iran," *Vacarmes*, 29 (2004). Available at http://www.vacarme.org/article1366.html (accessed on October 15, 2015).

Ruggie, J.G., "Territoriality and Beyond: Problematizing Modernity in International Relations," *International Organization*, 47(1) (1993): 139–74.

Rumford, C., *The European Union: a political sociology* (Hoboken, NJ: John Wiley & Sons, 2008).

Rushdie, S., *Shalimar the Clown* (New York: Random House, 2005).

Rutherford, P., *Endless propaganda: The advertising of public goods.* (Toronto: University of Toronto Press, 2000).

Samuel, B., "L'Education pour tous.' La production bureaucratique du réel," in Béatrice Hibou (ed.), *La bureaucratisation néolibérale* (Paris: La Découverte, 2013), pp. 263–90.

Sassen, S., "Land Grabs Today: Feeding the Disassembling of National Territory," *Globalizations* 10 (1) (2013): 25–46.

Sassen, S., *Expulsions: Brutality and Complexity in the Global Economy* (Cambridge, MA: Harvard University Press, 2014).

Schmitt, C., *The Nomos of the Earth in the International Law of Jus Publicum Europaeum*, transl. G. L. Ulmen (New York: Telos Press, 2003).

Schultz, T. W., "Investment in Human Capital," *The American Economic Review*, 51(1) (1961): 1–17.

Schultz, T. W., *Investing in People: The Economics of Population Quality*, (Berkeley: University of California Press, 1981).

Selby, J., "Engaging Foucault: Discourse, Liberal Governance and the Limits of Foucauldian IR," *International Relations*, 27(3) (2007): 324–345.

Sending, O. J. and I. B. Neumann, "Governance to Governmentality: Analyzing NGOs, States, and Power. *International Studies Quarterly* 50(3) (2006): 651–672.

Senellart, M., "Course context," in M. Foucault., *The birth of biopolitics: Lectures at the Collège de France, 1978–1979* (Basingstoke: Palgrave Macmillan, 2008), pp. 327–330.

Sibertin-Blanc, G., "Loi de population du capital, biopolitique d'État, hétéronomie de la politique de classe," in Franck Fischbach (ed.), *Relire Le Capital* (Paris, PUF, 2009).

Sibertin-Blanc, G., "Race, population, classe: discours historico-politique et bio-politique du capital de Foucault à Marx," in C. Laval, L. Paltrinieri, F. Taylan,

*Marx & Foucault. Lectures, usages, confrontations* (Paris, La Découverte, 2015), pp. 228–243.

Shapiro, M. J., *Studies in Trans-Disciplinary Method: After the Aesthetic Turn* (New York: Routledge, 2012).

Shapiro, M. J., *War Crimes: Atrocity, Justice and the Archives* (Cambridge, UK: Polity, 2014).

Slaton, A., J. Abbate, "The Hidden Lives of Standards. Technical Prescriptions and the Transformation of Work in America," in Michael T. Allen and G. Hecht (eds.), *Technologies of Power* (Cambridge, MA: MIT Press, 2001), pp. 95–144.

Smith, N., *Uneven Development: Nature, Capital and the Production of Space* (Atlanta: University of Georgia Press, third edition, 2008).

Marie-Claude Smouts, ed., *The New International Relations. Theorie and Practice* (London: Hurst Publishers, 2014 [1998]).

Spivak, G. C., *An Aesthetic Education in the Era of Globalization* (Cambridge, MA: Harvard University Press, 2012).

Spivak, G. C. and Harasym, S., *The Post-Colonial Critic: Interviews, Strategies, Dialogues* (Hove: Psychology Press, 1990).

Steele, B. J., *Defacing Power: The Aesthetics of Insecurity in Global Politics* (Ann Arbor: University of Michigan Press, 2012).

Stoler, A., *Race and the Education of Desire: Foucault's History of Sexuality and the Colonial Order of Things* (Durham: Duke University Press, 1995).

Stampnitsky, L., *Disciplining Terror: How Experts Invented Terrorism* (Cambridge: Cambridge University Press, 2013).

Steinbeck, J., *The Grapes of Wrath* (New York: Penguin, 2002 [1939]).

Stinchcombe, A. L., *When Formality Works. Authority and Abstraction in Law and Organizations* (Chicago: University of Chicago Press, 2001).

Supiot, A., *La Gouvernance par les nombres. Cours au Collège de France (2012–2014)*, (Paris: Fayard, 2015).

Suskind, R., "Without a Doubt," *New York Times*, 17 October 2004.

Swiffen, A., *Law, Ethics and the Biopolitical* (London: Routledge, 2011).

Tatz, C., "The Politics of Aboriginal Health," *Politics* (The Journal of the Australian Political Studies Association) 7(2) (November, 1972): 3–23.

Taylan, F., "L'interventionnisme environnemental, une stratégie néolibérale," *Raisons politiques*, 52(4) (2013): 77–87.

Taylan, F., *La Rationalité mésologique. Connaissance et gouvernement des milieux de vie (1750–1900)* (PhD thesis, Bordeaux University, 2014).

Tazzioli M., *Spaces of Governmentality: Autonomous Migration and the Arab Uprisings*, (London: Rowman & Littlefield International, 2014).

Thévenot, L., "Un gouvernement par les normes" in B. Conein, L. Thévenot (eds), *Cognition et information en société* (Paris: Editions de l'Ecole des Hautes Etudes en Sciences Sociales, 1997), pp. 204–242.

Thévenot, L., "Jugement ordinaire et jugement de droit," *Annales ESC*, 6, 1992: 1279–99.

Thévenot, L., "L'autorité à l'épreuve de la critique. Jusqu'aux oppressions du 'gouvernement par l'objectif'," in Bruno Frère (ed.), *Quel présent pour la critique sociale?* (Brussels, Desclée de Brouwer, 2012).

Tierney, B., *Foundations of the Conciliar Theory: The Contribution of The Medieval Canonists from Gratian to the Great Schism* (Cambridge: Cambridge University Press, 2010).

Thomas Y., "Fictio legis. L'empire de la fiction romaine et ses limites médiévales" in *Les Opérations du droit* (Paris, Le Seuil/Gallimard, 2011), pp. 133–186.

Urry, J. *Climate Change and Society* (Cambridge: Polity, 2011).

van der Ploeg I., *The Machine-Readable Body* (Maastricht: Shaker, 2006).

Vanel, G., "La normalisation financière internationale face à l'émergence de nouvelles autorités épistémiques américaines. Le cas de la filière des chiffres," *Revue de la régulation*, 3(4), 2008, available at http://regulation.revues.org/4443 (Accessed on October 26, 2015).

Veyne, P., *Writing History: Essay on Epistemology*, transl. Mina Moore-Rinvolucri (Middletown, CT: Wesleyan University Press, 1984).

Veyne, P., *Did the Greeks Believe in their Myths? An Essay on the Constitutive Imagination*, transl. P. Wissing (Chicago: University of Chicago Press, 1988).

Veyne, P., *Foucault: His Thought, His Character*, transl. J. Lloyd (Cambridge: Polity, 2010).

Vila, A. C., *Enlightenment and Pathology: Sensibility in the Literature and Medicine of Eighteenth-Century France* (Baltimore: Johns Hopkins University Press, 1998).

Walker, R. B. J., *Inside/Outside: International Relations as Political Theory* (Cambridge: Cambridge University Press, 1993).

Walker, R. B. J., *After the Globe, Before the World* (London and New York: Routledge, 2010).

Walker, R. B. J., *Out of Line: Essays on the Politics of Boundaries and the Limits of Modern Politics* (London and New York: Routledge, 2015).

Walter C. (ed.), *Nouvelles normes financières. S'organiser face à la crise* (Paris: Springer-Verlag France, 2010).

Walters, W., "Border/control," *European Journal of Social Theory*, 9(2) (2006): 187–203.

Walters, W., *Governmentality: Critical Encounters* (Abingdon: Routledge, 2012).

Waltz, K. N., "The Origins of War in Neorealist Theory," *The journal of interdisciplinary history*, 18(4) (1988): 615–628.

Watson, A., *A Evolução da Sociedade Internacional: Uma Análise Histórica Comparativa* (Brasília, Editora Universidade de Brasília, 2004).

Webber F., "How Voluntary are Voluntary Returns?" *Race & Class* 52(4) (2011): 98–107.

Weber, M., *The Protestant ethic and the spirit of capitalism*, ed. and transl. S. Kalberg (Chicago and London: Fitzroy Dearborn, 2001).

Weber, M., *Wissenschaftslehre* (Tübingen: Mohr, 1988).

Weber, M., *Economy and Society: an Outline of Interpretative Sociology, volume 1*, ed. G. Roth and C. Wittich (Berkeley, CA: University of California Press).

Weber, M., *From Max Weber: Essays in Sociology*, transl., ed., by H.H. Gerth and C. Wright Mills (New York: Oxford University Press, 1946).

Weizman, E., *Forensic Architecture: Notes from Fields and Forums* (English-German edition, Kassel: dOCUMENTA, 2012).

Weizman, E., *The Least of All Possible Evils: Humanitarian Violence from Arendt to Gaza* (London: Verso, 2012).

Whitehead, M., *State, Science and the Skies: Environmental Governmentality and the British Atmosphere* (Oxford: Wiley-Blackwell, 2009).

Wiles, D., *Mask and Performance in Greek Tragedy* (Cambridge: Cambridge University Press, 2014).

Wilcox L., *Bodies of Violence: Theorizing Embodied Subjects in International Relations* (Oxford: Oxford University Press, 2015).

Woodard, B., *On an Ungrounded Earth: Towards a New Geophilosophy* (Brooklyn, NY: Punctum Books, 2013).

Woodward, R., *Military Geographies* (Oxford: Wiley-Blackwell, 2004).

Young, R. J. C., "Foucault on race and colonialism," *New Formations* 25 (Summer 1995): 57–65.

Yusoff, K., Grosz E., Saldanha A., Nash C. and N. Clark, "*Geo*power: A Panel on Elizabeth Grosz's *Chaos, Territory, Art: Deleuze and the Framing of the Earth*," *Environment and Planning D: Society and Space* 30(6) (2012): 971–88.

Zamora D. & M. C. Berhent, *Foucault and Neoliberalism* (Cambridge: Polity Press, 2016).

# INDEX[1]

1968, 34, 38, 41, 52, 163, 181

## A

abnormal, 26, 43, 50, 124, 244

abstraction, 5, 159, 203–18, 249, 326, 332, 335

administration, 45, 50, 167, 169, 204, 206, 211, 228, 281, 285, 288, 290

aesthetics, 19, 129–30, 143, 144

Agamben, Giorgio, 49, 104, 113n38, 121, 132n27, 228, 234n23, 297, 307n9

alethurgy, 80, 82, 84–7, 91, 92

algorithm, 36, 88, 287

Althusser, 159, 172n5

amnesia, 278

anarchy, 47, 85, 223, 336

anatomy (political), 59–61, 67, 69

Anthropocene, 5, 261–73, 305–7, 311n63

archaeology, 20, 24, 25, 35, 155–73, 250, 251, 277–94

archive, 4, 29, 123, 160, 161, 324

army, 126, 128, 129, 142, 162, 247, 251, 272n1

art of government, 42, 47, 63, 73n27, 101, 108, 110, 227, 290

assemblage, 72n19, 101, 121, 182, 185

asylum, 62, 71n4, 115

austerity, 192, 219–35

authoritarianism, 141, 177

authority, 18, 21, 48, 64, 66, 146, 149, 162, 168, 197, 211, 222, 223, 229, 314, 318, 321, 331, 334, 336

## B

Barthes, Roland, 214, 218n41

Becker, Gary, 102, 112n29, 156, 199, 226, 252, 253, 259n65, 265

Bergson, Henri, 178

biometrics, 67, 288, 296, 297, 300, 303, 306

biopolitics (bio-politics), 4, 10, 25, 27, 35, 49–50, 61, 65, 97–101, 109,

[1] Note: Page number followed by n denote endnotes

© The Author(s) 2017
P. Bonditti et al. (eds.), *Foucault and the Modern International*,
The Sciences Po Series in International Relations and Political
Economy, DOI 10.1057/978-1-137-56153-4